JOURNAL FOR THE STUDY OF THE NEW TESTAMENT
SUPPLEMENT SERIES
106

Sheffield Academic Press

Jewish Responsibility for the Death of Jesus in Luke–Acts

Jon A. Weatherly

Journal for the Study of the New Testament
Supplement Series 106

Copyright © 1994 Sheffield Academic Press

Published by Sheffield Academic Press Ltd
Mansion House
19 Kingfield Road
Sheffield, S11 9AS
England

Typeset by Sheffield Academic Press
and
Printed on acid-free paper in Great Britain
by Bookcraft
Midsomer Norton, Somerset

British Library Cataloguing in Publication Data

A catalogue record for this book is available
from the British Library

ISBN 1-85075-503-5

CONTENTS

ACKNOWLEDGMENTS

This book represents a revision of my PhD thesis, submitted in 1991 to the University of Aberdeen, and I am grateful to acknowledge the many people who have assisted me in its completion. Their influence has been felt in various ways, but all have been important to the outcome. Dr Howard Marshall gave direction early on in my inquiries and offered helpful suggestions on a portion of the manuscript. More importantly, the impress of his careful scholarship and unselfish personality are felt through the Department of New Testament at Aberdeen; consequently, my work was conducted in an atmosphere that was both rigorous and charitable. Dr Max Turner, my supervisor, manifested those same qualities in providing astute counsel throughout my research and warm, collegial friendship during our sojourn in Aberdeen. My fellow postgraduates at Aberdeen provided many hours of stimulating discussion and many points of insightful criticism. Dr Lewis Foster and Mr Paul Friskney of Cincinnati Bible College and Seminary provided invaluable assistance in proofreading.

Financial assistance came through a variety of sources, including the Alexander Christian Foundation (Indianapolis, Indiana), South Side Christian Church (Munster, Indiana), Woodland Springs Christian Church (Carmel, Indiana), Grove City Church of Christ (Columbus, Ohio), Cincinnati Bible College and Seminary, and the Tyndale Fellowship. Floyd and Marjorie Kline were most generous on several occasions; without their liberality this work might never have been completed. My parents, C.D. and Mildred Weatherly, offered generous, steady assistance throughout my period of study, just as they have at every other juncture of my education.

Most of all I thank my immediate family. My son, Cale Daniel, provided joyous distraction at the beginning and end of each day of research. My daughter Allison, a late arrival in this process, has augmented that joy. And no one is more responsible for the completion of this thesis than my wife, Tammie. Her labor and thrift before we came to Aberdeen supplied the largest share of the money necessary for our maintenance. Her diligence and resourcefulness made our home a haven of warmth and love in what were often trying times. Her stamina and flexibility turned each new experience into an adventure. Most of all her unflagging confidence and patience—even in times of unexpected pain and loss—inspired me to persevere. With deepest affection and gratitude this work is dedicated to her.

ABBREVIATIONS

AB	Anchor Bible
AnBib	Analecta biblica
ANRW	*Aufstieg und Niedergang der römischen Welt*
ASNU	Acta seminarii neotestamentici upsaliensis
ASTI	*Annual of the Swedish Theological Institute*
ATANT	Abhandlungen zur Theologie des Alten und Neuen Testaments
BAGD	W. Bauer, W.F. Arndt, F.W. Gingrich and F.W. Danker, *Greek–English Lexicon of the New Testament*
BBB	Bonner biblische Beiträge
BDF	F. Blass, A. Debrunner and R.W. Funk, *A Greek Grammar of the New Testament*
BETL	Bibliotheca ephemeridum theologicarum lovaniensium
Bib	*Biblica*
BJRL	*Bulletin of the John Rylands University Library of Manchester*
BNTC	Black's New Testament Commentaries
BWANT	Beiträge zur Wissenschaften vom Alten und Neuen Testament
BZNW	Beihefte zur ZNW
CBQ	*Catholic Biblical Quarterly*
CNT	Commentaire du Nouveau Testament
ConBNT	Coniectanea biblica, New Testament
EBib	Etudes bibliques
EKKNT	Evangelisch-Katholischer Kommentar zum Neuen Testament
ETL	*Ephemerides theologicae lovanienses*
EvQ	*Evangelical Quarterly*
EvT	*Evangelische Theologie*
ExpTim	*Expository Times*
FB	Forschung zur Bibel
FRLANT	Forschungen zur Religion und Literatur des Alten und Neuen Testaments
GTA	Göttinger theologische Arbeiten
HNT	Handbuch zum Neuen Testament
HTKNT	Herders theologischer Kommentar zum Neuen Testament
HTR	*Harvard Theological Review*
HTS	Harvard Theological Studies
HUCA	*Hebrew Union College Annual*
ICC	International Critical Commentary

Int	*Interpretation*
JAAR	*Journal of the American Academy of Religion*
JBL	*Journal of Biblical Literature*
JBLMS	Journal of Biblical Literature Monograph Series
JES	*Journal of Ecumenical Studies*
JSNT	*Journal for the Study of the New Testament*
JSNTSup	*Journal for the Study of the New Testament*, Supplement Series
JSOTSup	*Journal for the Study of the Old Testament*, Supplement Series
JTS	*Journal of Theological Studies*
LD	Lectio divina
LSJ	Liddell–Scott–Jones, *Greek–English Lexicon*
NCB	New Century Bible
Neot	*Neotestamentica*
NIGTC	The New International Greek Testament Commentary
NovT	*Novum Testamentum*
NovTSup	*Novum Testamentum* Supplements
NTAbh	Neutestamentliche Abhandlungen
NTD	Das Neue Testament Deutsch
NTS	*New Testament Studies*
ÖTKNT	Ökumenischer Taschenbuch-Kommentar zum Neuen Testament
QD	Quaestiones disputatae
RB	*Revue biblique*
ResQ	*Restoration Quarterly*
RNT	Regensburger Neues Testament
SANT	Studien zum Alten und Neuen Testament
SBLDS	SBL Dissertation Series
SBLMS	SBL Monograph Series
SBLSCS	SBL Septuagint and Cognate Studies
SBLSS	SBL Semeia Studies
SBS	Stuttgarter Bibelstudien
SBT	Studies in Biblical Theology
SE	*Studia Evangelica*
SJ	Studia judaica
SJLA	Studies in Judaism in Late Antiquity
SNT	Studien zum Neuen Testament
SNTSMS	Society for New Testament Studies Monograph Series
SPB	Studia postbiblica
TDNT	G. Kittel and G. Friedrich (eds.), *Theological Dictionary of the New Testament*
THKNT	Theologischer Handkommentar zum Neuen Testament
TNTC	Tyndale New Testament Commentaries
TS	*Theological Studies*
TU	Texte und Untersuchungen

TynBul	*Tyndale Bulletin*
WBC	Word Biblical Commentary
WMANT	Wissenschaftliche Monographien zum Alten und Neuen Testament
WUNT	Wissenschaftliche Untersuchungen zum Neuen Testament
ZNW	*Zeitschrift für die neutestamentliche Wissenschaft*
ZTK	*Zeitschrift für Theologie und Kirche*

Chapter 1

A REVIEW OF RESEARCH ON JUDAISM AND THE DEATH OF JESUS
IN LUKE–ACTS

Is the New Testament anti-Semitic? Centuries of persecution of Jews by
Christians, the specter of the Nazi holocaust, and recent manifestations
of malice against Jews—all carried out with pretended theological
justification—give this question a particular urgency. As the question has
been posed and answers sought, the Lukan corpus has become a particular focus of investigation. Both the size of Luke and Acts (together
they comprise nearly a quarter of the New Testament) and the prominence with which they present the relationship of Judaism and
Christianity have thrust these books into the center of post-war debate
about the origins of anti-Semitism in Christianity.

But post-war interpretation is heir to an earlier legacy. The consensus
of critical opinion since the nineteenth century is that Luke writes for a
church which is predominantly comprised of Gentiles and has abandoned any mission to Jews.[1] That hypothesis has in turn influenced the
way every aspect of Luke's presentation of Jews and Gentiles is understood. Under this view, Luke depicts Jews negatively and Gentiles positively. He is pessimistic about the prospects for Jewish conversion and
sees the church's future in the Gentile world. In particular, Luke is
widely understood to depict the involvement of Jews in the crucifixion
of Jesus in order to place the entire Jewish nation under condemnation
for Jesus' death. Hence, the anti-Semitic calumny 'deicide race' has its
roots in Luke–Acts.

Can this conclusion be sustained on the evidence of the text itself?
This work will seek an answer to that question, and this chapter will justify yet another investigation of it. What emerges from a survey of

1. R.L. Brawley notes this consensus as a post-war phenomenon (*Luke–Acts
and the Jews: Conflict, Apology and Conciliation* [SBLMS, 33; Atlanta: Scholars
Press, 1987], pp. 2-3).

research on the role of Jews and Judaism in Luke–Acts is that although a wide consensus exists that Luke's perspective is hostile to the Jews as a people, important dissent from that consensus has been offered. From that dissent emerge two significant questions. First, precisely to whom does Luke assign responsibility for Jesus' death? Secondly, does Luke assign responsibility on the basis of sources or traditions which he received or is his treatment his own theological construct? These questions will become the focus of the balance of this work.

A complete survey of Lukan research is impossible within the constraints of this volume. Therefore, attention will be directed to three crucial areas. The first will be the developing consensus about Luke's approach to the Jews in what might be called the classical period of Lukan research, from F.C. Baur to M. Dibelius. Here attention will be given to a few seminal works which treat the subject in some detail. The second area will be the firming of that consensus in the period beginning with the publication of H. Conzelmann's epochal work on Lukan *Redaktionsgeschichte*.[1] Much of the attention here will be given to noting the distinct contribution of several redaction-critical works to the understanding of Luke's approach to the Jews, but consideration will be given as well to the dissemination of certain key assumptions in a wide body of scholarly publications. The third area will summarize recent objections to the consensus on Luke's approach to the Jews. Here the concern will be especially to note those areas left unresolved in the current discussion.

Luke–Acts and the Jews in the 'Classical' Period

The foundational issues of modern debate about the Jews in Luke–Acts took shape in critical studies prior to World War II. To this period attention will first be directed.

Ferdinand Christian Baur

According to F.C. Baur, the chief tension reflected in Acts is the one between Jewish Christianity and Gentile Christianity, not the one between Jews and Christians. Hence, he writes of scenes such as Peter and John's appearance before the Sanhedrin without the slightest suggestion that such scenes reflect the hostility between Christians and

---

1.   H. Conzelmann, *The Theology of St Luke* (New York: Harper & Brothers, 1960).

non-Christian Jews.[1] Indeed, Baur asserts, 'Acts consequently places the first disciples of Jesus as near as possible to the Jewish religion and the Jewish national cult',[2] and he endorses the position of Schenkenburger that Luke idealizes Paul as an observant Jew.[3] Acts 21 in fact obliterates the causes of tension between Paul and his non-Christian Jewish opponents as a consequence of Luke's desire to eliminate conflict between Jewish and Pauline Christianity.[4] Thus, if anything Acts reflects a tendency to treat Jews favorably and to minimize the conflict between Jews and Christians. According to Baur, Acts represents Jewish Christians as differing from non-Christian Jews in nothing save belief in Jesus as messiah.[5] But Baur's comments on Acts evince little interest on his part in pursuing the question of Luke's stance toward non-Christian Jews. The apology for Paul in Acts is made to the Jewish-Christian party, not to non-Christian Jews.[6]

Several ideas emerged from Baur's work which would prove crucial in subsequent discussion. One was the groundbreaking identification of the relationship of Christianity to Judaism as a significant factor in Luke's work. Baur asserted that the most important issue in the history of early Christianity is how the faith became an independent religion and not merely a sect within Judaism.[7] Baur's analysis of the tension between Jewish and Pauline Christianity would be rejected, but others would take up an implication which remained latent in his work: that Acts reflects conflict between church and synagogue. Moreover, Baur identified the question of the universal mission as the source of conflict between Jewish and Gentile Christianity.[8] After Baur, when analysis of Acts was set in the context of conflict between Christians and Jews, this issue would be recast: Christian universalism would be viewed as the assertion of Gentile primacy over Jews.

1.   F.C. Baur, *Paulus, der Apostel Jesu Christi: Sein Leben und Wirken, seine Briefe und seine Lehre: Ein Beitrag zu einer kritischen Geschichte des Urchristentums* (ed. E. Zeller; Leipzig: Fues [Reisland], 2nd edn, 1866–67), I, pp. 20-23.

2.   Baur, *Paulus*, I, p. 49. Throughout this book, works cited in German or French originals and quoted in English represent my own translations.

3.   Baur, *Paulus*, I, pp. 8-9, 233-34.

4.   Baur, *Paulus*, I, p. 221.

5.   Baur, *Paulus*, I, p. 49.

6.   Baur, *Paulus*, I, pp. 15-16.

7.   Baur, *Paulus*, I, pp. 5-6.

8.   Baur, *Paulus*, I, pp. 67-68.

Franz Overbeck

That recasting was largely accomplished by F. Overbeck in his revision of W.M.L. De Wette's commentary on Acts.[1] Overbeck explicitly denied the earlier position of De Wette that Acts was written to justify the Pauline Gentile mission to the Judaists.[2] But he likewise argued that Baur's view of Acts as a conciliatory work was inconsistent with what he saw as a pervasive tendency in the book: its 'national Anti-Judaism'.[3] Acts characteristically presents Jewish unbelief as the engine which drives the Gentile mission and which separates the Christians from the Jews at every turn. Consequently, it cannot be viewed as attempting to mollify Jewish Christians, who would trace their descent from those whom the book pilloried.[4] Its point of view, like that of the Fourth Gospel, reflects a standpoint which views Gentile Christianity as entirely predominant. What appears to be conciliatory, then, is in fact the attempt to vindicate Gentile Christianity by showing that it occupies 'the ground occupied by the original and proper Jewish Christianity'.[5] Having abandoned the antinomianism which was the essence of Pauline Gentile Christianity, the author of Acts justifies the existence of his brand of Gentile Christianity by an appeal to continuity with 'the old Apostolic Christianity' and to stubborn Jewish unbelief.[6]

The evidence to which Overbeck appealed in this analysis was that to which subsequent scholars would return repeatedly. On the one hand Acts emphasizes the continuity of the Gentile church with the primitive Jewish Christianity. Abandoning what Overbeck regarded as the authentic Paul's decisive break with Judaism, Acts stresses Paul's Jewish piety. His strict observance of the law is repeatedly suggested (7.58; 8.1, 3; 22.3ff., 19ff.; 26.9ff.) as is the mediation of a pious Jewish Christian in his conversion and call to a universal apostleship (9.10-19; 9.15).[7] As Paul's Gentile mission takes shape in the second part of Acts, he

---

1.   F. Overbeck, 'Introduction to the Acts from De Wette's Handbook', in E. Zeller, *The Contents and Origin of the Acts of the Apostles Critically Investigated* (ET; Edinburgh: Williams & Norgate, 1875), I, pp. 1-81. The substance of Overbeck's understanding of the Jews in Acts is contained in this introduction.

2.   Overbeck, 'Introduction', pp. 16-17.

3.   Overbeck, 'Introduction', p. 20.

4.   Overbeck, 'Introduction', pp. 21-22.

5.   Overbeck, 'Introduction', p. 22.

6.   Overbeck, 'Introduction', pp. 22, 24-25.

7.   Overbeck, 'Introduction', p. 25.

maintains his devotion to Judaism, visiting Jerusalem on three occasions, obtaining the approval of the Jerusalem church for his Gentile mission (15.1-33), scrupulously observing the law (18.18-19; 20.16; 15.23-24; 21.17ff.), and practicing 'an invariable recognition of the religious privileges of his Jewish associates'.[1]

On the other hand, Jewish unbelief is emphasized at key junctures in the narrative. While the newly founded Jerusalem church is 'flourishing in inward happiness', Jewish unbelief manifests itself in two persecutions (2.43–5.42).[2] But even before such conflict arises, Peter's speeches evince an 'Anti-Judaism' which anticipates the rupture to come.[3] Stephen's death proves to be a decisive turning point, leading as it does to preaching in 'semi-Gentile circles' by Hellenists with the blessing of the apostles (8.14-25).[4] Because the Paul of Acts is not an antinomian opposed by Jewish Christians, his opponents are identical with those of the Jerusalem church, namely, the unbelieving Jews.[5] Thus, preaching initially to Jews only, Paul is forced to flee from Damascus and then from Jerusalem because of Jewish hatred (9.19-30).[6] Paul returns to Jerusalem, but the Jews again instigate a persecution (11.27–12.25), manifesting their 'irreceptivity...for the new revelation' but also leading to Paul's work in Gentile areas.[7] But characteristic of his work among the Gentiles is Paul's confrontation with Jewish unbelief and hatred. To be sure, all Gentiles do not respond with faith. But Paul finds considerable faith among the Gentiles, and, more importantly, that faith is explicitly contrasted with Jewish unbelief (13.6ff., 48; 14.11ff.; 18.8-9; 28.20). Thus, the response of the Gentiles indicates the divine intention to send salvation to them (13.48).[8] The decisive indication of the relationship of Jews and Gentiles to the gospel is found in the narrative of Paul's trial. The product of 'Jewish hatred', the trial effectively has two consequences: Paul is acquitted but is able to use his imprisonment to continue his ministry to the Gentiles in Rome, the 'Gentile capital of the world'.[9]

1. Overbeck, 'Introduction', p. 25.
2. Overbeck, 'Introduction', pp. 24-25.
3. Overbeck, 'Introduction', p. 58.
4. Overbeck, 'Introduction', p. 25.
5. Overbeck, 'Introduction', p. 29.
6. Overbeck, 'Introduction', p. 25.
7. Overbeck, 'Introduction', p. 26.
8. Overbeck, 'Introduction', pp. 26-27.
9. Overbeck, 'Introduction', pp. 27, 75.

Both these tendencies serve to justify the existence of the author's brand of non-Pauline Gentile Christianity. On the one hand, the insistence on the Jewish piety of Paul establishes the continuity of Gentile Christianity with the primitive church. On the other, Jewish unbelief explains the existence of a predominantly Gentile church, one which no longer adheres to Pauline antinomian principles but which is decisively separated from the Jewish nation.[1] In this respect Acts has affinities with the second-century apologists like Justin, whose immediate forerunner it is.[2]

Overbeck's discussion set the agenda for subsequent studies of the Jews in Acts. He clearly identified two emphases which beg for explanation: the Jewish piety of the Jerusalem church and of Paul, and the persistent unbelief of the Jews. His explanation of these phenomena was widely accepted by later generations of scholars and provided the foundation for further studies of the issue. Some, however, questioned his conclusions, pointing out other features of the text and offering alternatives to his exegesis.

Alfred Loisy

A. Loisy is among those who largely followed Overbeck's lead. His works represent an advance on Overbeck's in two respects. First, Loisy found evidence for Luke's thoroughgoing anti-Judaism in his Gospel as well as in Acts. Secondly, he argued that Luke created or edited his material with allegorical significance and that much of this allegory had to do with the rejection of the gospel by the Jews and its acceptance by the Gentiles.

Loisy's procedure is clearly evinced in his privately published volumes on the Synoptic Gospels; his later work on Luke's Gospel largely recapitulates the earlier work.[3] Here he suggests that many Lukan pericopae are symbolic narratives which emphasize the reprobation of the Jews and the salvation of the Gentiles.[4] Hence, the Nazareth pericope (Lk. 4.16-30) symbolizes the disbelief and reprobation of the Jews, their stubborn demand for signs, their desire to kill Jesus and the sending of

---

1.   Overbeck, 'Introduction', p. 71-72.
2.   Overbeck, 'Introduction', p. 72.
3.   A. Loisy, *Les Evangiles synoptiques* (2 vols.; Ceffonds, près Montier-en-Der [Haute-Marne]: published by the author, 1907–1908), I, p. 168; *L'Evangile selon Luc* (repr.; Frankfurt: Minerva, 1971 [1924]), *passim*.
4.   Loisy, *L'Evangile selon Luc*, p. 460.

the gospel to the Gentiles. Luke transposes the pericope simply to maximize its symbolic value.[1] Similarly, the healing of the ten lepers (Lk. 17.12-19) indicates Israel's rejection of the gospel and the Gentiles' acceptance of it.[2] Even Zacchaeus (Lk. 19.1-10) is regarded by Loisy as a symbol of the salvation of the Gentiles.[3] This emphasis is particularly noteworthy in Luke's treatment of the death of Jesus. Luke is unaware of the contradiction between the favorable stance of the crowds in Jerusalem (e.g. Lk. 19.47) and Jesus' repeated statements of their unbelief (e.g. Lk. 13.33-35; 19.41-44).[4] The events of AD 70 have made such an impression on him that he is concerned only with the unbelief of the Jews and its consequences in the destruction of Jerusalem.[5] Luke is heir to the synoptic tradition which emphasizes the responsibility of the Jewish leaders, but he obscures this theme with his emphasis on the rejection of Jesus by all Israel.[6] Pilate, on the other hand, witnesses to the innocence of Jesus and transfers responsibility to the Jews; he is without blame in Luke's view.[7]

In his work on the book of Acts Loisy systematized these insights, offering hypotheses about their origin and further refining their implications. His symbolic interpretation continued in Acts, but with a clear assertion about Luke's motivation.[8] The great difficulty in early Christian apologetic was the unbelief of the Jews. Luke answers this problem by asserting that the stubbornness and hardening of the Jews is something consistent with their entire history and with the saving

---

1.   Loisy, *Synoptiques*, I, pp. 839, 845; *L'Evangile selon Luc*, pp. 159-62. The extent of the allegory is seen in the reference to three and a half years (Lk. 4.25), for which Loisy symbolizes the period of preaching the gospel to the Gentiles (*Synoptiques*, I, p. 847).

2.   Loisy, *Synoptiques*, II, pp. 179-82; *L'Evangile selon Luc*, p. 428.

3.   Loisy, *Synoptiques*, II, p. 257; *L'Evangile selon Luc*, pp. 453-54.

4.   Loisy, *Synoptiques*, II, pp. 127, 272, 281.

5.   Loisy, *Synoptiques*, II, p. 281.

6.   Loisy, *Synoptiques*, II, pp. 281, 652, 759. In isolated instances Loisy refers specifically to the Jews of Jerusalem as those who bring about Jesus' death (*Synoptiques*, II, pp. 179-82), but Loisy sees no attempt on Luke's part to distinguish these from the rest of the Jewish nation.

7.   Loisy, *L'Evangile selon Luc*, pp. 551-52.

8.   Examples of Loisy's allegorical interpretation of Acts can be found throughout his commentary; one example is his treatment of the blinding of Elymas in Acts 13.8-12 (*Les Actes des Apôtres* [repr.; Frankfurt: Minerva, 1973 (1920)], pp. 516-17).

purpose of God.[1] Emphasizing this stubbornness, he pushes the rejection of the gospel typical of Jews in his own time back to the ministry of Jesus. Consequently, in Luke's view the Jews who call for Jesus' death before Pilate are 'the Jews of every province', representatives of the entire nation.[2] Thus, the Jews rejected Jesus just as they reject Christianity, the authentic form of their own religion; the gospel is taken to the Gentiles only because of the stubbornness of the Jews.[3] Particularly important in Luke's development of these ideas are Stephen's speech (Acts 7.1-53) and the encounter between the Roman Jews and Paul (Acts 28.17-28). The former lays out the consistent pattern of Israel's stubborn unbelief; the latter is the definitive confrontation between Christianity and Judaism.[4]

Loisy's work anticipated subsequent developments in two significant ways. His symbolic interpretation, though not taken up by later critics, would prove similar to many of the redaction-critical studies of the post-war period. More particularly his emphasis on Luke's thorough anti-Judaism continued the trend established by Overbeck, a trend which would color the bulk of critical scholarship in the years to come.

Adolf Harnack

The perspective articulated by Overbeck clearly influenced the work of the famed German historian A. Harnack. Unlike Loisy, however, Harnack's response to Overbeck was to call attention to aspects of Luke's writings which tend to temper what was regarded as his anti-Judaism. Harnack suggests that Acts represents the first stage of developing Christian anti-Semitism. At this initial juncture individual differences among Jews are emphasized and the Jewish people as a whole are never condemned outright.[5] Hence, Harnack writes:

> The Jew is in a sense the villain in this dramatic history, yet not... the Jew in the abstract who has almost become an incarnation of the evil principle, but the real Jew without generalisation and exaggeration in his manifold gradations of Pharisee, Sadducee, aristocrat, Jew of Palestine or of the Dispersion. Where St Luke knows anything more favourable concerning

---

1. Loisy, *Actes*, pp. 115-17.
2. Loisy, *Actes*, pp. 212-13.
3. Loisy, *Actes*, pp. 212-13, 233, 509-10, 820, 899, 939.
4. Loisy, *Actes*, pp. 320, 934-38.
5. A. Harnack, *The Acts of the Apostles* (ET; New Testament Studies, 3; Crown Theological Library, 27; New York: Putnam's, 1909), pp. xxv n. 1, 286-88.

particular sections or persons among the Jews he does not keep silence,
and so sacrifice truth to his theology of history.[1]

Indeed, Harnack agrees that Luke emphasizes the hostility of Jews to
Christianity and tends to pardon the same behavior on the part of
Romans. However, such an emphasis is precisely what one would expect
of an author concerned to explain the spread of the gospel from the
sphere of Judaism to the Gentile world. Moreover, Luke's emphasis is
not unequivocal: he also notes instances of Roman hostility and positive
Jewish response.[2]

Likewise, Harnack notes that for Luke Christianity is the fulfillment of
the religion of the Jewish Scriptures. However, for Luke the promises to
Israel are still valid, and the law still has limited saving power for Jews.[3]
Unlike the second-century apologists and the *Epistle of Barnabas*, Luke
never suggests that the law is to be interpreted allegorically or that Israel
was never in possession of the promises of God.[4] Consequently, Luke
emphasizes the Jewish piety of Paul—not without historical warrant—
and regards such observance as worthy of admiration.[5]

The contrast between Harnack and his French contemporary epito-
mizes the debate that would develop in the coming decades. In large
part the scholarly community would follow the lead of Loisy, but the
caveats offered by Harnack would be raised again by those who questioned the developing consensus.

Martin Dibelius
The essays in Dibelius's *Studies in the Acts of the Apostles* never
directly address Luke's portrayal of Jewish involvement in the
crucifixion.[6] Dibelius does, however, emphasize some critical perspectives which proved influential in subsequent treatments of the issue.

One of those perspectives is his view of the nature of the speeches in
Acts. Dibelius declares repeatedly that for Luke the speeches serve pri-
marily as examples of Christian preaching to be followed by readers of
Acts.[7] Paul's defense speeches are no exception to this pattern. Their

1.   Harnack, *Acts*, p. xxiv.
2.   Harnack, *Acts*, pp. xxx-xxxi.
3.   Harnack, *Acts*, pp. 284-86.
4.   Harnack, *Acts*, p. 283.
5.   Harnack, *Acts*, pp. 284-88.
6.   M. Dibelius, *Studies in the Acts of the Apostles* (ET; ed. H. Greenven;
London: SCM Press, 1956).
7.   Dibelius, *Studies*, pp. 70, 79, 165-66, 213. This assertion appears to be at

purpose is not to tell the story of Paul's imprisonment, for the outcome is never given.[1] Rather, they serve as examples for Christians faced with Jewish hostility. They address the contemporary debate between Christians and Jews, demonstrating that Christianity is the proper development from true Judaism.[2]

This conclusion coincides with another: 'The Acts of the Apostles was written at a time when it was abundantly clear to all that Christianity was moving away from Judaism'.[3] Luke seeks to show that the Gentile mission is not the creation of any individual, such as Paul or even Peter, but is the direct work of God himself. Jewish rejection of the gospel is the fault of the Jews themselves, as demonstrated by the three episodes of Paul's denouncing Jewish unbelief and turning to the Gentiles (Acts 13.46; 18.6; 28.28).[4] Here Luke's distance from meaningful contact with Jews or Jewish Christianity is further demonstrated in his failure to substantiate these harsh judgments against the Jews.[5]

Dibelius's view of Luke's composition of the speeches and of his ecclesiological distance from Judaism has implications which remained for others to draw out. The speeches of Acts, of course, consistently ascribe responsibility for Jesus' crucifixion to Jews. If the speeches are intended as examples for Luke's readers, then it would appear that Luke regarded such an accusation against the Jews as an ordinary part of the preaching of his day. Luke would therefore regard his Jewish contemporaries as somehow responsible for the death of Jesus. Though Dibelius himself did not draw out this implication, it surfaces in the work of some who adopted his perspectives.

The Developing Post-War Consensus

With the rapid advancement in Lukan studies following World War II, critical opinion largely came into accord in its understanding of the Jews in Luke–Acts. The concern of this section will be to note the pervasiveness of that consensus and its particular effect on studies of the death of

odds with Dibelius's suggestion (*Studies*, pp. 88-90) that Acts circulated in secular circles until the end of the second century.

1.   Dibelius, *Studies*, p. 149.
2.   Dibelius, *Studies*, pp. 172-73.
3.   Dibelius, *Studies*, p. 173.
4.   Dibelius, *Studies*, pp. 173-74.
5.   Dibelius, *Studies*, pp. 149-50.

Jesus in Lukan theology. Specific attention will be given to works which give significant regard to the question of the Jews in Luke–Acts; the influence of the consensus on other Lukan studies will be noted briefly.

Hans Conzelmann

To the insights of Dibelius, Conzelmann added several suggestions which tended to fill out the portrait of Luke's relationship to Judaism. One of these is Conzelmann's understanding of Luke's view of the past. Luke clearly regards the early years of the church as characterized by exemplary Jewish piety: devotion to the temple is especially conspicuous in the initial chapters of Acts. But according to Conzelmann, the founding period of the church was unique in Luke's view. He cites several lines of evidence for this interpretation: the distinguishing between the past and the present in the preface to the Gospel (Lk. 1.1-4), the absence of any view of a decline since the church's founding which would necessitate a restoration, and the shift from legal piety to the law-free Gentile mission in Acts.[1] Temple devotion and legal piety therefore do not reflect the situation in Luke's community but are a feature of the distant past.

Another plank of Conzelmann's platform concerns the implication of Jewish involvement in the crucifixion. The rejection of Jesus by the Jews in Jerusalem is decisive for the Jewish nation, in Conzelmann's view. Again several Lukan emphases serve to make this point. One is the focus on the temple. Luke emphasizes the temple in his account of Jesus' activity in Jerusalem in order to show that the Jewish claim to the temple is illegitimate. Since the Jews rejected Jesus at the crucifixion, they occupy the temple illegally. Its destruction is therefore understood as a judgment against the nation that crucified Jesus.[2]

Luke likewise emphasizes the role of the Jews in the passion narrative proper. He omits Pilate's rendering of a verdict against Jesus (Mk 15.15) and suggests that the Jews themselves carried out the very act of crucifying (Lk. 23.25-26). Pilate is but a passive instrument of the Jewish will.[3] At Jesus' crucifixion the presence of the people during the leaders' scoffing reflects further Luke's placing the blame exclusively on the Jews.[4]

---

1. Conzelmann, *Theology*, pp. 14-15, 165, 211-12.

2. Conzelmann, *Theology*, pp. 78, 133-34, 165.

3. Conzelmann, *Theology*, pp. 87-88. For Conzelmann the exoneration of Pilate owes to Luke's efforts at political apology for the church (*Theology*, pp. 85-86).

4. Conzelmann, *Theology*, p. 90.

In keeping with this tendency, Luke has edited his sources in Acts to emphasize Jewish complicity in Jesus' death. Although in the source of Acts 2.23 ἀνόμων almost certainly referred to Gentiles, in Luke's version of the reference is to Jews.[1] Likewise in Acts 3.13; 4.27; 13.28 traditional material has been altered to play up Jewish involvement and play down Roman involvement.[2] Whatever remains of Roman responsibility merely survives from the sources and does not reflect Luke's perspective.[3]

In Conzelmann's view, Luke provides little by way of mitigating factors for the Jews' crucifixion of Jesus. Although they are indeed ignorant of Jesus' identity, and although complete knowledge of Jesus' identity is impossible before the resurrection, their ignorance is in fact the result of their rejection of Jesus. It does not excuse their action but stems from it. At most, ignorance provides the rationale for the conversion of individual Jews.[4] Likewise, although Jesus' death is foreordained by God to occur in Jerusalem, Jewish guilt is not thereby tempered. Jesus is crucified not just in Jerusalem but also by Jerusalem.[5] Divine predestination is indeed emphasized by the Jews' ignorance of the one they crucify, but their culpability remains.[6] The 'dogmatic' concern to show the death of Jesus as a part of the divine plan and the 'historical' concern to implicate the Jews and exonerate the Romans stand side by side in the narrative but are not integrated.[7]

Jewish rejection of Jesus results in the promises of Israel to the church. Those who reject the gospel cease to be 'Israel' and become 'the Jews'. Luke emphasizes the continuity between true Israel and the church by several means: the church's origin in Jerusalem, the legal piety of early Jewish Christianity, the imposition on the Gentiles of minimal legal observance in the apostolic decree, Christian possession of the Scriptures, and the stress on fulfillment of 'the hope of Israel' in the resurrection.[8] The Jewish nation is therefore now a profane nation; the

---

1. Conzelmann, *Theology*, pp. 90-92.
2. Conzelmann, *Theology*, pp. 91-92.
3. Conzelmann, *Theology*, pp. 90, 140 n. 1.
4. Conzelmann, *Theology*, pp. 92-93, 146, 162.
5. Conzelmann, *Theology*, pp. 133-34.
6. Conzelmann, *Theology*, pp. 92, 146.
7. Conzelmann, *Theology*, p. 140.
8. Conzelmann, *Theology*, pp. 146-48, 160-61, 212 n. 1, 213.

church is effectively, if not expressly, identified with Israel.[1]

Although in Conzelmann's view Luke emphasizes Jewish rejection of Jesus and the consequent judgment against the Jews, he apparently does not regard that rejection and judgment as unequivocal. The theme of ignorance does allow for the conversion of individual Jews.[2] Israel is divided by Jesus and the gospel, and it is the unbelieving portion which loses out on the promises.[3] But even this allowance appears to be a part of the past, for Acts 28.28 gives the 'final word' on Jewish conversion.[4] For Luke the church is a Gentile entity and was intended as such by God.[5]

Ernst Haenchen

Haenchen's view on the Jews in the Lukan corpus continue in the line of Dibelius and Conzelmann. They are found not only at appropriate points in his commentary on Acts but are also gathered together in a major article.[6] Again, Luke is a Gentile Christian who is far removed from the days of Jewish Christianity.[7] His perspective on the law, the temple and the Gentile mission all reflect the theology of late first-century Gentile Christianity.[8] The Jewish nation is characterized by its stubborn refusal of divine messengers.[9] By their refusal of the gospel, the Jews, not the church, are responsible for the rift between Christianity and Judaism.[10] Israel has therefore been replaced by the Gentiles as the nation of promise.[11] In this presentation of Judaism, Luke's aim is to establish salvation-historical and political continuity between Israel and the church; actual contact with Jews belongs to the past.[12]

Haenchen makes some comment about the presentation of guilt for

---

1. Conzelmann, *Theology*, pp. 25-26, 133-34, 145-46, 163-64, 190, 212.
2. Conzelmann, *Theology*, pp. 90, 92-93.
3. Conzelmann, *Theology*, pp. 21, 25-26, 145-46, 164.
4. Conzelmann, *Theology*, pp. 163, 190 n. 3.
5. Conzelmann, *Theology*, p. 212 n. 2.
6. E. Haenchen, *The Acts of the Apostles: A Commentary* (ET; Oxford: Basil Blackwell; Philadelphia: Westminster Press, 1971); 'Judentum und Christentum in der Apostelgeschichte', *ZNW* 54 (1963), pp. 155-89.
7. Haenchen, 'Judentum', p. 157.
8. Haenchen, *Acts*, pp. 101, 446, 459; 'Judentum', pp. 157, 164-65, 168.
9. Haenchen, 'Judentum', pp. 164-66.
10. Haenchen, *Acts*, pp. 101, 535, 539-40, 729; 'Judentum', p. 157.
11. Haenchen, *Acts*, pp. 209, 211; 'Judentum', pp. 168, 185.
12. Haenchen, *Acts*, pp. 101-102, 223.

the death of Jesus in the speeches of Acts. The death of Jesus in Luke's view is entirely the work of 'the Jews'; the Gentiles are merely their instruments.[1] Again, whatever remains of Gentile complicity is not indicative of Luke's essential view. But neither is it merely a surviving remnant of Luke's sources; rather, Luke's view is 'elastic enough' to accommodate contradictory statements.[2] Nevertheless, Luke's presentation of Jewish responsibility is not necessarily an anti-Jewish calumny. He is concerned less with the guilt of the Jews than with the innocence of Jesus, and he offers (however inconsistently) the excuse of ignorance to the Jews.[3] Haenchen never specifies whether Luke distinguishes between Jews who are responsible for the death of Jesus and those who are not, but his consistent use of 'the Jews' or 'Israel' without qualification in his comments on the relevant texts suggests that he assumes the indictment to be made without distinction.[4] It appears that Haenchen would consider any distinction among the Jews to have been unnecessary for a Luke to whom Judaism was an opponent and Jewish Christianity a distant memory.

Joachim Gnilka

The monograph by Gnilka on the use of Isa. 6.9-10 in the Synoptics makes a significant contribution to the discussion of Judaism in Luke–Acts.[5] Gnilka's analysis owes much to Conzelmann's epochal scheme.[6] Jesus' ministry represents the last opportunity for Israel to repent.[7] But because he goes to Jerusalem to die, that opportunity closes at the walls of the city.[8] Jerusalem is therefore not the 'central point' but the 'point of departure' of salvation.[9] In this connection Gnilka states explicitly a crucial point which is only implicit in his predecessors: Jesus is crucified by the entire Jewish nation (Acts 2.5, 22; 4.10).[10] The divine judgment

---

1. Haenchen, *Acts*, pp. 180, 183, 206.
2. Haenchen, *Acts*, p. 228.
3. Haenchen, *Acts*, pp. 207, 211, 416.
4. Haenchen, *Acts*, pp. 180, 183, 186, 206, 211, 416.
5. J. Gnilka, *Die Verstockung Israels: Isaias 6, 9-10 in der Theologie der Synoptiker* (SANT, 3; Munich: Kösel, 1961).
6. Gnilka, *Verstockung*, pp. 130-31, 149-50.
7. Gnilka, *Verstockung*, p. 132.
8. Gnilka, *Verstockung*, pp. 139-40.
9. Gnilka, *Verstockung*, pp. 139-40.
10. Gnilka, *Verstockung*, p. 139.

for this action is the destruction of Jerusalem.[1] Jewish responsibility for the death of Jesus is not mitigated by divine foreordination.[2]

But according to Gnilka the beginning of Acts offers yet another chance to the Jewish nation. According to a salvation-historical priority, repentance is again offered to the Jews, whose ignorance excuses in part their rejection of Jesus.[3] Those who repent retain the status of God's people which is otherwise forfeit.[4] Nevertheless, the Stephen episode and Paul's turning from the Jews to the Gentiles demonstrate the obduracy of the Jewish people.[5] The end of Acts marks the end of the Jewish mission, though the salvation of individual Jews is still possible.[6] The church assumes from Israel the identity of God's people and stands in opposition to the unrepentant 'Jews'.[7]

John C. O'Neill

A sharp anti-Jewish perspective in the Lukan corpus is alleged in the work of J.C. O'Neill.[8] Adopting the established viewpoint that Luke writes in a situation removed from Jewish Christianity, O'Neill finds similarities between Luke's presentation of Judaism and that of Justin. For both Luke and Justin the church finds its proper place only in the Gentile world.[9]

O'Neill argues several points to support his contention. One compares the role of Jerusalem to that of Rome. Just as Jerusalem is the final setting of the Gospel of Luke, so Rome is the final setting of Acts. But whereas Jesus meets death in Jerusalem, Paul's death in Rome is never narrated. Instead, the triumph of the gospel in Rome is emphasized. Jerusalem thus is associated with Jewish rejection of the gospel while Rome is associated with Gentile acceptance.[10] The divinely ordained

---

1. Gnilka, *Verstockung*, pp. 137-39.
2. Gnilka, *Verstockung*, p. 139.
3. Gnilka, *Verstockung*, pp. 141-43.
4. Gnilka, *Verstockung*, pp. 143-44.
5. Gnilka, *Verstockung*, pp. 144-49.
6. Gnilka, *Verstockung*, pp. 130, 154.
7. Gnilka, *Verstockung*, pp. 143-46, 149.
8. J.C. O'Neill, *The Theology of Acts in its Historical Setting* (London: SPCK, 2nd edn, 1970).
9. O'Neill, *Theology*, pp. 12-13.
10. O'Neill, *Theology*, pp. 61-63.

movement of the church is from Jerusalem to Rome, that is, from Jews to Gentiles.[1]

But more than just the success of the Gentile mission is at stake for Luke. O'Neill maintains that for Luke Paul's distinct contribution is not in taking the gospel to the Gentiles but in establishing churches that are institutionally separate from the synagogue.[2] 'Luke's thesis is that the gospel is free to travel to the ends of the earth only when it is free from the false form which the Jewish religion has taken.'[3] The critical junctures are in Corinth and Ephesus. In both cities Paul leaves the synagogue not to form a new synagogue—an action he could have taken in both situations—but to establish an altogether new institution composed of Jews and Gentiles.[4] Luke's Paul does not attack the Jews per se, but his forthright preaching has the effect of causing their rejection of the gospel, an outcome foreordained in the divine plan.[5]

Like Gnilka, O'Neill underlines Luke's presentation of Jewish involvement in the crucifixion. According to O'Neill, Luke not only places responsibility for the death of Jesus on the Jewish nation as a whole, he also emphasizes that the nation has rejected every opportunity for repenting of that action.[6] The last of these chances comes with the preaching of Stephen. In Stephen's speech Luke integrates his view of Jewish responsibility for the death of Jesus with a comprehensive view of Israel's history: Israel rejected Jesus in Jerusalem because Israel always rejects God's messengers.[7] Subsequent encounters with Jews only show that Jewish rejection serves to further the Gentile mission.[8] O'Neill quotes Overbeck with approval at this point: Luke uses Jewish responsibility for the death of Jesus as a part of his 'theoretical justification in the advance of Christianity's turning away from the Jews to the Gentiles, made in terms of the stubbornness of the Jews'.[9]

---

1.   O'Neill, *Theology*, pp. 75-76, 95, 178-79.
2.   O'Neill, *Theology*, pp. 74-75, 133-34.
3.   O'Neill, *Theology*, p. 75.
4.   O'Neill, *Theology*, pp. 74-75, 118-19.
5.   O'Neill, *Theology*, p. 75.
6.   O'Neill, *Theology*, pp. 79-81.
7.   O'Neill, *Theology*, pp. 83-84.
8.   O'Neill, *Theology*, pp. 84-86.
9.   O'Neill, *Theology*, p. 87; the precise source of the quotation of Overbeck is not identified.

Ulrich Wilckens

The influential study of the speeches of Acts by U. Wilckens likewise reflects the viewpoint that Luke writes for a church distant from Jewish contacts.[1] Adopting Conzelmann's epochal scheme, he confines the period of Jewish salvation to the early period of the church.[2] Jewish rejection of the gospel effects the transfer of salvation from Israel to the Gentiles. When Paul turns from the Jews to the Gentiles, the era of Jewish salvation ends and the era of Gentile salvation, Luke's own era, begins.[3]

But Wilckens does more than adopt Conzelmann's position: he seeks to reinforce and refine it. According to Wilckens Luke's perspective on Judaism is thoroughly Hellenistic and well removed from Jewish Christianity. The motif of responsibility for the death of Jesus demonstrates this point for Wilckens. He notes that each time the crucifixion is mentioned in Acts, the Jews are said to be responsible for it. Two contrasts—on the one hand between Pilate's verdict of innocence and the Jewish call for Jesus' death and on the other hand between the Jews' crucifying Jesus and God's raising him from the dead—serve ultimately to underline the sin of the Jews in the crucifixion.[4] In fact, in some instances the resurrection is grammatically subordinate to the Jews' action in crucifying Jesus.[5] Conversely, Roman involvement is played down.[6] The result is straightforward: 'That with Luke a clear tendency is present, to decide the question of responsibility unequivocally in the sense of solely Jewish responsibility, is a generally observed fact'.[7]

Wilckens observes that on at least one occasion Luke confines the accusation to Jerusalem Jews.[8] Nevertheless, he insists that Luke holds all Jews responsible for the death of Jesus. He bases this judgment partly on his understanding of Luke's theology: both the Jerusalemites' crucifixion of Jesus and the diaspora Jews' rejection of the gospel are prerequisites of the Gentile mission. Each group stands, therefore, for

---

1. U. Wilckens, *Die Missionsreden der Apostelgeschichte* (WMANT, 5; Neukirchen–Vluyn: Neukirchener Verlag, 3rd edn, 1973).
2. Wilckens, *Missionsreden*, pp. 96-99.
3. Wilckens, *Missionsreden*, pp. 52-53, 70-71, 96-97, 99.
4. Wilckens, *Missionsreden*, pp. 36-37, 39-40, 44-45, 51, 127, 134-35.
5. Wilckens, *Missionsreden*, p. 34.
6. Wilckens, *Missionsreden*, p. 128.
7. Wilckens, *Missionsreden*, p. 119.
8. Wilckens, *Missionsreden*, pp. 53, 97.

the entire Jewish nation which has forfeited its elect status and has been replaced by the Gentile church.[1] But it is Wilckens's tradition-critical argument on this point which makes a distinctive contribution to the ongoing debate. He maintains that the accusation of the death of Jesus in Acts stems from the same milieu as 1 Thess. 2.14-16. This text, according to Wilckens, is influenced by typical Hellenistic anti-Jewish attitudes, which are likewise reflected in Acts.[2] Luke has thus transferred a Hellenistic-Christian schema to the Jewish-Christian period of the church in order to create an *ordo salutis* in which the Jews must repent of the crucifixion as the Gentiles must repent of their paganism.[3] Although Wilckens traces the origin of ascription of responsibility to Jerusalem ultimately to the Hellenistic-Jewish-Christians expelled from Jerusalem, their intra-Jewish perspective is not reflected in Luke's use of the tradition as he received it.[4]

Robert Maddox

Reacting in part to the work of J. Jervell,[5] R. Maddox reasserts the predominantly Gentile setting of Luke–Acts. He reckons with Luke's apparent interest in Jewish matters but insists on a considerable anti-Jewish strain as well.[6] This latter orientation is seen especially in the confrontation with Jerusalem in the travel and passion narratives. Jesus 'set his face' to go to Jerusalem not in determination but in judgment.[7] The travel narrative consistently warns that judgment will come because of rejection of Jesus, and it assumes that Jerusalem's judgment is already sealed, as the apocalyptic discourse reiterates.[8] In Jerusalem Jesus is rejected by the entire Jewish nation, which calls for his crucifixion.[9] That rejection is anticipated as early as the Nazareth episode and is worked out in Acts.[10] Again, Stephen's speech and Paul's turning to the Gentiles emphasize the responsibility of the Jews for the rift between the

1. Wilckens, *Missionsreden*, pp. 52-53.
2. Wilckens, *Missionsreden*, pp. 119-21.
3. Wilckens, *Missionsreden*, pp. 85-86, 180-82.
4. Wilckens, *Missionsreden*, p. 207.
5. See the discussion of Jervell's work below.
6. R. Maddox, *The Purpose of Luke–Acts* (FRLANT, 126; Göttingen: Vandenhoeck & Ruprecht, 1982), p. 42.
7. Maddox, *Purpose*, pp. 46-47.
8. Maddox, *Purpose*, pp. 46-52.
9. Maddox, *Purpose*, pp. 45-46.
10. Maddox, *Purpose*, pp. 5, 44-45.

church and synagogue. The experience of the early Christians consistently shows them that God's will is for the gospel, rejected by the Jews, to go to the Gentiles.[1] Although Luke indicates divided response in Israel, his emphasis falls on rejection.[2] At the end of Acts the Jewish mission is over, but the Gentile mission has only just been entirely opened.[3] Jewish rejection and its consequent judgment, the loyalty of the early Christian leaders to Judaism, and the receptivity of the Gentiles always stand together for Luke.[4] The result is the end of the promises to Israel and their effective transfer to the (Gentile) church.[5]

Maddox offers a refined understanding of Luke's setting to account for the positive and negative aspects of Luke's approach to Judaism.[6] Luke's church is predominantly Gentile but finds its theological identity threatened by the ongoing existence of Judaism.[7] Luke therefore seeks to explain both the Jewish heritage of the church—as both a historical fact and a theological focus—and the rejection of the Christian gospel by Judaism. The Jewish orientation of much of Luke–Acts therefore does not indicate that Luke writes for a church which includes Jewish Christians; instead, the material explains the origins of the present situation.[8]

Stephen G. Wilson

The several contributions of S.G. Wilson to the study of Judaism in Luke–Acts have further refined scholarly debate.[9] Wilson's scope on

---

1. Maddox, *Purpose*, pp. 39, 53-54.

2. Maddox, *Purpose*, pp. 43, 62 n. 95.

3. Maddox, *Purpose*, pp. 42-44.

4. Maddox, *Purpose*, pp. 55-56. Pro-Romanism plays no part in this scheme (*Purpose*, pp. 93-95).

5. Maddox, *Purpose*, pp. 106-107, 183.

6. Maddox rightly notes that his reconstruction, like all others, amounts to 'reading between the lines' to determine what knowledge Luke assumed in his audience (*Purpose*, p. 45).

7. Maddox, *Purpose*, pp. 31-32, 46, 183-85.

8. Maddox, *Purpose*, pp. 16-17.

9. S.G. Wilson, *The Gentiles and the Gentile Mission in Luke–Acts* (SNTSMS, 23; Cambridge: Cambridge University Press, 1974); *Luke and the Law* (SNTSMS, 50; Cambridge: Cambridge University Press, 1983); 'The Jews and the Death of Jesus in Acts', in P. Richardson and D. Granskou (eds.), *Anti-Judaism in Early Christianity* (Studies in Christianity and Judaism, 2; Waterloo, Ontario: Wilfrid Laurier University Press, 1986), pp. 155-64.

this subject has been particularly broad; his monographs and essays touch on the whole range of issues related to Judaism in the Lukan corpus. Throughout his work he maintains the perspective of Dibelius and Conzelmann: although he knows that the church's origins were Jewish, Luke, in writing for a predominantly Gentile church in conflict with Judaism, regards Jewish Christianity and the Jewish mission as things of the past.[1] Although Luke views the religion 'Judaism' favorably, he views the people 'the Jews' as opponents of Jesus and the church.[2]

Wilson gives particular attention to the motif of responsibility for the death of Jesus in a recent essay.[3] Here he emphasizes that Luke, having received from Mark the tradition of Jewish involvement in the crucifixion, has further emphasized that involvement and played down the Romans' role.[4] In only two instances in Acts is Roman involvement intimated, and these do not remove the overwhelming impression of the narrative that the Jews bear responsibility for the crucifixion.[5] The culpability of the Jews is universal: Luke accuses the entire Jewish people, not merely the leaders, and places the crucifixion at the head of the list of Jewish rejections of God's prophets.[6] Nevertheless, Jewish culpability is mitigated somewhat by several factors, among them the distinction between the Jews of Jerusalem and those of the diaspora.[7]

Wilson's understanding of Jewish responsibility for the death of Jesus in Luke–Acts does not in itself represent a new contribution to the discussion. What he offers in particular is an observation about Luke's setting: if Luke's readers were indeed Gentile Christians for whom the Jewish mission was a part of the past but hostility from the synagogues an ever-present reality, the effect of the Lukan account—whatever its apparent nuances—could only have been markedly anti-Jewish.[8]

---

1.   Wilson, *Gentiles*, pp. 232-33, 236-37; *Law*, pp. 38-39, 53, 57-58, 107-108, 115-16. Wilson does allow for the possibility of ongoing contact with Jewish Christianity in the Lukan community (*Law*, pp. 102, 104-105), but he suggests that the evidence for that contact may well reflect criticism from Jews outside the Lukan church (*Law*, pp. 107-108, 113).

2.   Wilson, *Law*, pp. 115-16.

3.   Wilson, 'Jews and the Death of Jesus'.

4.   Wilson, 'Jews and the Death of Jesus', pp. 156-57, 160.

5.   Wilson, 'Jews and the Death of Jesus', pp. 156-57.

6.   Wilson, 'Jews and the Death of Jesus', p. 157.

7.   Wilson, 'Jews and the Death of Jesus', pp. 158-59, 163.

8.   Wilson, 'Jews and the Death of Jesus', p. 164.

Joseph B. Tyson

Examining Luke's presentation of Jesus' death with insights from literary criticism, J.B. Tyson follows in the main the consensus position concerning Luke's setting. The Lukan church has broken definitively with Judaism and seeks to place the onus for that break on the Jewish side.[1] To that end it emphasizes Jewish repudiation of Jesus and his followers by means of a persistent literary motif: initial acceptance followed by final rejection.[2] This motif develops in a number of ways. Although the Jewish leaders oppose Jesus and the Christians throughout the narrative, the Jewish people appear to be favorably disposed at the beginning of Jesus' ministry and in the early chapters of Acts.[3] But the inevitable rejection that is to come is foreshadowed in the Nazareth pericope.[4] In Luke's presentation of the passion that popular rejection comes to fruition in the arrest of Jesus.[5] For Luke, Judas's 'betrayal' is the offstage transformation of the previously supportive crowds into a hostile mob.[6] The cry of the crowd for crucifixion constitutes a definitive rejection of Jesus by the Jewish people.[7] Thus, Luke blames the Jewish people generally for Jesus' death, concurrently exonerating Rome.[8] Because of its final hostility to Jesus (and Paul), Jerusalem is for Luke associated with 'great danger and unreasonable, vicious hostility'.[9]

The same pattern of initial acceptance followed by final rejection is found in the Jerusalem section of Acts and in Paul's ministry.[10] In fact, the strength of the motif is seen in the logical inconsistencies it involves, such as Paul's repeated attempts at synagogue preaching despite his turning to the Gentiles.[11] In Paul's case the rejection becomes final in Rome, where the failed Jewish mission is terminated in favor of the successful Gentile mission.[12]

---

1. J.B. Tyson, *The Death of Jesus in Luke–Acts* (Columbia, SC: University of South Carolina Press, 1986), pp. 108-10, 169-70, 172.

2. Tyson, *Death*, pp. 29-30.

3. Tyson, *Death*, pp. 30-31, 78.

4. Tyson, *Death*, pp. 32-33.

5. Tyson, *Death*, pp. 34-35, 37-38.

6. Tyson, *Death*, pp. 120-21, 145-48.

7. Tyson, *Death*, pp. 37, 43.

8. Tyson, *Death*, pp. 118-19, 126-29, 138-39, 164.

9. Tyson, *Death*, pp. 100-101; cf. 110.

10. Tyson, *Death*, pp. 39, 42.

11. Tyson, *Death*, pp. 42-43.

12. Tyson, *Death*, pp. 43-44.

Jack T. Sanders

The viewpoint that Luke is far removed from Judaism is most thoroughly expressed in J.T. Sanders's recent monograph.[1] Sanders proposes that Luke's hostility to Jews is 'fundamental and systematic'.[2] Luke's narrative does not relent in its condemnation of Jews and Judaism. Regarding the particular issue of responsibility for the death of Jesus, Sanders insists that Luke implicates both the Jewish leaders and the Jewish people while exonerating the Romans.[3] The very deed of crucifixion is performed by Jewish soldiers.[4] Indeed, for Luke the Jews who crucify Jesus are all the Jews, so that all Jews bear guilt for the deed.[5] Neither divine foreordination nor ignorance provides for them an excuse.[6]

Sanders recognizes that certain elements of the text suggest a different viewpoint. Some appear to assert Roman complicity, but in these he finds indications that Luke has deliberately obscured the emphasis of his sources on Roman involvement.[7] Others appear to make distinctions among the Jewish people, dividing them into responsive and unresponsive groups.[8] But here Sanders proposes two explanations. One is that Jewish outcasts (tax collectors, sinners, Samaritans) are not Jews in Luke's view but a transitional group who represent the Gentiles in Luke's Gospel.[9] The other is that although some Jews are treated positively in the earlier portions of Luke's narrative, the Jews are universally condemned in the speech portions of Luke–Acts.[10] Those Jews who come in for positive treatment serve to establish salvation-historical continuity between Israel and the church.[11] But by the end of Acts, all Jews are opponents of Christianity. The result is that, in a manner similar to

1.   J.T. Sanders, *The Jews in Luke–Acts* (London: SCM Press, 1987). Cf. my preliminary critique of this work, 'The Jews in Luke–Acts', *TynBul* 49 (1989), pp. 107-17.

2.   Sanders, *Jews in Luke–Acts*, p. xvi.

3.   Sanders, *Jews in Luke–Acts*, pp. 3-9, 38-39.

4.   Sanders, *Jews in Luke–Acts*, pp. 10-13.

5.   Sanders, *Jews in Luke–Acts*, p. 53. Likewise, Luke indicts all Jews for the death of Stephen (*Jews in Luke–Acts*, pp. 73-74).

6.   Sanders, *Jews in Luke–Acts*, pp. 52, 63-64, 234-38.

7.   Sanders, *Jews in Luke–Acts*, pp. 13-15.

8.   Sanders, *Jews in Luke–Acts*, pp. 47-50, 85-89.

9.   Sanders, *Jews in Luke–Acts*, pp. 133-39, 144.

10.   Sanders, *Jews in Luke–Acts*, pp. 36, 48-50.

11.   Sanders, *Jews in Luke–Acts*, pp. 97-99.

Tyson's scheme, the Jews 'become what they are' through the course of the narrative.[1] Identified in the speeches as evil and unrepentant, they behave as such in the end of the narrative. The closing scene of Acts drives home this point and indicates that for Luke the Jews are now confirmed in their condemnation.[2] The church is a Gentile entity (as God had always intended), and the Jewish mission is closed.[3] Those Jewish Christians whom Luke knows (represented by the Pharisees in the narrative) he condemns as hypocrites and legalists.[4]

Sanders's work represents the culmination of the pervasive trend in studies on Judaism in Luke–Acts since Overbeck. In large measure his conclusions are reached by rigorously pursuing the lines of inquiry already mapped out. He not only sets forth with greater thoroughness the evidence of Luke's hostility to Judaism but also addresses those elements of the text which appear to moderate it. The major contribution of his work lies in presenting a thorough, comprehensive account of Luke's approach to Judaism.

The Extent of the Consensus
A number of monographs on various aspects of Lukan theology reflect this consensus on Luke's approach to the Jews. Appearing at various times throughout the post-war period, these works agree in asserting that Luke presents the death of Jesus as the rejection of Jesus by the entire Jewish nation.[5] Each then suggests implications of that view in a

---

1. Sanders, *Jews in Luke–Acts*, pp. 81, 129-30.
2. Sanders, *Jews in Luke–Acts*, pp. 53, 273-75, 279, 298.
3. Sanders, *Jews in Luke–Acts*, pp. 76, 128-29, 250, 283-84, 299.
4. Sanders, *Jews in Luke–Acts*, pp. 94-103, 110-11, 123-24, 128-29.
5. Statements on the responsibility of the entire nation of Israel for the death of Jesus can be found in G. Schneider, *Verleugnung, Verspottung und Verhör Jesu nach Lukas 22, 54-71* (SANT, 22; Munich: Kösel, 1969), pp. 148, 153, 169; K. Löning, 'Lukas—Theologe der von Gott geführten Heilsgeschichte (Lk, Apg)', in J. Schreiner (ed.), *Gestalt und Anspruch des Neuen Testaments* (Würzburg: Echter Verlag, 1969), p. 219; E. Kränkl, *Jesus der Knecht Gottes: Die heilsgeschichtliche Stellung Jesu in den Reden der Apostelgeschichte* (Münchener Universitäts-Schriften, Katholisch-Theologische Fakultät; Regensburg: Pustet, 1972), pp. 102-105, 108, 208; F. Keck, *Die öffentliche Abschiedsrede Jesu in Lk 20, 45–21, 36* (Forschung zur Bibel, 25; Stuttgart: Katholisches Bibelwerk, 1976), pp. 198, 205; H.L. Egelkraut, *Jesus' Mission to Jerusalem: A Redaction Critical Study of the Travel Narrative in the Gospel of Luke, Lk 9.51–19.48* (Europäische Hochschulschriften, Reihe 23, Theologie 80; Frankfurt: Peter Lang;

variety of areas. Several may be cited briefly here. G. Schneider presses Conzelmann's suggestion that in Luke's passion narrative Jewish soldiers perform the actual deed of crucifying.[1] K. Löning argues that the movement of the church outward from Jerusalem is a reversal of Jesus' journey to Jerusalem in consequence of Israel's rejection of Jesus and the gospel.[2] Similarly, F. Keck suggests that the Lukan confrontations in the temple with the Jewish leaders indicate that the breach between the church and Judaism comes about as a result of Jewish refusal.[3] H.L. Egelkraut, on the other hand, submits that during Jesus' journey to Jerusalem he was rejected by a cross-section of Jewish society representing the nation as a whole, who seal that rejection in the crucifixion of Jesus and the refusal of the gospel in Acts.[4] E. Kränkl notes the Lukan emphasis on the death of Jesus as divinely initiated but insists that Jewish culpability is not thereby ameliorated.[5]

Among such works, however, are some which note elements that tend to soften the prevailing portrait of Luke as anti-Jewish. A. Büchele, for example, notes that the leaders of Israel, not the people, are the real opponents of Jesus, and Israel's response to the gospel is not so much outright rejection as division.[6] But for Büchele this tension is left unresolved; Luke's presentation of responsibility for the death of Jesus is, in the final analysis, ambiguous.[7] Similarly, C.H. Talbert argues that Israel is divided by Jesus and his ministry in Luke–Acts.[8] Still, Jesus' rejection by the Jerusalem leadership is representative of the entire

---

Bern: Herbert Lang, 1976), pp. 133, 178; A. Büchele, *Der Tod Jesu im Lukasevangelium: Eine redaktionsgeschichtliche Untersuchung zu Lk 23* (Frankfurter Theologische Studien, 26; Frankfurt: Knecht, 1978), pp. 27, 29-30, 33, 38-39, 47, 65-66, 105, 108-109, 123-26, 155, 184; C.H. Talbert, 'Martyrdom in Luke–Acts and the Lucan Social Ethic', in R.J. Cassidy and P.J. Scharper (eds.), *Political Issues in Luke–Acts* (Maryknoll, NY: Orbis Books, 1983), p. 102; J.H. Neyrey, *The Passion according to Luke: A Redaction Study of Luke's Soteriology* (New York and Mahwah: Paulist Press, 1985), pp. 70-73, 82-83.

1. Schneider, *Verleugnung*, p. 195.
2. Löning, 'Heilsgeschichte', pp. 219-20.
3. Keck, *Öffentliche Abschiedsrede*, pp. 24-26, 187.
4. Egelkraut, *Mission to Jerusalem*, pp. 132, 192, 232-33.
5. Kränkl, *Knecht*, p. 103.
6. Büchele, *Tod*, pp. 105-10, 136, 165-66, 180-81.
7. Büchele, *Tod*, p. 188.
8. Talbert, 'Martyrdom', pp. 100-101.

nation's rejection.[1] Talbert does not address the question of how division and national rejection are integrated in Luke's theology. Likewise, J. Neyrey argues that the trials of Jesus in Luke are in fact the trials of the nation of Israel.[2] Nevertheless, even though those trials encompass the entire nation, Israel's rejection of Jesus is not permanent; the nation is ultimately divided in its response to the gospel.[3]

The breadth of scope represented in these works indicates the pervasiveness of the supposition that Luke charges all Israel with the guilt for Jesus' death as part of a larger, anti-Jewish theological venture. The conclusions of Overbeck, Loisy, Conzelmann, Haenchen *et al.* are unmistakably reproduced in the preponderance of post-war criticism.

Dissent from the Consensus

Although the predominant critical opinion has been that Luke's perspective on Jews is essentially negative, a number of recent works have challenged that view. These works raise significant questions about Luke's approach to Judaism and the death of Jesus, many of which remain unaddressed.

Gerhard Lohfink

Although allowing that the Jewish mission was a matter of the past for Luke's church, G. Lohfink's seminal study on Lukan ecclesiology nevertheless suggests that Luke the Gentile Christian shared the essentially Jewish-Christian perspective of his sources.[4] For Lohfink's Luke the church is the true Israel, gathered through the ministries of the Baptist, Jesus and the apostles.[5] The Jewish people are divided through their preaching into two camps.[6] Those who accept the message become part of the true Israel. Those who do not lose their elect status and become 'Jews'.[7]

Lohfink argues from several converging lines of evidence that in the

---

1. Talbert, 'Martyrdom', p. 102.
2. Neyrey, *Passion*, pp. 75, 82, 89-92.
3. Neyrey, *Passion*, pp. 110-11, 121-23, 132.
4. G. Lohfink, *Die Sammlung Israels: Eine Untersuchung zur lukanischen Ekklesiologie* (SANT, 39; Munich: Kösel, 1975), pp. 21, 61.
5. Lohfink, *Sammlung*, pp. 22-23, 93-95.
6. Lohfink, *Sammlung*, pp. 61-62.
7. Lohfink, *Sammlung*, pp. 23-25, 30, 54-58.

journey narrative Jesus gathers together all of Israel.[1] The λαός in Jerusalem at the passion is thus the entire nation of Israel. Therefore it is the entire nation which, in Luke's one departure from a positive depiction of Israel, calls for Jesus' crucifixion.[2] The significance of this action is revealed in Acts. At Pentecost, the same crowd which called for Jesus' death accepts the gospel proclaimed by Peter.[3] The rejection of Jesus by the entire nation is thus a salvation-historical necessity: it allows for the announcement of repentance and forgiveness after the resurrection.[4] The emphasis on mass conversions of Jews in Acts continues the theme of the gathering of all true Israel.[5] The Gentile mission is the result not merely of Jewish rejection of the gospel; it fulfills the scriptural promises to Israel and has as its prerequisite the gathering of Israel.[6] The λαός of God only comes to reality when all of true Israel is gathered and the Gentiles are added.[7]

Eric Franklin

Reading Luke–Acts from the supposition that Luke's church is composed of both Jews and Gentiles, E. Franklin attempts to understand Luke's presentation of Judaism as an apology aimed at justifying Christian claims in light of Jewish rejection.[8] Thus he finds an emphasis in Luke–Acts on the recognition among the faithful in Israel of God's initiative to renew Israel through Jesus.[9] Those who reject Jesus (largely identified as the Jewish leaders) do so from an obstinacy which is consistent with one element of Israel's history.[10] Thus, Israel is divided.[11] Luke therefore ameliorates the judgment which comes on Israel because of the obstinate faction: Jerusalem is destroyed in judgment for rejecting Jesus in accordance with God's will, but that destruction is not an

---

1.   Lohfink, *Sammlung*, pp. 35-42.
2.   Lohfink, *Sammlung*, pp. 42-46.
3.   Lohfink, *Sammlung*, pp. 48-50.
4.   Lohfink, *Sammlung*, pp. 51, 74-77.
5.   Lohfink, *Sammlung*, pp. 52-54.
6.   Lohfink, *Sammlung*, pp. 28-30.
7.   Lohfink, *Sammlung*, pp. 58-61.
8.   E. Franklin, *Christ the Lord: A Study in the Purpose and Theology of Luke–Acts* (London: SPCK, 1975), pp. 77, 110-12, 136.
9.   Franklin, *Christ the Lord*, p. 78.
10. Franklin, *Christ the Lord*, pp. 78, 88-89, 103.
11. Franklin, *Christ the Lord*, pp. 88-89, 104.

eschatological act of God but a purely political and historical event.[1] The pronouncements of Jerusalem's destruction thus exhibit no hostility toward the city of the Jewish nation per se.[2]

The climax of Jesus' rejection by the obstinate element in Israel is, of course, the crucifixion. According to Franklin, Luke's emphasis on the culpability of the Sanhedrin cannot be squared with the hypothesis of a political apologetic directed to Rome, for Luke depicts the Romans in a less than favorable light.[3] Nevertheless, although Rome is involved in Jesus' death, the Sanhedrin bears all the responsibility.[4] In their call for the crucifixion, the Jewish people (who act as the entire nation) are separated from their leaders in two ways: (1) they act in ignorance; (2) they fulfill the divine purpose and thus act as the covenant people.[5] They are therefore not held to account for their actions at the beginning of Acts.[6] In Acts they repeat their behavior toward Jesus in the rejection of Stephen, but the gospel continues to win adherents in the city even after this decisive action.[7] Similarly, Paul's preaching meets with widespread acceptance among the Jews of the Diaspora as well as definitive rejection.[8] The final 'turning to the Gentiles' is therefore not an absolute end to the Jewish mission but an explanation of Jewish rejection and the Gentile mission in light of Luke's understanding of Israel's history.[9]

Because Franklin's Luke views Jesus as the one who restores Israel, he holds out considerable hope for the future of the Jewish people. Luke does not deny the hope of a restoration of the kingdom to Israel. For the present that restoration is effected by the obedient response of the Jews to God's initiative in Jesus.[10] 'Israel' therefore no longer means 'empirical Israel' but 'repentance Israel'.[11] In the future Israel's promises will be fulfilled in Jesus' return.[12]

---

1. Franklin, *Christ the Lord*, pp. 89-92, 130.
2. Franklin, *Christ the Lord*, pp. 89-90.
3. Franklin, *Christ the Lord*, p. 93.
4. Franklin, *Christ the Lord*, p. 93.
5. Franklin, *Christ the Lord*, p. 94.
6. Franklin, *Christ the Lord*, pp. 94-95.
7. Franklin, *Christ the Lord*, pp. 102-103.
8. Franklin, *Christ the Lord*, pp. 110-11.
9. Franklin, *Christ the Lord*, pp. 113-15, 122, 138-39.
10. Franklin, *Christ the Lord*, pp. 94-95.
11. Franklin, *Christ the Lord*, p. 99.
12. Franklin, *Christ the Lord*, pp. 95-96.

Jaques Dupont

While accepting the supposition that Luke writes to explain the institutional separation between Christianity and Judaism, J. Dupont's various essays on Judaism in Luke–Acts provide some perspectives different from many of the common ideas in critical literature.[1] In particular, Dupont removes the attribution of responsibility for the death of Jesus from discussion of Luke's alleged hostility to Judaism by insisting that Luke restricts blame among the Jews to the people of Jerusalem and their leaders only.[2] That accusation in Acts is based on Luke's redaction

1.   J. Dupont, 'La conclusion des Actes et son rapport à l'ensemble de l'ouvrage de Luc', in J. Kremer (ed.), *Les Actes des Apôtres: Traditions, rédaction, théologie* (BETL, 48; Gembloux: Duculot; Leuven: Leuven University Press, 1979), pp. 386, 403; 'Un peuple d'entre les nations (Actes 15.14)', *NTS* 31 (1985), p. 330.

2.   J. Dupont, 'Les discours missionaires des Actes des Apôtres d'après un ouvrage récent', *RB* 69 (1962), pp. 45-46; *idem*, 'Les discours de Pierre dans les Actes et le chapitre XXIV de l'évangile de Luc', in F. Neirynck (ed.), *L'Evangile de Luc: Problèmes littéraires et théologiques: Mémorial Lucien Cerfaux* (BETL, 32; Gembloux: Duculot, 1973), pp. 337, 339. Dupont has been followed in this observation by several exegetes: G. Delling, 'Die Jesusgeschichte in Acts', *NTS* 19 (1972–73), pp. 380-81; M.F.-J. Buss, *Die Missionspredigt des Apostels Paulus im Pisidischen Antiochien* (FB, 38; Stuttgart: Katholisches Bibelwerk, 1980), pp. 67-68, 149; J. Roloff, *Die Apostelgeschichte* (NTD, 5; Göttingen: Vandenhoeck & Ruprecht, 1981), pp. 51, 206; E.J. Via, 'According to Luke, Who Put Jesus to Death?', in R.J. Cassidy and P.J. Scharper (eds.), *Political Issues in Luke–Acts* (Maryknoll, NY: Orbis Books, 1983), pp. 135, 138; M. Rese, 'Die Aussagen über Jesu Tod und Auferstehung in der Apostelgeschichte', *NTS* 30 (1984), pp. 344-45; R. Pesch, *Die Apostelgeschichte* (EKKNT, 5; 2 vols.; Zürich: Benziger Verlag; Neukirchen–Vluyn: Neukirchener Verlag, 1986), I, p. 121; R.C. Tannehill, Review of *Luke–Acts and the Jews: Conflict, Apology and Conciliation*, by Robert L. Brawley, *Bib* 70 (1989), p. 281; and F.J. Matera, 'Responsibility for the Death of Jesus according to the Acts of the Apostles', *JSNT* 39 (1990), p. 79. L. Gaston assigns this view to Proto-Luke only (*No Stone on Another* [NovTSup, 23; Leiden: Brill, 1970], pp. 330-31); elsewhere he concludes that the present text of Luke–Acts assigns responsibility to all Jews (*idem*, 'Anti-Judaism and the Passion Narrative in Luke and Acts', in Richardson and Granskou, *Anti-Judaism in Early Christianity*, pp. 128-30). G. Schneider allows that only Jerusalemites are accused (*Die Apostelgeschichte* [HTKNT, 5; 2 vols.; Freiburg: Herder, 1980–82], I, p. 271 n. 68; I, p. 468; II, p. 129) but understands that they represent the entire nation (*Die Apostelgeschichte*, I, p. 347; II, p. 78; *idem*, 'Das Verfahren gegen Jesus in der Sicht des dritten Evangeliums [Lk 22,54–23,25]: Redaktionskritik und historische Rückfrage', in K. Kertelge [ed.], *Der Prozess gegen Jesus: Historische Rückfrage und theologische Deutung* [QD, 112; Freiburg: Herder, 1989], pp. 117-18, 121).

of the passion narrative, which gives particular emphasis to the Jerusalemites' involvement.[1]

Similarly, Dupont has challenged the notion that for Luke the Gentile mission comes merely as a result of either the rejection or the acceptance of the gospel by the Jews.[2] He notes in particular Luke's emphasis on prophetic fulfillment and divine initiative in the establishment of the Gentile mission.[3] Nevertheless, Jewish rejection of the Christian message is still important to Luke. The closing scene of Acts especially emphasizes its role. The Jews who hear Paul's pronouncement represent the entire Jewish nation which rejects the gospel, for whom the Gentiles are a virtual substitute in God's design.[4] Still, the condemnation of Israel is not entire: the relatively small number who believe do not constitute 'this generation'; instead, they receive the salvation which is the object of Israel's hope.[5] Division in Israel, not wholesale rejection, is the Lukan emphasis.[6] Thus, rejection of the gospel by the Jews and the divine intention to save the Gentiles stand as coexistent and inseparable facts behind the Gentile mission.[7]

Augustin George
In two essays of comprehensive scope, A. George sets forth an interpretation which departs at several points from the prevailing consensus about Luke's hostility to Judaism. George accepts the notion that Luke wrote for a church which was predominantly Gentile, separated from the synagogue and well removed from its Jewish origins.[8] Nevertheless, it is division, not absolute rejection, which Luke characterizes as Israel's response to Jesus and the gospel.[9] Indeed, for Luke that division is nothing new, for he finds the same pattern in the history of biblical

1. Dupont, 'Les discours des Pierre', p. 337.
2. Dupont, 'La conclusion des Actes', pp. 393-95, 403.
3. J. Dupont, 'Le salut des gentils et la signification theologique du livre des Actes', *NTS* 6 (1959–60), p. 155; 'La conclusion des Actes', pp. 359-60; 'Un peuple d'entre les nations', p. 329.
4. Dupont, 'La conclusion des Actes', pp. 364, 376.
5. Dupont, 'La conclusion des Actes', pp. 379-80, 393; 'Un peuple d'entre les nations', pp. 324-26.
6. Dupont, 'La conclusion des Actes', pp. 380, 393-95.
7. Dupont, 'La conclusion des Actes', pp. 402-403.
8. A. George, 'Israël dans l'oeuvre de Luc', *RB* 75 (1968), pp. 481, 487-88, 491; 'Le sens de la mort de Jésus pour Luc', *RB* 80 (1973), p. 203.
9. George, 'Israël', pp. 484-86.

Israel.[1] When Jesus appears on the scene, the division is already an accomplished fact, manifested in Israel's response to the preaching of John.[2] In Jesus' ministry opposition is confined to the doctors of the law who adhere to traditional interpretations and to the political leaders who reject Jesus' rule over Israel.[3] The Jewish people are favorably disposed to Jesus and his apostles; even in the passion account they do not call for Jesus' crucifixion.[4] In fact, Jews in the narrative are assumed to be favorable unless the contrary is indicated.[5] The rejection by the leaders does not therefore serve as a representative rejection by the entire nation.[6] Although judgment for the crucifixion comes in the destruction of Jerusalem, that judgment can be escaped through repentance made possible by Jewish ignorance.[7] Nevertheless, after the Stephen episode Luke reckons with popular Jewish rejection of the gospel.[8] Thereafter, those of the house of Israel who reject the gospel become 'the Jews' and lose their status as God's people.[9]

Although after Stephen's murder the possibility of national conversion is clearly gone, individual Jewish conversions remain possible.[10] In Rome, having reached the ends of the earth, the gospel receives its definitive rejection by the Jewish people. But that rejection only ends the priority of addressing the gospel to Jews and leaves open the possibility of individual Jewish conversions.[11]

1. George, 'Israël', pp. 486, 522-23.
2. George, 'Israël', pp. 488-89.
3. George, 'Israël', pp. 493-94, 502-503; 'Le sens de la mort', pp. 199-200. Other adversaries, including Pilate, are of little significance for Luke according to George ('Israël', p. 503; 'Le sens de la mort', pp. 202-203).
4. George, 'Israël', pp. 496-98, 507-508. He opts for the reading ἄρχοντες τοῦ λαοῦ in Lk. 23.13 ('Israël', pp. 503-504) and asserts that the ascription of responsibility for the death of Jesus to the people in Acts is kerygmatic and does not reflect Luke's theology ('Le sens de la mort', pp. 200-201). Nevertheless, he suggests that Luke deliberately includes some indictment of the people of Jerusalem ('Le sens de la mort', pp. 201-203) which complicates the perspective on the death of Jesus. In any case, George follows Dupont in asserting that those responsible for the death of Jesus are confined to Jerusalem ('Le sens de la mort', p. 204).
5. George, 'Israël', pp. 494-95.
6. George, 'Israël', p. 504.
7. George, 'Israël', pp. 504-506; 'Le sens de la mort', pp. 203-204, 206-207.
8. George, 'Israël', pp. 510-11.
9. George, 'Israël', pp. 512, 519-20, 522.
10. George, 'Israël', p. 512.
11. George, 'Israël', pp. 520-24.

Jacob Jervell

A conscious and thorough attempt to redraw the agenda for critical study of Judaism in Luke–Acts is found in the work of the Scandinavian J. Jervell. He differs emphatically with the scholarly consensus concerning Luke's setting. Jewish Christianity is not a matter of the past for Luke. Although the church by Luke's time is primarily composed of Gentiles, Jewish Christians comprise a powerful minority with a cohesive self-consciousness.[1] Luke writes with this Jewish element of the church clearly in mind.[2] In fact, much of Acts is aimed at addressing issues of controversy within Jewish Christianity.

Jervell finds several lines of evidence which confirm this view. He argues that evidence outside Luke–Acts indicates that the ongoing strength of Jewish Christianity survived the Jewish War and continued as a distinct entity within the larger Christian movement.[3]

More particularly, Jervell argues that Luke's presentation of the Jewish mission only makes sense if read from a perspective which reckons with Jewish-Christian interests. He agrees with others in suggesting that Luke presents not Israel's rejection of the gospel but its division through the gospel. The believing portion is the true Israel, to which the Gentiles are added as an associate people who share in Israel's promises.[4] Luke's emphasis on the mass conversion of Jews in Jerusalem indicates his interest in the acceptance, not the rejection, of the gospel by Jews.[5] Even in the diaspora large numbers of Jewish conversions are the regular feature.[6] It is in fact Jewish acceptance of the gospel, not rejection, which is the presupposition of the Gentile mission; and the Gentile mission, not the Jewish mission, requires theological justification.[7] Jewish acceptance of the gospel always interplays with rejection, but Luke's viewpoint cannot be that Israel *en masse* rejected the Christian message, for those who reject are not

1. J. Jervell, *The Unknown Paul* (Minneapolis: Augsburg, 1984), pp. 13, 20, 27, 30, 33-34; 'Paulus in der Apostelgeschichte und die Geschichte des Urchristentums', *NTS* 32 (1986), pp. 387-88.
2. Jervell, *Unknown Paul*, pp. 14, 40-41.
3. J. Jervell, *Luke and the People of God* (Minneapolis: Augsburg, 1972), p. 54; 'Paulus in der Apostelgeschichte', pp. 388-90.
4. Jervell, *People of God*, pp. 41-43; *Unknown Paul*, pp. 41-42.
5. Jervell, *People of God*, pp. 44-45.
6. Jervell, *People of God*, p. 46.
7. Jervell, *People of God*, pp. 51-55, 60-63; *Unknown Paul*, p. 24; 'Paulus in der Apostelgeschichte', p. 386.

legitimate representatives of Israel.[1] The Jewish mission ends in Rome, but not because the gospel is definitively repudiated there. In Rome as elsewhere, Israel is divided. Rather, the Jewish mission ends in Rome because there it has reached the ends of the earth and the purified, true Israel has been gathered.[2]

Luke's depiction of Paul's ministry is a particularly telling feature in Jervell's interpretation. Paul's missionary endeavors always involve work among Jews, and no church is established where there are no Jewish converts.[3] Even after leaving the synagogue, Paul continues his ministry to Jews and never pursues an exclusively Gentile mission.[4] Paul maintains connections to the Jewish church of Jerusalem throughout Acts.[5] The content of Paul's defense speeches shows that Luke is concerned to answer not charges of sedition against Rome but charges of infidelity to Judaism.[6]

Jervell's proposals have met with considerable acclaim as well as considerable criticism. Although certain details of his exegesis appear to be ill-founded, he has nevertheless suggested that the study of the Lukan corpus is in need of fundamental reappraisal. Several scholars have followed his lead and approached Luke–Acts from the perspective he suggests.

David L. Tiede
The American D.L. Tiede has produced a study of Jewish rejection of the gospel in Luke–Acts which follows Jervell's suggestions about the setting of the work.[7] Noting the cultural and ethnic diversity of the first-century synagogue, Tiede begins with the caveat that Luke's work must

---

1.   Jervell, *People of God*, pp. 47-49, 53-54, 61-62.
2.   Jervell, *People of God*, pp. 48-49, 63-64, 68, 174-75; *Unknown Paul*, pp. 41-42.
3.   Jervell, *Unknown Paul*, p. 16.
4.   Jervell, *Unknown Paul*, p. 16.
5.   Jervell, *Unknown Paul*, p. 18.
6.   Jervell, *People of God*, pp. 167, 174-75; 'Paulus in der Apostelgeschichte', p. 386.
7.   D.L. Tiede, *Prophecy and History in Luke–Acts* (Philadelphia: Fortress Press, 1980). The essential perspective of this work is also found in a number of the author's articles subsequent to it, most recently '"Fighting against God": Luke's Interpretation of Jewish Rejection of the Messiah Jesus', in C.A. Evans and D.A. Hagner (eds.), *Anti-Semitism and Early Christianity: Issues of Faith and Polemic* (Minneapolis: Fortress Press, 1993), pp. 102-12.

not be unconsciously evaluated from the later perspective in which Christians and Jews defined themselves in opposition to each other.[1] Like Jervell, he notes Luke's assumption of Israel's ongoing election, his concern to justify the Gentile mission and his interest in the question of what constitutes fidelity to Judaism.[2] He suggests that Luke adopts Jewish scriptural traditions which view the prophets as those who reveal or even cause obduracy in Israel.[3] Luke claims that Jesus is the prophet like Moses and urges that Jews evaluate that claim not precipitously, as did those who rejected Jesus in his lifetime, but in light of the entirety of his work, according to the traditional test for false prophets.[4] As a prophet Jesus divides Israel into believing and unbelieving camps, of which only the former receives the fulfillment of Israel's promises.[5] Such a perspective cannot be assumed to have been adopted by the Gentile Luke to use against the synagogue because prophetic language is inevitably sharp, even when the prophet stands squarely within the tradition criticized.[6] In particular, Luke gives no evidence of a replacement theology and appears to hold out hope for Israel's eventual restoration.[7]

Tiede offers limited observations about the responsibility for the crucifixion. He suggests that for Luke divine necessity is of more importance than human involvement: in the passion the people of Jerusalem are swept up in events over which they have no power.[8] He denies that Luke's purpose is pro-Roman apology and consequent anti-Jewish polemic, insisting instead that locating responsibility for the death of Jesus in Israel is consistent with prophetic patterns.[9] Luke's sensitive treatment of the 'compromised role' of the Jewish people, who on Tiede's reading are trapped by circumstances into calling for crucifixion,

---

1. Tiede, *Prophecy and History*, pp. 7-11.
2. Tiede, *Prophecy and History*, pp. 50-51, 70, 116-17.
3. Tiede, *Prophecy and History*, pp. 30-31, 76.
4. Tiede, *Prophecy and History*, pp. 46-47, 77-78.
5. Tiede, *Prophecy and History*, pp. 55, 62, 77, 114. Tiede sees this division as a part of a larger theodicy in which 'God's determined will encounters rejection and faith in the arena of human history' ('Contending with God: The Death of Jesus and the Trial of Israel in Luke–Acts', in B.A. Pearson *et al.* [eds.], *The Future of Early Christianity: Essays in Honor of Helmut Koester* [Minneapolis: Fortress Press, 1991], p. 304).
6. Tiede, *Prophecy and History*, pp. 48-49, 80-83, 88-89, 121-22.
7. Tiede, *Prophecy and History*, pp. 94-95, 131.
8. Tiede, *Prophecy and History*, pp. 104-105.
9. Tiede, *Prophecy and History*, pp. 107-108, 110.

is clear evidence of his intra-Jewish perspective.[1] The 'people' are culpable because of their complicity in Jesus' death, but the rulers are more culpable because of their active role.[2] Furthermore, some indictment of Rome is the inevitable consequence of Luke's narrative.[3]

Robert L. Brawley

The recent monograph by R.L. Brawley explicitly states as its goal the recovery of the Lukan portraits of Jesus and Paul through the 'erasing' of the negative assessment of Judaism assumed in the common reading of Luke's ecclesiology.[4] Luke's interest, according to Brawley, is in the story of Jesus, not in the justification of the Gentile composition of the church. Material like the Nazareth pericope therefore emphasizes Jesus' identity, not the transfer of salvation from Jews to Gentiles.[5] Luke evinces no interest in a transfer as such; Paul's turning to the Gentiles, for example, serves to justify to a Jewish audience the actual course of his mission.[6] Jewish rejection of Jesus and his followers serves to legitimate them, not to condemn the Jews as Jews.[7] Likewise, Jewish rejection is not the motivation for the Gentile mission; divine initiative is (although Luke's interest in the Gentile mission as such has been exaggerated, in Brawley's view).[8] Nor does Jewish rejection precipitate an end to the Jewish mission: Paul's turning to the Gentiles is always followed with more preaching among Jews, and the Jews continue to occupy his attention at the end of the narrative.[9] Luke's purpose is thus to offset the scandal of Jesus' rejection and explain Jewish unbelief rather than to justify an ecclesiological rift with Judaism.[10]

Like others who emphasize Luke's affinity to Judaism, Brawley sees division rather than outright rejection as the Lukan view of Jewish response to the gospel.[11] Those who reject Jesus and the Christian gospel, such as the Sadducees and high priests, are not true

1. Tiede, *Prophecy and History*, pp. 111-13.
2. Tiede, 'Contending with God', p. 306.
3. Tiede, *Prophecy and History*, pp. 108-10.
4. Brawley, *Luke–Acts and the Jews*, p. 3.
5. Brawley, *Luke–Acts and the Jews*, pp. 7-11.
6. Brawley, *Luke–Acts and the Jews*, pp. 8, 39-40, 48-49, 51-63, 68-69, 78.
7. Brawley, *Luke–Acts and the Jews*, pp. 16-18, 23-25.
8. Brawley, *Luke–Acts and the Jews*, pp. 70-72.
9. Brawley, *Luke–Acts and the Jews*, pp. 71-74, 140-44.
10. Brawley, *Luke–Acts and the Jews*, pp. 20, 23-24, 75-77.
11. Brawley, *Luke–Acts and the Jews*, pp. 77, 135-39.

representatives of Judaism.[1] By contrast, in the Pharisees, whose belief in the resurrection parallels Christian belief and among whom Jesus and the gospel received some acceptance, Luke seeks to establish a link to Judaism.[2] Luke does not seek to justify the church's claim to the heritage of Israel as an institution separate from empirical Israel; instead he stresses the inclusion of a significant portion of Israel in the church.[3]

Brawley gives little attention to Jewish involvement in the crucifixion. He observes that although Jerusalem experiences judgment as a result of the crucifixion, that judgment is limited by the Lukan themes of forgiveness, ignorance and the fulfillment of 'the times of the Gentiles'.[4] Ultimately for Luke the purpose was not to emphasize the culpability of Jerusalem but to understand its destruction in light of its promised restoration.[5] Concerning Acts 4.23-28 Brawley argues that Luke's emphasis is on the culpability of the leaders, not on a general condemnation of the Jews, which the logical structure of the passage will not allow.[6]

David P. Moessner
Another American scholar, D.P. Moessner, suggests that Luke's presentation of Jesus as the Deuteronomistic prophet like Moses serves to connect Luke–Acts to Jewish concerns. In particular, Luke's presentation of Jewish rejection of Jesus and the gospel matches the Deuteronomistic view of Israel's history.[7] Jesus repeatedly announces on his journey to Jerusalem that the disobedient nation as a whole will be judged.[8] In the apocalyptic discourse, Jesus defines that judgment as apocalyptic events

1. Brawley, *Luke–Acts and the Jews*, pp. 107-17.
2. Brawley, *Luke–Acts and the Jews*, pp. 84-106.
3. Brawley, *Luke–Acts and the Jews*, p. 153.
4. Brawley, *Luke–Acts and the Jews*, pp. 125-26.
5. Brawley, *Luke–Acts and the Jews*, pp. 126, 132.
6. Brawley, *Luke–Acts and the Jews*, pp. 146-47.
7. D.P. Moessner, 'Luke 9.1-50: Luke's Preview of the Journey of the Prophet like Moses of Deuteronomy', *JBL* 102 (1983), p. 602; '"The Christ Must Suffer": New Light on the Jesus–Peter, Stephen, Paul Parallels in Luke–Acts', *NovT* 28 (1986), pp. 225-26; *Lord of the Banquet: The Literary and Theological Significance of the Lukan Travel Narrative* (Minneapolis: Augsburg Fortress, 1989), *passim* (cf. my review of this book in *EvQ* 63 [1991], pp. 270-73).
8. Moessner, '"The Christ Must Suffer"', p. 242; 'Paul in Acts: Preacher of Eschatological Repentance to Israel', *NTS* 34 (1988), pp. 96-98; *Banquet*, pp. 62-64, 93-96, 113-14.

that will take place in the lifetime of the hearers.[1] Through the insidious influence of the Jewish leaders, the Jewish people (comprising the entire nation and including the disciples), once favorable to Jesus, ultimately turn on him.[2] The Sanhedrin, which takes the lead in putting Jesus to death, acts on behalf of the Jewish nation as its official court.[3] Hence, 'this generation', an expression referring to Israel as a whole, is responsible for the death of Jesus.[4] However, judgment is not precipitated by the crucifixion; rather, Jewish rejection of Jesus at the passion allows his death to effect blessing and deliverance for Israel, just as Moses' death does in Deuteronomy.[5] The definitive rejection of the gospel by the nation as a whole does, however, occur in Acts.[6] Stephen's speech connects this rejection to Israel's history, and Paul's ministry confirms the rejection in the diaspora.[7]

Although this scheme might appear hostile to Jewish concerns, Moessner finds it consistent with a more favorable perspective. He asserts that 'Israel' for Luke includes both the believing and unbelieving portions; believing Israel is the eschatological remnant which calls the rest of the nation and the Gentiles to repentance.[8] Jewish rejection is but one aspect of the picture: at the end of plotted time (Acts 28) some Jews still respond positively to Paul's message.[9] Luke emphasizes that rejection because it is the most puzzling aspect of the picture.[10] Thus, fulfillment both of Israel's promises and of Israel's judgment are part of Luke's expectation.[11]

---

1. Moessner, 'Paul in Acts', pp. 98-100; 'The "Leaven of the Pharisees" and "This Generation": Israel's Rejection of Jesus according to Luke', *JSNT* 34 (1988), p. 40.

2. Moessner, '"Leaven of the Pharisees"', pp. 24, 30-35, 41; *Banquet*, pp. 183, 217.

3. Moessner, '"Leaven of the Pharisees"', p. 37.

4. Moessner, *Banquet*, pp. 67-69, 118-19.

5. Moessner, *Banquet*, pp. 68-69.

6. Moessner, '"The Christ Must Suffer"', p. 226.

7. Moessner, '"The Christ Must Suffer"', pp. 227-28; 'Paul in Acts', pp. 101-102.

8. Moessner, 'Paul in Acts', p. 102; '"Leaven of the Pharisees"', pp. 30-31; *Banquet*, p. 310.

9. Moessner, 'Paul in Acts', pp. 102-103; *Banquet*, p. 311.

10. Moessner, '"Leaven of the Pharisees"', p. 41.

11. Moessner, 'Paul in Acts', pp. 102-103.

Observations and Proposals

As indicated at the beginning of this chapter, this *Forschungsbericht* suggests two key points which justify another study of Luke's presentation of responsibility for the death of Jesus.

1. Comprehensive treatments of the motif of Jewish responsibility for the death of Jesus have to this point reflected the post-war consensus that Luke writes for a church profoundly separate from, if not outright hostile to, Jews and Judaism.[1] The ongoing debate of this very point, however, suggests that the question should be reopened. How does Luke understand Jewish involvement in the death of Jesus? To what larger theological context does that understanding belong? In particular, Dupont's suggestion that Luke ascribes responsibility for the death of Jesus only to the Jews of Jerusalem has gone largely undeveloped. Made as a passing observation by Dupont and repeated by a handful of others, the considerable exegetical difficulties attendant to it have not been addressed. Particularly in light of J.T. Sanders's forceful assertion that Luke ascribes responsibility to all Jews, it requires reassessment. More than that, it must be placed into the larger context of Luke's presentation of Jewish response to Jesus and the gospel.

2. No evaluation of the place of responsibility for the death of Jesus in the pre-Lukan tradition has been attempted since Wilckens. His view that Luke's ascription of responsibility to the Jews is an element of Hellenistic anti-Judaism is considerably less likely if in fact Luke places responsibility only on the Jerusalem Jews. If such is the case, then a new tradition-critical inquiry is justified.

These, then, are the questions to be explored in this work. The question of Luke's assessment of responsibility for the death of Jesus will be addressed in the first part of the study (Chapters 2–3). The origin of this assessment will be the subject of the second part (Chapters 4–7). A final chapter (Chapter 8) will summarize the conclusions reached and suggest some implications.

---

1. The recent study by Matera deals only with the material in Acts ('Responsibility', p. 78).

Chapter 2

JERUSALEM'S RESPONSIBILITY FOR THE DEATH OF JESUS
IN LUKE–ACTS

According to Luke, who killed Jesus of Nazareth? The previous
chapter's review of the critical literature reveals the common answer:
'He says the Jews did it'. But do the data of the text support this conclusion? Does Luke implicate certain Roman officials, such as Pilate,
Roman soldiers and Herod?[1] On the other hand, does he regard all Jews
or only some Jews as sharing in culpability? The current state of debate
about the Jews and the death of Jesus in Luke–Acts indicates that these
questions should be addressed again.

In the reexamination of this issue that follows, a distinct pattern in the
Lukan text emerges: Luke implicates Pilate, his soldiers, Herod, the
Jerusalemites and especially the Jewish leaders of Jerusalem in Jesus'
death. For Luke, not all Jews are responsible for Jesus' death, and not all
those responsible are Jews. The discussion of the data will naturally
divide itself into two major sections. The first will explore the more
important theme of Jerusalem's responsibility. It will demonstrate that
Luke implicates in the crucifixion of Jesus the leaders of Jerusalem and,
to a lesser extent, a crowd of people explicitly identified in Acts as
Jerusalemites, but never the Jews generally. The second major section
will present the evidence that Luke assigns a measure of responsibility to
others, particularly Pilate. Here a partial response will be given to the

---

1.   Those positing apology for the church before Rome are numerous.
P.W. Walaskay argues that Luke presents an apology for Rome to the church (*'And
So We Came to Rome': The Political Perspective of St Luke* [SNTSMS, 49;
Cambridge: Cambridge University Press, 1983]). Such a view naturally suggests
that Luke sought to exonerate Rome. On the other hand, D. Slingerland has argued
that the presentation of responsibility for the death of Jesus in Acts actually mitigates
Jewish responsibility by emphasizing Roman involvement ('The Composition of
Acts: Some Redaction-Critical Observations', *JAAR* 56 [1988], pp. 103-104).

view that Luke seeks to absolve the Romans of blame by playing down their responsibility.

Certain methodological assumptions underlie this study. The first is that Luke–Acts is a unified narrative by one author which exhibits a congruous theological perspective in both its major parts. The Gospel of Luke and Acts have different emphases, to be sure, so caution must be exercised in equating the perspective of one with that of the other. Indeed, an important difference between the two volumes in the presentation of popular responsibility for the death of Jesus will be noted. Nevertheless, scholarship of this century has repeatedly demonstrated the essential unity of the corpus.

The second assumption, which concerns Luke's sources, is more controversial. Although the two-source theory has been widely accepted in the study of the Synoptics, it no longer holds incontrovertible status. Competing 'solutions' to the Synoptic problem continue to cast doubt on the erstwhile 'assured conclusion' that Luke used Mark and Q as his major sources. The existence of Q as a distinct and unified source appears particularly questionable,[1] and the possibility that Luke used Matthew[2] or had traditions parallel to Mark at several

1.   The Q hypothesis has attracted criticism from various perspectives. A.M. Farrer ('On Dispensing with Q', in D.E. Nineham [ed.], *Studies in the Gospels: Essays in Memory of R.H. Lightfoot* [Oxford: Basil Blackwell, 1955], pp. 55-88) and S. Petrie ('"Q" Is Only What You Make It', *NovT* 3 [1959], pp. 28-33) argue that there is no evidence that the Q material was ever a single, distinct, coherent document. A different approach is offered by M. Goulder, who argues that Luke depends on Matthew for the so-called Q material ('A House Built on Sand', in A.E. Harvey [ed.], *Alternative Approaches to New Testament Study* [London: SPCK, 1985], pp. 1-24). The debate between Goulder and W.R. Farmer, advocate of the so-called Griesbach hypothesis, is highlighted in C.M. Tuckett (ed.), *Synoptic Studies: The Ampleforth Conferences of 1982 and 1983* (JSNTSup, 7; Sheffield: JSOT Press, 1984).

2.   Matthean priority has been championed in modern times by B.C. Butler (*The Originality of St Matthew* [Cambridge: Cambridge University Press, 1951]) and most notably by W.R. Farmer (*The Synoptic Problem: A Critical Analysis* [Dillsboro, NC: Western North Carolina Press; Macon, GA: Mercer University Press, rev. edn, 1976]). Farmer's view has won a number of adherents, including D.L. Dungan ('Mark—The Abridgement of Matthew and Luke', in *Jesus and Man's Hope* [Pittsburgh: Pittsburgh Theological Seminary, 1970], pp. 51-97); J.B. Orchard (*Matthew, Luke and Mark* [Manchester: Koinonia Press, 1976]); H.-H. Stoldt (*History and Criticism of the Marcan Hypothesis* [ET: Macon, GA: Mercer University Press, 1980]); M. Lowe ('The Demise of Arguments from Order

points[1] cannot be dismissed out of hand. But neither can another theory of Synoptic relationships be assumed; opponents of the two-document

for Markan Priority', *NovT* 24 [1982], pp. 27-36; *idem*, 'From the Parable of the Vineyard to a Pre-Synoptic Source', *NTS* 28 [1982], pp. 257-63); C.S. Mann (*Mark* [AB, 27; Garden City, NY: Doubleday, 1986]); and many of the contributors to W.O. Walker (ed.), *The Relationships among the Gospels: An Interdisciplinary Dialogue* (San Antonio: Trinity University Press, 1978); to W.R. Farmer (ed.), *New Synoptic Studies: The Cambridge Gospel Conference and Beyond* (Macon, GA: Mercer University Press, 1983); and to E.P. Sanders (ed.), *Jesus, the Gospels and the Church: Essays in Honor of William R. Farmer* (Macon, GA: Mercer University Press, 1987). Seminal essays supporting both Markan and Matthean priority are collected in A.J. Bellinzoni (ed.), *The Two-Source Hypothesis: A Critical Appraisal* (Macon, GA: Mercer University Press, 1985). The arguments of Farmer are criticized in C.H. Talbert and E.V. McKnight, 'Can the Griesbach Hypothesis Be Falsified?', *JBL* (1972), pp. 338-68. These criticisms are addressed by G.W. Buchanan, 'Has the Griesbach Hypothesis Been Falsified?', *JBL* 93 (1974), pp. 550-72. Interestingly, Talbert later argued that interpretation of Luke must be done without reference to any particular theory about his sources ('Shifting Sands: The Recent Study of the Gospel of Luke', *Int* 30 [1976], pp. 381-95).

1.   Apart from advocates of Markan or Matthean priority stand those scholars who suggest that the Synoptic Gospels developed through a more 'organic' process in which oral traditions circulated among various Christian communities and were gradually assimilated into the present Gospel narratives. Sometimes called 'multi-stage theories', such hypotheses allow for mutual interrelationships as primitive 'gospels' developed and circulated in oral or written form, influencing in various ways the composition of the Synoptic Gospels (and probably also the Fourth Gospel). Those suggesting such a view include E.P. Sanders (*The Tendencies of the Synoptic Tradition* [SNTSMS, 9; London: Cambridge University Press, 1969]; cf. his later refinements and caveats in *idem* and M. Davies, *Studying the Synoptic Gospels* [London: SCM Press, 1989], pp. 112-17), X. Léon-Dufour ('Redaktionsgeschichte of Matthew and Literary Criticism', in *Jesus and Man's Hope* [Pittsburgh: Pittsburgh Theological Seminary, 1970], pp. 9-35), J.A.T. Robinson (*Redating the New Testament* [London: SCM Press, 1976], pp. 93-107), J.W. Wenham ('Synoptic Independence and the Origin of Luke's Travel Narrative', *NTS* 27 [1980–81], pp. 507-15), D. Wenham (*The Rediscovery of Jesus' Eschatological Discourse* [Gospel Perspectives, 4; Sheffield: JSOT Press, 1984]; *idem*, 'Paul's Use of the Jesus Tradition: Three Samples', in *idem* [ed.], *The Jesus Tradition Outside the Gospels* [Gospel Perspectives, 5; Sheffield: JSOT Press, 1985], pp. 39-62), and B. Reicke ('Die Entstehungsverhältnisse der synoptischen Evangelien', *ANRW*, II.25.2.1758-91; and *idem*, *The Roots of the Synoptic Gospels* [Philadelphia: Fortress Press, 1986]). Concerning Luke's relationship to non-Matthean and non-Markan traditions, cf. the remark of B. Gerhardsson on the prologue to Luke's Gospel (*The Gospel Tradition* [ConBNT, 15; Malmö: Gleerup,

theory have been more successful in eroding confidence in the established view than in inspiring confidence in a different one.[1] In this study a final judgment on the Synoptic question will therefore be suspended: no theory of Synoptic relationships will be assumed, and the relationship of different traditions will be evaluated *ad hoc*.[2] The method employed here will therefore differ from that of redaction-critical studies which assume the use of Mark and Q. The possibility that Luke followed Matthew dictates that his text be compared to Matthew in the triple tradition as well as in 'Q' sections. Furthermore, in every case the possibility that Luke follows other documents or traditions parallel to Mark must be considered, although in this case the likelihood that Luke used Mark, Matthew or something very much like one of them requires that his choice in following a tradition independent of either of them be explained.[3] Moreover, any conclusion based on Luke's apparent

---

1986], p. 29): '"Many (πολλοί) is certainly a conventional exaggeration, but Luke would hardly use this phrase if he was just thinking of one or two *specific* predecessors'. Cf. also the observation of T. Wright concerning the implications for Synoptic studies of Jesus' having said similar things in different places during his itinerant ministry (in S. Neill and *idem*, *The Interpretation of the New Testament 1861–1981* [Oxford: Oxford University Press, 2nd edn, 1988], p. 397).

1. Hence the judgments of E.E. Ellis: 'In the present state of affairs source criticism appears either to have come full circle or to have reached something of an impasse' ('Gospels Criticism', in P. Stuhlmacher [ed.], *Das Evangelium und die Evangelien* [WUNT, 2.28; Tübingen: Mohr (Paul Siebeck), 1983], pp. 27-54); and of H.F.D. Sparks: 'In the future we shall either have to be content with one of the simpler solutions or admit frankly that on the basis of the existing evidence alone the problem is insoluble' (Review of *Synopse des quatres évangiles en français*, by P. Benoit and M.-E. Boismard, *JTS* NS 25 [1974], pp. 485-89).

2. Various factors demand that relative antiquity of Gospel parallels be evaluated *ad hoc*. E.P. Sanders observes that possibilities such as the overlapping of Mark and Q, the existence of Ur-Mark, or continuing circulation of oral tradition—including Aramaic material—require that the antiquity of traditions be determined individually (*Tendencies*, pp. 4-7). This has always been recognized as the method of necessity for the so-called Q material; uncertainty about Synoptic relationships demands that the same method be applied to the Markan or triple tradition as well, as Robinson observes (*Redating*, pp. 93-94).

3. Such an explanation need not relate to a peculiarity of Luke's theology. He may follow a non-Markan or non-Matthean tradition because it is more familiar to him or to those for whom he writes. This observation urges additional caution in basing judgments on Luke's theology on deviations from the other Gospels. Cf. also the statement of Gerhardsson (*The Gospel Tradition*, p. 53): 'Only if we know for sure that an evangelist intends his book to be the exclusive Gospel for his community

alterations of his sources should be confirmed by appeal to broader considerations, such as the presentation of similar ideas in other texts which can be assigned to Luke's hand with a degree of confidence. On the other hand, any element of the text which appears to have been part of Luke's sources cannot thereby be taken as irrelevant for determining Luke's own intention. The author's selection of traditional material can be as deliberate as his rewriting of tradition. Although the author may employ traditional material which reflects ideas he does not hold, the presence of a particular idea or theme in disparate strata of tradition within a work, or its presence in both traditional and redactional material, may indicate that the author consciously adopts the perspective of the source. All in all, these assumptions demand that the text of the Gospel of Luke be interpreted with caution in regard to sources which must always remain hypothetical and with attention to the wider scope of the entire narrative.[1]

Jerusalem's Responsibility for the Death of Jesus

Luke gives the greatest attention to the responsibility of Jewish people in the death of Jesus. But the texts asserting their responsibility do not assign it indiscriminately to all Jews. Although Jesus and his representatives encounter opposition from Jewish people in a variety of locations, only those in Jerusalem—and especially the Sanhedrin leadership—bear guilt for the crucifixion. This section will consider the evidence from the text of Luke–Acts which indicates that the author so ascribed responsibility to this circle. References which associate 'Jerusalem' with the

can we take his book as a full presentation of his own total view'.

1.   This caution in using source-critical assumptions to interpret the Synoptics is reflected in a number of recent works, for example O'Neill, *Theology*, pp. 172-73; M. Wilcox, 'A Foreword to the Study of the Speeches in Acts', in J. Neusner (ed.), *Christianity, Judaism and Other Greco-Roman Cults: Studies for Morton Smith at Sixty* (SJLA, 12; Leiden: Brill, 1975), I, p. 214; J.B. Tyson, 'Source Criticism of the Gospel of Luke', in C.H. Talbert (ed.), *Perspectives on Luke–Acts* (Edinburgh: T. & T. Clark, 1978), pp. 37-39; *idem*, 'Scripture, Torah and Sabbath in Luke–Acts', in Sanders (ed.), *Jesus, the Gospels and the Church*, p. 92; *idem*, *Death*, p. 4; Wilson, *Law*, pp. 12-13; R.T. France, *The Gospel according to Matthew* (TNTC; Leicester: Inter-Varsity Press, 1985), pp. 37-38; A. Sand, *Das Evangelium nach Matthäus* (RNT; Regensburg: Pustet, 1986), pp. 25-27. Such statements are even found in the work of staunch advocates of the two-document hypothesis: for example, D.A. Carson, *Matthew* (Expositor's Bible Commentary, 8; Grand Rapids: Zondervan, 1984), pp. 16-17.

crucifixion will be considered first. The specific involvement of the Jerusalem leadership, which receives most attention in Luke–Acts, will then be examined, followed by consideration of the involvement of the wider circle of Jerusalemites.

General References to Jerusalem

Luke's structuring of the 'travel narrative' with Jerusalem as its destination is well known. For present purposes it is only necessary to draw attention again to the presentation of Jerusalem as the setting of Jesus' coming death.[1] What makes these references relevant to the thesis pursued here is their particularity: Jesus only speaks about his death as occurring specifically in Jerusalem and at the hands of Jerusalemites, even when he travels among other Jews, some of whom are hostile, in Galilee and Judea.

Jerusalem is first named specifically in reference to Jesus' death in Lk. 9.31. The allusion to the fate of Jesus is oblique: ἔξοδος is sufficiently vague to leave the outcome in doubt. The significance, however, is clarified by the earlier direct reference to Jesus' death in 9.22, where the agents of the death include the high priests whom Luke associates directly with Jerusalem. Similar observations apply to the pivotal statement in 9.51, where the significance of ἀνάλημψις is seen only against the backdrop of earlier predictions of the passion, which now include 9.44. The indirectness of these references is removed in the later parallel text, Lk. 18.31-34, where Luke follows the tradition (//Mt. 20.18//Mk 10.33) in naming Jerusalem directly as the site of the passion.

In Lk. 13.31-35 the ordering of material suggests Jerusalem as the site and agent of Jesus' death. Here Jesus refuses to act on the Pharisees' warning about Herod's deadly intentions. He continues his journey to Jerusalem, for a prophet must die there, not elsewhere. In the oracle that follows, Jerusalem is named not only as the site of the deaths of the prophets but is personified as the agent of those deaths. That Jesus will meet the same fate on his arrival is implied by the juxtaposition of the Pharisees' warning of Herod's plans (v. 31), the determination of Jesus to continue his journey (vv. 32-33a), the necessity of a prophet's dying nowhere but Jerusalem (v. 33b) and the designation of Jerusalem as the one who kills the prophets (v. 34).

---

1. The relationship between Jerusalem's responsibility for the death of Jesus and the people of Israel as a whole will be considered in the following chapter.

With this material in its background the oracle of Lk. 19.41-44 has similar implications. The visitation of Jerusalem which the city fails to recognize hints at the rejection of Jesus that leads to his crucifixion.[1] Jerusalem's destruction is intimated in the oracle as the result of this failure. Therefore, although the discourse of 21.5-34 makes no direct allusion to Jesus' death, the connection between his impending demise and the destruction of the city is nevertheless in its background.[2]

Likewise, the fate of the 'daughters of Jerusalem' is tied to the things done 'in the green wood' as Jesus goes to his death (23.27-30). Whatever the precise meaning of the proverb of v. 30, it clearly draws a connection between the imminent execution of Jesus and the fate of Jerusalem.

The Jewish Leaders of Jerusalem

The intention of Luke's references to Jesus' death in or at the hands of Jerusalem as a general entity is clarified with a variety of elements in the narrative. These primarily, but not exclusively, specify the involvement of the Jewish leaders of Jerusalem as the agents of Jesus' death. Furthermore, these leaders are repeatedly distinguished from the other Jews. To these features of the text our attention now turns.

Specific Attribution of Responsibility. Like all the Evangelists, Luke foreshadows the climactic events of the passion throughout the first part of his narrative. In the infancy narratives Luke alludes to opposition and painful rejection (Lk. 2.34-35), and in the inauguration of Jesus' public ministry that opposition proves deadly (Lk. 4.28-30). It is therefore significant that Luke does not follow the triple tradition in implicating the Pharisees in an early plot against Jesus' life (Lk. 6.11; diff. Mt. 12.14;

---

1.   C.H. Giblin argues that this failure to recognize the visitation is the failure of the Jerusalemites to join the disciples (19.37) in acclaiming Jesus (*The Destruction of Jerusalem according to Luke's Gospel: A Historical-Typological Moral* [AnBib, 107; Rome: Biblical Institute, 1985], pp. 55-56). This conclusion neglects the material that follows the narrative, however, which indicates Jesus' popular acclaim among the people of Jerusalem (v. 48). The particular designation 'disciples' for those who acclaim Jesus is discussed below.

2.   Moessner notes a number of elements in Lk. 21.5-36 which imply indirectly a connection between the destruction of the city and the fate of Jesus ('Paul in Acts', pp. 98-100).

Mk 3.6). Although the Pharisees appear as opponents, the fateful plot against Jesus is reserved to others.[1]

Who those others will be is indicated in the first passion prediction (Lk. 9.22), which implicates the elders, chief priests and scribes. Luke follows a traditional formulation here: his variations from Mark and Matthew are slight. With Matthew he omits the articles with ἀρχιερέων and γραμματέων. Although this may indicate independent alterations by both Evangelists to tie the three groups together, the presence of other minor agreements against Mark (ἀπό in place of ὑπό, ἐγερθῆναι in place of ἀναστῆναι) could be explained by either a common source parallel to Mark or dependence on Matthew. Matthew includes a direct reference to Jerusalem (Mt. 16.21) which is absent from Luke. If this was available to Luke its omission can be explained by Luke's reserving direct mention of Jerusalem for the pivotal statements in 9.31, 51. But the retention of the traditional formulation here still tacitly implies a connection to Jerusalem, the venue of the chief priests.

Luke's presentation in this text of the responsibility of the Jerusalem leaders is qualified by a number of elements. One is his choice to follow the traditional formulation without major alteration. The word order suggests that the elders, chief priests and scribes are agents of ἀποδοκιμασθῆναι but not necessarily of ἀποκτανθῆναι.[2] At this point Luke does not go beyond his sources to assert the leaders' responsibility for Jesus' death itself as well as for the rejection that leads to it.[3] More interesting is his apparent omission of reference to the chief

1.   Moessner argues that because the same things are predicated of the 'scribes' in the passion narrative as are predicated of the 'Pharisees' earlier in Luke's Gospel, Luke intends the reader to understand that the 'scribes' are in fact Pharisees (*Banquet*, p. 193). This argument is unconvincing in that in the passion narrative the same things are also predicated of the high priests, who obviously are not regarded as Pharisees by Luke. What is true is that Luke makes similar statements about all of Jesus' opponents, not that he identifies one group with another.

2.   The passive ἀποκτανθῆναι may conceivably be a divine passive, but ἀποδοκιμασθῆναι cannot be because of the explicit agent, *contra* Büchele, *Tod*, p. 134.

3.   Luke's retention of the traditional ἀποδοκιμάζειν in 9.22 may be intentional. The verb occurs in Ps. 117.22 LXX, to which Luke refers twice. In the first instance, Lk. 20.17, he follows the formulation of the triple tradition in retaining the verb in the quotation. In the second, Acts 4.11, he alters it to ἐξουθενεῖν. This latter term is found in Lk. 18.9, where it is likely to have come from Luke's hand, and Lk. 23.11, which also may be Lukan. Its use in Acts 4.11 can therefore be assigned

priests and scribes in a parallel text, the third passion prediction (Lk. 18.31). So puzzling is this omission in light of the emphasis on their role in the passion narrative that G. Schneider cites this text as an example of Luke's use of a passion source other than Mark.[1] What Schneider's suggestion does not explain, however, is Luke's reason for following a source that omits this reference if one was available to him that included it. Here again it appears that Luke does not press the responsibility of the Jerusalem leadership at every available point. But neither does he neglect it: the leaders' involvement is a prominent theme of Luke's Jerusalem narrative, as examination of that material will show. Büchele is therefore likely correct in his assertion that the reference in the first passion prediction to the Jerusalem leaders serves as a 'superscription' for the rest of the narrative, in which the succeeding texts emphasize other significant features of the passion.[2]

Luke's emphasis on the responsibility of the Jerusalem leadership takes shape after Jesus' entry into Jerusalem. In 19.47 the high priests, the scribes and οἱ πρῶτοι τοῦ λαοῦ are said to be seeking to kill Jesus.[3] The origins of this verse are uncertain. The parallel at Mk 11.18 names the high priests and scribes, though in the reverse order from Luke and with considerable differences in the rest of the sentence. The expression οἱ πρῶτοι τοῦ λαοῦ appears at the end of Luke's sentence apart from the rest of the compound subject, perhaps added by the author.[4] These 'first of the people' appear to correspond to the groups

---

to Luke's hand with some confidence. If in that instance Luke alters ἀποδοκιμάζειν in his source, his retention of it here may indicate a conscious choice *not* to alter his source to implicate the Jerusalem leadership further.

1. Schneider, *Verleugnung*, pp. 36-37.

2. Büchele, *Tod*, p. 136. Note that the second Lukan passion prediction does not include reference to the actual death of Jesus but gives greater emphasis than the parallels to the disciples' ignorance (Lk. 9.44-45//Mk 9.31-32//Mt. 17.22-23). Each of the Lukan passion predictions gives emphasis to a different aspect of the passion: note the introduction of Gentile involvement in 18.31-34.

3. M. Bachmann presents a long and persuasive argument that this triad composes the Sanhedrin for Luke (*Jerusalem und der Tempel: Die geographisch-theologischen Elemente in der lukanischen Sicht des jüdischen Kultzentrums* [BWANT, 6.9; Stuttgart: Kohlhammer, 1980], pp. 188-94).

4. The expression πρῶτοι τοῦ λαοῦ appears only here in the New Testament, with or without the definite article. Elsewhere Luke uses similar expressions (ἄρχοντες τοῦ λαοῦ, Acts 4.8; πρῶτοι τῶν Ἰουδαίων, Acts 25.2), but parallels are found in Matthew as well (Mt. 2.4; 21.23; 26.47; 27.1), so the phrase may have

named in 9.22. In the narrative that follows, Jesus' opponents are named as 'the priests and the scribes with the elders' (20.1). Again the formula is largely based on tradition, although Luke's hand may be perceived in the alteration of the third member of the triad to a prepositional object. Luke is alone in placing the controversies introduced in 20.1 in proximity to the note about the plot in 19.47; his apparent omission of the cursing of the fig tree allows the two to be brought together, giving stress to the portrayal of the leaders' plot against Jesus.

This pattern continues in 20.19, where the high priests and scribes seek to lay hands on Jesus. Luke's specification of the subject here may stress their role beyond the emphasis of his sources, but because the implied subject is the same in the parallels (Mt. 21.45; Mk 11.27), the insertion may be more for clarity than for emphasis. Whether the difference in Luke's selection of expressions here (Mt. 21.46//Mk 12.12 have κρατῆσαι where Luke has ἐπιβαλεῖν ἐπ' αὐτὸν τὰς χεῖρας) is intended to strengthen the expression is largely a subjective judgment. What is clear is that Luke continues to attribute the plot against Jesus to the same leadership groups. Furthermore, that plot begins to take specific shape in the following verse, Lk. 20.20, where the unnamed subjects, clearly the scribes and high priests of v. 19, seek to trap Jesus so that he can be turned over to the governor. This element is another apparent elaboration of Luke's source which served to highlight the involvement of the leaders.

The specification of those responsible for the crucifixion is left aside in the material which immediately follows Lk. 20.20. In 20.27 the Sadducees are named as opponents (//Mt. 22.23//Mk 12.18), but their opposition is not connected to a plot against Jesus and they disappear from the Jerusalem narrative thereafter. The unrelenting opposition is even qualified in 20.39, where τινες τῶν γραμματέων applaud Jesus' response to the Sadducees. Specific attribution of responsibility to the

some basis in tradition. Similar expressions in Josephus (οἱ γνώριμοι τῶν Ἰουδαίων, *War* 2.240; οἱ δυνατοὶ τῶν Ἰουδαίων, *War* 2.287; οἱ πρῶτοι τῶν Ἰουδαίων, *Ant.* 13.165) indicate that the expression is not unusual (all references to the works of Josephus are from the edition of H.StJ. Thackeray [LCL; London: Heinemann, 1926–29]). It would appear from the variety of terms used to name those who plot against Jesus in his passion narrative that Luke used a fairly free hand in selecting terms. Nevertheless, the phrase πρῶτοι τοῦ λαοῦ and its position in the sentence carry an important emphasis in the context, as the discussion below will show.

leaders begins again in Lk. 22.1-6. Luke's apparent omission of the Bethany pericope brings together the two parts of the plot divided by that pericope in Matthew and Mark, but his motive for the omission may not have been related to his emphasis on the leaders' plot (perhaps avoiding repetition; cf. Lk. 7.36-50).[1] Luke follows the traditional (and by now in his narrative, stereotypical) formulation of 'high priests and scribes' in 22.2 but to ἀρχιερεῖς adds στρατηγοί in v. 4. This addition prepares for the arrest in Lk. 22.47-53. There Luke goes beyond the other Synoptics in stating that the ὄχλος which comes to arrest Jesus includes high priests, captains of the temple and elders (vv. 47, 52).[2] By addressing the saying of vv. 52-53 to the leaders, Luke indicates more clearly than the other accounts that responsibility lies primarily with those who instigated the arrest and not merely with those ordered to carry it out. The position of this designation late in the pericope serves to make the subject of the verb in Lk. 22.54 clearer than in the parallels, although this clarification may have been an accidental result of Luke's editing.

Luke's use of sources in his account of the mocking (22.63-65) and the Sanhedrin trial (22.66-71) is notoriously difficult to ascertain.[3] His transposition of the mocking scene, elimination of witnesses and separation of the high priests' questions may be his own redaction or part of a non-Markan (or non-Matthean) source. If he does follow another source, his choice of that source over the other(s) available to him was deliberate, so the unique features of these verses, where they are corroborated by similar emphases elsewhere in the narrative, can provisionally be regarded as indicating Luke's intention. Nevertheless, the precise force of some of the distinctively Lukan features is unclear.

One such feature is the position of the mocking before the convening of the Sanhedrin. This element has been understood as tending to implicate the Sanhedrin less, occurring as it does before the group

---

1. Schneider does not consider that other motives may be at work (*Verleugnung*, p. 153).

2. L.T. Johnson, *The Literary Function of Possessions in Luke–Acts* (SBLDS, 39; Missoula, MT: Scholars Press, 1977), p. 118.

3. Schneider (*Verleugnung*, p. 38) argues that Luke must have had a continuous source other than Mark, while M.L. Soards (*The Passion according to Luke: The Special Material of Luke 22* [JSNTSup, 14; Sheffield: JSOT Press, 1987], pp. 103-104) argues that Luke followed Mark and supplemented the account with other, non-continuous traditions and his own compositions.

gathers.[1] But since those who mock are apparently those who arrest (22.63; only Luke supplies a specific subject here), among whom are the high priests (v. 52) counted among the Sanhedrin (v. 66), such an amelioration of involvement could only be slight. On the other hand, the position of the mocking has been taken as sharpening the culpability of the Sanhedrin, since it indicates their unwillingness to accept Jesus' testimony about himself even before the trial.[2] This suggestion may have more to commend it, since it corresponds to Luke's emphasis on the clandestine plot of the leadership. However, the likelihood that the position of the mocking serves to sharpen the contrast with the denials of Peter and/or to bring the Sanhedrin and Pilate scenes into greater continuity urges caution in drawing other conclusions.[3]

Similarly, the note of the convening of the Sanhedrin and list of those who compose it (v. 66) has been understood as an indication of special stress on their blameworthy activity.[4] On the other hand, the expression is based on tradition (//Mt. 27.1//Mk 15.1), and Luke's alterations of it can largely be attributed to clarification and improvement of style. Furthermore, factors other than emphasis on the Sanhedrin's culpability more readily explain the transposition. The more likely scenario involves a difference in Luke's passion chronology, perhaps suggested by his special sources.

The omission of the witnesses and sentence from the hearing is another element that is difficult to assess. Some suggest that it indicates a sharpening of the Sanhedrin's culpability;[5] others, a lessening of it.[6]

1. Schneider argues that the transposition has the effect of effacing the Sanhedrin's involvement in the mocking (*Verleugnung*, pp. 98-99). From this conclusion he argues further that the transposition therefore indicates that Luke follows a non-Markan source at this point, since he would not miss an opportunity to implicate the Jews in the passion. However, other elements of the text preserve the implication, although it is not as wide an implication as Schneider suggests.

2. Neyrey argues that the position of the mocking emphasizes Jesus' inevitable rejection by Israel (*Passion*, p. 70).

3. Büchele suggests that Luke transposes the mocking and rewrites Peter's denials to give the narrative continuity and conciseness (*Tod*, pp. 26-27).

4. Neyrey, *Passion*, p. 71. Neyrey sees this verse as indicating that 'the broadest possible official representation of Israel was present', and thereby indicting all Israel for its rejection of the supreme prophet. Neyrey's analysis is flawed here, as it is at several points, by his uncritical equation of one segment of Israel with all Israel.

5. Franklin, *Christ the Lord*, p. 92.

6. Schneider sees it as uncharacteristic, given what he accepts as Luke's

But it appears likely that these omissions, whether part of Luke's source or not, were not intended by Luke either to play up or to play down the Sanhedrin's accountability. Since neither a trial based on false testimony nor a trial without testimony would be legal, Luke's omission of the witnesses was probably not intended to sharpen or ameliorate the hearing's illegitimacy.[1] Furthermore, his earlier emphasis on the plot fomented against Jesus' life by a part of the Sanhedrin suggests that Luke may have regarded the sentence of death, or at least the intention to seek Jesus' death, as implicit in the high priest's reply (v. 70). The knowledge Luke gives the reader concerning the plot against Jesus also affects the way the high priest's rhetorical question, 'What need have we of testimony?', is understood. The intention of the priests having been revealed as early as 22.1-2, this question suggests that those who conducted the hearing actively sought a decision against Jesus. No further testimony is needed for them to reach the verdict they desired, since Jesus' own words are sufficiently self-condemning. Similarly, the statement before Pilate in 23.2, τοῦτον εὕραμεν διαστρέφοντα τὸ ἔθνος ἡμῶν, implies that the hearing reached some decision of guilt. This observation is not affected by the possibility that Luke omits the formal pronouncing of sentence because he reserves *ius gladii* to the Romans, for in any case he depicts the Sanhedrin as actively and illegally seeking Jesus' death.[2]

The response of Jesus in 22.67b-68 is easier to assess. This saying, whether based on tradition or composed by Luke, continues the earlier portrayal of Jesus' opponents as thoroughly committed to his ruin. J.P. Heil correctly notes that like the rest of the scene, this response is conditioned by the readers' knowledge of the high priests' plot: Jesus

disposition to blame the Jews and exonerate the Romans, and so understands it as an indication that Luke follows a source (*Verleugnung*, pp. 29-30).

1.   Neyrey apparently ignores this point when he sees the omission of false witnesses as rendering the trial 'solemn, valid, and formal' (*Passion*, p. 71). Johnson may be correct that the omission of false witnesses further confines responsibility for the death of Jesus to the leaders apart from the people (*Possessions*, p. 118), although Luke certainly does not eliminate all popular responsibility.

2.   Schneider rightly points out that the omission of formal sentence in the Sanhedrin scene makes the trial before Pilate, with its threefold pronouncement of innocence, the climax of the narrative but does nothing to lessen the Sanhedrin's responsibility, which he characteristically generalizes as Jewish responsibility (*Verleugnung*, pp. 38-39). This observation is corroborated by the fact that the Sanhedrin's persistence in seeking Jesus' death is emphasized in the Pilate scene.

ironically understates the deadly opposition of the Sanhedrin as mere unbelief.[1] The saying makes explicit what was implicit in the controversy dialogues with their repeated notes about the developing plot: the opponents make their enquiries as a pretext for doing away with Jesus.[2]

In summary, the mocking and Sanhedrin scenes involve a complex series of elements, some of which probably appear because of factors other than Luke's view of responsibility for the crucifixion. Taken as a whole, however, they suggest that Luke preserved the implication in his sources that the Jerusalem leadership instigated the affair and that he gave it additional emphasis at certain points.

As the scene shifts to Pilate's court, the involvement of the Jerusalem leaders continues. The expression ἅπαν τὸ πλῆθος αὐτῶν in 23.1 has been taken as a widening of the accusers to include, or at least prepare for, the appearance of a crowd of common people in later verses (cf. 22.4, 13).[3] The expression is either Luke's rewriting of a traditional phrase (cf. ὅλον τὸ συνέδριον, Mk 15.1) or may be part of a special Lukan source. Whatever the phrase's origin, the participle ἀναστάν indicates that the multitude here is composed of the same groups which convened in 22.66 and who now arise from the συνέδριον. Furthermore, the remarks made by Jesus' accusers in 23.2 suggest that a leadership group is still intended. The verb εὕραμεν, although certainly not a technical term, suggests a judicial finding, and in the context the phrase τὸ ἔθνος ἡμῶν suggests a degree of responsibility for—not merely identity with—the nation on the part of the speaker.[4] What is reported, in other words, is the accusation not of a popular mob but of an official body. A similar conclusion applies to the expression τοὺς ἀρχιερεῖς καὶ τοὺς ὄχλους in 23.4. Although ὄχλος refers elsewhere in Luke to crowds of ordinary people, the term denotes not ordinary

---

1. J.P. Heil, 'Reader-Response and the Irony of Jesus before the Sanhedrin in Luke 22.66-71', *CBQ* 51 (1989), pp. 277-81.

2. Schneider sees the saying as indicating Luke's belief that discussion of the gospel with the Jews is always unsuccessful (*Verleugnung*, pp. 172-73). In drawing this conclusion he ignores Luke's emphasis, discussed below, on the receptivity of the people, which is portrayed in direct contrast to the antagonism of the leaders. It is therefore fallacious to generalize Luke's portrait of the Jerusalem leaders to apply to Jews generally. Büchele assesses this point more accurately (*Tod*, p. 181).

3. Sanders, *Jews in Luke–Acts*, p. 222.

4. Cf. the more limited observations of Johnson (*Possessions*, p. 118).

people per se but any group unsystematically organized.[1] In this context again the accusations which are made imply that the accusers are not common Jerusalemites. The charge of 22.5 is that Jesus stirs up τὸν λαόν, an expression which has verisimilitude only if it is understood as coming from the mouths of persons who do not count themselves among the masses.[2] By contrast, after the summoning of the λαός in 23.13, the crowd shouts not accusations of sedition but demands for the crucifixion of Jesus and the release of Barabbas, the genuine insurrectionist. In other words, the cries of the ὄχλος in 23.4ff. suggest a crowd composed of leaders; whereas the cries of the λαός in 23.13ff. suggest a crowd composed of ordinary people. Thus, it appears that Luke uses the expression τοὺς ἀρχιερεῖς καὶ τοὺς ὄχλους in 23.4 to signify a sizable, unorganized gathering of the leadership, led by the high priests. It is even possible that Luke has prepared for the appearance of this group with the phrase ἅπαν τὸ πλῆθος αὐτῶν in v. 1.[3] This understanding is confirmed in the scene before Herod which follows, where 'the high priests and the scribes' are specified as the accusers (v. 10).[4] Hence, the consistent perspective of the passion narrative to this point is that Jesus' adversaries are the Jerusalem leadership only.

Leaving aside for the moment the question of popular involvement in 23.13, we note that in this verse the leadership is again involved. The term ἄρχοντες appears here for the first time in the Jerusalem narrative. The frequent recurrence of the term in Luke–Acts (Lk. 23.35; 24.20; Acts 3.17; 4.5, 8, 26; 13.27; 14.5; 16.19) as well as its absence

---

1.   Lohfink misstates the case when he says that if ὄχλος means a group composed of the leaders here, it is a unique usage in Luke (*Sammlung*, pp. 42-43). The ὄχλος which arrests Jesus (22.47) is explicitly composed of high priests, captains of the temple and elders (22.52).

2.   Luke ironically notes the people's outcry against the one charged with stirring them to revolt in 23.13-23 (see the discussion below), but he never puts the charge of sedition itself on the people's lips.

3.   Büchele oversteps the evidence when he sees this expression as indicating that the entire Sanhedrin is held responsible for Jesus' death (*Tod*, p. 27). Later Luke will show that some in the Sanhedrin objected to the decision (23.51). Nevertheless, it is true that Luke stresses the opposition of the Sanhedrin as a whole to Jesus.

4.   Sanders argues that the ὄχλος, which he understands as a popular mob, disappears here to allow the leaders to appear as the primary actors (*Jews in Luke–Acts*, pp. 67-68). This argument explains v. 10 on Sanders's view, but it leaves unexplained the other difficulties.

from the other passion narratives suggests that it is a Lukan term. Here it appears to serve as a comprehensive designation for the various leadership groups which Luke has named earlier (scribes, elders), allowing for conciseness in what otherwise might become a long list. The leaders' earlier accusation of inciting popular revolt is reviewed in 23.14, again indicating that the high priests and other leaders propel the events.

A *crux interpretum* regarding responsibility for the death of Jesus in Luke–Acts is Lk. 23.25-26. In v. 25 Pilate 'turns [Jesus] over (παρέδωκεν) to their will [i.e., the will of those who called for crucifixion]'. Then in v. 26 the nearest antecedent to the implied subject of ἀπήγαγον is αὐτῶν in v. 25. It would appear that the same subject is implied in 23.33 for both ἦλθον and ἐσταύρωσαν. Does Luke thereby imply that the Jewish leaders—or even a wider circle of Jews—carried out the crucifixion? A number of factors enter into the decision about this expression.

1. Luke does not always carefully specify the subjects of third person verbs or the antecedents of third person pronouns.[1] In Lk. 5.33 the subject of εἶπαν is unclear: the closest referent is 'Pharisees', but the direct discourse which follows refers to the Pharisees in the third person and to the disciples of John in such a way as to make it unlikely that the speaker is a Pharisee. In Lk. 14.35 the subject of βάλλουσιν is unspecified in a proverbial saying. In Lk. 16.4 the subject of δέξωνται is specified not in the preceding context but in the following verse, and in 16.9 the verb reappears, again without an expressed subject. No subject is specified for ἐροῦσιν in the gnomic expression of Lk. 17.21. One critic inclined to see firm emphasis on Jewish agency in the crucifixion says in the case of Lk. 20.41 that the antecedent of αὐτούς is 'indeterminate'.[2] Similarly in Lk. 21.5 the τινων who talk about the temple are of uncertain identity, either people or disciples (cf. 20.45). In Lk. 21.12 the subjects are again indefinite. Likewise in Lk. 24.13 the 'two of them' may refer either to the eleven of v. 9 or to τοῖς λοιποῖς of the same verse or to the apostles in v. 10. Perhaps the most familiar example is the uncertain antecedent of πάντες in Acts 2.1. In Acts 15.2 the nearest explicit antecedent for the subject of ἔταξαν is τινες κατελθόντες ἀπὸ τῆς Ἰουδαίας, but the following context explicitly

---

1.   Harnack asserts that it is characteristic of Luke's style in Acts to change syntactical subjects abruptly; he cites ἤγαγον and παρακλήθησαν in Acts 20.12, which have different subjects, as an example (*Acts*, p. 226).

2.   Sanders, *Jews in Luke–Acts*, pp. 214-15.

demands that the subject be understood as the church of Antioch (οἱ...προπεμφθέντες ὑπὸ τῆς ἐκκλησίας, v. 3). Likewise, the antecedent of αὐτούς in Acts 15.5 is not stated in the immediate context.[1] In several cases the referent is separated from the pronoun or verb by considerable distance. In Acts 4.13-21 the subjects of the third person plural verbs and antecedents of the third person plural pronouns appear only as near as 4.5. In Acts 19.28 the subject occurs in v. 24. In Acts 22.22 the subject of the verb ἤκουον is specified twenty verses previously (Acts 21.40, ὁ λαός).

2. Evidence is overwhelming that crucifixion was regularly carried out by Roman soldiers throughout the empire. This fact in itself would not prevent Luke from narrating a crucifixion at the hands of Jews. But it does suggest that he would be compelled to spell out clearly any direct involvement of non-Romans, since his readers would naturally assume that the executioners were Roman if the matter were left in doubt.

3. On the other hand, ἀπήγαγον αὐτόν in 23.26 is one of a series of similar expressions in the Lukan passion narrative. In 22.54, 66; 23.1 ἄγω or compounds of it appear in the aorist tense, and all have the Jewish leaders as their expressed or implied subjects. Nevertheless, it should be noted that these occur before the Romans appear on the scene and that none has any of the ambiguity attached to 23.26. Furthermore, the phrase and its variations are undoubtedly traditional (Mt. 26.57// Mk 14.53; Mt. 27.2//Mk 15.1; Mt. 27.27//Mk 15.16; Mt. 27.31b// Mk 15.20b), serving as the stock phrases which signal the changes in scene in the passion narrative. By contrast, in the transfer of Jesus from Pilate to Herod and back to Pilate, which Luke alone narrates, a different expression, ἀνέπεμψεν αὐτόν, appears (Lk. 23.7, 11). Therefore, adherence to tradition, not a consistent usage with Jewish subjects, appears to dictate the use of ἀπήγαγον αὐτόν in 23.26.

4. The crucifixion scene which follows mentions the Jewish leaders and the soldiers as separate groups (23.35b-37). The likely explanation for the soldiers' presence is that they perform the act of crucifying.[2]

---

1.   Pesch, *Apostelgeschichte*, II, p. 72.

2.   Cf. *Mart. Isa.* 5.1, 12, where Manasseh (or the evil spirit Beliar through the agency of Manasseh, in whom he dwells) is first said to saw Isaiah in half but then is among those who watch others do it (all references to the Old Testament Pseudepigrapha are taken from the edition of J.H. Charlesworth [Garden City, NY: Doubleday, 1983]). Manasseh's instigation of the execution appears to account for the discrepancy.

Furthermore, their use of the distinctively un-Jewish phrase 'the king of the Jews' suggests that they are indeed Roman soldiers. Against this understanding, J.T. Sanders has argued that Luke has prepared for this scene by carefully introducing Jewish soldiers attached to the temple earlier in the narrative (22.4, 52). According to Sanders, Luke depicts these soldiers as having authority to go into the city and make arrests. Their un-Jewish mocking is explained by the *titulus*, which they quote (23.38).[1] But against Sanders it must be observed that elsewhere Luke has used στρατηγοί and στρατευόμενοι, not στρατιῶται, to refer to Jewish military figures.[2] Elsewhere in Luke–Acts στρατιῶται are always Roman or at least Herodian.[3] Sanders argues that Luke's temple police are like the praetors (στρατιῶται) of a Roman provincial city who administer a beating to Paul as Jesus receives a beating in the passion (Acts 16.22; Lk. 22.63). However, this hypothesis does not explain Luke's consistent usage elsewhere of στρατιῶται for Romans and his similarly consistent usage of στρατηγοί for the military contingent of the temple. Furthermore, the *titulus* is introduced not as an explanation of the mocking of the soldiers but as a successive element in a series of taunts linked with δὲ...καί (23.35b, 36, 38); syntactically it is equal, not subordinate, to the mocking of the soldiers. Finally, Jewish soldiers as crucifiers renders the appearance of the centurion at the cross (whom Sanders argues is Roman) a mystery.[4]

---

1. Sanders, *Jews in Luke–Acts*, pp. 11-13. Gaston argues the same point ('Passion Narrative', p. 149). He adds that the soldiers' words of mocking are ascribed to Jews in Mark. Although the relevance of this point is difficult to see in any event, it should be noted that the words in question, 'save yourself', are found with minor variations on the lips of everyone who mocks Jesus on the cross in Mark and in Luke.

2. Brawley, *Luke–Acts and the Jews*, pp. 146-47. Luke uses στρατηγοί only in connection with the temple; στρατευόμενοι appears in the John the Baptist narrative (Lk. 3.14) and indicates Jewish soldiers without explicit reference to the temple. It appears that Luke is consistent with the Synoptic tradition in reserving στρατιῶται for Roman soldiers (cf. Mt. 27.27//Mk 15.16).

3. The Herodian soldiers of Acts 12.4, 6, 18 are decidedly un-Jewish. Herod, who commands these soldiers, is regarded by the text not as a Jewish figure but as one who seeks to please οἱ 'Ιουδαῖοι. The soldiers of Herod in Lk. 23.10 are στρατεύματα. Whether Luke regards these soldiers as properly Roman or not is difficult to determine and irrelevant for purposes here: it is sufficient that they are distinguished from the temple military identified with the Jerusalem leadership.

4. Sanders's argument on this point hinges ultimately on his judgment that neither Pilate nor Herod has anything to do with the order to crucify, so that soldiers

The difficulties thus appear to outweigh the positive evidence for seeing the crucifiers as Jewish in Luke. The problem of the unspecified subject's antecedent appears to stem from Luke's adherence to the traditional formulation in 23.26 coupled with his omission or transposition of the mocking scene.[1] Nevertheless, his emphasis on Pilate's concession to the will of those who call for crucifixion in 23.24-25 is significant. Luke appears less concerned with who drove in the nails than with who instigated the affair. On that issue his stress remains on the Jewish leaders of Jerusalem.

If the leaders are not the actual executioners, they nevertheless appear among Jesus' tormentors in the crucifixion scene. In 23.35b Luke has apparently altered the traditional ἀρχιερεῖς (Mt. 27.41//Mk 15.31) to ἄρχοντες. Since Luke elsewhere retains the traditional emphasis on the high priests as the leaders in the conspiracy against Jesus, his alteration here may be for the purpose of widening the group of mockers to include the other leadership groups (scribes, elders).[2] Nevertheless, as D. Tiede points out, the indictment of the leaders is at least marginally ameliorated by 23.34, 50-51. The leaders' rejection of Jesus is qualified by their ignorance and by some dissent.[3] These verses introduce themes repeated later in Acts.

Emphasis on the leaders' responsibility is undeniable in the first retrospective comment on the passion, Lk. 24.20. Luke's tendencies, observed elsewhere, to retain the traditional expressions like ἀρχιερεῖς on some occasions and to characterize the various leadership groups

under the command of either one cannot carry out the execution (*Jews in Luke–Acts*, pp. 11-15). On this subject see the discussion below. Elsewhere Sanders argues that early copyists understood that the crucifiers were Jewish and so omitted Lk. 23.34 because of their anti-Semitic predilections (*Jews in Luke–Acts*, p. 227). Of course, a converse of this argument is that other copyists of pro-Roman sentiment may have allowed 23.34 to stand, or even inserted it, because they understood that the crucifiers were Roman. Likewise, if the motive for deleting an authentic 23.34 was anti-Semitism, the excising scribes may have understood the objects of the intercession as including those who instigated the crucifixion as well as those who carried it out. Thus, the textual history of 23.34 sheds no light on the identity of the crucifiers.

1.   Cf. the remarks of M.L. Soards, 'Tradition, Composition and Theology in Jesus' Speech to the "Daughters of Jerusalem" (Luke 23, 26-32)', *Bib* 68 (1987), pp. 226-27.

2.   Further discussion of this element in relation to Luke's apparent redaction in 23.35a appears below.

3.   Tiede, *Prophecy and History*, p. 111.

as ἄρχοντες are both at work here. The manner in which responsibility is assigned to these leaders in this verse urges caution in assigning importance to certain details of the passion narrative. The leaders are said to have turned Jesus over for judgment of death, though no clear sentence of death is ever rendered in the narrative. As previous discussion has shown, however, it is likely that Luke regards the sentence as implicit. Likewise, the leaders are said to have crucified Jesus; whereas earlier we have argued that Luke does not regard the Jewish leaders as the actual crucifiers. What is apparently at stake in this text is again the identity not of the actual executioners but of those who instigate the execution. In other words, the entire passion is here condensed into brief compass to emphasize the points relevant to Luke's interests.[1] Again, subsequent discussion will aim at bringing out the intended emphasis.

Indictment of the Jerusalem leaders continues in Acts. In Acts 3.17 the leaders (ἄρχοντες) and the people are said to have acted in ignorance in crucifying Jesus.[2] Emphasis on the leaders' culpability appears particularly in the speeches of Peter and the apostles in the Sanhedrin. In 4.5-6 the same leadership groups who appear in the passion account (ἄρχοντες, πρεσβύτεροι, γραμματεῖς) are mentioned with particular emphasis on the high priest and members of high priestly families, who are listed by name (v. 6). The speech that follows accuses them directly: 'You [emph.] crucified...rejected by you' (vv. 10-11). Likewise, in 5.30, 'the high priest and those with him' (5.17) are again blamed.[3] Similarly, Luke indicates with the words of the high priest himself that the apostles assign responsibility for Jesus' death to the Jerusalem leadership (5.28). Outside Jerusalem, Paul makes a similar attribution of responsibility to Jerusalem's leaders (13.27).

1.   Cf. the similar condensation in Acts 13.29, which would appear to assert that the people of Jerusalem and their leaders bury Jesus.

2.   R.F. Zehnle inaccurately states that this verse is unique in excusing the leaders' responsibility because of their ignorance (*Peter's Pentecost Discourse: Tradition and Lukan Reinterpretation in Peter's Speeches of Acts 2 and 3* [SBLMS, 15; Nashville and New York: Abingdon Press, 1971], p. 134). This appears to be the exact force of Lk. 23.34.

3.   Sanders recognizes that the accusation of this verse is directed specifically at the leadership (*Jews in Luke–Acts*, pp. 241-42).

In summary, then, we may observe the following:

1.   The attribution of responsibility for the death of Jesus to the Jerusalem leaders was a part of the traditions which Luke used throughout his Gospel, especially in the passion account.
2.   Luke preserves that attribution at most points and emphasizes it at some points.
3.   Luke's approach to the leaders' responsibility for the death of Jesus is not confined to issues like the passing of formal sentence or the actual act of crucifying. Those responsible are primarily the ones who set in motion the events which lead to the crucifixion, not those who perform the deed itself.
4.   Luke is not concerned with the leaders' responsibility for the death of Jesus beyond other considerations. At some points he condenses or eliminates material in harmony with his view of that responsibility in order to make other points not related to it.

The Contrast between Leaders and People. Luke emphasizes the Jerusalem leaders' involvement in the crucifixion by repeatedly contrasting it with Jesus' popular support. This contrast has not escaped the attention of Lukan scholars.[1] In particular J. Kodell has argued convincingly that Luke uses λαός in the Jerusalem narrative to draw out the contrast between the people and the leaders.[2] Although the contrast is

---

1.   It is noted in Büchele, *Tod*, pp. 165-66; Tiede, *Prophecy and History*, pp. 111-12; George, 'Le sens de la mort', pp. 200-201; Moessner, 'Prophet like Moses', pp. 603-604; Neyrey, *Passion*, pp. 121-23, 132; Schneider, *Verleugnung*, p. 148; V. Taylor, *The Passion Narrative of St Luke: A Critical and Historical Investigation* (SNTSMS, 19; Cambridge: Cambridge University Press, 1972), p. 86; Tyson, *Death*, pp. 30-31; Wilckens, *Missionsreden*, pp. 60-61; Sanders, *Jews in Luke–Acts*, pp. 68-69, 213, 239, 244; R.J. Cassidy, 'Luke's Audience, the Chief Priests and the Motive for Jesus' Death', in *idem* and P.J. Scharper (eds.), *Political Issues in Luke–Acts* (Maryknoll, NY: Orbis Books), pp. 150-51; F. O'Fearghail, 'Israel in Luke–Acts', *Proceedings of the Irish Biblical Association* 11 (1988), p. 29; J.B. Chance, *Jerusalem, the Temple and the New Age in Luke–Acts* (Macon: Mercer University Press, 1989), pp. 68-70.

2.   J. Kodell, 'Luke's Use of *LAOS*, "People", Especially in the Jerusalem Narrative', *CBQ* 31 (1969), p. 328 and *passim*. Both H. Strathmann ('λαός', *TDNT*, IV, p. 34) and H. Bietenhard ('People, Nation, Gentiles, Crowd, City', in C. Brown [ed.], *The New International Dictionary of New Testament Theology* [Grand Rapids: Zondervan, 1978], II, pp. 795-96) observe that λαός is used to

firmly rooted in the Synoptic tradition (cf. Mt. 26.5//Mk 14.2), Luke develops it well beyond the parallels and so probably beyond his sources. To Kodell's analysis the following observations can be added.

One concerns the pattern of Luke's usage of λαός. Not only does the Jerusalem narrative contain a preponderant number of Luke's uses of λαός, it also contains the greatest concentration of uses which stand in contrast to the Jerusalem leadership. Of the eighteen occurrences of the term before 19.47, only two contrast the receptivity of the people with the antagonism of the leaders: Lk. 6.17 (cf. vv. 7, 11) and 7.29. In those instances the contrast is between ὁ λαός and the Pharisees and lawyers, who do not appear in the Jerusalem narrative. Furthermore, in Luke 19–24 λαός only occurs once outside of the contrast schema, 21.23. The Jerusalem section of Acts (chs. 1–7) follows the same pattern. In only six of twenty-four occurrences does λαός appear in these chapters other than in contrast to the Jerusalem leadership; and of those, four are taken from the LXX (3.23; 4.25, 27; 7.34), while two appear to signify Israel as covenant people (3.10; 7.17). The interest and favor of ὁ λαός in chs. 2–5 contrasts with the antagonism of the leaders. In Acts 2.47 the favor of the people is announced as a prelude to the events of chs. 3–4, where the leaders' antagonism is first directed against the apostles. Peter's address to ὁ λαός (3.9, 11-12; 4.1) provides the occasion for and stands in contrast to the leaders' action against him (4.2, 17). The contrast is reiterated with further mention of people's continuing support (4.21). The apostle's favor with the people continues to contrast with the leaders' opposition in ch. 5 (5.12, 13, 20, 25, 26; cf. v. 17). Gamaliel is distinguished from his Sanhedrin colleagues by his honor among the people (5.34) and compares the apostles and their followers to uprisings among ὁ λαός (5.37). Only in 6.12 does this pattern change, although semantically ὁ λαός still signifies people outside leadership circles and may be limited by the context to those among certain Hellenistic synagogues.

contrast ordinary people with leaders in classical sources and the LXX (cf. LSJ, pp. 1029-30). In the LXX this usage is especially prominent in 1 Esdras (cf. 1.7, 12, 13, 47; 5.45, 56-62 [versification follows Rahlfs's edition]). N.A. Dahl provided the crucial observation that λαός in Luke–Acts 'can stand for Israel as a totality, but also for any group of Israelites present at a specific place and moment' ('"A People for his Name" [Acts XV, 14]', *NTS* 4 [1957–58], p. 326). K. Löning observes that λαός is limited to Palestinian Jews in Acts 13.31 (*Die Saulustradition in der Apostelgeschichte* [NTAbh, 9; Münster: Aschendorff, 1973], p. 153).

Another observation concerns the redaction in Lk. 19.47–20.1. As noted above, Luke's omission of the fig tree narrative brings these texts together and so emphasizes the leaders' animosity. Beyond this, this Lukan text is arranged chiastically to sharpen the contrast between the people and leaders:

A: High priests, scribes and first of all the people seek to kill Jesus but are unable to do (ποιέω, Luke only) anything against him (19.47-48a).

B: All the people hang on to hear Jesus (19.48b).

B':   Jesus teaches and evangelizes the people (20.1a).

A':   The priests and the scribes with the elders ask Jesus by what authority he does (ποιέω) these things (20.1b-2).

The structure depends on several elements of Luke's redaction (absence of the fig tree narrative, double use of λαός, emphasis on teaching and hearing, insertion of ποιέω) and thus appears to be deliberate. The result is a more obvious contrast between the receptivity of the people and the enmity of the leaders.

Moreover, Luke's insertion of πρῶτοι τοῦ λαοῦ in 19.47 further sharpens the contrast. Such τοῦ λαοῦ phrases appear to be more characteristic of Matthew than of Luke (Mt. 2.4; 21.23; 26.3, 47; 27.1), but the particular combination here is distinctively Lukan (cf. Acts 4.8; 25.2; 28.7). The insertion of the phrase after the rest of the compound subject and the verb is also unusual.[1] In this instance it serves to bring this element of the subject into closer proximity with what follows. In the succeeding material, the approbation of the people is introduced. Thus, the point of this insertion appears again to be a sharpening of the contrast between leaders and people.

The contrast is likewise highlighted by the parable of the wicked tenants (Lk. 20.9-19). Although the parable is addressed to ὁ λαός (v. 9), who exclaim μὴ γένοιτο at the result (v. 16), the scribes and high priests understand that it is spoken against them (v. 19).[2] These elements

1.   A computer search of the New Testament text using GRAMCORD software (Deerfield, IL: GRAMCORD Institute, 1987) reveals only one other such structure in Luke–Acts (Acts 22.5) and only five others in the New Testament (Mt. 2.3; Gal. 5.6; 1 Jn 2.17; Rev. 21.16).

2.   Sanders overstates his case when he argues that the address to the people and their response indicates that the parable is aimed at the Jews generally (*Jews in Luke–Acts*, p. 62). This judgment ignores both the continuing Lukan motif of the people's support and the function of a public indictment against the leaders as a warning to the

suggest that C. Giblin is right to see the parable as an indictment of the Jerusalem leadership for its perversion of its office.[1] Caution is required, however, in connecting this parable too closely to the crucifixion. Although the reference to the crucifixion in the murder of the vineyard owner's son is unmistakable in all the Synoptics, the Lukan order of the tenants' casting out the son before murdering him probably does not refer to Jesus' death outside the city. Luke's treatment of this sentence appears to be aimed at making the actual death of the son the climax;[2] the death outside the city does not figure in the passion narrative and is not developed theologically by Luke.[3] Likewise, caution is required in pressing the allegorical elements of the parable: L.T. Johnson may be correct that the vineyard represents Israel which endures despite a change in leadership,[4] but there is little which positively indicates that Luke so understood the parable.

Luke's use of a traditional element in this pericope may be explicated by its usage elsewhere. Luke recapitulates the reference to Ps. 118.22 (117.22 LXX) in Acts 4.11. There the setting is thoroughly colored by the contrast between the leaders and the people, as it is in Luke 20.

---

people whom they lead. His attempt to deal with the problem of the parable's address by separating speech from narrative (*Jews in Luke–Acts*, pp. 212-13) likewise fails: the indication that the speech is addressed to the people is a part of the narrative (v. 9), which Sanders views as positively disposed to the people at this point. Likewise, the fact that Luke inserts the reference to the people into a Markan context is not decisive (*contra* Sanders, *Jews in Luke–Acts*, pp. 212-13). The antecedent of αὐτοῖς in Mk 12.1 is ambiguous (cf. Mk 11.32-33), as is the subject of the verbs in Mk 12.12. Luke's apparent insertion of the people and of the scribes and high priests thus merely serves to clarify what is otherwise unclear. Even Sanders himself admits that the dual reference maintains the people/leaders dichotomy (*Jews in Luke–Acts*, p. 213).

1. Giblin, *Destruction*, p. 66.

2. Matthew's order is similar (Mt. 21.39), although arranged paratactically. The agreement with Luke may be coincidental, but it may also be either that the two depend on the same or similar traditions parallel to Mark or that Luke depends on Matthew. In any case, the rendering of ἐκβάλλω as a participle probably is Lukan: cf. the similar treatment in Lk. 18.31-34, where the use of passive verbs and the participle μαστιγώσαντες again presents ἀποκτείνω as the climax of the sentence.

3. Giblin notes that elsewhere in Luke the passion is said to take place 'in Jerusalem' (13.33; 24.18; *Destruction*, pp. 69-70). His view that the casting out is a part of the tenants' attempt to make the vineyard their own is less transparent than the emphasis Luke's order and syntax gives to the death itself.

4. Johnson, *Possessions*, pp. 119-20.

Peter, having been arrested by the temple leadership while speaking to ὁ λαός, addresses his adversaries sharply in the second person. In v. 10 they are accused of putting Jesus to death (as Jesus alludes to his death in Lk. 20.15), and in v. 11 they are specifically identified with the stone-rejecting builders of Ps. 118.22 with the conspicuous insertion of ὑμῶν into the citation.[1] The striking parallels between these two contexts suggests that the same identification is at work in Lk. 20.17. This reading is confirmed by the likely direction of v. 18 (Luke only). If v. 17 serves as an announcement and interpretation of the leaders' manifest rejection of Jesus, v. 18 warns the λαός who listen to Jesus to repudiate the leadership, accept the one they reject, and so escape their punishment. This understanding preserves the dual address of the parable and does justice to the continuing contrast between the people and the leaders which underlies the rest of the narrative.

Likewise, the editorial conclusion in Lk. 21.37-38 sharpens the contrast between people and leaders already present in the tradition behind 22.1-6. Luke reiterates Jesus' popularity with ὁ λαός, keeping before the reader the contrast with the leaders' hostility and illuminating the necessity of their plot in the verses that follow. Likewise, in 22.6 Luke has apparently added the phrase ἄτερ ὄχλου, which not only clarifies the nature of the betrayal but continues to distinguish the leaders from the people.[2]

These observations make a telling point against the view of G. Lohfink that λαός in the Jerusalem sections of Luke and Acts indicates the entire people of Israel.[3] Admitting that Luke knows that all

---

1.   J.T. Sanders has argued that the common use of Ps. 118.22 in Lk. 20.17 and Acts 4.11 indicates that all Israel is addressed in both instances ('The Prophetic Use of the Scriptures in Luke–Acts', in C.A. Evans and W.F. Stinespring [eds.], *Early Jewish and Christian Exegesis: Studies in Memory of William Hugh Brownlee* [Scholars Press Homage Series, 10; Atlanta: Scholars Press, 1987], pp. 195-97). He neglects the repeated use of the second person plural which indicates that the leaders alone are in view. Sanders argues that Luke clarifies the reference to all Israel in Acts 4.11 because his narrative structure has the people favorably disposed to Jesus in Lk. 20.17. However, in Sanders's view of Luke's structure the people are still favorably disposed in Acts 4.11; the critical shift of opinion has yet to occur on his reading. Thus, his understanding of both texts is inconsistent.

2.   Johnson, *Possessions*, p. 118.

3.   Lohfink, *Sammlung*, pp. 36-39, 48-50. Cf. Schneider, *Verleugnung*, pp. 192-93; Chance, *Jerusalem*, p. 61; J.T. Carroll, 'Luke's Crucifixion Scene', in D.D. Sylva (ed.), *Reimaging the Death of the Lukan Jesus* (BBB, 73; Frankfurt:

Israel is not gathered in Jerusalem for the passion as they were gathered in the wilderness for the exodus, Lohfink nevertheless maintains that Luke intends to suggest such a gathering with his repeated use of λαός.[1] In support of this assertion, Lohfink appeals to several features of the text. One is the emphasis that Luke places on the gathering of large numbers of people in the travel narrative, which suggests the gathering of all Israel on Jesus' journey to Jerusalem.[2] In each instance, however, these texts introduce a word of warning which appears to be occasioned by the presence of large crowds. In 11.29 the implication seems to be that the large crowds illegitimately seek miraculous signs. The crowds in 12.1 are the backdrop for Jesus' warning to the disciples about hypocrisy. The crowds themselves are warned in 12.54 about their inability to discern the time. 14.25 introduces the sayings about the cost of discipleship, again suggesting that the very size of the crowds indicates their inadequate commitment. In each case, then, the mention of large crowds serves as an introduction to the warning; any inference about their belonging to a motif of the gathering of all Israel appears to be unwarranted. Lohfink is probably correct when he observes that Luke has altered certain geographical references in his sources to include all of Judea (Lk. 4.44; 5.17; 6.17 cf. 23.5; Acts 10.36, 39),[3] but in other cases the alterations appear to be more for stylistic reasons (Lk. 3.21; 4.43). The material which suggests unbelief among a part of the crowds, largely dismissed by Lohfink as traditional,[4] suggests that his interpretation must be modified as well. The identity of this λαός in Luke's Gospel is indeterminate, but the speeches of Acts leave little doubt about who Luke understands them to be. The designation of the crowd at Pentecost as εἰς Ἰερουσαλὴμ κατοικοῦντες Ἰουδαῖοι (i.e. residents of Jerusalem, Acts 2.5) with origins in the diaspora suggests at the very least that they are accused of putting Jesus to death (2.23, 36).[5] Luke certainly emphasizes that John and Jesus address their message to all

Hain, 1990), pp. 108, 112-13. Moessner's analysis is virtually identical to Lohfink's, but Moessner nowhere indicates knowledge of Lohfink's work (*Banquet*, p. 217). Brawley takes issue with Lohfink's view (*Luke–Acts and the Jews*, pp. 137-38).

1. Lohfink, *Sammlung*, pp. 35-36.
2. Lohfink, *Sammlung*, pp. 38-39.
3. Lohfink, *Sammlung*, pp. 39-40.
4. Lohfink, *Sammlung*, pp. 43-46.
5. Lohfink, *Sammlung*, p. 48. Cf. the discussion below.

Israel (Lk. 3.21; 6.17); his emphasis appears to be on the necessity for every Israelite to repent in order to receive the promised salvation. Likewise, Luke asserts that Jesus fulfills Israel's hope (1.17; 2.10, 31, 37; 7.16). But it appears less likely that he represents Jesus as gathering all Israel around himself on the way to Jerusalem. The evidence to which Lohfink appeals to make this case is better explained on other grounds.[1]

The repeated, deliberate contrast between the leaders of Jerusalem and the people of Jerusalem is a part of Luke's presentation of responsibility for the death of Jesus. It serves to emphasize what other elements of the text assert: that the high priests, scribes and elders of Jerusalem willfully sought and accomplished the crucifixion of Jesus.

The People

Despite the clear emphasis in Luke–Acts on the responsibility of the Jerusalem leadership for the crucifixion, and despite the sharp contrast between the leaders and the people of Jerusalem in much of the narrative, Luke assigns a measure of responsibility to the people also. In the passion narrative their identity is obscure, but the speeches of Acts clarify Luke's understanding of their identity.

The Passion Narrative. The focus for seeing popular involvement in the crucifixion in the Lukan passion is Lk. 23.13. The summoning of 'the high priests and the leaders and the people (λαός)' is the prelude to the cry for crucifixion that follows (vv. 18, 21, 23). The tension between the apparent implication of this text, that the people cried out for Jesus' death, and the contrast elsewhere between the leaders' antagonism and the people's support for Jesus has led G. Rau to suggest that the text should read ἄρχοντες τοῦ λαοῦ.[2] He supports the reading by noting that earlier the leaders are referred to with terms that suggest a large crowd (22.47, 52, 66; 23.1, 4) such as that which appears in the scene

---

1.   O'Fearghail is probably closer to the truth when he observes that the crowd that surrounds Jesus in the travel narrative is one entity among many in Luke–Acts which appear to stand for the people of God in the age of fulfillment ('Israel', pp. 31, 36).

2.   G. Rau, 'Das Volk in der lukanischen Passionsgeschichte: Eine Konjektur zu Lk 23, 13', *ZNW* 56 (1965), pp. 41-51. He is followed by George, 'Israël', pp. 503-504. Gaston originally followed this reading (*No Stone*, pp. 331-32) but later reversed his view ('Passion Narrative', pp. 146-47).

that follows 23.13 (note παμπληθεί, v. 18).[1] Furthermore, the absence of explanation for the cry for Barabbas's release (v. 18) is explained by accepting τοῦ λαοῦ: the leaders are in a position to make such a demand of the governor, even without the custom of a clemency at Passover.[2] Rau recognizes that if only the leaders are summoned in 23.13, then it is difficult to see what the summoning signifies, since the leaders are already gathered in 23.1. But he counters that the summoning of 23.13 includes the secular as well as spiritual leaders; ἄρχοντες τοῦ λαοῦ, he asserts, 'has an authoritative ring'.[3] Rau also recognizes that Acts asserts popular involvement in the crucifixion. But he suggests that in Acts Luke was more concerned with conflict between the church and the entire Jewish people; hence, the differentiation between leaders and people also disappears after 6.12.[4] The reading καὶ τὸν λαόν would thus have appeared through either deliberate harmonization or unconscious correction.[5]

Several problems emerge from Rau's defense of the τοῦ λαοῦ reading. Apart from its weak external support, it leaves unexplained other, more essential aspects of the cry for Barabbas's release (see discussion above). The demand of the crowd in 23.18 for the release of Barabbas, whom Luke identifies as an insurrectionist in v. 19, is incongruous on the lips of a crowd composed of leadership figures who seek to have Jesus executed on charges of insurrection. The fact that Luke does not explain the Passover clemency custom is irrelevant: it hardly lacks verisimilitude for a mob, offered the release of a controversial figure, to counter with a demand for a popular insurrectionist's release. Elsewhere Luke does not distinguish Jewish secular and religious leaders; thus, such a distinction is difficult to press in this passage. Rau's suggestions about Acts are not compelling either, since the attribution of popular responsibility continues well after the dissolution of the tension between the leaders and the people (Acts 13.27). If καὶ τὸν λαόν is original, then the variant may be explained as assimilation to the very texts which Rau cites to suggest that ἄρχοντες τοῦ λαοῦ has an authoritative ring: Acts 4.8; 23.5; Mt. 21.23; 26.3, 47; 27.1. The tension

1. Rau, 'Das Volk', pp. 48-49.
2. Rau, 'Das Volk', p. 49.
3. Rau, 'Das Volk', p. 49 n. 35.
4. Rau, 'Das Volk', p. 47 n. 32.
5. Rau, 'Das Volk', p. 50.

with the people's otherwise positive demeanor must therefore be allowed to stand.

There is, however, another, more immediate tension. Following the summoning of τὸν λαόν (23.13), Pilate reviews the charge against Jesus of ἀποστρέφοντα τὸν λαόν (v. 14). The connection between these elements has led to three imaginative hypotheses. R. Cassidy has argued that the people are summoned by Pilate to counter the demands of the high priests. In other words, Pilate assumes that Jesus' popularity will carry the day and that his supporters will silence the high priests. Thus, he argues that the ones who call for crucifixion, unnamed in the text, are to be understood as only the high priests and leaders; the people remain silent.[1] Similarly, D. Tiede argues that the people are effectively trapped by the situation. Jesus is charged with stirring up the people, so that their support would only needlessly incriminate him further and implicate themselves in the sedition.[2] J.B. Chance suggests that because Pilate apparently addresses only the leaders in v. 14, the antecedent of the subject of v. 18 may be restricted to the leaders only.[3] None of these hypotheses, however, explains the repeated emphasis on popular responsibility in Acts, and Cassidy's and Chance's have the additional weakness of leaving unexplained the cry for Barabbas noted above.

All these hypotheses neglect what may provide the answer to this dilemma: the Lukan insistence on Jesus' innocence. As is well known, Luke emphasizes that Pilate three times pronounces Jesus innocent (23.4, 14-15, 22; cf. 23.41, 47; Acts 3.13; 13.28). The juxtaposition of the people's appearance (v. 13) and the charge of stirring up the people (v. 14) may be partly explained by this Lukan interest. By placing the two together Luke demonstrates to his readers the manifest falsehood of the accusation, inasmuch as the very people Jesus is said to have stirred up call for his death and demand the release of a genuine insurrectionist. Nevertheless, the indictment of the people of Jerusalem in Acts (see discussion below) suggests that Luke does not intend to implicate the entire nation at this point of the passion account: Luke's use of λαός elsewhere does not suggest that all Israel appears in 23.13.[4]

---

1. Cassidy, 'Audience', pp. 151-52.
2. Tiede, *Prophecy and History*, p. 112.
3. Chance, *Jerusalem*, p. 70.
4. *Contra* D.P. Moessner, 'Jesus and the "Wilderness Generation": The Death of the Prophet like Moses according to Luke', in *Society of Biblical Literature*

If the people turn against Jesus in 23.13, do they ever turn back, and if so at what point? It appears that Luke effects the change in the very next scene, Lk. 23.27-31. There a large multitude of the people (λαός) and women follow Jesus, weeping and mourning him. Some have argued that the multitude of the people should be distinguished from the women who are said to mourn, so that 'the people' are still hostile to Jesus at this point.[1] The structure of v. 27 argues against this understanding, however: both genitive nouns govern the nominative πολὺ πλῆθος, so that the group is conceived of as a single entity.[2] Why, then, are the women singled out, and why does the relative clause refer grammatically only to them? Here the answer would appear to lie in the nature of the saying that follows and its relationship to the narrative that introduces it. The relationship of saying and setting here is an example of the conundrum of the chicken and the egg. The degree to which vv. 27-31 are based on tradition cannot be resolved with certainty. What is clear, however, is that the language of v. 29 is reminiscent of, if not directly based on, oracles addressed to women as the particular victims of siege warfare and built on references to childbearing and motherhood ('daughters', 'barren', 'wombs', 'breasts'; cf. Lk. 21.23//Mt. 24.19// Mk 13.17; Lam. 2.20). In other words, the traditional form of such sayings requires women as addressees. Whether Lk. 23.29 is traditional or a Lukan composition, the feminine orientation of its language is necessary for its connection to the wider tradition of prophetic oracles. The same necessity would then apply to the setting of the sayings, which must prepare for the particularity of the address. Again, whether Luke followed a traditional introduction in v. 27 or composed it himself, the reference to women is necessitated by the inherent structure of the saying it introduces.[3]

Seminar Papers 1982 (Chico, CA: Scholars Press, 1982), pp. 334-37; *Banquet*, p. 183.

1.   Soards, 'Daughters', pp. 229-30; Sanders, *Jews in Luke–Acts*, pp. 67-68.

2.   *Contra* Tannehill, Review of Brawley, p. 281. It is probably not correct to see the article τοῦ as governing both λαοῦ and γυναικῶν, as does Giblin (*Destruction*, pp. 97-98). The women are an indefinite group and are likely anarthrous; conversely λαός is predominantly articular in Luke–Acts, especially when referring to Israel or any part of it. Giblin is correct to conclude from the dual epexegetic genitive that the women are representative of the crowd.

3.   A similar example may be found in an earlier part of Luke's Gospel. It has often been observed that Luke has edited the account of the triumphal entry so that Jesus is acclaimed by 'disciples' (Lk. 19.37). Explanations for this alteration are

The implication of this analysis is that no limitation or division of the crowd that follows Jesus should be assumed from the specification of the mourners as women in 23.27. The syntax of the sentence runs against such a division, and the particular form the sentence takes is determined by the saying that it introduces, not by some restriction of those in sympathy with Jesus.

Another argument against a positive disposition of the people toward Jesus in 23.27-31 concerns the nature of their mourning. More than one critic has suggested that what the people and women mourn is not Jesus' fate but their own.[1] This interpretation, however, can only be advanced by ignoring the obvious implication of v. 28: the command not to weep for Jesus assumes that the women have been weeping for him to that point.[2] Whether their weeping signifies repentance at having called for Jesus' death or grief at the execution of an innocent man is irrelevant here, since on either understanding the people's disposition toward Jesus is positive.

Another objection to seeing in these verses a positive disposition

numerous, but one plausible hypothesis has apparently gone unexplored. Luke alone reports the objection of the Pharisees and Jesus' reply (vv. 39-40). In the Pharisees' protest, Jesus is called on to rebuke his 'disciples'. Clearly, the reference to disciples in v. 37 prepares for these words. But beyond that, the nature of the Pharisees' remark requires that such a term be used. Their demand assumes that Jesus has the authority over his followers to order their silence. Such authority is implied by referring to them as disciples (cf. Lk. 5.33). In this instance as well, then, it appears that Luke has composed the introduction to a saying according to the intrinsic structure of that saying.

1.   Gaston interprets the verse in this way because of Luke's perspective after the destruction of Jerusalem which makes that destruction an accomplished fact ('Passion Narrative', pp. 149-50). But that perspective is irrelevant to the issue of whether Luke regards some Jerusalemites as sympathetic to Jesus, and it does not account for the implicit assumption of v. 28. Neyrey offers a variation on this view: ὁ λαός is to be understood as positively disposed here, according to the pattern before 23.13, while the phrase 'daughters of Jerusalem' signifies Jerusalem which rejects and so is antagonistic (*Passion*, pp. 110-11). He likewise sees a post-70 CE perspective as determinative. Moessner, on the other hand, asserts that the women mourn both the death of the condemned Jesus and the fate of the nation but suggests that Acts was written before the destruction of Jerusalem (*Banquet*, pp. 183, 314-15).

2.   Soards, 'Daughters', pp. 228-29. If Brawley is correct that 'they' of v. 31 are the crucifiers (*Luke–Acts and the Jews*, p. 125), then the mourners of v. 27 are further distinguished from Jesus' opponents.

toward Jesus among the mourners is his evident pronouncement of judgment against them. Elsewhere, however, the judgment against Jerusalem
is expected to have its effect on innocent people. In Lk. 21.20-21 Luke
includes the traditional instructions to flee the city on the arrival of the
surrounding armies, instructions which assume that all who remain in
the city, the guilty as well as the innocent, will suffer in what follows. As
did the destruction of 587 BCE, so will the coming destruction affect the
people of the city indiscriminately.[1]

Furthermore, the specificity of the address 'daughters of Jerusalem' is
suggestive. It could imply that at least the women, if not the entire
crowd, are Jerusalemites, not Israelites or Jews generally.[2] Of course,
Jerusalem may stand by synecdoche for all Israel: an evaluation of this
possibility depends on examining other Lukan statements about popular
responsibility for the death of Jesus and his wider approach to Israel in
general. But what is important to note at this juncture is that Luke's
language is particular and does not directly suggest that those who witness the crucifixion in Jerusalem are other than the residents of
Jerusalem.

The restoration of the people's positive stance toward Jesus continues
in the crucifixion narrative. In contrast to those who mock, ὁ λαός is
said to stand beholding (θεωρῶν, 23.35a). This beholding has been
understood as itself an indication of mocking: the term is associated with
mocking in Ps. 22.8 (21.8 LXX), to which it appears Luke refers with
ἐξεμυκτήριζον in v. 35b, and the double conjunction δὲ καί suggests
that the two be taken together.[3] Other considerations make this view
less likely, however. Although the use of θεωρῶν may be suggested by
Ps. 21.8 LXX, its meaning need not be determined by it. Had Luke so
intended, a more definite implication of mocking by the beholders could
have been delivered with the allusion to Ps. 21.8 LXX by preserving the
close syntactical connection between the participle and verb in the
Psalm. By assigning them to different subjects, altering the plural
θεωροῦντες to the singular θεωρῶν and employing it circumstantially
instead of attributively, Luke has preserved the allusion while altering
the force.[4] The act of beholding is not inherently hostile for Luke:

---

1. So Tiede, *Prophecy and History*, pp. 104-105; Giblin, *Destruction*, p. 96.
2. Tyson, *Death*, p. 35.
3. Gaston, 'Passion Narrative', p. 150.
4. Carroll comes to similar conclusions ('Crucifixion Scene', pp. 111-12). Cf.
also Tiede, 'Contending with God', pp. 305-306.

beholders appear again in 23.48 (θεωρίαν...θεωρήσαντες), where they react to what they have seen by beating their breasts, a response that is at the very least not hostile. Moreover, since the final figure around the cross, the second of the evildoers, evinces a positive disposition toward Jesus, it may well be that Luke frames the mocking with instances of positive behavior at the end with the second evildoer and at the beginning with the people. Some details of these verses even suggest that the scene is arranged chiastically:

A: The people (sympathetically) behold (v. 35a).
B: The leaders cry, 'Save yourself if you are the Christ' (v. 35b).
C: The soldiers cry, 'If you are the king of the Jews' (vv. 36-37).
C':   The *titulus* says, 'King of the Jews' (v. 38).
B':   One evildoer says, 'Aren't you the Christ? Save yourself and us' (v. 39).
A':   The other evildoer expresses sympathy/support (vv. 40-42).

Furthermore, if Luke had available to him Mt. 27.39; Mk 15.29 or the tradition underlying them, then his choice of expression in 23.35a suggests a decision against a definite implication of the ordinary people in the mocking.[1] The very ambiguity of v. 35a compared to its parallels indicates that it is to be understood in at least a neutral, if not a sympathetic, sense.[2] And if the sense of v. 35a is neutral, the neutrality becomes remorse or grief in v. 48, either of which indicates disapproval of Jesus' death.

The Speeches of Acts. Although the people's responsibility for the death of Jesus appears to be narrowly limited in the passion account, it is emphatically asserted in Acts. Numerous texts affirm their involvement in the crucifixion (Acts 2.23, 36; 3.13-15; 10.39; 13.27-29).[3] The

---

1.   Johnson, *Possessions*, p. 118.

2.   Cf. P.F. Esler, *Community and Gospel in Luke–Acts: The Social and Political Motivation of Lucan Theology* (SNTSMS, 57; Cambridge: Cambridge University Press, 1987), p. 255 n. 4.

3.   The volume of this material makes it difficult to agree with Johnson that Luke shifts blame from the people to the leaders in Acts (*Possessions*, p. 84). In both volumes Luke stresses the leaders' involvement, but he does not thereby exonerate the people of Jerusalem. C.A. Evans rightly observes that the failure to mention the leaders in such texts as Acts 10.39 does not indicate a shift of responsibility away from them to a wider group ('Is Luke's View of the Jewish Rejection of Jesus Anti-Semitic?', in D.D. Sylva [ed.], *Reimaging the Death of the Lukan Jesus* [BBB, 73; Frankfurt: Hain, 1990], p. 177 n. 29).

question that they raise is not whether the people are implicated but how many are among the implicated group. Although some have argued, and many others assumed,[1] that in Acts Luke sees popular responsibility for the death of Jesus as an indictment of all Jews, the evidence of the text suggests that he limits that indictment to the people of Jerusalem only. Thus, Acts specifies what is only latent or implicit in Luke's Gospel (Lk. 23.28): the crowd who called for Jesus' death was composed of Jerusalemite Jews.

In Acts 2 Peter's audience is the group implicated with the second person plural declarations of vv. 23, 36. Some have argued that the extensive catalogue of vv. 9-11 serves to introduce a group representative of world-wide Jewry so that all can be accused of killing Jesus in the speech which follows.[2] Without question, these verses introduce something important for Luke's purpose, but it is highly doubtful that his purpose is the indictment of all Jews for the crucifixion. The only positive evidence advanced to support such an understanding is the generalized address of vv. 14, 22, 36 (ἄνδρες Ἰουδαῖοι, ἄνδρες Ἰσραηλῖται, πᾶς οἶκος Ἰσραήλ).[3] The point of the address, however, is more likely the establishing of the audience's relationship to the promises which are declared fulfilled in Jesus. In v. 36, 'all the house of Israel' is grammatically distinct from the emphatic second person plural subject which is said to have crucified Jesus. A number of factors other than a universal indictment of Jews appear to have motivated the inclusion of the catalogue of nations. A wide diversity of languages is required to portray the character of the miracle (v. 4); this is the immediate use to which the author puts the catalogue (vv. 11-12). Furthermore, the catalogue may be one element among others which foreshadows the universal extension of the gospel in Acts (cf. 1.8; 2.39), whether that extension is conceived geographically or ethnically. Other

1.   J.R. Wilch speaks of a 'subliminal, almost unconscious' ascription to all Jews of responsibility for the death of Jesus in much exegesis of Acts ('Jewish Guilt for the Death of Jesus—Anti-Judaism in the Acts of the Apostles?', *Lutheran Theological Journal* 19 [1984], p. 53).

2.   N.A. Beck, *Mature Christianity: The Recognition and Repudiation of the Anti-Jewish Polemic of the New Testament* (London: Associated University Presses, 1985), pp. 212-15; Sanders, *Jews in Luke–Acts*, p. 233.

3.   Sanders, *Jews in Luke–Acts*, pp. 51, 233-34; cf. Kränkl, *Knecht*, pp. 102-103; Lohfink, *Sammlung*, p. 48; Büchele, *Tod*, p. 188; C.F. Evans, '"Speeches" in Acts', in A. Descamps and A. de Halleux (eds.), *Mélanges bibliques en homage au R.P. Béda Rigaux* (Gembloux: Duculot, 1970), pp. 291-92.

factors indicate that Luke conceives of these people as diaspora Jews who have taken up residence in Jerusalem.[1] As E. Haenchen has observed, following their conversion they do not scatter to their homelands but remain in Jerusalem as an ongoing community.[2] Additionally, they are assumed to know of the ministry of Jesus and have had miracles performed in their midst (v. 22).[3] Moreover, Luke heads the catalogue with the comprehensive designation εἰς Ἰερουσαλὴμ κατοικοῦντες Ἰουδαῖοι and again employs οἱ κατοικοῦντες Ἰερουσαλήμ in the direct address in v. 14. Elsewhere in Acts κατοικέω is used for permanent residence, not temporary residence in Jerusalem or elsewhere (Acts 1.19; 4.16; 7.2, 4, 48; 9.22, 32, 35; 11.29; 13.27; 17.24, 26; 19.10, 17; 22.12), as R.N. Longenecker notes.[4] In particular, it is used in reference to the residents of Jerusalem as those responsible for the death of Jesus in 13.27 (see discussion below). It is especially interesting that in 1.19 and 4.16 events in Jerusalem (Judas's death, the healing of the lame beggar) are said to be known to all the residents of the city, just as the ministry of Jesus is known to Peter's audience in v. 22. All these factors suggest that Luke has combined multiple concerns in this text: foreshadowing of the universal extension of the gospel, initial restriction of the gospel to Jews, and specification of

---

1. G. Stählin (*Die Apostelgeschichte* [NTD, 5; Göttingen: Vandenhoeck & Ruprecht, 13th edn, 1970], p. 33) and A. Wickenhauser (*Die Apostelgeschichte* [RNT, 5; Regensburg: Pustet, 4th edn, 1961], p. 38) both suggest that diaspora Jews commonly retired to Jerusalem to end their lives in proximity to the temple. Bachmann suggests that Luke may have been aware that not many diaspora Jews came to Jerusalem for Pentecost (*Tempel*, p. 303).

2. Haenchen, *Acts*, pp. 168, 175.

3. Bachmann, *Tempel*, p. 303. Lohfink argues that because Luke reports no miracles of Jesus in Jerusalem, the crowd is therefore composed of the people of Israel whom Jesus gathered on his journey to Jerusalem (*Sammlung*, p. 49). This argument obviously depends on the assumption that Luke intended his silence about Jerusalem miracles definitively. In fact, his omission of the cursing of the fig tree appears to have other motives. But even if Lohfink is correct that the text assumes that the audience are Palestinian Jews who came to Jerusalem with Jesus, their presence in Jerusalem for the passion is thereby assumed and the interpretation taken here is confirmed.

4. R.N. Longenecker, *The Acts of the Apostles* (Expositor's Bible Commentary, 9; Grand Rapids: Zondervan, 1981), p. 272. Harnack noted that Luke uses the phrase οἱ κατοικοῦντες τὴν Μεσοποταμίαν in Acts 2.9 because there was no established term for people from Mesopotamia, not because he understands οἱ κατοικοῦντες in v. 5 as anything other than permanent residence (*Acts*, p. 65).

the Jerusalemites as the ones responsible for the death of Jesus.[1]

A similar pattern develops in the speech of Acts 3. Again the setting is Jerusalem when the accusation is made in the second person plural (vv. 13-15). As was argued above, the designation of the audience as ὁ λαός (v. 12) serves to differentiate them from the temple leadership which will arrest Peter and John as the narrative develops, not to identify them with the entire people of Israel.[2]

The same implication is made in 4.25-28. In this case the use of λαός is determined by its usage in Ps. 2.1, not the distinction between people and leaders found elsewhere; the influence of the Psalm citation extends even to the plural form here. Therefore, the term need not exclude the Jerusalem leaders in this context and in fact probably is comprehensive, including both people and leaders. But its comprehension should probably be understood as encompassing only the different classes of the Jerusalem Jews. The illegitimacy of understanding λαοῖς Ἰσραήλ to implicate the Jews generally, as some have done,[3] is demonstrated by the immediate context: Luke hardly intends by ἔθνεσιν to implicate all Gentiles.[4] The general term λαοί is retained by Luke to connect the fulfillment to the Psalm text; it is appropriate because those referred to are Jews, though they are hardly all the Jews.[5] In other words, Luke finds fulfillment of the generalized language of the Psalm in the involvement of the particular group of Jews whom he has implicated elsewhere.

Because the early chapters of Acts have their setting in Jerusalem, the restriction of responsibility to the Jerusalemites may be accidental. But texts set outside Jerusalem indicate that the limitation is intentional. Two

1. A. Weiser notes these concerns except for responsibility for the death of Jesus (*Die Apostelgeschichte* [ÖTKNT, 5; 2 vols.; Gütersloh: Gerd Mohn, 1981], I, p. 87).

2. *Contra* Sanders, *Jews in Luke–Acts*, p. 236; Kränkl, *Knecht*, pp. 105, 208.

3. Kränkl, *Knecht*, pp. 110-11; Bachmann, *Tempel*, pp. 218-20; H.J. Hauser, *Strukturen der Abschlusserzählung der Apostelgeschichte (Apg. 28.16-31)* (AnBib, 86; Rome: Biblical Institute, 1979), p. 162; Carroll, 'Crucifixion Scene', p. 195 n. 11.

4. Brawley, *Luke–Acts and the Jews*, pp. 146-47.

5. Cf. the observation of Dahl that Luke uses λαός on some occasions to refer to all Israel but on others to refer only to a part ('People', p. 326). Note as well that Luke apparently regards Herod and Pilate as filling the roles of οἱ βασιλεῖς and οἱ ἄρχοντες, even though both terms are plural. Obviously, if Luke could regard one king and one governor as representing οἱ βασιλεῖς and οἱ ἄρχοντες, he could also regard some Jews as representing λαοί.

texts, Acts 10.39 and 13.27-29, indicate the deliberate specification of Jerusalemites as those responsible for the death of Jesus.[1]

At first glance Acts 10.39 appears to violate the confinement of responsibility to Jerusalem. The unexpressed subject of ἀνεῖλαν is widely taken as having its antecedent in τῶν Ἰουδαίων, thus implying culpability shared by all Jews. However, several factors suggest that this text does not abandon the pattern followed elsewhere in the Lukan corpus. These may be enumerated as follows.

1. Although τῶν Ἰουδαίων is the nearest plural noun to ἀνεῖλαν, Ἰερουσαλήμ intervenes. The term is singular but is also a collective and could be logically referred to with a subsequent plural. Several examples can be cited which show that Luke used plurals to refer to collective nouns relatively frequently.[2] In Lk. 1.21 the subject of ἐθαύμαζον is evidently the collective ὁ λαός. The plural is again used with ὁ λαός in Lk. 21.23-24 (πεσοῦνται, αἰχμαλωτισθήσονται); Acts 3.9-10 (ἐπεγίνωσκον) and 19.4 (πιστεύσωσιν). Similar usages occur in Lk. 6.19, where the verb is ἐζήτουν and the subject is ὁ ὄχλος; in 9.12, where the subject is ὁ ὄχλος (Mt 14.15//Mk 6.36 have plurals) and the verbs πορευθέντες, καταλύσωσιν and εὕρωσιν; and in Acts 2.6, where τὸ πλῆθος is followed by the plural verb ἤκουον. In Lk. 13.34-35 (//Mt. 23.37-39) the personification employed in the saying requires that Jerusalem be treated as a singular, as it initially is, but the reference to τὰ τέκνα σου is followed by a consistent use of second person plural. In the quotation of Gen. 15.13-14 in Acts 7.6 σπέρμα serves as the subject for δουλώσουσιν and κακώσουσιν. Most directly relevant is Acts 22.18-19, where Ἰερουσαλήμ serves as the logical subject for παραδέξονται and antecedent for αὐτοί. Luke also refers to collectives with plural pronouns: Acts 7.34 (LXX); 8.5; 13.1-2 (possible); 13.17. This body of data suggests that the reference of the plural subject of ἀνεῖλαν is to the collective Ἰερουσαλήμ in Acts 10.39. If it is, then this text is also consistent with the restriction of responsibility to Jerusalem found elsewhere in Luke–Acts.

2. The expression χώρα τῶν Ἰουδαίων is primarily geographical,

---

1.   Evans notes the critical shift from the second person to the third in these texts ('Luke's View', p. 33).

2.   S. Antoniadis notes this phenomenon in the Gospel of Luke only (*L'évangile de Luc: Esquisse de grammaire et de style* [Collection de l'Institut Néo-hellénique, 7; Paris: Société d'édition 'Les belles lettres', 1930], pp. 157-58).

not ethnic or religious; it signifies 'country of the Judeans'.[1] It is one of the expressions Luke uses to signify Judea in summaries of various periods of ministry (cf. Lk. 4.44; Acts 8.1; 9.31; 10.37; 26.20). Hence, if τῶν Ἰουδαίων provides the antecedent for the unexpressed subject of ἀνεῖλαν, it can logically refer only to Judean Jews, not to all Jews. But beyond this observation there is evidence which suggests that this particular expression was not necessarily chosen over χώρα τῆς Ἰουδαίας in order to provide an antecedent for the unspecified subject of ἀνεῖλαν. Josephus uses the expression ἡ Ἰουδαίων...χώρα in *War* 1.134 and τῆς Ἰουδαίων τε καὶ πέριξ χώρας in *War* 3.58, and in neither case does Ἰουδαίων provide an antecedent for any pronoun. In *Ant.* 14.250 τῆς Ἰουδαίων χώρας again appears, and Ἰουδαίων serves as antecedent for a pronoun that follows. Similarly, in *Ant.* 13.204 τοῖς ὅροις τῶν Ἰουδαίων appears, followed by a plural pronoun (τούτων). But in this instance the particular expression appears to have been chosen not to supply an antecedent for this pronoun but to suggest both the territory and its inhabitants in the sentence in which it appears: 'No one shall raise auxiliary troops in the territories of the Jews' (i.e., no one shall raise Jewish auxiliaries in Palestine). In *Ant.* 15.121 the phrase ἡ γῆ τῶν Ἰουδαίων is followed by the note that 30,000 ἄνθρωποι were killed. In this case the opportunity to use Ἰουδαίων as an antecedent was clearly neglected, so the expression must have been chosen merely because it was deemed appropriate to the context concerned with the victims of an earthquake. In *Ant.* 17.222 τὰς ἄκρας ὅσαι γε ἐν τοῖς Ἰουδαίοις appears, and Ἰουδαίοις does not serve as an antecedent for any subsequent expression. Likewise, in *Ant.* 20.133 Jerusalem is referred to as τὴν τῶν Ἰεροσολυμίτων πόλιν. The sentence that follows then refers to the observance of a festival there with a feminine singular subject, neglecting the personal reference to the Jerusalemites potentially supplied by the expression in favor of the synecdotal reference. These examples illustrate that an expression like χώρα τῶν Ἰουδαίων may be chosen to supply an antecedent for some subsequent expression but is at least equally likely to be employed for some other reason. In Acts 10.39 the phrase provides a fitting emphasis on the people—Jews in contrast to the Gentile Cornelius—among whom

---

1.   M. Lowe has observed that the geographical meaning of Ἰουδαῖος (one who lives in Judea) was generally the most important in the first century, although the importance of different meanings varied according to the setting ('Who Were the ΙΟΥΔΑΙΟΙ?', *NovT* 18 [1976], pp. 104-107).

Jesus ministered. Thus, it does not appear to represent a deliberate semantic choice to stress the involvement of either the entire Jewish people or the Judeans in the subsequent discourse.

3. The phrase 'in the country of the Judeans and [in] Jerusalem' summarizes Jesus' ministry according to the pattern of Luke's Gospel: Jesus passes through Judea (in the broader sense) on his way to Jerusalem, where he meets his death. It is thus in harmony with the Gospel's emphasis on Jerusalem as the site and agent of the death of Jesus. This observation makes it unlikely that Luke intends τῶν Ἰουδαίων as the antecedent of the subject of ἀνεῖλαν.

4. The use of the third person plural ἀνεῖλαν appears to be related to the earlier second person plural usage of the same verb in a similar context at Acts 2.23. Luke may simply have altered the verb to the third person to conform to the setting and left the subject unspecified, considering it sufficiently clear from other indications that only the Jerusalemites slew Jesus.

At most, then, Acts 10.39 can indicate that Luke regards Palestinian Jews as the widest circle of culpability, though it is more consistent with Luke's narrative and with his style elsewhere to understand a specification of Jerusalem alone. In particular, the specificity of the subsequent reference to responsibility for the death of Jesus, Acts 13.27-29, suggests the latter. Set in the diaspora, this text provides the ideal opportunity for the author to implicate a circle of Jews wider than Jerusalem's residents, whether that circle includes all Palestinian Jews or all Jews everywhere. However, the specification of the Jerusalemites is utterly transparent: οἱ κατοικοῦντες ἐν Ἰερουσαλὴμ καὶ οἱ ἄρχοντες αὐτῶν (v. 27). Indeed, unless Luke simply had no consistent view of responsibility for the death of Jesus, this text indicates with the greatest clarity exactly how he understood Jewish responsibility.

Despite the fact that Acts 13.27-29 appears to limit responsibility to Jerusalem in a straightforward way, dispute still surrounds relevant aspects of the text. J.C. O'Neill asserts that responsibility is limited in order not to blame the audience and so to leave the way open for them to believe.[1] But this assertion ignores the restriction of responsibility to Jerusalem in other texts where no such motive can be assumed. M. Dumais notes this restriction elsewhere but asserts that in Jerusalem the accusation is direct because truth gets the better of Luke's

---

1.   O'Neill, *Theology*, p. 86.

diplomacy.[1] But to judge that the author's procedure is inconsistent is unnecessary when an explanation is available that allows for consistency. E. Schweizer suggests that Luke specifies Jerusalemites so as not to indict the Gentiles in Paul's audience with a second-person accusation.[2]

U. Wilckens sees in the apparent ascription of the burial to the Jerusalemites a broadening of their culpability.[3] But as Kränkl has pointed out, the burial is not the only anomaly in this section: the finding of innocence is also credited to the Jerusalemites instead of Pilate.[4] Both these apparent departures from the norm of Luke's passion account can be explained as the result of the condensation of the passion story into brief compass. In fact, another result of that condensation is the omission of any direct mention of Jesus' death, though the implication is nonetheless obvious. Furthermore, since burying the righteous was highly regarded in Jewish circles (Tob. 1.17-20; 2.3-10; 12.11-14; 14.11-13), it is unlikely that Luke broadens the Jerusalemites' guilt even if he does ascribe the burial to them. These considerations suggest that Luke does not here revise or contradict his depiction of the passion found elsewhere.

Another argument is advanced by Bachmann, who proposes that Luke specifies the people of Jerusalem here because the audience includes both Jews and Gentiles and cannot therefore be addressed in the second person.[5] But in this case it is not clear why Luke specifies Jerusalemites instead of designating the crucifiers with ὁ λαὸς Ἰσραήλ, οἱ Ἰουδαῖοι, or some other general expression. Furthermore, Luke appears deliberately to subsume the Jewish and Gentile elements of the audience under inclusive terms (τοὺς πατέρας ἡμῶν, v. 17; ἄνδρες ἀδελφοί, v. 26; ἡμῖν [var. ὑμῖν], v. 26). His concern appears to be less to distinguish the two elements of the audience than to stress the availability to both of the same salvation. The more consistent explanation of the specification of Jerusalem in v. 27 is therefore that Luke understands

---

1.   M. Dumais, *Le langage de l'évangélisation: L'annonce missionnaire en milieu juif (Actes 13, 16-41)* (Recherches 16, Théologie; Tournai: Desclée; Montreal: Bellarmin, 1976), pp. 234-35.

2.   E. Schweizer, 'Concerning the Speeches in Acts', in L.E. Keck and J.L. Martyn (eds.), *Studies in Luke–Acts* (Nashville and New York: Abingdon Press, 1966), pp. 210, 214.

3.   Wilckens, *Missionsreden*, pp. 135-36.

4.   Kränkl, *Knecht*, pp. 116-17.

5.   Bachmann, *Tempel*, pp. 231-35.

that among the Jews only the Jerusalemites were responsible. This confirms what is consistently indicated elsewhere in Luke–Acts.

Thus, what is indeterminate or only hinted at in the Gospel of Luke is clarified by statements of Acts: Luke restricts popular Jewish responsibility for the death of Jesus to the people of Jerusalem. No broader ascription of Jewish responsibility is in evidence.

Others' Responsibility for the Death of Jesus

The prevailing view in critical literature on the death of Jesus in Luke–Acts is that Luke's indictment of the Jews (even if those Jews are limited to the Jerusalemites) has the exoneration of the Romans as its counterpart.[1] But does one necessarily imply the other? Luke unquestionably assigns the bulk of the blame to the Jews of Jerusalem, as is argued above. But at key points in his narrative he indisputably implicates others in the crucifixion. Their role is secondary, but it is not denied.

This section will examine those texts of Luke–Acts which implicate persons other than the Jewish leaders and people of Jerusalem. Because of the help they supply in interpreting Luke's passion account, attention will first be given to those texts which comment on others' responsibility outside of the passion narrative proper. Then the passion account will be examined in light of those other Lukan texts.

Texts outside the Passion Account
Luke 18.31-34. The assertion of this text that Jesus will be turned over to the Gentiles (παραδοθήσεται γὰρ τοῖς ἔθνεσιν, v. 32) is striking. This phrase is traditional, but its inclusion in a context in which Jewish involvement is omitted (cf. Mt. 20.18-19//Mk 10.33) suggests that it cannot be dismissed as an incongruent element of the tradition unconsciously transmitted by Luke. Indeed, because of the omission of the Jerusalem leadership in this text, greater stress falls on the involvement of the only remaining agents, the Gentiles.

J.T. Sanders has recently argued that Luke does not assert any Gentile responsibility for the death of Jesus anywhere in his narrative. Concerning this text he says that Luke has rendered Mark's active verbs into passives and then shifted back to active to obscure the reference to

---

1.   For example F. Schütz, *Der leidende Christus: Die angefochtene Gemeinde und das Christuskerygma der lukanischen Schriften* (BWANT, 89; Stuttgart: Kohlhammer, 1969), pp. 126-37.

the agent. Thus, when the pericope closes with the reference, not found in the parallels, to the disciples' inability to understand, Sanders finds here an indication that Luke has deliberately rendered the saying impossible for the reader to understand. In this way, the passage does not assert Gentile complicity; it in fact asserts nothing.[1]

Sanders's analysis of this text has a number of weaknesses. They can be enumerated briefly.

1. Luke has passive verbs where the other Synoptics have actives not only in the case of the verbs of which τοῖς ἔθνεσιν might be construed as the subject or agent but also with παραδοθήσεται (Mark and Matthew have παραδώσουσιν), of which τοῖς ἔθνεσιν is an indirect object. This passive verb does nothing to obscure Gentile involvement and suggests that the others are rendered in the passive for another purpose as well. In fact, they all put 'the Son of Man' in the center of the syntactical stage by making him the subject of a series of polysyllabic future passive verbs. In his shift back to active, furthermore, Luke renders μαστιγόω as a participle before ἀποκτενοῦσιν, focusing attention on the latter verb in climactic fashion.[2] Stylistic motives are more clearly at work in the syntax here than the motives that Sanders proposes.

2. The reference to the disciples' ignorance, although absent in the immediate parallels, is present in a different form in the second passion prediction in Mark and Luke. If Sanders is correct about the significance of the disciples' ignorance in the third passion prediction, then we must ask if it has the same meaning in the second. But the second prediction includes no note of Gentile involvement. If the disciples' ignorance had the same meaning in the second prediction as in the third, it could well be concluded that something other than obscuring Gentile involvement in the crucifixion was Luke's intention. But if it does not, then one

1.   Sanders, *Jews in Luke–Acts*, p. 13.

2.   In the rendering of verbs in the passive voice, Schneider finds Luke's attempt to give the passage greater unity, since it begins with the passive παραδοθήσεται (*Verleugnung*, p. 38). The weakness of this hypothesis is twofold: (1) παραδοθήσεται is passive by necessity: the identity of the betrayer cannot be revealed to the disciples yet; (2) if unity is the purpose, it is poorly accomplished, since not all the verbs are rendered in the passive and none of the others can share the agent of παραδοθήσεται. Büchele asserts that the verbs are divine passives, but the implication that the Gentiles are the agent of Jesus' suffering urges that such is not the case (*Tod*, p. 132).

wonders why Luke employs the motif of ignorance in such strikingly different ways.[1]

3. Sanders fails to observe that among the differences between Luke and the other Synoptics in his third passion prediction is the one noted above: his omission of a clear assertion of Jewish involvement. If elsewhere in the passage Luke was attempting to obscure Gentile involvement without omitting τοῖς ἔθνεσιν, his reason for omitting Jewish involvement altogether is a mystery. Even if Jewish involvement was not in Luke's source at this point, his assertion of it in the first passion prediction (9.22) could easily have been reproduced here.[2]

Acts 4.25-28. In the exegesis of Ps. 2.1-2 Luke again asserts the involvement of ἔθνη, naming Pilate and Herod specifically. The word-for-word correspondence between the Psalm and its fulfillment in this passage has been noted frequently. What appears significant, however, is that the identification of Pilate with οἱ ἄρχοντες is uncharacteristic of Luke. Elsewhere he uses ἄρχοντες primarily of Jewish leaders (Lk. 14.1; Acts 3.17; 13.27; 14.5), especially in the immediate context and the passion account (Acts 4.5, 8; Lk. 23.13, 35). Moreover, the term is plural and would therefore have served as a more apt description of the collective Jewish leadership than of the individual Roman governor. It does not appear, then, that Luke was compelled by the language of the Psalm to assign responsibility where he would not otherwise, since he could easily have named the Jewish ἄρχοντες in place of Pilate.

J.T. Sanders has sought to interpret this text in accord with his view that Luke never asserts Gentile involvement in the crucifixion. He finds three elements in this text which mitigate Gentile involvement. One is the use of ἐπί with the accusative in v. 27. Sanders admits that G. Schneider has shown that Luke uses this construction as a Septuagintalism to mean 'against'. But he nevertheless insists that

---

1. Büchele is probably right that the ignorance motif here and elsewhere belongs to Luke's assertion that understanding only comes when Jesus gives it after the resurrection (Lk. 24.25-27; *Tod*, pp. 133-35). The necessity of the death of Jesus can only be perceived after Easter.

2. Schneider asserts that the omission of Jewish involvement in this passage in light of Luke's emphasis on it elsewhere indicates that he follows a source other than Mark at this point (*Verleugnung*, pp. 36-37). This conclusion fails, however, to supply a motive for Luke's following a source which does not present the concerns he evinces elsewhere.

because Luke uses it 'many, many times' to indicate place, and because the unambiguous κατά was available in the preceding quotation of Ps. 2.2, the choice of ἐπί here serves 'to introduce a note of ambiguity into the meaning of the exegesis'. Secondly, Sanders notes that v. 28 introduces divine foreordination into the picture, further ameliorating Gentile involvement. Finally, Sanders says that the passage says nothing about what anyone actually did to Jesus.[1]

Again, Sanders's arguments suggest special pleading. While ἐπί with the accusative may well indicate place, the personal object here suggests a different meaning. Since Luke has already indicated place with ἐν τῇ πόλει ταύτῃ, an additional designation of place would be redundant. The meaning 'against' presents none of the problems which 'at' introduces; all that Sanders can offer by way of evidence against it is that Luke does not always use ἐπί to mean 'against'.

Sanders's argument that divine foreordination ameliorates Gentile responsibility has some force, but it is force that he applies with curious inconsistency. Elsewhere he claims that references to predestination do *not* lessen Jewish responsibility for the crucifixion.[2] Sanders has obviously struggled with this passage, since his treatment of it in the latter section of his book is different. He writes, 'Since Jesus' death was God's plan, the four entities "convened" were merely instruments in that plan, as Peter's earlier sermons have made clear'.[3] Nevertheless he goes on to write,

> In no sense does v. 27 reduce Jewish guilt in the death of Jesus, since
> [Acts] 2.23 has already explained the relation between Jews and Gentiles
> in the matter of Jesus' execution. If God used all four entities, neverthe-
> less the Jews used the Gentiles.[4]

But concerning Acts 2.23 he has elsewhere asserted that the ἄνομοι are the Jewish leaders, not the Gentiles.[5] Perhaps Sanders means to suggest that Luke has inconsistently applied the theme of predestination in order to excuse Gentiles and condemn Jews. If so, he does not indicate how to recognize the inconsistency.

As to the omission of specifics about what was done to Jesus, one can

1. Sanders, *Jews in Luke–Acts*, p. 14.
2. Sanders, *Jews in Luke–Acts*, p. 234.
3. Sanders, *Jews in Luke–Acts*, p. 240.
4. Sanders, *Jews in Luke–Acts*, p. 240.
5. Sanders, *Jews in Luke–Acts*, p. 10. Sanders contradicts this point later in his work (p. 234).

hardly call it a surprising factor. The author probably considered the details to be sufficiently clear from the passion narrative. The omission of specifics here has significance only if the reader would have under ordinary circumstances expected specifics, and such is not the case. The emphasis of this passage is on the wide array of human forces gathered against the Anointed of God; the reader is assumed to know what the gathered forces did.

These factors, taken together, indicate that Luke throws the net of responsibility beyond the circle of the Jews in Jerusalem. Pilate, Herod and unnamed ἔθνη are among those who gathered in Jerusalem to accomplish God's purpose in the passion of Jesus.

Acts 13.27-29. This text suggests that Pilate participates in Jesus' execution along with the Jerusalemites and their leaders. Against this indication J.T. Sanders argues two points. One is that the text never says that Pilate gave in to the request of the Jews for Jesus' execution. The other is that 'they', that is, 'those dwelling in Jerusalem and their leaders', are the ones who do the deed and so are the ones who are guilty.[1] Again it is true that the people of Jerusalem and their leaders are the primary actors on the stage: they are the subject of the main clause in vv. 27-28. Nevertheless, they are not the only ones who appear. Luke indeed does not indicate explicitly that Pilate accedes to their request for execution. But unless it is assumed that Pilate fulfilled the request to do away with Jesus, Jesus' death is nowhere indicated, although his removal from the death of Jesus, burial and resurrection are. To assume, therefore, that Pilate did not acquiesce in the request for death makes nonsense of the text. A specific indication that Pilate had Jesus killed at the request of those dwelling in Jerusalem and their leaders would be entirely redundant in the context. The text betrays no interest in protecting Pilate from a share of the responsibility, though clearly it is primarily concerned with the responsibility of Jerusalem.

The Passion Narrative
The vagaries of interpreting narratives without reference to the narrator's editorial comments have allowed many to see an exoneration of the Romans in the Lukan passion account. But the references discussed above suggest that Luke reserves a measure of responsibility for the

---

1.   Sanders, *Jews in Luke–Acts*, pp. 14-15.

Romans, including Pilate, and for Herod. Is this perspective confirmed by the passion account itself, or is the Lukan passion narrative in tension with his comments elsewhere?[1] It has already been argued above that the soldiers of Luke's crucifixion scene are Roman. What remains is to examine his presentation of Pilate and Herod.

The pronouncement of Jesus' innocence by Pilate (Lk. 23.4, 14-15, 22) and Herod (23.15a) is commonly seen as exonerating them of any culpability in the crucifixion. In this regard they are frequently compared to the second thief and the centurion who likewise pronounce Jesus innocent (23.41, 47) and are treated sympathetically by the author. But Pilate's threefold pronouncement of Jesus' innocence may serve purposes other than Pilate's own vindication. Luke's interest in Jesus' innocence of all charges is clear, as has already been noted. Pilate's pronouncements make that point plainly but may nevertheless imply nothing about his own guiltlessness. In fact, by pronouncing Jesus innocent three times and then turning him over to be crucified, Pilate appears all the more culpable for having knowingly turned an innocent man over to execution.[2] Herod's similar pronouncement of innocence is accompanied by mocking and beating (Lk. 23.11). Not only is such treatment hardly commendable handling of an innocent, it also corresponds to the description of Jesus' sufferings through the agency of ἔθνη in Lk. 18.32.[3] Even if Herod has Jesus beaten as a troublemaker who is nevertheless innocent of the charges brought against him, his

1. Kränkl finds contradiction between the Lukan passion narrative and Acts 4.25-28 (*Knecht*, pp. 110-11).

2. Esler correctly observes that if Luke's purpose had been to counter Christian resentment toward Rome, he would not have included the reference to Pilate's violence in Lk. 13.1 (*Community and Gospel*, pp. 209-10). What Esler misses, however, when he refers to Luke's 'whitewashing of Pilate's role in the condemnation and death of Jesus' (pp. 202-203) is that Pilate's acquiescence to the demand for the death of an innocent man is no less negative. Indeed, it is consistent with Luke's depiction of other Roman governors of Palestine, namely Felix and Festus, as, in Esler's own words, 'self-seeking and corrupt'. Carroll properly observes that Pilate's pronouncement vindicates Jesus, not the Roman administration ('Crucifixion Scene', p. 196 n. 12).

3. Gaston insists that Herod's soldiers are Jewish ('Passion Narrative', pp. 147-48). Although the connection of the account of their beating may not correspond to the beating from ἔθνη in Lk. 18.32, the precise identity of these soldiers is ultimately a matter of indifference for purposes here. The point is that they act under the authority of Herod, not under that of the high priests and scribes.

action cannot be positively regarded from Luke's editorial perspective. Luke is concerned to show that Jesus is innocent before Rome, and that concern may reflect his respect for Roman law.[1] But the implication of the narrative is that Pilate's actions were a perversion of that law.

Furthermore, the verb παραδίδωμι in Lk. 23.25 may carry a sinister connotation. The verb is used 31 times in Luke–Acts, and in 18 of those cases it indicates a giving over in persecution, betrayal, arrest or execution (Lk. 9.44; 12.58; 18.32; 21.12, 16; 22.4, 6, 21, 22, 48; 23.25; 24.7, 20; Acts 3.13; 8.3; 12.4; 21.11; 22.4). Particularly important is the fact that it is the regular verb for betrayal in the passion predictions. And aside from 23.25, in the passion narrative it refers only to the act of betrayal. Furthermore, each time παραδίδωμι appears with a personal object in Luke, it connotes at least callous disregard and at most outright hostility toward its object (Lk. 12.58; 20.20; 22.4, 6; 23.25). Given the circumstances of Pilate's handing over of Jesus and the consistent use of παραδίδωμι earlier in the narrative, the word may carry this sinister connotation in Lk. 23.25.

Other telling details indicate that Pilate has charge over the crucifixion. One is the second person singular verb σταύρου in Lk. 23.21, which clearly implies the crowd's expectation that Pilate is the one who will crucify. Luke appears to have chosen this form deliberately, since he differs from Mark (15.13-14) in using the present instead of the aorist and from Matthew (27.22) in using the active. In fact, Matthew's passive rendering demonstrates that Pilate's involvement could be minimized without eliminating the crowd's cry. Luke is, of course, readily able to transform actives into passives to suit his purposes (cf. Lk. 18.31-34). But here he makes no effort to efface the suggestion of Pilate's involvement in the crucifixion. Similarly, Luke follows the traditional account of Jesus' burial in which Joseph of Arimathea goes to Pilate for Jesus' body (Lk. 23.52//Mt. 27.58//Mk 15.43).[2] If Pilate is the authority who disposes of Jesus' body, it can reasonably be assumed that Pilate is the authority under whom Jesus is executed. Indeed, it is the plan of the conspirators from the beginning to turn Jesus over to the 'rule and authority of the governor' (20.20, Luke only). Pilate's concession to the will of the Jerusalemites (23.24-25) does not therefore

---

1. Esler correctly emphasizes that preceding the hearing before Pilate Luke incorporates material which refutes the charges brought against Jesus (*Community and Gospel*, pp. 202-203).

2. Cassidy, 'Audience', p. 147.

appear to be an abdication of his authority in Jesus' execution; it indicates weakness, not innocence. Rome continues to exercise the final control.[1]

These considerations, taken together, present a consistent picture. The instigators of the crucifixion are the Jerusalem leaders associated with the temple. They are supported in the decisive moment by the people of Jerusalem. But the political authorities are involved as well. Although they recognize Jesus' innocence and, in Pilate's case, seek to release him, ultimately they surrender to pressure and exercise their power against Jesus. Luke may reduce the emphasis on Roman involvement, although such a judgment depends on a thorough knowledge of Luke's sources which is unavailable to us. In any case, he does not eliminate Roman involvement, and he does sharpen it at some points. What is clearer is his emphasis on the involvement of the leaders of Jerusalem, whose provocation of the crucifixion is always at the forefront of the narrative.[2]

Conclusions

The preceding analysis has repeatedly confirmed that Luke holds directly responsible for the death of Jesus only the Jerusalemites and their leaders among the Jews. In both Luke's Gospel and Acts the responsibility of the leaders is repeatedly and explicitly expressed. The identity of the Jewish crowd that calls for Jesus' death is indefinite in Luke's Gospel, although there are hints that the crowd is Jerusalemite (23.28). But Acts explicitly implicates the people of Jerusalem in Jesus' death. Furthermore, in both his volumes Luke maintains a degree of responsibility for Herod, Pilate and his Roman soldiers. This finding establishes a strong prima facie case against the common view that Luke exonerates Rome and implicates the Jews as a whole in his presentation of Jesus' death.

1.   Bachmann has argued that the same pattern appears in Acts, where the Romans continue to exercise the decisive authority over Paul; cf. Acts 21.30ff.; 25.9 (*Tempel*, pp. 257-58).

2.   E.P. Sanders concludes that the essence of this scenario, that Jesus was killed by the Romans at the behest of the Jewish leadership, is the best explanation of the available, indisputable 'facts' about Jesus' death (*Jesus and Judaism* [London: SCM Press, 1985], pp. 317-18).

The case cannot be considered conclusive, however, until other material related to Luke's presentation of the Jews is examined. It is possible that in Luke's narrative Jerusalem's involvement in the death of Jesus serves as a token by which all Jews are condemned.[1] Many have found in Luke–Acts just such a tendency to condemn the Jewish people as a whole. Whether such a view can be sustained is the next question to be addressed.

---

1.   Moessner, for example, considers it 'beyond question' that Jerusalem stands for all Israel (*Banquet*, p. 118).

Chapter 3

JERUSALEM'S RESPONSIBILITY IN RELATION TO ALL ISRAEL

In the previous chapter it was argued that Luke restricts responsibility for the death of Jesus among the Jews to the Jerusalemites. But does this attribution of responsibility still implicate Israel as a whole? Several elements might suggest as much: Jerusalem is the capital of Israel, and the Sanhedrin of Jerusalem is the supreme judicial body of Israel. Either could reasonably stand for the entire nation. Luke's partiality to expressions which suggest the Jewish people as a whole (ὁ λαός, ἡ γενεὰ αὕτη, οἱ Ἰουδαῖοι) lends plausibility to such a figurative function for Jerusalem.

If Jerusalem's role in the crucifixion does somehow implicate all Israel for Luke, how can such an implication be recognized? If Luke directly accused Jews outside Jerusalem of complicity in the crucifixion, the implication would be clear. But the previous chapter has shown that such is not the case. However, in other, more subtle ways, Luke may still indict Israel as a whole. Any indication that he regards the Jewish nation as a whole as having rejected Jesus and the gospel or that he regards the Jewish nation as a whole as standing under God's condemnation could well be related in Luke's thought to some form of national responsibility for the crucifixion. Suggestions that either or both of these ideas are present in Luke–Acts are numerous. But are they well founded? This chapter will evaluate their supporting evidence.

The Use of Generalized Expressions

Luke's predilection for terms which appear to refer to the Jewish nation as a whole is well known. The use of one such expression, ὁ λαός, has already been discussed in the previous chapter. But the use of other expressions, particularly ἡ γενεὰ αὕτη and οἱ Ἰουδαῖοι, may also suggest a general rejection of Jesus and the gospel by the nation as a whole or the condemnation of the nation as a whole. The evidence of the text, however, demonstrates that Luke does not intend such a generalized reference with either expression, as the following discussion will show.

'This Generation'

Luke's use of ἡ γενεὰ αὕτη has suggested to some exegetes that he views the entire Jewish nation as standing under condemnation. Aside from the occurrence in Lk. 21.32 (cf. 16.8, ἡ γενεὰ ἡ ἑαυτῶν), the phrase in Luke–Acts is used negatively, mostly in statements of judgment spoken by Jesus to his (Jewish) audience (Lk. 7.31; 11.29-32, 50-51; 17.25; cf. Acts 2.40; Lk. 9.41).[1] Various approaches have been taken to show that Luke intends the judgment pronounced on ἡ γενεὰ αὕτη to be understood as judgment against the Jews generally.

J.T. Sanders and H. Egelkraut have appealed to a variety of features in Luke's redaction of these statements and their contexts which tend to reinforce the suggestion that he insinuates a blanket condemnation of the Jewish people. Sanders notes that the usage in 7.31 is preceded by the statement about the Pharisees' rejection of the plan of God, from which Sanders infers a condemnation of Jewish rejection of Jesus, and is followed by references to the rejection of John and Jesus by the Jews. This emphasis on Jewish rejection, coupled with the reference in context to the faith of a Gentile in the healing of the centurion's slave and to the faith of a Jewish 'outsider' in the person of the sinful woman, suggests to Sanders a Lukan predilection to condemn Jews and commend non-Jews.[2] Similarly, in Lk. 11.29 Sanders insists that Luke has sharpened the anti-Jewish overtones of the expression by using πονηρά in a copulative sentence instead of as an attributive adjective and by moving the reference to Nineveh to the end of the discourse (cf. Mt. 12.39; Mk 8.12).[3] Likewise, H. Egelkraut suggests that the condemnation of

---

1. Except for Lk. 17.25 and, of course, Acts 2.40, every Lukan use of ἡ γενεὰ αὕτη is paralleled in Matthew, Mark or both; it is clearly a traditional expression. Care must be taken, however, neither to overemphasize its traditional nature (as does Lohfink, *Sammlung*, pp. 43-44) nor to ignore it altogether (as do the studies cited below, most of which are influenced by narrative-critical methods which eschew source-critical considerations). Luke's inclusion of the phrase from the tradition is deliberate and may well indicate something of his intentions, but evidence of his own emphases must be sought in the contexts where the phrase occurs.

2. Sanders, *Jews in Luke–Acts*, pp. 175-76.

3. Sanders, *Jews in Luke–Acts*, pp. 57-58, 185. He does not consider that μοιχαλίς (Mt. 12.39) may have appeared in Luke's source and been omitted in his redaction, rendering the saying less emphatic.

the Jewish audience for seeking a sign in a context in which a sign is given emphasizes Jewish callousness. According to Egelkraut, this condemnation has a particular anti-Jewish accent with the use of 'finger of God' in Lk. 11.20, a reference to Exod. 8.15 (LXX), where the (Gentile) Egyptian magicians recognize God's activity in Moses, in contrast to this (Jewish) generation's failure to recognize the same activity in Jesus.[1] In Lk. 11.46-52, Sanders suggests that Luke connects the Pharisees' interpretation of Torah to the killing of the prophets, the culmination of which is the death of Jesus. Thereby, Luke condemns the Pharisees, who are excluded from the Lukan passion narrative, for the crucifixion.[2]

J.M. Dawsey has brought other considerations to bear on the discussion of ἡ γενεὰ αὕτη in Luke–Acts. He begins with a statistical overview of Luke's use of the expression. Luke uses γενεά 14 times in Luke–Acts, 11 times in the speech of Jesus and never in the narrator's voice. By contrast, he uses λαός 37 times, 24 of which are in the narrator's voice and only one of which is in Jesus' speech. Especially important is Lk. 7.29-31, where the narrator uses λαός and Jesus uses γενεά of the same people.[3] The explanation for this phenomenon is to be found in a conflict of voices in the narrative. For the narrator the people of God as a whole support Jesus, although only a few recognize the true significance of his actions; popular rejection of Jesus is a well-intentioned misunderstanding. Thus, the narrator is inclined to use λαός for the people, implying with it that they are indeed the people of God.[4] In contrast, Jesus views his rejection as a full rejection by a wicked generation. The narrator fails to appropriate this perspective because he wishes to reinterpret the story to accommodate the universal Jewish and Gentile church and extend the message to his own generation.[5] Dawsey suggests that while Luke supports the view of Jesus over that of the narrator, he nevertheless purposely allows the two perspectives to stand in tension in the narrative.[6]

---

1. Egelkraut, *Mission to Jerusalem*, pp. 95-97.
2. Sanders, *Jews in Luke–Acts*, p. 104-105, 187-88. The involvement of ἡ γενεὰ αὕτη in the death of Jesus is made explicit by Luke in Lk. 17.25, a text which Sanders fails to note in this connection.
3. J.M. Dawsey, *The Lukan Voice: Confusion and Irony in the Gospel of Luke* (Macon, GA: Mercer University Press, 1986), p. 75-76.
4. Dawsey, *Lukan Voice*, pp. 78-80.
5. Dawsey, *Lukan Voice*, pp. 81-82.
6. Dawsey, *Lukan Voice*, pp. 103-24.

For D.P. Moessner ἡ γενεὰ αὕτη is tied in Luke to the malicious influence of the Pharisees. The 'leaven of the Pharisees' is at work in the people to transform their support for Jesus to rejection in the passion narrative.[1] Thus, Jesus regards the earlier rejection by some (the Pharisees prominent among them) as the rejection by all and condemns all under the rubric 'this generation'. Moessner sees the connection thus:

> It is as though Luke has drawn a line from a sample of the evidence (skepticism on the part of some) to an arraignment of the accused (the whole evil generation) to the prime source of the crime (the baneful influence of the Pharisees and their scribes).[2]

Thus, although Luke distinguishes various reactions among the Jews of Jesus' 'generation', rejection by some is condemned in Deuteronomistic terms as rejection by all. The entire nation—including even the disciples—stands under judgment because of an unrepentant faction.[3] Consistent with this perspective, Luke implicates the entire 'generation' in Jesus' death.[4]

Although each of these perspectives calls attention to significant features of the Lukan text, none can be judged entirely satisfactory. Each assumes that the expression ἡ γενεὰ αὕτη is used by Luke to refer to the Jewish people in general. Hence, the condemnation of 'this generation' is used to interpret positive response to Jesus as inadequate. But usage elsewhere suggests that a more restrictive reference is more likely. The phrase and its near equivalents are relatively rare in the LXX,[5] where they are mostly used with temporal emphasis for a generation in a specific period of history (Noah's generation, Gen. 7.1; the wilderness generation, Num. 32.13 and Deut. 32.5; the present generation as compared to eternity, Ps. 11.8 [12.7]; cf. ἡ γενεὰ ἐκείνη used temporally in Exod. 1.6; Judg. 2.10). The phrase ἡ γενεὰ αὕτη does not occur in Josephus, but his use of γενεά is suggestive. On three occasions γενεά designates the rebellious Jewish faction under the command of John of

---

1. Moessner, 'Prophet like Moses', pp. 603-604; 'Leaven of the Pharisees', pp. 31-32.

2. Moessner, 'Leaven of the Pharisees', p. 30.

3. Moessner, 'Leaven of the Pharisees', pp. 31-32.

4. Moessner, 'Wilderness Generation', pp. 328-36. Moessner integrates this conclusion into his exegesis of the travel narrative of Luke in *Banquet*, pp. 62-64, 66, 68-69, 93, 95-96, 101-102, 104-105.

5. M. Wilcox notes the rarity of the phrase in the LXX in his analysis of Acts 2.40 (*The Semitisms of Acts* [London: Oxford University Press, 1965], p. 30).

Giscala at the destruction of Jerusalem (*War* 5.442, 566; 6.408).[1] In each case the faction is regarded as evil and the rest of the city as relatively blameless except for its toleration of the rebels. The setting is different from Luke's: Josephus does not deliver prophetic pronouncements of judgment (and so the exact phrase ἡ γενεὰ αὕτη does not appear). But the referents are strikingly similar. The only other instance where Josephus uses γενεά to refer to a group of people other than a family (his predominant usage) is *Ant.* 4.4, where he refers to the Jewish nation with ἡ Ἀβραμου γενεά, emphasizing their common Abrahamic descent. Such limited occurrences demand that conclusions be drawn with reserve. Nevertheless, it is interesting that Josephus uses γενεά without qualification in a partitive sense and only uses it to refer to the nation as a whole with explicit qualification to that effect. Josephus' usage indicates that γενεά does not necessarily carry an inclusive connotation.

E. Lövestam has recently noted the use of similar expressions in the targums and rabbinic literature. His conclusion is that 'this generation' refers to one of a series of generations distinguished by its unfaithfulness to God and therefore subject to judgment.[2] But the 'generation' is not monolithic: in each 'generation' are those distinguished by their faithfulness (for example, Noah, Caleb and Joshua) who escape the judgment which comes on their fellows.[3]

Several factors in Luke's redaction suggest that he does not understand ἡ γενεὰ αὕτη to carry an inclusive meaning in the sayings where it appears. The statement of Lk. 7.31 is qualified by Luke with the preceding context. The notes about the contrasting responses to John of ὁ λαὸς...καὶ οἱ τελῶναι on the one hand and the Pharisees and lawyers on the other (vv. 29-30), although based on traditional material (cf. Mt. 21.32), appear to have been inserted by Luke into this context. The description of ἡ γενεὰ αὕτη is connected to these verses in two ways: (1) 'this generation' rejects John, as do the Pharisees and lawyers (v. 33); (2) 'this generation' criticizes Jesus' associations with τελῶναι, the very people who received John's baptism (v. 34). The insertion of vv. 29-30 thus logically restricts the epithet ἡ γενεὰ αὕτη to the Pharisees and lawyers. The saying of v. 35 further reinforces the implied

---

1. Only the first of these references is cited by F. Büchsel, 'γενεά κτλ', *TDNT*, I, p. 663.

2. E. Lövestam, 'Der Rettungsappel in Ag 2, 40', *ASTI* 12 (1983), pp. 85-86.

3. Lövestam, 'Rettungsappel', pp. 86-87.

division, indicating as it does that 'wisdom's children' accept the ministries of John and Jesus.[1] Sanders and Moessner are thus incorrect in asserting that the Pharisees' rejection sets the stage for a denunciation of the Jews generally; Luke sharply differentiates between the response of the Pharisees and that of the Jewish people and outcasts and applies the denunciation only to the former. Likewise, Dawsey incorrectly assumes a conflict in the use of γενεά and λαός in this context: neither term carries the inclusive import he suggests.[2]

Similar observations can be made about the use of ἡ γενεὰ αὕτη in Lk. 11.50-51. Again the statement is traditional (//Mt. 23.35-36), although it is difficult to know whether Matthew and Luke used the same recension of the material and what their particular recensions actually included. But Luke's version either preserves or inserts various elements which suggest again that he understood the reference of ἡ γενεὰ αὕτη to be restricted to a particular group of Jews. The text is linked to the preceding context through the reference to the killing of the prophets (vv. 47, 49, 50-51), which is ascribed in the first case to the νομικοί.[3] The preservation or insertion of τῶν προφητῶν in v. 50, despite the fact that Abel was clearly not a prophet in the ordinary sense, serves to link the saying closely to the preceding material with its

---

1. Cf. the brief discussion in Johnson, *Possessions*, pp. 101-102. Moessner admits that this group constitutes an exception to the condemnation of 'this generation' but asserts that it is a peculiar characteristic of the Deuteronomistic perspective to condemn all despite exceptions (*Banquet*, pp. 102-105; cf. 113-14). In general Moessner notes Luke's tendency to portray Israel as divided but insists that expressions like 'this generation' still imply a monolithic rejection of Jesus (*Banquet*, p. 221). He insists repeatedly on this point despite his observations that similar expressions are used in Jewish literature with reference to the unfaithful portion of the nation (1QS 3.14; *Banquet*, p. 248 n. 289) and that the Deuteronomic tradition included the concept of a faithful remnant (*Banquet*, p. 91).

2. See the discussion of Luke's use of λαός in the preceding chapter. The fact that γενεά and λαός do not indicate a conflict between Jesus and the narrator here lends credence to the general criticism of Dawsey's thesis offered by R.C. Tannehill (*The Narrative Unity of Luke–Acts: A Literary Interpretation. I. The Gospel according to Luke* [Philadelphia: Fortress Press, 1986], p. 7).

3. R.J. Miller rightly notes that there is a missing proposition in the logic of Lk. 11.49-51 ('The Rejection of the Prophets in Q', *JBL* 107 [1988], p. 230). But he wrongly assumes that the missing proposition is the persecution of the Q prophets. Rather it is the rejection of Jesus by the νομικοί (v. 47) which provides the link. The saying is not incongruent in the context, as Miller suggests.

address to the νομικοί.[1] The reference of ἡ γενεὰ αὕτη in v. 50 thus appears to be restricted to those whose building of the tombs of the prophets connects them to the murder of the prophets. Even if Matthew's second person reference in this verse was in Luke's source (Mt. 23.35), the phrase ἡ γενεὰ αὕτη occurs later in the Matthean version (v. 36) and so was presumably in Luke's source as well. In such a case ἡ γενεὰ αὕτη could have been reproduced by Luke in the previous sentence to lend greater unity to the discourse, the restrictive meaning of the term being implicit in both instances.

The possibility of a comparison between ἡ γενεὰ αὕτη as the entire Jewish nation and various Gentile representatives in Lk. 11.29-32 is likewise undermined by certain distinctive Lukan features. In the saying about the Queen of the South (v. 31//Mt. 12.42) Luke apparently inserts τῶν ἀνδρῶν before τῆς γενεᾶς ταυτῆς and alters the pronoun which follows to agree with the former expression (αὐτούς). Several factors suggest that these are Lukan elements: (1) in 11.32 no qualifying phrase is attached to τῆς γενεᾶς ταύτης; (2) in Lk. 7.31 τῆς γενεᾶς ταύτης is similarly qualified with τοὺς ἀνθρώπους (diff. Mt. 11.16), with a corresponding shift in the grammar that follows (ὅμοιοι); (3) these are the only differences in wording from the Matthean version of Lk. 11.32. The emphasis of the comparison is thus shifted from ἡ γενεὰ αὕτη to a particular group within that generation, that is, the men, whose rejection of God's messenger contrasts with the positive response of a woman. Luke thus appears to have edited the saying in such a way that places at least as much emphasis on the comparison between male rejection and female acceptance of God's messenger as between Jewish rejection and Gentile acceptance, which remains the accent in v. 32. His interest does not therefore appear to lie in the possibilities which the saying of v. 31 presented for applying a blanket condemnation to the Jewish nation in

---

1. It cannot be decided with certainty whether τῶν προφητῶν in v. 50 is original and was altered by Matthew or his source to δίκαιον or whether δίκαιον was original and was altered to τῶν προφητῶν by Luke or his source to explicate the connection to the preceding context. I.H. Marshall suggests the former alternative, based on the assumption that Matthew seeks to remove the problematic identification of Abel as a prophet (*The Gospel of Luke* [NIGTC; Exeter: Paternoster Press, 1978], p. 505). But it is nevertheless possible that τῶν προφητῶν was substituted for an original δίκαιον at a later stage in the tradition, perhaps by Luke himself, whose interest in the killing-of-the prophets motif would supply the motivation.

comparison to Gentiles.[1] Instead, both comparisons appear to be united in their interest in the positive response of 'outsiders' (Gentiles, women) as opposed to the negative response of 'insiders' (Jews, men). Therefore, even if, as Sanders suggests, Luke has sharpened the assertion that 'this generation' is evil, or, as Egelkraut argues, Luke emphasizes the callousness of those who reject by juxtaposing the demand for a sign with the giving of a sign, he does not appear thereby to indict the Jews as a people but to sharpen the condemnation of those among them who fail to repent.[2]

These observations suggest that Luke does not intend the statement of Lk. 17.25 as an indictment of the Jewish nation as a whole for the crucifixion. It is again impossible to determine with certainty whether the verse is Lukan or traditional,[3] although if it is Lukan, it appears to have been based on the other passion predictions. The phrase ἡ γενεὰ αὕτη, although absent from the other passion predictions, is found in the Synoptic apocalyptic discourse (Mt. 24.34//Mk 13.30//Lk. 21.32), and could well have been inserted from it into this related context by Luke or his source. The occurrence in the apocalyptic discourse carries a decidedly temporal emphasis: 'This generation will not pass away until...'[4] The same kind of emphasis is likely in Lk. 17.25 as well, where it would indicate that the imminent suffering of the Son of Man is the prerequisite to the coming of the kingdom of God. Additionally, however, the context—with references to Noah (vv. 26-27), Lot (vv. 28-29, 32), and those 'taken' and 'left' (vv. 34-35)—again suggests not a blanket condemnation of an entire people but a division among that people. The restricted reference of the saying is likewise indicated by the

---

1. Moessner notes the comparison between 'men' and a woman in this text but asserts that it is merely a stylistic device (*Banquet*, p. 93). Luke's willingness to introduce such stylistic improvements rather than to develop the potential for condemnation of the entire nation in the saying still suggests something about his interests.

2. Similar conclusions can therefore also be drawn for similar Lukan comparisons where ἡ γενεὰ αὕτη does not appear (Lk. 4.25-27; 13.29).

3. The different opinions are summarized by Marshall, *Gospel of Luke*, pp. 661-62; cf. Wenham, *Eschatological Discourse*, pp. 159-60.

4. The argument of R. Morgenthaler and C. Brown ('Generation', in C. Brown [ed.], *The New International Dictionary of New Testament Theology* [Grand Rapids: Zondervan, 1978], II, pp. 37-38), that ἡ γενεὰ αὕτη refers to Israel as a class of people in Lk. 21.32, depends on assumptions which will be addressed in the discussion of the 'turning episodes' of Acts.

similarity of the verse with the saying in Lk. 9.22, where τῶν πρεσβυτέρων appears instead of τῆς γενεᾶς ταύτης. Luke's usage of ἡ γενεὰ αὕτη elsewhere already indicates that he uses the phrase to refer to such specific groups. The text gives little evidence, therefore, that Luke intended with it to broaden the more restricted ascription of responsibility for the death of Jesus to Jerusalem so that all Israel was included.

The restrictive sense of ἡ γενεὰ αὕτη appears likely in Acts 2.40 as well. The assumption of the sentence is clearly that the entire 'generation' stands under a judgment which individuals can only escape through repentance. M. Wilcox has demonstrated that Semitic antecedents may lie behind this expression,[1] and Lövestam's more recent work confirms that judgment.[2] Even if the phrase does originate in Semitic—and hence Jewish-Christian—circles, Luke might still employ it in an anti-Jewish fashion. But the context suggests no such anti-Jewish thrust. The identity of the generation depends on the speech which precedes this verse, where repentance is offered to the people of Jerusalem who stand accused of the crucifixion (vv. 23, 36-38).[3] In a manner similar to Josephus's usage and to targumic and rabbinic usage, Luke thus appears to designate the people of Jerusalem implicated in the crucifixion, not the Jews as a whole, as ἡ γενεὰ αὕτη.

In summary, then, there is little evidence that Luke uses ἡ γενεὰ αὕτη as an inclusive term for the Jewish people as a whole. Neither the relevant parallels nor the details of his own usage suggest that such is the case. The judgment of those critics who understood the phrase as having a restricted reference can therefore be affirmed with greater confidence.[4]

'The Jews'

Luke's use of οἱ Ἰουδαῖοι has likewise indicated to some a tendency to view all Jews as opponents of Christianity. Although the critical literature shows considerable disagreement about exactly how often οἱ Ἰουδαῖοι appears in Acts with a negative implication,[5] a general

1. Wilcox, *Semitisms of Acts*, p. 30.
2. Lövestam, 'Rettungsappel', pp. 84-87.
3. See the discussion in the previous chapter.
4. For example, Gnilka, *Verstockung*, p. 134; George, 'Israël', p. 498; Dupont, 'La conclusion des Actes', pp. 379-80; Tyson, *Death*, pp. 62-64.
5. R.R. Ruether counts 45 hostile uses of οἱ Ἰουδαῖοι in Acts and only ten as

pattern of usage is clear. After the Stephen episode, the term appears repeatedly and in many instances is used without immediate qualification for opponents of Christianity, especially of Paul. Because of this pattern of usage, the conclusion has persistently been drawn that Luke seeks to characterize the Jewish nation in its entirety as opposing Christianity,[1] so that, in J.T. Sanders's words, 'Apostles are not Jews and Jews are not Christians'.[2] Some have even suggested that the relative frequency of λαός in the earlier chapters of Acts and its disappearance in favor of Ἰουδαῖοι following the death of Stephen indicates that Luke views the unrepentant people of Israel as having forfeited their membership in the λαός of God and become members of the merely secular nation, οἱ Ἰουδαῖοι.[3]

descriptions of Christians (*Faith and Fratricide: The Theological Roots of Anti-Semitism* [New York: Seabury, 1974], pp. 89-90). J. Koenig, responding to Ruether, counts only 30 negative references, 18 of which refer to particular groups of Jews (*Jews and Christians in Dialogue: New Testament Foundations* [Philadelphia: Westminster Press, 1979], p. 168). Hauser finds 34 instances where the phrase appears with relative self-sufficiency, 26 of which are hostile (*Apg 28*, pp. 98-99). Sanders counts a total of 74 occurrences of Ἰουδαῖοι or οἱ Ἰουδαῖοι in all of Luke–Acts, only eight of which (all without hostility) occur before Stephen's death; but he does not suggest how many of the 68 remaining uses are hostile (*Jews in Luke–Acts*, pp. 71-72). The differences in these evaluations depend largely on the different criteria used to determine what constitutes a hostile usage.

1.   In addition to those listed in the previous note, the following works also draw this conclusion: F.J. Foakes-Jackson and K. Lake (eds.), *The Beginnings of Christianity.* Part I. *The Acts of the Apostles* (Grand Rapids: Baker, 1979 [1933]), IV, p. 291; J.T. Sanders, 'The Parable of the Pounds and Lucan Anti-Semitism', *TS* 42 (1981), p. 668; Gaston, 'Passion Narrative', pp. 133, 137-39; D. Slingerland, '"The Jews" in the Pauline Portion of Acts', *JAAR* 54 (1986), pp. 305-21; *idem*, 'Composition of Acts', pp. 99-100; Beck, *Mature Christianity*, pp. 222-24; Wilson, *Law*, pp. 113, 115-16. D.R.A. Hare sees Luke's use of οἱ Ἰουδαῖοι as an element of 'gentilizing anti-Judaism', but insists nevertheless that Luke's total work indicates that he does not despise Judaism or the Jewish people ('The Rejection of the Jews in the Synoptic Gospels and Acts', in A. Davies [ed.], *Antisemitism and the Foundations of Christianity* [New York: Paulist Press, 1979], pp. 36-38).

2.   Sanders, *Jews in Luke–Acts*, p. 264.

3.   Conzelmann, *Theology*, pp. 145-46; Gnilka, *Verstockung*, pp. 145-46; George, 'Israël', pp. 510-12; Lohfink, *Sammlung*, pp. 57-58. Cf. the preceding chapter, where it was argued that the frequent use of λαός in the early chapters of Acts has to do with the differentiation between the people and the leaders, not the theological conception of Israel as the λαός of God.

Are such judgments justified by the evidence of the text? A statistical overview does indicate a transition in Luke's usage of 'Ιουδαῖος after the Stephen narrative. But characterizing the Jews as opponents is not the only possible explanation for that transition. J.T. Townsend has suggested that Luke uses 'Ιουδαῖος in the latter chapters of Acts as a part of his tendency to accommodate his language to the Hellenistic setting of these chapters:

> When writing about events in Palestine, [Luke] tends to distinguish among the various Jewish groups as any Palestinian Jew would do. In a gentile setting, Luke refers to Jews as a gentile would, and lumps them together as 'The Jews' without distinction.[1]

Townsend's observation is clearly correct in many instances. The usage in Lk. 7.3 appears to be influenced by the focus on the Gentile centurion. The occurrences of 'Ιουδαῖος in the Cornelius episode are appropriate not only on the lips of Cornelius's messengers (Acts 10.22) but also as a term of self-designation for Peter (10.28).[2] Likewise, the frequent use of 'Ιουδαῖος in the account of Paul's missionary work in the diaspora (chs. 13–14, 16–20) stems at least in part from the adaptation of language to setting. The term is also appropriate in the material on Paul's defense, which is delivered largely before Roman magistrates (chs. 23–28). It is interesting in this regard to note that in ch. 15, where the focus shifts back to Jerusalem, 'Ιουδαῖος does not appear. Likewise, when the scene shifts back to the temple in Acts 21, Luke employs λαός (vv. 28, 30, 36, 40) except for Paul's conversation with the Roman centurion (v. 39) and his identification of himself (not his opponents) as a Jew as opposed to a Gentile (22.3). All this indicates that the shift to designating Jewish people as 'Ιουδαῖοι is at least as likely to be a matter of style as a matter of theology.

But does the absolute, unqualified use of οἱ 'Ιουδαῖοι nevertheless

---

1. J.T. Townsend, 'The Gospel of John and the Jews', in Davies, *Antisemitism*, p. 80. Cf. the discussion of Luke's adaptation of language to setting in H.J. Cadbury, *The Making of Luke–Acts* (London: SPCK, 2nd edn, 1958), pp. 221-38. B. Vawter notes the tendency of the Gospels and Acts to use absolute language like that of the Hebrew Bible ('Are the Gospels Anti-Semitic?', *JES* 5 [1968], pp. 480-82).

2. K.G. Kuhn notes that 1 Maccabees demonstrates that 'Ιουδαῖος was employed even by Palestinian Jews as a term of self-designation when communicating with non-Jews ('Ισραήλ, κτλ', *TDNT*, III, pp. 360-61). Cf. Cadbury, *Making*, p. 338 n. 28.

indicate a tendency to view the entire Jewish people as opponents of the gospel or to see Jews and Christians in mutually exclusive categories?[1] Similar usage in Josephus illustrates that οἱ 'Ιουδαῖοι could be used absolutely but with reference only to a specific group of Jews. J. Ashton has noted that Josephus uses Γαλιλαῖοι in such a way that might suggest that the people of Sepphoris were not Galileans, though in fact he simply expects the reader to understand the implied qualifications (*Life* 38-39, 123, 325; *War* 3.61).[2] In fact, Josephus's usage of οἱ 'Ιουδαῖοι follows the same pattern. He uses οἱ 'Ιουδαῖοι absolutely or with modifiers which suggest a general reference in contexts where the reference is clearly to specific groups of Jews.[3] Several examples can be noted.

Throughout the *Jewish War* Josephus repeatedly indicates that the Jews of Palestine were divided over the rebellion against Rome. He attributes the rebellion to a relatively small group and depicts the rest of the population as either passively acquiescent, vacillating, or firmly opposed to it.[4] Indeed, in *War* 4.182-83 Ananus speaks derisively of the rebels as those 'calling themselves Jews' ('Ιουδαίους καλουμένους), and in *War* 4.326 Josephus writes that the Ζηλωταί and Idumean hordes butchered τὸν λαόν. Nevertheless, Josephus regularly refers to the rebel forces simply as 'Ιουδαῖοι or οἱ 'Ιουδαῖοι.[5] Occasionally

---

1.   Brawley suggests that the use of οἱ 'Ιουδαῖοι for the opponents of the church is mostly confined to material about Paul (*Luke–Acts and the Jews*, pp. 139-40). On this basis, he seeks to refute the notion that the term is used to identify all Jews as opponents of Christianity by suggesting that the rejection of Paul is not the rejection of Christianity per se. It may still be true, however, that Luke regards this rejection as characteristic of Jews generally, a concept which may play a role in a larger depiction of the Jews as those who always reject divine messengers. Furthermore, it is not clear that Luke would distinguish between the rejection of a divine messenger (Paul) and the divine message. Brawley's observation, even if correct, nevertheless does not settle the controversy.

2.   J. Ashton, 'The Identity and Function of the 'Ιουδαῖοι in the Fourth Gospel', *NovT* 27 (1985), p. 72.

3.   Lowe notes that terms of ethnic identification, including 'Ιουδαῖος, can carry a variety of denotations in context and often identify a subgroup within the larger ethnic category ('ΙΟΥΔΑΙΟΙ', pp. 104-107).

4.   *War* 1.10; 2.334, 345-46, 402-407, 408-11, 422, 455; 3.3, 30-33, 492-501, 532, 542; 4.161-67, 193ff., 375-77, 401, 490; 5.52, 420, 6.205-207; 7.111, 113, 254, 257, 259, 409-19.

5.   *War* 2.47, 51, 172, 177, 454, 506, 514, 517, 519, 521-23, 543, 551-53; 3.9, 17-19, 22, 113-14, 211, 218, 239, 270, 276-77, 452, 473, 475, 479-80, 488;

'Ιουδαῖοι is modified so as even more to appear universal (πάντας 'Ιουδαίους, *War* 3.28; τὸ πλῆθος τῶν 'Ιουδαίων, *War* 3.471), but the referents in the context are clearly the rebel military forces. Similarly, Josephus can refer to the forces under his own command simply as οἱ 'Ιουδαῖοι (*War* 3.130, 142, 147, 149, 150, 157, 161, 165, 167, 170, 189), again on occasion using emphatic expressions that could appear to be universal (πᾶν τὸ τῶν 'Ιουδαίων πλῆθος, *War* 3.151; cf. *Life* 113). That a limited reference is intended is clear not only by the context of the expressions and the assumptions which underlie Josephus's work but also by the way οἱ 'Ιουδαῖοι alternates with more specific terms elsewhere. In *War* 5.109-10, οἱ 'Ιουδαῖοι is first used but then is replaced with στασιασταί. Likewise, in *War* 6.251 οἱ στασιασταί attack the Romans, but the Romans rout τοὺς 'Ιουδαίους.

Other conflicts in Jewish history call forth similar usage from Josephus. In local conflicts between Jews and their neighbours of other nationalities, the Jews involved can simply be called οἱ 'Ιουδαῖοι. Hence, οἱ ἐν Καισαρείᾳ 'Ιουδαῖοι (*War* 2.285) are also called οἱ 'Ιουδαῖοι (*War* 2.289); the Jews of Damascus are first οἱ παρ' ἑαυτοῖς 'Ιουδαῖοι (*War* 2.559) and then οἱ 'Ιουδαῖοι (*War* 2.561); τοῖς ἐπὶ τῆς 'Αντιοχείας 'Ιουδαίοις (*War* 7.54) become [οἱ] 'Ιουδαῖοι (*War* 7.55, 56, 60, 62); and Jews in Babylon are οἱ 'Ιουδαῖοι without qualification (*Ant.* 18.371, 373, 374, 376). Likewise, in wider conflicts Jewish military forces are simply called οἱ 'Ιουδαῖοι. οἱ 'Ιουδαῖοι appears without qualification in narratives about confrontations with Arabs (*War* 1.366, 382-84; *Ant.* 15.11, 113, 115-17, 119, 147, 150, 154), Philistines (*Ant.* 6.26, 30, 96-97), Syrians (*Ant.* 7.108; 9.245), Babylonians (*Ant.* 10.87), Samaritans (*Ant.* 20.122) and Idumeans (*Apion* 2.112-14). Jews may be divided in their loyalties, yet one faction may still be called οἱ 'Ιουδαῖοι. Thus, although Alexander Jannaeus is opposed by large numbers of Jews, his forces are called οἱ 'Ιουδαῖοι when they are in combat with those of Ptolemy Lathyrus (*Ant.* 13.342-43, 356, 359, 362). The forces which oppose Herod's

4.36, 43, 60, 75, 424; 5.76, 78, 80, 82, 85, 88, 92, 94, 119, 121, 129, 132, 155, 264, 271, 284-89, 295-96, 299, 304-309, 312-19, 331-33, 341, 464, 478-79, 481-92, 541; 6.9, 13, 20, 23-25, 30, 37-39, 42, 62, 64, 71, 74, 79, 82, 86, 91, 102-107, 140, 143, 148, 152-54, 159-61, 164, 166, 175, 180, 185, 187, 190, 223, 226, 233, 239-41, 244, 247, 253, 326, 361, 411; 7.18, 194, 195, 200, 206, 211, 212, 214, 454; *Ant.* 17.257-58, 261; *Life* 182.

assumption of the crown are οἱ Ἰουδαῖοι (*Ant.* 14.327, 397), despite the fact that he also enjoys Jewish support (*Ant.* 14.398, 410).

Conflict is not the only setting for such absolute usage with partitive reference. Josephus refers to the Jews who returned to Jerusalem from Babylon simply as οἱ Ἰουδαῖοι (*Ant.* 11.29), despite his knowledge that many Jews did not return (*Ant.* 11.67, 113, 131) and many others went elsewhere in Palestine (*Ant.* 11.74). Likewise, he calls the rebuilding of Jerusalem ἡ τῶν Ἰουδαίων ἀποκατάστασις (*Ant.* 11.63) and refers to those rebuilding the city as οἱ Ἰουδαῖοι (*Ant.* 11.11, 88, 89, 96, 97, 101, 102, 108, 173). In other contexts οἱ Ἰουδαῖοι refers only to the Jews of Jerusalem (*War* 2.319; *Ant.* 12.4) or of Palestine (*Ant.* 12.133, cf. 136). Diaspora Jews can be the referents of such expressions as well: Jews in Mesopotamia (*Ant.* 15.15-18), Ionia (*Ant.* 16.27, 30), and Asia (*Ant.* 16.167-68) are all so named. Claudius's edict concerning the Jews of Alexandria refers simply to οἱ Ἰουδαῖοι (*Ant.* 19.278-85, 286), despite the fact that another edict is issued to τὴν ἄλλην οἰκουμένην (*Ant.* 19.287). Such local references may be intended even when other terms are included which suggest a more general reference. Thus Herod summons Ἰουδαῖοι from παντὸς τοῦ ἔθνους to Jerusalem as mourners for his impending death (*Ant.* 17.174), but these obviously include only Jews who live within the borders of Herod's kingdom, since they are compelled on pain of death. Likewise in *Ant.* 11.322 the phrase τῶν δὲ Ἰουδαίων ὅμου πάντων μίᾳ φωνῇ in *Ant.* 11.332 can refer only to Jerusalemites; the generalizing modifiers suggest the unanimity of the Jews gathered on that occasion, not the crying out of the entire nation. Similarly, τοὺς Ἰουδαίους ἅπαντας in *Ant.* 12.107 are the Jews of Alexandria who were not involved in translating the LXX. Delegations which represent the interest of various Jewish groups before the imperial authorities are also called οἱ Ἰουδαῖοι (*Ant.* 17.315; 18.266).

In several contexts Josephus's usage of Ἰουδαῖος shows considerable flexibility within a brief compass. An example is *War* 1.92-96. There Demetrius the Unready is joined by οἱ Ἰουδαῖοι, though his opponent, Alexander Jannaeus, has the loyalty of τὸ εὐνοοῦν Ἰουδαϊκὸν εἰς μυρίους. Demetrius hopes to win over Alexander's (Greek) mercenaries, and Alexander hopes to win over τοὺς ἅμα Δημητρίῳ Ἰουδαίους. But neither οἱ Ἰουδαῖοι nor οἱ Ἕλληνες are persuaded. After defeating Alexander, Demetrius is deserted by his Jewish supporters. Alexander is joined by Ἰουδαίων ἑξακισχίλιοι, and Demetrius believes that πᾶν τὸ ἔθνος is going over to Alexander. Nevertheless he retains the support of τὸ λοιπὸν πλῆθος. In a parallel account, Josephus adds that after the defection of six thousand Jews to Alexander, οἱ Ἰουδαῖοι ἐπολέμουν Ἀλεξάνδρῳ (*Ant.* 13.379), though eventually οἱ Ἰουδαῖοι welcome Alexander because of his military success (*Ant.* 13.394). Similarly, in *Ant.* 20.173-82 a quarrel between the Jewish and Syrian inhabitants of Caesarea is narrated. After introducing the situation, the Caesarean Jews are called οἱ Ἰουδαῖοι, but then are referred to as οἱ κατὰ τὴν πόλιν Ἰουδαῖοι in 176 and 177 and back again to τῶν τὴν Καισαρείαν κατοικούντων Ἰουδαίων in 182 and οἱ κατὰ τὴν Καισαρείαν Ἰουδαῖοι in 184.

Certainly Josephus can and does refer to all Jews on some occasions. Phrases such as νόμος τῶν Ἰουδαίων or ἔθη τῶν Ἰουδαίων are frequent. In *Ant.* 11.184 he writes that τῶν Ἰουδαίων ἔθνος ἅπαν was threatened under Artaxerxes and in *Ant.* 11.292 that πάντες οἱ ἐν τῇ οἰκουμένῃ Ἰουδαῖοι observe Purim (cf. *Ant.* 14.110). Furthermore, there can be no doubt that Josephus regards the Jewish War as a tragedy for all Jewish people. What is relevant for the purposes here—and what justifies this extensive citation of Josephus's usage—is that he frequently employs Ἰουδαῖος either without qualification or with such qualification as could appear to indicate all Jews when referring to only a specific group of Jews.[1]

Josephus's usage suggests that Luke may simply employ a common mode of expression when he refers to the opponents of the Christians as οἱ Ἰουδαῖοι.[2] In fact, several elements of the text indicate that Luke intends neither to characterize the entire nation as opponents nor to deny the Jewish identity of a considerable segment of the church by using οἱ Ἰουδαῖοι without qualification. Three contexts in which Ἰουδαῖος occurs several times in brief compass illustrate what appears to be characteristic of Luke's usage.

---

1.   Josephus' usage, of course, is not unique in this respect. The second-century Christian writer Hegesippus is quoted by Eusebius as referring to the death of James at the hands of τῶν Ἰουδαίων καὶ γραμματέων καὶ Φαρισαίων (*Eccl. Hist.* 2.23.10; references to this work are from the edition of H.J. Lawlor [LCL; London: Heinemann, 1944–45]). Clearly here οἱ Ἰουδαῖοι are Jews other than the scribes and Pharisees.

2.   Harnack's comment, 'To apply again and again the general name of a nation or of a religious society to a distinct group of the same is an unusual procedure', therefore appears unwarranted (*Acts*, p. 54).

The first is Acts 14.1-5.[1] Here Ἰουδαῖος first occurs in v. 1, where Luke notes that through Paul and Barnabas's preaching in the synagogue τῶν Ἰουδαίων, Ἰουδαίων τε καὶ Ἑλλήνων πολὺ πλῆθος come to faith. Those who oppose the missionaries are first designated as οἱ...Ἰουδαῖοι with the attributive qualification ἀπειθήσαντες (v. 2). These opponents, already explicitly differentiated from the believing Jews, are then designated simply as τοῖς Ἰουδαίοις in v. 4. They in turn arouse opposition to the Christians among both Jews and Gentiles (v. 5). The context previous to v. 4 suggests that Luke did not intend to identify the Jews in their entirety as the sole opponents of the church. He does not ignore his note in v. 1 that a large contingent of Jews believed;[2] nor does he imply that those Jews who did believe are no longer Jews. Instead, he appears to assume that the reader understands the restricted sense of his absolute expression in v. 4.[3]

The second context is Acts 23.12-21. Here the absolute οἱ Ἰουδαῖοι occurs first: 'the Jews' form a conspiracy against Paul (v. 12). But this absolute usage is followed by the note that the plot was formed by πλείους τεσσεράκοντα, who in turn enlisted the help of the chief priests and elders (vv. 13-14). Later in the context the same sequence occurs again: Paul's nephew reports to Claudius Lysias that οἱ Ἰουδαῖοι have requested Paul's delivery to the Sanhedrin (v. 20), but he goes on to indicate that more than forty of them had sworn to kill Paul (v. 21). In this instance οἱ Ἰουδαῖοι apparently includes the priests and elders who are party to the conspiracy, since the ἄνδρες πλείους τεσσεράκοντα are here reckoned as ἐξ αὐτῶν (v. 21). But in both cases Luke's procedure is to identify the limited circle of Paul's Jewish opponents simply as οἱ Ἰουδαῖοι, not to characterize all Jews as Paul's opponents. Were the latter the case, the specification of the forty-plus conspirators would only serve to undermine Luke's intention.[4]

1.   D.L. Tiede notes the importance of this text for understanding Luke's use of Ἰουδαῖος ('"Glory to Thy People Israel": Luke–Acts and the Jews', in J.B. Tyson [ed.], *Luke–Acts and the Jewish People: Eight Critical Perspectives* [Minneapolis: Augsburg, 1988], pp. 141-42 n. 18).

2.   This is implied by Beck, *Mature Christianity*, pp. 226-27.

3.   See the discussion of this point in Dupont, 'La conclusion des Actes', pp. 378-79; M. Lowe, 'Real and Imagined Anti-Jewish Elements in the Synoptic Gospels and Acts', *JES* 24 (1987), pp. 270-71. Conzelmann sees this usage as polemical but also as allowing for individual Jewish conversion (*Theology*, p. 145 n. 2).

4.   Even Sanders is forced to admit that Luke does not intend to suggest in 23.12 that all the Jews conspired to kill Paul (*Jews in Luke–Acts*, pp. 290-91). He

The third context is Acts 25.1-24. Here again the opponents of Paul are first identified specifically as οἱ ἀρχιερεῖς καὶ οἱ πρῶτοι τῶν Ἰουδαίων (v. 2). Then the identification shifts in v. 7 to οἱ ἀπὸ Ἱεροσολύμων καταβεβηκότες Ἰουδαῖοι, that is, those who come to Caesarea in response to Festus's invitation in v. 5 as representatives of the leaders mentioned in v. 2. It is therefore this group to which Luke refers when he indicates that Festus wished to do a favor for οἱ Ἰουδαῖοι in v. 9: these are the ones who wanted Paul to return to Jerusalem in the first place. Likewise, ἅπαν τὸ πλῆθος τῶν Ἰουδαίων (v. 24), offered on the lips of Festus with some ironic hyperbole, can refer in context to none other than those opponents named in v. 2.[1] Again Luke's method appears to be to use οἱ Ἰουδαῖοι without qualification where it is clear that he refers to a particular group of unbelieving Jewish opponents.

To these examples can be added another of a different kind which reinforces this understanding. In Acts 24.5 Tertullus refers to πᾶσιν τοῖς Ἰουδαίοις. An unbelieving Jew, Tertullus can hardly be understood to use the expression as one of disparagement. Rather, it appears as the appropriate term in a speech before a Roman magistrate.

J.B. Tyson has observed that Luke's use of Ἰουδαῖος has a certain flexibility. His explanation of the variation in usage is that while Luke uses the singular Ἰουδαῖος neutrally, the plural, though not always negative, has its 'characteristic and most striking uses' in identifying the opponents of Christianity.[2] Tyson recognizes that Luke indicates a positive response among some Ἰουδαῖοι, but he insists that this positive response does not affect Luke's view that the Jews as a whole reject the gospel in Acts. Hence, although some Ἰουδαῖοι are converted, οἱ Ἰουδαῖοι are opposed to the gospel.[3] But because Luke's shifts in usage are so similar to Josephus's, and because both Ἰουδαῖος and

nevertheless insists that Luke is 'serious' about claiming that 'the Jews' sought to kill Paul, and that the distinction between 'some Jews' and 'all Jews' means little to him (p. 79). But these statements ignore the fact that Luke does distinguish among Jews at key points in the narrative.

1.   Sanders suggests that Festus's words are an official opinion which indicates that all Jews want Paul dead (*Jews in Luke–Acts*, p. 294). He fails to consider that Festus speaks in the narrative as a Roman who, portrayed with Lukan verisimilitude, is inclined to ignore the distinctions among Jewish groups.

2.   J.B. Tyson, 'The Problem of Jewish Rejection in Acts', in *Luke–Acts and the Jewish People*, pp. 131-32.

3.   Tyson, 'Jewish Rejection', pp. 132-33.

'Ιουδαῖοι are used in Acts for both believers and opponents, Tyson's explanation appears to be inadequate. Luke's flexibility of usage was characteristic of other writers of his age; his readers would not have found it particularly noteworthy.

These observations suggest that similar conclusions can be drawn about other occurrences of οἱ 'Ιουδαῖοι in Acts. In Pisidian Antioch οἱ 'Ιουδαῖοι who oppose Paul (13.45, 50) do not therefore include those who are persuaded by his message (v. 43).[1] Likewise, οἱ 'Ιουδαῖοι who are jealous of Paul in Thessalonica (17.5) respond thus because some of their number (ἐξ αὐτῶν, i.e. τῶν 'Ιουδαίων, vv. 1, 4) have joined certain Gentile synagogue-goers in following Paul. Later these opponents are designated as οἱ ἀπὸ τῆς Θεσσαλονίκης 'Ιουδαῖοι (17.13),[2] differentiated explicitly from the Berean Jews but no less differentiated implicitly from the Jewish believers of Thessalonica whose conversion initiated the conflict. Again in Corinth, Jews are converted (18.4), but those Jews who oppose Paul are designated οἱ 'Ιουδαῖοι without qualification (18.5, 12, 14). The point is again not to characterize all the Jews of Corinth as opponents, since even after the introduction of Jewish opposition Luke notes the conversion of a notable Jew (v. 8). Hence, the indication that οἱ 'Ιουδαῖοι arise against Paul 'with one accord (ὁμοθύμαδον, v. 12) suggests not so much the work of the entire Jewish community as the united, vigorous action of Paul's Jewish opponents.

The designation of those in Damascus who wish to kill Paul (ἀνελεῖν) as οἱ 'Ιουδαῖοι (9.23) is paralleled in the next venue, Jerusalem, by a similar plot by τοὺς Ἑλληνιστάς (9.29, also ἀνελεῖν). The Hellenists had, of course, already been identified as a group from which came both believers and opponents (6.1, 9); likewise, Luke exhibits no reserve in identifying Christians in Damascus as Jews (22.12). In neither case, then, is the reader justified in inferring a characterization of either all Jews or all Hellenists as opponents. Indeed, this example

---

1. So rightly observes B.J. Koet (*Five Studies on Interpretation of Scripture in Luke–Acts* [Studiorum Novi Testamenti Auxilia, 14; Leuven: Leuven University Press, 1989], pp. 115-16).

2. Elsewhere Luke also notes that Jewish opponents travel from one city to another and incite conflict against Paul (14.19; 21.27). These are likewise characterized as 'Ιουδαῖοι or οἱ 'Ιουδαῖοι, but that they do not represent the entire Jewish communities of their cities is assumed. Indeed, elsewhere the Asian Jewish opponents are characterized as τινὲς... ἀπὸ 'Ασίας 'Ιουδαῖοι (24.19).

probably illustrates best the tendency of Luke to 'lump together' the various Jewish groups in Hellenistic settings, as suggested by Townsend. In Jerusalem, the Hellenists are distinguished from other groups in the city. In the diaspora, Paul's opponents are simply 'the Jews'. But it must be observed that in neither instance does Luke pursue a course which characterizes the entire group, whether οἱ Ἑλληνισταί or οἱ Ἰουδαῖοι, as enemies of the church.

The use of οἱ Ἰουδαῖοι in Acts 12 can also be explained according to this pattern.[1] The phrase is appropriate in the context inasmuch as the narrative at this point treats Herod as a Roman ruler: Herod pleases οἱ Ἰουδαῖοι (12.3), a group to which he does not himself belong (and distinctions among whose various sects might not interest him). But does this term nevertheless suggest that the Jews as a whole are pleased by James's death? Later when the narrative returns to Jerusalem, Luke refers to μυριάδες...ἐν τοῖς Ἰουδαίοις τῶν πεπιστευκότων (21.20), a detail which suggests that he does not regard all the Jews of Jerusalem as hostile to the Christian leaders. Instead, it appears that οἱ Ἰουδαῖοι in 12.3 again refers to those already shown to be antagonistic to the church in Jerusalem (the chief priests, the Sanhedrin and certain Hellenists) without calling attention to the obvious distinction between them and the Jewish believers. The fact that the opponents in Jerusalem largely come from circles of power suggests that Luke could regard the identity of those whom Herod wishes to please to be confined to such circles in which a ruler would have particular interest (cf. Acts 25.27). On the other hand, Peter is to be brought before τῷ λαῷ (v. 4) and is delivered from πάσης τῆς προσδοκίας τοῦ λαοῦ τῶν Ἰουδαίων (12.11). But Luke has already suggested more than once the capriciousness of the Jerusalem λαός, most recently as the object of agitation of the Hellenistic opponents (6.12) but most notably in the trial of Jesus.[2] The point appears to be that the uncommitted elements of the Jerusalem populace have been incited to malevolence by the opponents of the church, not that the entire λαός of Israel expects Peter's death.[3] The

---

1. Gaston ('Passion Narrative', p. 133) and Beck (*Mature Christianity*, pp. 224-25) both insist on the presence of a sharp anti-Jewish invective in the use of οἱ Ἰουδαῖοι in this chapter.

2. Dupont correctly notes that Paul's later emphasis on his call to preach to ὁ λαός (26.17, 23) indicates that Luke does not view the entire λαός as opposed to the gospel in this instance ('La conclusion des Actes', p. 379).

3. F.F. Bruce suggests that the goodwill of the Jerusalem public was lost with

situation for the church in Jerusalem is more polarized than in the earlier chapters, but unbelief by no means characterizes the entire city or the entire Jewish people.

J.T. Sanders has drawn attention to Paul's two encounters with magicians identified as Ἰουδαῖοι, Elymas (13.6ff.) and the sons of Sceva (19.13ff.). He characterizes these scenes as incidents of 'spiritual warfare between the evil magic of Judaism and the power of the gospel'.[1] Sanders finds evidence for their typical significance in the following details: (1) the use of the number seven with the sons of Sceva; (2) the connection to a high priest; (3) the fact that the only magicians in Acts are Jews; (4) the position of the episodes at the beginning and end of Paul's career.[2] But considerable objections can be raised against this interpretation. One is the fact that these are not the only 'magicians' in Acts. Inasmuch as Luke does not characterize the sons of Sceva as μάγοι (cf. 13.6), Sanders obviously allows that Luke can present an individual in the narrative as a 'magician' without calling him such. But then there seems little reason not to introduce into the classification the Gentile masters of the girl with the divining spirit (16.16ff.). There can be even less objection to viewing Simon the Samaritan as a magician, inasmuch as Luke characterizes his activity as μαγεύων (8.9) and his deeds as μαγείαι (8.11). Elymas and the sons of Sceva thus are clearly not the only magicians in Acts. And neither can it be said with any certainty that they appear at the beginning and end of Paul's career. It is difficult to know what Luke regards as the beginning and end of Paul's 'career', though certainly he regards both Paul's conversion and the events after his arrest in Jerusalem to be significant. Nevertheless, it may be conceded that Cyprus and Ephesus could mark the beginning and end of a distinct phase in Paul's life as represented by Luke. What makes even that observation difficult to square with Sanders's

Peter's conversion of Cornelius and his colleagues' 'acquiescence in it', with the result that James was executed and Peter imprisoned for execution ('The Church of Jerusalem in the Acts of the Apostles', *BJRL* 67 [1984–85], pp. 651-52). Nevertheless, although the attack went on with the approval of the Jewish leaders, it ended with Agrippa's death. This historical reconstruction also explains the ascent of James the Just to a position of prominence, indirectly indicated in 12.17: he became the leader of the Jerusalem church because he was not associated with the approach to the Gentiles. To Bruce's reconstruction the observation must be added that Luke regards conversions among the Jews of Jerusalem as continuing (cf. Acts 21.20).

1.   Sanders, *Jews in Luke–Acts*, p. 280.
2.   Sanders, *Jews in Luke–Acts*, pp. 280-81.

interpretation is that the Ephesus material ends not with the sons of Sceva but with the riot provoked by the Gentile silversmith Demetrius (19.23ff.). No deliberate structuring of the narrative to emphasize Jewish opposition in these episodes is therefore in evidence.

Several observations can be offered which suggest an alternative to Sanders's proposal. One is that Jewish magicians were apparently a common feature in the ancient world. M. Simon has noted the extensive influence in the Roman Empire of Jewish magicians and of magical formulae based on Jewish religious symbols.[1] Their presence in a narrative like Acts cannot therefore be regarded as significant in itself. The characterization of Elymas and the sons of Sceva as Jews also appears to serve interests of the narrative other than the negative portrayal of Jews. Elymas's Jewish identity serves to indicate the interest of his master, Sergius Paulus, in Jewish religious ideas, thus supplying a link to the gospel similar to the one repeatedly suggested with the appearance of Gentile God-fearers in the synagogues. Likewise, the fact that the sons of Sceva are Jewish explains their inclination to adopt the name of a Jewish figure, Jesus, in their formulae. These concerns are more readily apparent in the text than an interest in deriding of the Jews as magicians. Furthermore, they are consistent with Luke's pattern elsewhere of grounding the impact of the Pauline mission in the Jewish community.

In conclusion, then, Luke's usage of Ἰουδαῖος does not indicate that he seeks to characterize the Jews as a whole as opponents of Christianity. Instead, his employment of the term gives consistent evidence of his recognition that the gospel had produced a sharp division within the Jewish community. He was concerned neither to deny the presence of a Jewish element in the church nor to identify all Jews as enemies of the faith.

Narrative Structure

Recent interpretations of Luke–Acts have suggested that more than the use of any specific term, the structure and direction of Luke's narrative indicate a general rejection of the gospel by the Jewish nation and the consequent condemnation of the nation as a whole. Three monographs

---

1.   M. Simon, *Verus Israel: A Study of the Relations between Christians and Jews in the Roman Empire (135–425)* (ET; Oxford: Oxford University Press, 1986), pp. 340-56. Cf. H.J. Cadbury, *The Book of Acts in History* (New York: Harper & Brothers; London: A. & C. Black, 1955), p. 95.

make it a matter of major concern. Their views can be briefly summarized here.

J.B. Tyson distinguishes between the negative response of the Jewish leaders and the positive response of the Jewish people. The leaders reject Jesus from the first, while the people accept him. But Luke then indicates that the people's initial acceptance is followed by final rejection.[1] This pattern applies to the Gospel, where the public's acceptance becomes final rejection at the crucifixion, and recapitulates in Acts, where the acceptance of the early chapters is followed by the rejection of Paul in the latter chapters. In both cases the transition from acceptance is foreshadowed at key points in the narrative before it finally occurs.[2] Tyson asserts that the apparent inconsistency of the Jerusalem crowd's acceptance of the apostles in the early chapters of Acts after their rejection of Jesus indicates Luke's dogged adherence to the literary pattern of acceptance followed by rejection. Because he develops the pattern in two great cycles, Luke accepted the logical inconsistency in the transition from the Gospel to Acts.[3] This pattern likewise explains the apparent inconsistency in Paul's continuing to preach in the synagogue even after having turned to the Gentiles (Acts 13.46; 18.6): these episodes are repeated minor cycles of acceptance and rejection which foreshadow the denouement (Acts 28.28).[4]

The interpretation of J.T. Sanders is similar to Tyson's but represents a refinement of his position. Like Tyson, Sanders sees in Luke–Acts a pattern whereby the acceptance of Jesus and the gospel in earlier chapters gives way to a final rejection by the entire nation.[5] To this scheme, however, he adds another factor: the distinction between speech and narrative. Taking his cue from M. Bachmann's study of the two spellings of Jerusalem,[6] Sanders suggests that it is initially in speech, not in narrative, that the view of the author of Luke–Acts is readily apparent.[7] Although the Jewish people respond positively in the narrative,

---

1.   Tyson, *Death*, pp. 29-30.
2.   Tyson, *Death*, pp. 40-42.
3.   Tyson, *Death*, p. 42.
4.   Tyson, *Death*, pp. 42-43. M.J. Cook adopts Tyson's position ('The Mission to the Jews in Acts: Unraveling Luke's "Myth of the Myriads"', in Tyson [ed.], *Luke–Acts and the Jewish People*, pp. 117-19).
5.   Sanders, *Jews in Luke–Acts*, p. 27.
6.   Bachmann, *Tempel*, pp. 13-66.
7.   Sanders, *Jews in Luke–Acts*, pp. 36, 50.

they are everywhere condemned in the speech.[1] But then the two elements are brought together as the Jews in the narrative 'become what they from the first were' and as a body reject the gospel at the end of Acts.[2] Two elements thus stand together in Sanders's interpretation: the universal condemnation of the Jews in speech and the transition from acceptance to rejection in the narrative.

R.C. Tannehill's perspective differs from those of Tyson and Sanders but nevertheless offers similar evidence to reach a similar conclusion. Tannehill's focus is on the fulfillment of the promise of Israel's political redemption made at the beginning of Luke's Gospel (e.g. 1.32-33, 68-71, 74; cf. 24.21) and repeated in Acts (1.8; 2.30-36; 3.20-21; 13.22-23, 32-34).[3] This promise establishes a set of expectations in the narrative which go unfilled according to a tragic pattern. Israel is in fact not redeemed by the end of the narrative, and the failure of the promise owes to the nation's rejection of the proffered redemption at the moment of fulfillment.[4]

These works have in common a view of Luke–Acts which sees an emphasis on a final, decisive rejection of Jesus and the gospel by Israel as a whole. Together they raise two key questions for the purposes of this study: (1) Does Luke indicate that the entire Jewish nation rejects the gospel at the end of the narrative? (2) Does he indicate that the rejection of the gospel by the Jews causes the promises made to the nation to go tragically unfulfilled? Because these two questions in part address the same data in the text, they can be treated together.

Several portions of Luke–Acts are cited by Tyson, Sanders and Tannehill to demonstrate their positions, but certain texts are of particular significance for them. These especially include the Nazareth pericope (Lk. 4.16-30), the Stephen episode (Acts 6.8–7.60), the three episodes of Paul's 'turning to the Gentiles' (Acts 13.46; 18.6; 28.28)[5] and Paul's

---

1. Sanders, *Jews in Luke–Acts*, pp. 53-54, 63-64.

2. Sanders, *Jews in Luke–Acts*, p. 81; cf. pp. 78-79. Cf. the earlier view of O'Neill that the direction of the narrative in Acts signifies the movement of the gospel from the Jews, represented by Jerusalem, to the Gentiles, represented by Rome (*Theology*, pp. 63, 67-68, 72-73, 178-79).

3. Tannehill, *Narrative Unity*, I, pp. 25-26, 259, 280-81.

4. Tannehill, *Narrative Unity*, I, pp. 8-9, 25-26.

5. Others have noted the connections between the Nazareth pericope and the turning episodes in the presentation of Judaism in Luke–Acts, for example Cadbury, *Making*, pp. 255-57; Maddox, *Purpose*, pp. 44-45.

assertion about his own faithfulness as a Jew in his trial defense (22.1, 3; 23.1, 6; 26.4, 6, 7; 28.19). Careful analysis of these texts will serve to evaluate the validity of these interpretations.

The Nazareth Pericope (Luke 4.16-30)

Literature on Luke's version of the Nazareth pericope is enormous, and the questions which it raises are numerous. Attention here can be restricted to three issues: (1) Does the pericope fit a pattern of initial acceptance followed by final rejection? (2) Does it represent, prefigure, or symbolize the rejection of Jesus and the gospel by the entire Jewish nation, especially in the crucifixion? (3) Does it imply a transfer of salvation from the Jews to the Gentiles?

Initial Acceptance. Tyson assumes a widely held position when he asserts that the initial reaction of the Nazarenes to Jesus is positive.[1] Most studies of the passage have concluded that the expression καὶ πάντες ἐμαρτύρουν αὐτῷ καὶ ἐθαύμαζον indicates a positive reaction, both because Luke ordinarily uses μαρτυρέω with a positive connotation and because θαύμαζω also suggests a positive reaction.[2] But several factors suggest that Luke understands the Nazarenes' initial reaction to Jesus to be considerably less than full acceptance.

1. It has been repeatedly observed that the rhetorical question 'Is this not Joseph's son?' in light of Lk. 3.23 presents a view of Jesus which Luke regards as superficial at best and inimical to true faith at worst.[3]

---

1.   Tyson, *Death*, pp. 32-33.
2.   Cf. J. Wellhausen, *Das Evangelium Lucae* (Berlin: Georg Reimer, 1904), p. 10; E. Preuschen, 'Das Wort vom verachteten Propheten', *ZNW* 17 (1916), p. 37; Loisy, *L'Evangile selon Luc*, pp. 158-59; A.R.C. Leaney, *The Gospel according to St Luke* (BNTC; London: A. & C. Black, 1958), p. 119; J.C. O'Neill, 'The Six Amen Sayings in Luke', *JTS* NS 10 (1959), p. 3; J.M. Creed, *The Gospel according to St Luke* (London: Macmillan, 1965), pp. 66-67; Lohfink, *Sammlung*, pp. 44, 46; W. Radl, *Paulus und Jesus in lukanischen Doppelwerk: Untersuchungen zu Parallelmotiven im Lukasevangelium und in der Apostelgeschichte* (Europäische Hochschulschriften, 13.49; Frankfurt: Peter Lang, 1975), pp. 94-95; W. Schmeichel, 'Christian Prophecy in Lucan Thought: Luke 4, 16-30 as a Point of Departure', *SBL Seminar Papers* 10 (1976), p. 299; J.A. Fitzmyer, *The Gospel according to Luke* (AB, 28; 2 vols.; Garden City, NY: Doubleday, 1981, 1985), I, p. 534; Sanders, *Jews in Luke–Acts*, pp. 64, 166-67.
3.   A. Plummer, *A Critical and Exegetical Commentary on the Gospel according to S. Luke* (ICC; Edinburgh: T. & T. Clark, 1896), p. 124; E.E. Ellis, *The Gospel*

The initial reaction cannot, therefore, be judged to be entirely positive from Luke's perspective.

2. F. O'Fearghail has recently made an impressive case for viewing ἐμαρτύρουν in this context as part of a negative reaction to Jesus, although the verb itself retains a positive connotation. He notes first that the sequence of verbs in the imperfect (ἐμαρτύρουν, ἐθαύμαζον, ἔλεγον) suggests a continuous response without a shift in tenor from positive to negative.[1] The verb μαρτυρέω, however, always carries in Luke–Acts a connotation of positive testimony from personal experience.[2] How can these two elements be reconciled? O'Fearghail proposes that Luke indicates with ἐμαρτύρουν that the Nazarenes offer positive testimony about their previous experience of Jesus, but that testimony does not lead them to expect such a declaration as the one in v. 21.[3] Therefore, they express skepticism about Jesus' claims, if not outright rejection of them.[4]

3. The words of Jesus in v. 23 appear to be less a prophetic forecast of what the Nazarenes will say in the future than an articulation of the unspoken thoughts of the Nazarenes in the present.[5] Those thoughts are

---

of Luke (NCB; London: Nelson, 1966), p. 97; H. Flender, *St Luke: Theologian of Redemptive History* (London: SPCK, 1967), p. 155; W. Eltester, 'Israel im lukanischen Werk und die Nazarethperikope', in *Jesus in Nazareth* (BZNW, 40; Berlin and New York: de Gruyter, 1972), pp. 138-39; B. Reicke, 'Jesus in Nazareth—Luke 4, 14-30', in H. Balz and S. Schulz (eds.), *Das Wort und die Wörter: Festschrift G. Friedrich* (Stuttgart: Kohlhammer, 1973), pp. 48-49; H.J.B. Combrink, 'The Structure and Significance of Lk 4, 16-30', *Neot* 7 (1973), p. 37; U. Busse, *Das Nazareth-Manifest: Eine Einführung in das lukanische Jesusbild nach Luke 4, 16-30* (SBS, 91; Stuttgart: Katholisches Bibelwerk, 1978), pp. 31, 37-38; Brawley, *Luke–Acts and the Jews*, pp. 10, 13-14.

1. F. O'Fearghail, 'Rejection in Nazareth: Lk 4.22', *ZNW* 75 (1984), pp. 64-65.

2. O'Fearghail, 'Rejection', pp. 65-70.

3. O'Fearghail suggests that the appearance of οὗ ἦν τεθραμμένος in v. 16 is superfluous except to emphasize the previous experience of the Nazarenes with Jesus which forms the basis for their 'testimony' ('Rejection', p. 65).

4. O'Fearghail, 'Rejection', pp. 70-72.

5. J.-N. Aletti stresses that Jesus' articulation of the Nazarenes' unspoken thought is part of Luke's use of Jesus in the role of omniscient narrator in this pericope, by which means he reinforces the motif of Jesus as prophet ('Jésus à Nazareth [Lc 4, 16-30]: Prophétie, écriture et typology', in F. Refoulé (ed.), *A cause de l'évangile: Etudes sur les Synoptiques et les Actes offertes au P. Jaques Dupont, O.S.B. à l'occasion de son 70ᵉ anniversaire* [LD, 123; Paris: Cerf, 1985], pp. 434-36). In this case the future ἐρεῖτε is not an introduction to a prediction of what the

skeptical, demanding an authenticating sign, an attitude which Jesus condemns elsewhere in Luke as rejection of him (11.29-30).

All these factors indicate that the initial reaction of the Nazarenes is not presented positively by Luke. Tyson's pattern apparently does not correspond to the details of this so-called 'programmatic' episode.

Rejection by Israel as a Whole. W. Eltester's striking metaphor, that the Nazareth pericope 'functions within the entire Lukan work like a minus-sign before a mathematical bracket',[1] is but one expression of a commonly held view. Much of the critical literature asserts that the episode prefigures or symbolizes the rejection of Jesus and the gospel by the entire Jewish nation.[2] Final judgment on the exact significance of the pericope in this regard must await the determination of whether Luke actualizes such a rejection later in the narrative. But certain issues can be addressed concerning the episode itself and its immediate context.

One such issue is the connection of the text to the surrounding material. Although the Nazareth pericope is the first incident of Jesus' Galilean ministry narrated by Luke, it is of course not the first mention of that ministry. The editorial summary of 4.14-15 assumes that position. Its tenor is entirely positive, indicating the glorification of Jesus ὑπὸ πάντων. And that tenor appears to be distinctively and deliberately Lukan: it is without parallel in the other Synoptics. Likewise, the Capernaum material which follows the Nazareth pericope suggests unmitigated popular acceptance of Jesus (4.31-43). J. Dupont is probably correct when he asserts that the Nazareth and Capernaum episodes are connected as two panels of a diptych through the reference to Capernaum in v. 23 and the common use of Isaiah 61 in vv. 18-19 and 43.[3] Again, the insertion of the allusion in v. 43 is apparently Lukan. But these are not the only verbal links which tie together the Nazareth

Nazarenes will say in the future but a substitute for the potential optative introducing what they could say in the present; cf. Loisy, *L'Evangile selon Luc*, p. 160; N.B. Stonehouse, *The Witness of Luke to Christ* (London: Tyndale Press, 1951), p. 74; Reicke, 'Jesus in Nazareth', pp. 47-48; Marshall, *Gospel of Luke*, p. 187; BDF § 385.

1. Eltester, 'Israel', p. 146.

2. For example, George, 'Israël', p. 493; Löning, 'Heilsgeschichte', pp. 218-19; Büchele, *Tod*, pp. 123-24; Marshall, *Gospel of Luke*, p. 178.

3. Dupont, 'La conclusion des Actes', p. 397; followed by O'Fearghail, 'Israel', p. 26.

episode, the Capernaum scenes and the editorial summary. 'Galilee' appears in 4.14 (//Mt. 4.12//Mk 1.14) and at the beginning of the Capernaum section (v. 31, Luke only). Nazareth is identified earlier as a city of Galilee in 1.26; 2.4, 39. Just as in Nazareth Jesus refers to Capernaum (v. 23), in Capernaum he is identified as a Nazarene (v. 34).[1] These details suggest that Luke has deliberately embedded the Nazareth pericope within a context of Jesus' popular acceptance.

How, then, is the contrast between this acceptance and rejection to be understood? It is difficult to see how, as Eltester suggests, the rejection at Nazareth can negate the popular acceptance suggested by the other material, particularly in light of Luke's deliberate emphasis on that acceptance in 4.15. Instead, it appears that the two elements are intended by the author to stand side by side. D. Tiede and R. Brawley are therefore correct when they indicate that the rejection of Nazareth is matched by the acceptance found in the surrounding context.[2] Luke appears to suggest here an Israel divided in its response to Jesus, a theme consistent with the pivotal announcement of Simeon in the infancy narrative (2.34).[3] If it stands for anything, Nazareth's rejection stands not for the response of the entire nation but for the response of one part of the nation.

In this respect the connection between the Nazarene rejection and the Samaritan rejection (9.52-55) is instructive. These two incidents, of course, stand in parallel positions at the beginning of Luke's major divisions of Jesus' public ministry. Tiede notes that both incidents are followed by parallel examples of the faith from members of both rejecting groups (the Jewish leper in 5.12-16, the Samaritan leper in 17.11-19).[4]

---

1.   The term is paralleled in Mk 1.24. If the term appeared in his source, Luke's retention of it in this context may be intentional, however. Elsewhere he either omits the Markan Ναζαρηνός (Mk 14.67//Lk. 22.56) or alters it to Ναζωραῖος (Mk 10.47//Lk. 18.37), the term he apparently prefers (Acts 2.22; 3.6; 4.10; 6.14; 22.8; 24.5; 26.9), although the former term is also found in Lk. 24.19, where it may appear in Luke's source (cf. Mk 16.6). More decisive is the proximity of the allusion to Jesus' Nazarene origins to the rejection at Nazareth in Luke's narrative.

2.   Tiede, *Prophecy and History*, p. 55; Brawley, *Luke–Acts and the Jews*, pp. 23, 26-27.

3.   C.A. Evans notes the significance of this text as setting forth the theme of Israel's division ('Prophecy and Polemic: Jews in Luke's Scriptural Apologetic', in *idem* and J.A. Sanders [eds.], *Luke and Scripture: The Function of Sacred Tradition in Luke–Acts* [Minneapolis: Fortress Press, 1993], p. 174).

4.   Tiede, *Prophecy and History*, p. 62.

This factor suggests that neither Nazareth nor the Samaritan village is intended by Luke to characterize the response of their entire people. To this assertion Sanders has offered a rejoinder. He notes two key differences between the two episodes: (1) Lk. 9.53 provides a rationale for the Samaritans' rejection; (2) Jesus offers no word of judgment against the Samaritans as he does against the Nazarenes (4.24-27). These differences, says Sanders, are more significant than the similarities.[1] But several objections can be offered against Sanders's view. One is that the Nazareth pericope does indeed provide a 'rationale' for the Nazarenes' rejection: as O'Fearghail has shown, they reject Jesus' claims because of their previous experience of him. Secondly, it is doubtful that Luke would regard the 'rationale' of either group as providing a legitimate excuse for their rejection of Jesus. The Samaritans are hardly less culpable on that count. As to the omission of 'judgment' against the Samaritans, it is difficult to draw any conclusions based on that factor alone. Luke may intend just as much to emphasize the fact that on both occasions Jesus took no retaliatory action against his opponents. Both incidents end with the note that Jesus (and his disciples in the latter case) traveled on (πορεύομαι, 4.30; 9.56). In both cases the interest appears to be less in what happens to those who reject than in the fact that their rejection does not deter the ministry of Jesus. At the very least, then, Luke does not emphasize the differences between the two incidents, and much suggests that he was aware of the similarities. Those similarities weigh against the judgment that Luke regarded the Nazarenes' rejection of Jesus as typical or symbolic of his rejection by the Jewish nation as a whole and that he regarded such rejection as a peculiarly Jewish tendency.

Nevertheless, the connection between the Nazareth pericope and the Lukan passion narrative appears to be valid. Although the verbal parallel between Lk. 4.23 and 23.35 may be merely coincidental,[2] a foreshadowing of Jesus' death in the murderous actions of the Nazarenes appears likely. What does *not* appear likely, however, is the implication that the Nazarenes' action implies the involvement of the entire nation in the

---

1. Sanders, *Jews in Luke–Acts*, pp. 143-44, 181.

2. Sanders cites the parallel as an indication that 'the Jews', not merely the Nazarenes, fulfill Jesus' 'prophecy' in 4.23 (*Jews in Luke–Acts*, p. 56). Against this view is the judgment that Jesus' 'prophecy' has to do not with the future but with the articulation of the Nazarenes' unspoken thoughts; see the discussion above.

crucifixion. Rather, their action is treated by Luke as typical only of one part of the nation's response to Jesus.[1]

Transfer of Salvation to the Gentiles. The statement of Jesus in 4.25-27 is widely taken as Luke's foreshadowing of the transfer of salvation from Israel to the Gentiles.[2] Again, final judgment on this issue awaits a decision as to whether such a transfer actually occurs in the ensuing narrative.[3] But certain observations can still be made concerning the text at hand.

In his provocative analysis of the Nazareth pericope, R. Brawley notes the parallel between v. 24 and vv. 25-27. The point is to show an analogy between Jesus' relationship to his πατρίς and Elijah and Elisha's relationship to Israel. However, in this analogy Jesus' πατρίς is not equated with Israel; the comparison is between the larger complexes, not the details of the complexes.[4] Were the comparison drawn between the

---

1. Esler's suggestion (*Community and Gospel*, pp. 56-57) that Luke inserts the Nazareth episode because his own community faced rejection by the Jews thus can be only a partial explanation. The immediate literary interest in foreshadowing Jesus' death supplies at least part of the motivation.

2. For example Ruether, *Faith and Fratricide*, p. 86; S. Sandmel, *Anti-Semitism in the New Testament?* (Philadelphia: Fortress Press, 1978), p. 77; Maddox, *Purpose*, p. 5; Dupont, 'La conclusion des Actes', pp. 399-402. Sanders goes so far as to suggest that the sayings indicate not that salvation is transferred from the Jews to the Gentiles but that it was never intended for the Jews in the first place (*Jews in Luke–Acts*, p. 167). He is followed in this by Cook ('Mission to the Jews', p. 121).

3. The different opinions offered by L. Gaston illustrate the importance which judgments about the developing narrative in Acts have had in the exegesis of these verses. In his study of proto-Luke, Gaston urges that 4.25-27 serve not as an announcement of the Gentile mission but as a warning to Israel to repent before it is too late (*No Stone*, p. 313). But he insists that the difference in perspective of the final (Gentile) redactor, writing after the destruction of Jerusalem, transforms such statements from warnings to *ex eventu* predictions which are anti-Judaic ('Passion Narrative', pp. 139-40, 143, 150-51). Cf. Büchele who explicitly relies on the narrative of Acts to interpret the Nazareth pericope (*Tod*, pp. 109-10). Brawley likewise notes the importance of how Luke–Acts as a whole is read for the understanding of this material (*Luke–Acts and the Jews*, p. 7).

4. Brawley, *Luke–Acts and the Jews*, pp. 9-10. Esler suggests that the comparisons with the widow and Namaan were suggested by their possibilities for representing the extremes of the social scale, not by their Gentile ethnicity (*Community and Gospel*, pp. 35, 180-83). Luke's interest in such themes may

details as well, the implication would be that Jesus was about to launch a ministry to Gentiles, which of course he does not. The alternative is to see Capernaum as a symbol of the Gentile mission. But, in fact, Luke closes the Capernaum material with the note that Jesus continued to preach in the synagogues τῆς Ἰουδαίας (4.44; diff. Mk 1.39).[1] To Brawley's observations it may be added that Luke retains the emphasis of his sources on the synagogue and the sabbath (vv. 31, 33, 38), which suggests that he did not wish to obscure the Jewishness of Capernaum in order for it to function as a symbol of the Gentiles. Likewise, Luke retains the condemnation of Capernaum with the other Galilean cities (Lk. 10.15), a detail which suggests no interest in using the city as a symbol for the Gentile reception of salvation.[2]

It appears, then, that little in the Nazareth pericope suggests the acceptance–rejection pattern of Tyson and Sanders. The passage does not begin with Jesus' acceptance by the Nazarenes, and their rejection is not viewed as the rejection of Jesus by Israel as a whole which yields a transfer of salvation to the Gentiles. If such notions were intended by the author, he must have expected them to be understood only after reading the entire narrative, especially Acts. But does the rejection of the gospel by Israel as a whole and the concomitant transfer of salvation to the Gentiles occur in Acts? The following sections address that question.

The Stephen Episode (Acts 6.8–8.3)

The material in Acts about Stephen has been the subject of numerous scholarly treatises. Questions of its origin and historical value can for the most part be left aside for the purposes here. The issue raised by the present inquiry concerns Luke's use of the material in his presentation

---

indeed have motivated their inclusion, though one might still ask whether he might have selected similar Jewish figures. Koet suggests that the comparisons were included to encourage Israel's own repentance, since the vocation of the prophets Elijah and Elisha was to stimulate Israel's repentance (*Five Studies*, p. 50). Evans argues that Luke here takes issue with the idea that God's blessings are exclusively for the Jewish people, a concept which leads many to reject the Christian gospel ('Prophecy and Polemic', pp. 176-77).

1.   Brawley, *Luke–Acts and the Jews*, pp. 10-11; Combrink, 'Lk 4, 16-30', p. 38.

2.   Cf. the discussion of the contrast between Gentile faith and Jewish unbelief above, and the discussion below of the condemnation of the Galilean cities. Evans offers the suggestion that for Luke the Nazareth pericope does not assert a transfer of salvation to the Gentiles but denies that salvation is offered exclusively to Jews ('Luke's View', p. 30).

of Jewish response to the gospel. Do various details of the text indicate that Luke holds all Israel responsible for Stephen's death, and so also for its parallel, the crucifixion of Jesus? Does Stephen's speech, especially with its negative survey of Israel's history and possible disparagement of the temple, suggest a condemnation of the entire Jewish nation? Or does the structure of the narrative indicate that the Stephen episode is a watershed, marking the decisive rejection of the gospel by the Jews?

The Identity of Stephen's Opponents. At the beginning of the Stephen narrative, Luke identifies Stephen's opponents as certain diaspora Jews in Jerusalem (6.9). But in the development of the narrative some have found a broadening of the opposition to include a wider circle, until by the end of Stephen's speech all Israel has been identified as his opponents.[1] The rejection and murder of Stephen by Israel is viewed further as a deliberate parallel to the death of Jesus, and the implication is drawn that Luke indicts all Israel for the death of both.[2]

The evidence cited for this view is various. The diaspora Jews stir up τὸν λαὸν καὶ τοὺς πρεσβυτέρους καὶ τοὺς γραμματεῖς (6.12), so that all are included among Stephen's opponents.[3] The length of Stephen's speech separates the accusations at the end from the identification of his opponents in the introduction. The effect is that by the time 7.51 is reached, the reader has forgotten the specific identity of the opponents and understands them simply as the Jews, who habitually kill the prophets.[4] Luke allows such an understanding by not specifying the subjects of the verbs in 7.54-60 beyond 'the witnesses' in v. 58.[5]

Again, certain details of the text which suggest another meaning can be noted. First of all, the syntax of 6.12-13, though not without ambiguities, does not necessarily suggest that Luke's emphasis is on the fact that those 'stirred up' by the Hellenists seize Stephen and take him into the Sanhedrin. The conjunction τε in vv. 11-13 serves to emphasize a

---

1. So J. Bihler, *Die Stephanusgeschichte im Zusammenhang der Apostelgeschichte* (Münchener theologische Studien, 1.16; Munich: Hueber, 1963), pp. 12, 81; O'Neill, *Theology*, p. 91; Gaston, 'Passion Narrative', p. 133; Sanders, *Jews in Luke–Acts*, pp. 50-51, 73-74, 247-49.

2. So Eltester, 'Israel', p. 114; Talbert, 'Martyrdom', p. 102; Gaston, 'Passion Narrative', p. 133.

3. Eltester, 'Israel', p. 114; Sanders, *Jews in Luke–Acts*, p. 247.

4. Gaston, 'Passion Narrative', p. 133; Sanders, *Jews in Luke–Acts*, pp. 50-51.

5. Sanders, *Jews in Luke–Acts*, pp. 73-74, 249.

series of three verbs: ὑπέβαλον (v. 11), συνεκίνησαν (v. 12) and ἔστησαν (v. 13).[1] These verbs all indicate that although a variety of people are involved in the hostilities against Stephen, the opposition is orchestrated and manipulated by a distinct group, the diaspora opponents. Thus, although Luke notes the involvement of a wider group in v. 12, his attention is immediately drawn back to the instigators in v. 13. In this opportunity to broaden the focus of opposition, he keeps the accent on the narrower group.[2]

Secondly, other texts show the same tendency to separate third-person verbs from their subjects with the intervention of a long discourse. Paul's temple speech, although not as long as Stephen's speech, nevertheless separates the verb ἤκουον (Acts 22.22) from the antecedent of its unspecified subject (ὁ λαός, Acts 21.40).[3] In that instance, it is difficult to ascribe to Luke any desire to obscure the specific subject to imply a more generalized attribution: the opponents of Paul apparently already include all the Jews on the scene. Instead, it appears in both instances that Luke's habit of omitting subjects is at work without any conscious design.

Thirdly, Luke gives an indication elsewhere that he did not regard the murderers of Stephen as comprising a larger group. In Acts 22.20 Paul identifies them simply as τῶν ἀναιρούντων αὐτόν, whose garments he watched over. The expression is straightforward; it gives no evidence that Luke assigned some broad, national responsibility for the death of Stephen. Earlier, of course, Luke identified those who left their garments with Paul as οἱ μάρτυρες (7.58), which likewise indicates no interest in broadening the circle of responsibility.

Fourthly, the leadership of the high priests in the ensuing persecution

1.   Bihler rightly notes the importance of these verbs in characterizing Stephen's opposition but fails to notice the limitation of the subjects (*Stephanusgeschichte*, p. 11).

2.   Luke does, of course, implicate the (false) witnesses brought forward by the diaspora opponents as among those who stoned Stephen (7.58). But the point here is not that Luke exonerates all but the diaspora instigators. It is rather that he maintains the emphasis on the instigators in 6.9-15 despite the involvement of others and the opportunity that it presented to suggest a wider circle of culpability. The witnesses' action is also consistent with the demands of the Torah (Lev. 24.14; Deut. 17.7) and may well reflect Luke's source or the event itself. Hence, Johnson is correct when he says that Luke limits the involvement of the λαός in Stephen's death and implicates only the Jerusalem leaders (*Possessions*, p. 51 n. 3).

3.   Cf. the discussion in Chapter 2.

(9.1-2), suggests, as Evans has pointed out, that Luke still views the chief opponents of the church as the priestly aristocracy. Indeed, the sandwiching of the first notice of the persecution between the death and burial of Stephen (8.1) closely links the two events.[1]

Fifthly, as Jervell notes, the Stephen episode is not entirely characterized by opposition. It is introduced with a note of the further success of the Christian mission in Jerusalem (6.7).[2] The juxtaposition of Jewish conversions and Jewish opposition is found here as it is in other Lukan contexts.[3]

Stephen's Use of Israel's History. Stephen's recitation of Israel's history is frequently viewed as a thoroughgoing indictment of the Jewish people. On this view, Stephen characterizes Israel's history as an unrelenting tale of disobedience and rebellion. In particular, the temple is a testimony to Israel's rebelliousness; its construction was tantamount to idolatry. The actions of the recent past bear out this interpretation in Stephen's view: in keeping with earlier murders of prophets, the Jews killed Jesus, just as they finally kill Stephen.[4]

Again a variety of details within the text suggest another perspective. First of all, it is less than certain that in Stephen's speech Luke presents Israel's entire history as characterized by disobedience. It also high lights faithful personages like Abraham, Joseph, Moses and David. T.L. Donaldson rightly recognizes that the speech holds one part of Israel's history in high esteem.[5] Moreover, as has been frequently

1. Evans, 'Luke's View', p. 37.
2. Jervell, *People of God*, p. 47.
3. The interruption of Stephen's speech by his opponents has recently been addressed by G.H.R. Horsley, who notes that the interruption is a Lukan literary device that does not in itself imply hostility and is not in any way confined to Jewish audiences ('Speeches and Dialogue in Acts', *NTS* 32 [1986], pp. 610-11).
4. So, with varying emphases, Gnilka, *Verstockung*, pp. 144-45; O'Neill, *Theology*, p. 91; Schneider, *Verleugnung*, pp. 200-201; Franklin, *Christ the Lord*, p. 103; Ruether, *Faith and Fratricide*, pp. 76-77; Maddox, *Purpose*, pp. 53-54; C.K. Barrett, 'Old Testament History according to Stephen and Paul', in W. Schrage (ed.), *Studien zum Text und zur Ethik des Neuen Testaments: Festschrift zum 80. Geburtstag von Heinrich Greeven* (BZNW, 47; Berlin: de Gruyter, 1986), pp. 68-69; Sanders, *Jews in Luke–Acts*, pp. 34, 50-51, 73-74.
5. T.L. Donaldson, 'Moses Typology and the Sectarian Nature of Early Christian Anti-Judaism', *JSNT* 12 (1981), pp. 28-30. F.F. Bruce notes that the speech holds the promised land in high esteem ('Stephen's Apologia', in

noted,[1] the recitation of Israel's history in Acts 7 is in many respects supplemented by the recitation in Acts 13.17-25. On that occasion the promise to Israel is emphasized, and little if anything of disobedience is to be found.

Similar remarks can be made concerning the presentation of the temple. If Stephen's speech reflects a decidedly anti-temple perspective (perhaps with origins in a radical Hellenistic Jewish or Gentile-Christian circle),[2] then it is difficult to square with the apparent reverence in which Luke holds the temple elsewhere. In fact, Luke expressly labels as false the charge that Stephen blasphemed the temple (6.13).[3] The appeal to Isa. 66.1 appears to be less an indictment of temple worship per se than a correction of what Luke regards as a serious misunderstanding of the nature of the temple.[4]

B.P. Thompson [ed.], *Scripture: Meaning and Method: Essays Presented to Anthony Tyrrell Hanson for his Seventieth Birthday* [Hull: Hull University Press, 1987], p. 42), and Koet emphasizes its positive view of Moses and, consequently, the law (*Five Studies*, pp. 78-79). Lohfink notes that for Luke Israel has always included those who were just and devout, as illustrated in the infancy narratives (*Sammlung*, pp. 94-95).

1.   For example, by Barrett, 'Old Testament History', pp. 57-69.

2.   Donaldson has shown that the use of the law and the reverence for the Aaronic cult found in certain elements of the speech indicate that it could not have originated in a radical Hellenistic environment and that the exegetical traditions employed indicate a Palestinian Jewish milieu ('Moses Typology', pp. 28-32).

3.   Jervell, *Unknown Paul*, pp. 13-14. It is therefore difficult to agree with Bruce that Stephen's speech does not refute the charge against him ('Stephen's Apologia', pp. 39-40). Esler is more likely correct that it represents a 'defense on the law', demonstrating that even if the charges are true, they do not represent a breach of the law (*Community and Gospel*, pp. 123-25). Cf. the more general remarks of J. Dupont, 'La structure oratoire du discours d'Etienne (Actes 7)', *Bib* 66 (1985), pp. 162-63.

4.   Barrett's assertion that there is no parallel in Jewish literature to the attitude of Stephen to the temple reflected in his use of Isa. 66.1-2 ('Old Testament History', p. 68) apparently overlooks the Deuteronomistic account of Solomon's prayer at the temple's dedication (1 Kgs 8.27; cited by Bruce, 'Stephen's Apologia', p. 46; and Dupont, 'Discours d'Etienne', pp. 159-60). The statement in 1 Kings is clearly aimed at misunderstanding of the temple, not the temple itself. Evans points to several complementary Jewish texts indicating that true worship is possible without a physical temple ('Prophecy and Polemic', pp. 198-99 n. 107). That this is also the perspective of Stephen's speech is pointed out by J.J. Kilgallen ('The Function of Stephen's Speech [Acts 7, 2-53]', *Bib* 70 [1989], pp. 177-79). He notes that the affirmation of the tabernacle, the portability of which is never mentioned in the

The effect of this presentation is to divide Israel's history into two streams: the faithful, which proclaims the prophetic message and properly esteems the cult, and the unfaithful, which kills the prophets and misappropriates the cult.[1] This perspective is reflected in certain details of the language of Acts 7 as well. The common Jewish heritage of Stephen and his audience is stressed throughout the speech (ἀδελφοὶ καὶ πατέρες, v. 2; τὸ γένος ἡμῶν, v. 19; ὃς ἐδέξατο λόγια ζῶντα δοῦναι ἡμῖν, v. 38). The expression οἱ πατέρες ἡμῶν is particularly frequent (vv. 11, 12, 15, 19, 38, 39, 45 [twice]). But in vv. 51-53 this heretofore static mode of expression shifts, and Stephen addresses his audience in the second person and refers to οἱ πατέρες ὑμῶν, with whom the audience stands in solidarity in the persecution of the prophets and disobedience to the law (cf. vv. 39-42).[2] The shift serves to identify his audience's opposition to him and the gospel with the opposition faced by Moses and the prophets.[3] Likewise, the charge that fathers of the audience killed the prophets (v. 52) stands in contrast to the statement 'You are the sons of the prophets' in Acts 3.25. On two different occasions two different elements of Israel's heritage are emphasized, but in neither case is one element thereby denied.

---

speech, indicates that localized places of worship as such are not condemned, only improper attitudes to them. Nevertheless, Bruce is correct in saying that the speech could be understood by Stephen's audience as blasphemous ('Church of Jerusalem', p. 648; 'Stephen's Apologia', p. 46), though Kilgallen ('Stephen's Speech', p. 183) is correct to observe that it is the mention of Jesus, not the statements about the temple, that prompt the stoning.

1.   Donaldson notes how such a view of Israel's history is characteristic of sectarian Judaism, in which the sect lays claim to the heritage of the faithful stream of Israel's history and identifies opponents with the unfaithful stream ('Moses Typology', pp. 39-40). Cf. also Koet, *Five Studies*, p. 81. Slingerland ignores the possibility that Luke held such a view when he hypothesizes that an anti-Jewish redactor added the negative elements to the essentially pro-Jewish original account of Stephen ('Composition of Acts', pp. 106-10).

2.   Bihler observes this shift but asserts that Luke has Stephen distance himself from the Jewish audience because of the accusations made (*Stephanusgeschichte*, pp. 77, 81). He fails to consider the implications of Stephen's earlier use of the first person plural. Likewise, Franklin notes the contrast but does not allow the implications drawn here because he sees the point of the speech to be the apostasy of all Israel (*Christ the Lord*, p. 104). Slingerland also observes the shift but, failing to see the compatibility of the two perspectives, posits two levels of redaction to explain it ('Composition of Acts', pp. 109-10).

3.   Cf. the discussion below.

The Stephen Episode as Turning Point. Luke clearly rounds off one portion of his narrative and begins another with the story of Stephen. After his death, the scene shifts outside of Jerusalem for the first time. A number of scholars have concluded that this transition marks a decisive turning point for the fate of the Jews in Acts. Talbert, for example, sees the death of Stephen as the second and decisive rejection of God's messenger by the Jews. Although Jesus' death could be ascribed to ignorance, Stephen's is clearly deliberate, and the Jews are culpable. Therefore, the period of Jewish salvation, or at least of mass Jewish conversion, comes to a close. The gospel makes its way to the Gentiles, and its encounter with Judaism from this point is characterized by conflict.[1]

One important element in this interpretation has already been dealt with: the use of οἱ Ἰουδαῖοι following the Stephen episode. To that observation others can be added. One is that conversions of large numbers of Jews do not end with the Stephen episode. Paul's converts in the diaspora (13.43; 14.1; 16.1; 17.4, 12; 18.8; 19.17; 28.24) and the 'myriads' of Palestinian Jewish believers (21.20) indicate ongoing success for the Christian mission among Jews.[2] A second relevant point is

1.   Talbert, 'Martyrdom', p. 102; cf. Schneider, *Verleugnung*, pp. 200-201; O'Neill, *Theology*, pp. 84-87; J. Zmijewski, *Die Eschatologiereden des Lukas-Evangeliums* (BBB, 40; Bonn: Peter Hanstein, 1972), pp. 167-68; Johnson, *Possessions*, p. 73-76; Gaston, 'Passion Narrative', p. 133; Sanders, *Jews in Luke–Acts*, pp. 55, 283; and, more cautiously, George, 'Israël', p. 512; and Lohfink, *Sammlung*, pp. 54-55.

2.   Sanders supplies several motives for the inclusion of these conversions despite what he sees as the end of the epoch of Jewish salvation in Acts 6.7: (1) the gospel cannot be powerless and so must produce a few Jewish conversions (*Jews in Luke–Acts*, p. 250); (2) Luke knows of some Jewish Christians in the diaspora and must account for them (p. 250); (3) Luke introduces these conversions to vary his narrative and avoid 'woodenness' (p. 76); (4) for Luke these conversions belong to the past (pp. 283-84). But it is difficult to see the evidence for these explanations. Jewish conversions demonstrate the power of the gospel, to be sure, but so do Gentile conversions. If for Luke the day of Jewish salvation ends with Stephen and subsequent preaching to Jews is intended only to pronounce judgment, the power of the gospel could more consistently be demonstrated with massive Gentile conversions accompanied only by ringing denunciations of the Jews without Jewish conversions. For Luke to demonstrate the gospel's power with results that were contrary to what he thought was its purpose is a strikingly inconsistent procedure. The same inconsistency is evident if his motive is narrative variety. The final argument, that these conversions belong to the past, does not address the issue, since they still

raised by Brawley: the narrative, far from leaving Jerusalem behind, repeatedly returns to it (8.25; 9.26-29; 11.2, 27-30; 15.2-7; 21.15; 28.17).[1] No doubt Luke has a firm historical basis for seeing a dispersion of the church from Jerusalem following the death of Stephen.[2] But if he regards the event as the watershed of salvation history for the Jews, the rest of the narrative gives no evidence of such a view.

Paul's Turning to the Gentiles (Acts 13.46; 18.6; 28.28)

Most analyses of Luke's approach to Judaism which conclude that he was hostile to the Jews emphasize Luke's account of Paul's turning from the Jews to the Gentiles (Acts 13.46; 18.6; 28.28). These are understood as indicating that (1) the Jews as a whole reject the gospel which Paul presents; (2) Paul's turning to the Gentiles signifies a transferral of salvation from the Jews to the Gentiles; (3) Paul delivers a judgment against the entire Jewish nation.[3] However, at several points this view does not accord with the data of the text, as the discussion which follows indicates. Instead, Luke appears to stress the division that the gospel brings to the Jews of the diaspora and to contrast the refusal of salvation by some Jews with the potential for salvation among the Gentiles.

---

follow the epochal turning point of Stephen's death. And if 'individual' Jewish conversions are possible after the turning point, and if the gospel is still actively preached to the Jews, it is difficult to see what the turning point signifies.

1. Brawley, *Luke–Acts and the Jews*, pp. 35-36.

2. Bruce suggests that following the death of Stephen the Jerusalem church made no further inroads among the Hellenists of Jerusalem ('Church of Jerusalem', pp. 648-49). The evidence he cites is compelling, but it is all incidental to Luke's motives. Luke displays no interest in such a transition, instead stressing the success of the mission efforts of Hellenistic Jewish Christians outside Jerusalem.

3. Wilcox provides what could be a fourth argument that Paul's turning to the Gentiles indicates Luke's anti-Jewish orientation (*Semitisms of Acts*, pp. 65-66). He argues that the statement of Paul in Acts 18.6, τὸ αἷμα ὑμῶν ἐπὶ τὴν κεφαλὴν ὑμῶν, alludes to 2 Kgdms (2 Sam.) 1.16 (LXX), where David pronounces a similar judgment on the Amalekites for slaying τὸν χριστὸν κυρίου, i.e., Saul. If this is indeed the intended allusion, then the rejection of the gospel could be equated with the killing of Jesus (Wilcox does not make this connection). However, the next clause in Acts 18.6, καθαρὸς ἐγώ, indicates that the allusion is probably to Ezek. 33.1ff., which contrasts the guilt of the recalcitrant audience with the innocence of the faithful messenger.

Rejection by Israel as a Whole. Luke is clearly interested in the rejection of Paul's gospel by the Jews; he repeatedly emphasizes it in the course of the narrative. But whether he viewed that rejection as characteristic of all or part of the Jewish people is not settled by simply noting that Jews reject Paul's message and that he subsequently turns to the Gentiles.[1] Attention must be given to the contexts of the turning episodes to determine exactly what Jewish reaction prompts Paul's turning to the Gentiles. In fact, each includes details which suggest that Luke viewed Jewish rejection of Paul's gospel as a rejection by only a part of the Jewish community.[2]

This characteristic of the turning episodes is clearest in the episode in Corinth (18.6). Following Paul's announcement of 'turning' and his departure from the synagogue (vv. 6-7), Luke notes the conversion of the synagogue leader, Crispus, and his household (v. 8).[3] This conversion might appear to be included by Luke as an exception to the general pattern of Jewish rejection. It is not, however, the only such note which Luke includes in the turning episodes. In Pisidian Antioch, earlier in the scene at Corinth, and at Rome Luke indicates that at least a sizable minority of Paul's Jewish audience accepts his message (13.43; 18.4; 28.24). Likewise, when Paul departs from the synagogue in Ephesus, he takes disciples with him (19.9), apparently having converted them in the synagogue. Thus, a consistent pattern appears to be at work: Paul turns to the Gentiles after some Jews accept his message and others refuse.

Against this view, Sanders has argued that Luke uses πείθω,

---

1. Both Egelkraut (*Mission to Jerusalem*, pp. 228-30) and Slingerland ('"The Jews"', p. 317) ignore the possible distinction between a rejection by some Jews and a rejection by all in the turning episodes. Likewise, Wilson's judgment that the turning episodes represent Luke's view of all Jews while the conversions explain the presence of a Jewish minority in the church neglects the issue of whether Luke regards the instigation of Paul's turning to the Gentiles to be rejection by the whole or by a part (*Gentiles*, pp. 232-33).

2. The division among the Jews caused by Paul's preaching in Acts was noted by P. Schubert but left undeveloped ('The Final Cycle of Speeches in the Book of Acts', *JBL* 87 [1968], pp. 9-10). The implications were better realized by Johnson (*Possessions*, pp. 54-57).

3. R.C. Tannehill, 'Rejection by Jews and Turning to Gentiles: The Pattern of Paul's Mission in Acts', in Tyson (ed.), *Luke–Acts and the Jewish People*, p. 91. The fact that Luke notes Crispus's conversion after Paul's departure from the synagogue weighs heavily against Tyson's view (*Death*, p. 39) that rejection follows acceptance according to a consistent literary pattern.

common to all these incidents, to indicate a positive response to the gospel that falls short of actual conversion.[1] But Luke's pattern of usage suggests otherwise.[2] In the Gospel, Luke uses the perfect passive of πείθω to indicate belief in something (Lk. 18.9; 20.6). In Acts the active refers to the process of Christian preaching (18.4; 19.8, 26), the result of which is 'to make a Christian' (26.28). In Acts 28, the process of Paul's preaching is 'persuading' (28.23), which yields those who are persuaded (28.24), just as in Acts 19 Paul's 'persuading' (v. 8) produces some (τινες) who are 'unpersuaded' (ἠπείθουν, v. 9).[3] Furthermore, in at least one instance in Acts, those who 'are persuaded' unquestionably refer to believers. In 17.4, some in the Thessalonian synagogue 'are persuaded' and attach themselves to Paul and Silas. Later, the text refers to those 'brothers' who assist Paul and Silas on their way to Berea following their persecution in Thessalonica (17.10).[4] It appears to be beyond question that the 'brothers' are the ones who were persuaded in 17.4 and are regarded by Luke as genuine believers. In 18.4 those persuaded include both Jews and Greeks, and little suggests that Luke is reticent to suggest the genuine conversion of Greeks.[5] It is likewise noteworthy that in Acts 28.24, persuasion is contrasted with unbelief.[6] The difference

1. Sanders, *Jews in Luke–Acts*, pp. 273-75, 279, 298.

2. Dupont reaches a conclusion exactly opposite to Sanders's, namely, that πείθω regularly indicates conversion for Luke ('La conclusion des Actes', pp. 375-76). R.F. O'Toole notes that Luke's usage may have been influenced by the LXX, which uses ἀπειθής and ἀπείθω for anyone who disobeys God, but especially for disobedient Jews (*The Unity of Luke's Theology* [Good News Studies, 9; Wilmington, DE: Michael Glazier, 1984], p. 81). Evans offers a brief and telling critique of Sanders's view of πείθω in these verses ('Luke's View', p. 37).

3. Sanders notes this antithesis and acknowledges that it occurs elsewhere in Acts but fails to consider it in his analysis of πείθω elsewhere (*Jews in Luke–Acts*, p. 280). More satisfactory are the observations of Koet (*Five Studies*, p. 127).

4. This point has also been observed by C.A. Evans (*To See and Not Perceive: Isaiah 6.9-10 in Early Jewish and Christian Interpretation* [JSOTSup, 64; Sheffield: JSOT Press, 1989], p. 126).

5. Dupont's assertion that only Jewish conversions are noted in Corinth appears to neglect this detail ('La conclusion des Actes', pp. 385-86).

6. Hauser notes the opposition with the μὲν... δέ construction in 28.24 but says that the point of the opposition is unclear (*Apg 28*, pp. 62-63). He observes correctly that the point could be to contrast outright unbelief with theoretical agreement or a positive inclination without actual conversion (*Apg 28*, pp. 64-66; cf. Haenchen, *Acts*, pp. 723-24, 729; this possibility is missed by Brawley, *Luke–Acts and the Jews*, pp. 141-42). But Luke's usage of πείθω elsewhere indicates that the

between those persuaded and the unbelievers is underlined with the note in v. 25 that the audience is ἀσύμφωνοι.[1] The opposite is true in Acts 14.1-2, where belief is contrasted with 'unpersuasion'.[2] Luke thus appears comfortable using either πιστεύω in the active or πείθω in the passive to indicate conversion.[3]

Are there other indications that Luke understands these Jewish responses to be less than full conversion? Sanders suggests that Paul's admonition 'to abide in the grace of God' in Acts 13.43 means 'to remain fixed in their accustomed religious development', that is, to remain non-Christian Jews.[4] Against this view is the fact that 'the grace of God' elsewhere for Luke signifies the content of the Christian gospel (Acts 20.24).[5] The verb προσμένω is only surprising in this context if, as Sanders apparently assumes, Luke views Christian belief as discontinuous with the Jewish faith of Paul's synagogue audience. Sanders's admission 'that the rebuff is not immediately obvious' reveals the weakness of his position.[6]

F.F. Bruce proposes that the imperfect tense of ἐπείθοντο in Acts 28.24 implies the meaning 'take heed', a response short of actual conversion.[7] However, both the immediate context and Luke's use of

---

opposition is between authentic conversion and unbelief. Hauser rightly grasps the implications that ἠπίστουν indicates refusal of the gospel in 28.24 but ignores the converse that ἐπείθοντο indicates belief (cf. *Apg 28*, pp. 131-32). Cf. also the opposition between πιστεύω and ἀπιστέω in Josephus, *War* 2.187.

1. Dupont suggests that the structure of the scene indicates that v. 25a was inserted by Luke as an introduction to vv. 25b-28, which form 'le coeur et le sommet de tout le passage Ac 28, 16-31' ('La conclusion des Actes', p. 365). If this is the case, then division within the Jewish community, not outright rejection, prompts Paul's pronouncement.

2. O'Fearghail, 'Israel', p. 42 n. 86.

3. Dupont correctly observes that the only factor which suggests that πείθω does not indicate full conversion in 28.24 is the statement of blanket condemnation in vv. 26-28 ('La conclusion des Actes', pp. 375-76).

4. Sanders, *Jews in Luke–Acts*, pp. 261-62. Only by holding such a view can Sanders assert that the quotation of Hab. 1.5 in Acts 13.47 shows that the Jews are preordained not to believe ('Use of the Scriptures', p. 197); otherwise, some of Paul's Jewish audience do believe.

5. Cf. the discussion of this point by Evans, who notes also Luke's view of grace in Acts 11.23 ('Luke's View', pp. 35-36).

6. Sanders, *Jews in Luke–Acts*, p. 262.

7. F.F. Bruce, *The Acts of the Apostles: The Greek Text with Introduction and Commentary* (Grand Rapids: Eerdmans, 1951), p. 479. He is followed by Hauser,

the imperfect elsewhere indicate that the imperfect tense here has another significance. The same imperfect tense is used for the unbelieving response of the rest of the audience in 28.24 (ἠπίστουν), and nothing suggests that their response was short of actual unbelief.[1] Furthermore, in v. 23 Paul's preaching is expressed in the imperfect (ἐξετίθετο) and elaborated with present participles (διαμαρτυρόμενος, πείθων). The durative aspect appears to be intended in this series of verbs, particularly with the emphasis on the length of the encounter (ἀπὸ πρωὶ ἕως ἑσπέρας, v. 23). The appearance of an aorist participle (εἰπόντος, v. 25) then indicates the end of the scene described with the previous series of imperfects and present participles.[2] All this suggests a group of people who respond individually with belief or unbelief at various times through the course of Paul's preaching, a process which comes to an end with Paul's pronouncement as they depart.

Luke's usage elsewhere indicates that this interpretation is the correct one. The identical imperfect form occurs in Acts 5.36, 37, where it signifies 'conversion' to the movements of the messianic pretenders Theudas and Judas the Galilean. Likewise, the genuine believing response of a group of people is expressed with the imperfect in 6.7 (ὑπήκουον), 13.48 (ἔχαιρον καὶ ἐδόξαζον) and 18.8 (ἐπίστευον καὶ ἐβαπιτόζοντο). Corresponding unbelief among a group is also indicated with the imperfect in 17.32 (ἐχλεύαζον) and 19.9 (ἐσκληρύνοντο καὶ ἠπείθουν). It is especially significant that Luke uses the imperfect of πείθω in the context of the two other episodes of turning to the Gentiles (Acts 13.43; 18.4), where the actions of the opposition are likewise in the imperfect (ἀντέλεγον, 13.45) or the equivalent present participle (ἀντιτασσομένων...βλασφημούντων, 18.6) and the encounter ends with a Pauline pronouncement introduced with the aorist (13.46; 18.6).[3] Particularly in ch. 18 it is unmistakable

Apg 28, pp. 64-66; and Tannehill, 'Rejection by Jews', pp. 96-97.

1. O'Fearghail, 'Israel', p. 42 n. 86.

2. Cf. BDF § 327.

3. Cf. Acts 5.33-35, where the plotting of the Sanhedrin (διεπρίοντο καὶ ἐβούλοντο, v. 33) is brought to an end with the pronouncement of Gamaliel (εἶπεν, v. 35); and 9.20-23, where Paul's preaching in Damascus (ἐκήρυσσεν, v. 20; ἐνεδυναμοῦτο καὶ συνέχυννεν, v. 22) and the response to it (ἐξίσταντο...ἔλεγον, v. 21) comes to an end with the plot of the Damascene Jews (συνεβουλεύσαντο, v. 23).

that a portion of Paul's Jewish audience genuinely believes (18.4, 8). The similarities of language suggest that the same is true in ch. 28.

For Sanders, notes of conversions in the first two episodes are relatively unimportant. By separating speech from narrative, he allows that Luke includes Jewish conversions in the narrative for variety while still denouncing all Jews in Paul's speech.[1] However, the fact that conversions also occur at the end of the narrative demonstrates the weakness of Sanders's position; on his view, the Jews must become 'monolithic' in their opposition by the end of Acts.[2] Likewise for Tyson, rejection at the end of the narrative must be decisive and final.[3] Although Luke is concerned with the phenomenon of Jewish refusal, the text does not indicate that he neglected or suppressed the reality of Jewish conversions.[4] Apparently recognizing the difficulties in maintaining this view of Acts 28, Tyson has recently suggested that Luke indicates that although the conversion of individual Jews is possible, the Jews have rejected the gospel corporately.[5] Tyson's only objection to the view that Israel is divided in Acts 28 is that Paul addresses Isa. 6.9-10 to ὁ λαός, which, according to Dahl's analysis, 'almost always applies to the Jewish people'.[6] However, Dahl's article in fact argues that λαός is used by Luke to refer to Israel or *any part of Israel*.[7] Luke obviously follows the text of the LXX in using λαός in Acts 28.26, but it may still be significant that the precise phrase is τὸν λαὸν τοῦτον. The use of the demonstrative may be significant: Luke may understand 'this' people to refer to that portion which refuses the message of salvation, the people who fail to 'hear'. But even if the demonstrative is not significant, Luke's use of λαός elsewhere indicates that he uses it for a portion of Israel.[8] Division, not

---

1.   Sanders notes that in Pisidian Antioch and Corinth Paul experiences 'considerable success' among the Jews (*Jews in Luke–Acts*, p. 65). But he allows that such success is only included to avoid 'woodenness' in the narrative (*Jews in Luke–Acts*, p. 264).

2.   Sanders, *Jews in Luke–Acts*, p. 264.

3.   Tyson, *Death*, pp. 31, 172.

4.   *Contra* Tyson, *Death*, p. 43.

5.   Tyson, 'Jewish Rejection', pp. 126-27. A similar opinion is offered by Tannehill, 'Rejection by Jews', pp. 96-100.

6.   Tyson, 'Jewish Rejection', p. 126; cf. Tannehill, 'Rejection by Jews', p. 97.

7.   Dahl, 'People', p. 326; cf. O'Fearghail, 'Israel', p. 43 n. 90.

8.   Cf. the discussion above, where it was argued that Luke uses λαός in the passion narrative to refer to the people of Jerusalem.

unequivocal rejection, characterizes Luke's view of Jewish response to the gospel.[1]

Transfer of Salvation to the Gentiles. That the words of judgment delivered by Paul in the turning episodes are directed against all Jews is often inferred from the apparent comparison between Jewish unbelief and Gentile receptivity. This comparison is said to be most clearly set forth in Acts 28.28. There καί is taken in an adversative sense, so that the emphatic pronoun αὐτοί stands in contrast to the Jews.[2] The verb ἀκούσονται is thus understood to signify a favorable response, to listen and heed.[3] Hence, the Gentiles are viewed as receptive to the gospel in contrast to the stubborn, recalcitrant Jews: '*they* (in contrast to you Jews) will listen (and believe)'.[4] In view of this essential difference between the two groups, salvation is effectively transferred from the Jews to the Gentiles.[5]

That this understanding was not Luke's intention is indicated by a combination of elements in the text. These indicate that Luke does not

1. Hence, the view of Löning (*Salustradition*, pp. 157-58, 176) that Paul's function as a witness to the Jews is to bring about their rejection of the gospel is also incorrect, ignoring as it does the substantial number of Jewish converts that Luke continues to ascribe to Paul (*Saulustradition*, pp. 161-62). V. Stolle is correct to observe that the divided reaction of the Jews in Acts 28 is typical in Luke's view (*Der Zeuge als Angeklagter: Untersuchungen zum Paulusbild des Lukas* [BWANT, 102 (6.2); Stuttgart: Kohlhammer, 1973], p. 88). Cf. also the remarks of Jervell (*People of God*, pp. 61-63), Brawley (*Luke–Acts and the Jews*, pp. 140-41), Moessner (*Banquet*, p. 311) and Koet (*Five Studies*, pp. 132-33) concerning the divided response here. Evans's view that Acts 28 explains the rejection of the gospel by 'the nation of Israel in general' is correct inasmuch as it serves as an apologetic point for Luke, establishing the truth of the Christian gospel despite Jewish rejection and allowing for previous and ongoing conversions of substantial numbers of individual Jews ('Luke's View', p. 179 n. 44). If this view is correct, then the Western insertion of v. 29 represents a proper understanding of Luke's intention.

2. For example Hauser, *Apg 28*, p. 40.

3. For example Maddox, *Purpose*, pp. 43-44, 46. Hauser (*Apg 28*, pp. 79-80) notes the range of meaning for ἀκούω in Luke–Acts.

4. For example Hauser, *Apg 28* pp. 75-76, 107.

5. Hauser's comment is typical (*Apg 28*, p. 224): 'Hier in Rom finde die definitive Konfrontation des Judentums mit dem Christentum, eine endgültige Absage an die Juden statt. Dabei wird die Verstockung der Juden entweder als Anlaß oder gar als Grund für das Heil für die Heiden gesehen: Nun sie der καιρός der Heiden gekommen; nun löse sich das Christentum von jüdischen Partikularismus und werde zur Weltreligion.'

contrast the response of Jews to that of Gentiles but announces that the gospel will go to the Gentiles with the potential of their accepting it in contrast to the unconverted segment of Paul's audience.[1]

The first element is the word καί. Luke's use of καί as an adverb with either additive ('also') or ascensive ('even') force, as it appears in 28.28, follows a remarkably regular pattern.[2] Luke consistently inserts adverbial καί into a clause immediately *before* the word or phrase expressing a new point added to the previous clause.[3] Several examples may be cited. Often καί appears before an element which is substituted for a corresponding element of the previous clause. Thus, adverbial καί appears before subjects or their equivalents in clauses whose predicates are similar to those in the clauses that precede them. For example in Lk. 2.4 Ἰωσήφ, preceded by adverbial καί, 'goes up' (ἀνέβη) to his home city, as do πάντες and ἕκαστος in the preceding clause (v. 3). Substituted subjects are also introduced with adverbial καί in 9.60-61 (εἶπεν δὲ αὐτῷ...εἶπεν δὲ καὶ ἕτερος); 11.17-18 (πᾶσα βασιλεία ἐφ' ἑαυτὴν διαμερισθεῖσα...εἰ δὲ καὶ ὁ Σατανᾶς ἐφ' ἑαυτὸν διεμερίσθη); Acts 5.1-2 (Ἀνανίας...ἐνοσφίσατο ἀπὸ τῆς τιμῆς, συνειδυίης καὶ τῆς γυναικός); 19.27 (τὸ μέρος εἰς ἀπελεγμὸν ἐλθεῖν, ἀλλὰ καὶ τὸ...ἱερόν). Objects are also introduced with adverbial καί when the subject and verb in their clauses are similar to those in the preceding verbal phrase or clause. In Lk. 11.40 adverbial καί introduces τὸ ἔσωθεν, which corresponds to τὸ ἔξωθεν in the preceding participial phrase. Similar constructions can be found in 14.7-12 (ἔλεγεν δὲ πρὸς τοὺς κεκλημένους...ἔλεγεν δὲ καὶ τῷ κεκληκότι); and Acts 19.21 (πορεύεσθαι εἰς Ἱεροσόλυμα, εἰπὼν ὅτι μετὰ τὸ γενέσθαι με ἐκεῖ δεῖ με καὶ Ῥώμην ἰδεῖν).

Likewise, verbs are preceded by adverbial καί when their subjects or

---

1. Hauser (*Apg 28*, p. 39) rightly observes that in Acts 28.28 ὑμῖν contrasts with τοῖς ἔθνεσιν, which stands in an emphatic position at the beginning of the clause. But this leaves open the issue of the point of the contrast.

2. Cf. the classification of adverbial uses, as opposed to conjunctive uses, in BAGD, p. 393. The study of καί in Luke's Gospel by Antoniadis does not consider postpositive uses (*Esquisse de grammaire*, pp. 298-316). Similarly, S.H. Levinson considers only copulative καί and limits his study to narrative sections of Acts (*Textual Connections in Acts* [SBLMS, 31; Atlanta: Scholars Press, 1987]).

3. Luke's usage here appears to be distinctive: Paul often separates adverbial καί from the element to which it is logically joined (BDF § 442 [12]; C.F.D. Moule, *An Idiom Book of New Testament Greek* [Cambridge: Cambridge University Press, 2nd edn, 1959], p. 167).

objects are the same as those in the preceding clause. In Acts 1.3 παρέστησεν is introduced with adverbial καί; its implied subject, ὁ 'Ιησοῦς, is also the subject of the verbs in vv. 1b-2. Other examples are found in Acts 1.10-11 (ἄνδρες δύο παρειστήκεισαν...οἳ καὶ εἶπαν); 3.24 (πάντες δὲ οἱ προφῆται...ὅσοι ἐλάλησαν καὶ κατήγγειλαν); 7.44-45 (ἡ σκηνὴ τοῦ μαρτυρίου ἦν τοῖς πατράσιν ἡμῶν...ἣν καὶ εἰσήγαγον...οἱ πατέρες ἡμῶν); 12.3-4 (προσέθετο συλλαβεῖν...Πέτρον...ὃν καὶ πιάσας ἔθετο); 13.22 (ἤγειρεν τὸν Δαυὶδ...ᾧ καὶ εἶπεν); 22.28 (ἐγὼ...τὴν πολιτείαν ταύτην ἐκτησάμην...ἐγὼ δὲ καὶ γεγέννημαι); 26.9-10 (δεῖν πολλὰ ἐναντία πρᾶξαι, ὃ καὶ ἐποίησα).

In all such instances the new element which is added to the idea of the previous clause—the word or phrase emphasized by adverbial καί—is the one that follows καί, not the one that precedes it. Luke's consistency in this pattern even extends to inserting καί into the appropriate position before the element of addition or emphasis where it was apparently lacking in his source (Lk. 6.36 [καθὼς καὶ ὁ πατήρ (var.)]; 11.34 [καὶ ὅλον τὸ σῶμά σου φωτεινόν ἐστιν]; 14.34 [ἐὰν δὲ καὶ τὸ ἅλας μωρανθῇ]; 17.26 [οὕτως ἔσται καὶ ἐν ταῖς ἡμέραις τοῦ υἱοῦ τοῦ ἀνθρώπου], 37 [ἐκεῖ καὶ οἱ ἀετοὶ ἐπισυναχθήσονται]; 19.19 [εἶπεν δὲ καὶ τούτῳ]; 20.12 [οἱ δὲ καὶ τοῦτον τραυματίσαντες ἐξέβαλον], 31 [ὡσαύτως δὲ καὶ οἱ ἑπτά], 32 [ὕστερον καὶ ἡ γυνὴ ἀπέθανεν]; 21.16 [παραδοθήσεσθε δὲ καὶ ὑπὸ γονέων]). Similarly, καί may have been dropped from Lk. 6.16 (ὃς ἐγένετο προδότης; diff. Mt. 10.4//Mk 3.19: ὁ/ὃς καὶ παραδοὺς/παρέδωκεν αὐτόν) because it did not conform in this instance to Luke's ordinary usage. One exception to the pattern appears to have been adopted from Luke's source (Lk. 21.31//Mt. 24.33// Mk 13.29: οὕτως καὶ ὑμεῖς). The emphasis falls on the word following adverbial καί in every other instance in Luke–Acts where, as it is in Acts 28.28, adverbial καί is preceded by a pronoun (Lk. 6.13 [οὓς καὶ ἀποστόλους ὠνόμασεν], 14 [ὃν καὶ ὠνόμασεν Πέτρον]; 7.49 [ὃς καὶ ἁμαρτίας ἀφίησιν]; 10.30 [οἳ καὶ ἐκδύσαντες αὐτὸν], 39 [ἣ καὶ παρακαθεσθεῖσα πρὸς τοὺς πόδας τοῦ κυρίου]; Acts 1.3 [οἷς καὶ παρέστησεν ἑαυτὸν ζῶντα], 11 [οἳ καὶ εἶπεν]; 7.45 [ἣν καὶ εἰσήγαγον διαδεξάμενοι οἱ πατέρες ἡμῶν]; 10.39 [ὃν καὶ ἀνεῖλαν]; 11.30 [ὃ καὶ ἐποίησαν]; 12.4 [ὃν καὶ πιάσας ἔθετο εἰς φυλακήν]; 13.22 [ᾧ καὶ εἶπεν]; 22.5 [παρ' ὧν καὶ ἐπιστολὰς δεξάμενος], 28 [ἐγὼ δὲ καὶ γεγέννημαι]; 24.6 [ὃς καὶ τὸ ἱερὸν ἐπείρασεν βεβηλῶσαι, ὃν καὶ ἐκρατήσαμεν], 15 [ἐλπίδα...ἣν καὶ αὐτοὶ οὗτοι προσδέχονται]; 26.10 [ὃ καὶ ἐποίησα ἐν Ἰεροσολύμοις], 26 [πρὸς ὃν καὶ παρρησιαζόμενος λαλῶ]; 28.10 [οἳ καὶ πολλαῖς τιμαῖς ἐτίμησαν ἡμᾶς]) or followed by a verb (see list above). If this consistent pattern carries through in Acts 28.28, the emphasis of adverbial καί falls on the verb ἀκούσονται, not on the pronoun αὐτοί.[1] This element, then, does not by itself suggest a contrast between Jews and Gentiles which disparages the former. Instead, it puts the focus on ἀκούσονται.

A contrast between Jews and Gentiles which disparages the former is nevertheless still possible within the broader structure of the context.[2] But whether it is consistent with the other aspects of Luke's usage of καί is another question. On one occasion Luke uses adverbial καί to suggest a contrast of the lesser with the greater. In Acts 22.28 Claudius Lysias's purchase of Roman citizenship is contrasted with Paul's birth into citizenship with ἐγὼ δὲ καὶ γεγέννημαι. Elsewhere, however, the construction is used to indicate not contrast but continuity. Furthermore, on no occasion does Luke use adverbial καί to contrast the negative with the positive, as would be the case if the Gentiles' 'listening' were contrasted with the Jews' 'not listening'. This pattern of usage suggests a presumption in favor of a similar meaning for καί in Acts 28.28, but such a presumption must be confirmed by other elements of the text.

An emphasis on continuity is entirely within the semantic range of ἀκούω. The verb can, of course, carry the neutral meaning 'hear'

---

1.   *Contra* Dupont, who asserts that καί emphasizes the preceding pronoun in Acts 28.28 ('La conclusion des Actes', pp. 373-74). The pronoun αὐτοί in Acts 28.28 is, nevertheless, still emphatic in its own right. Haenchen (*Acts*, p. 724) in connection with 28.28 refers to an earlier note (p. 140) where he asserts that καί following a relative pronoun should not be translated. Of course, αὐτοί is not a relative pronoun, but Haenchen apparently means to apply the maxim to it as well. But the fact that καί is not translatable does not mean that it is without syntactical force, and such force is readily apparent in the examples cited where καί follows a pronoun.

2.   Dupont finds an antithesis between the message sent 'to this people' (v. 26) and the one sent 'to the Gentiles' (v. 28; 'La conclusion des Actes', pp. 369-70). However, the Lukan introduction to the quotation (v. 25) indicates an application not to 'the people' as a whole but to the unbelieving segment (see below). This suggests that any antithesis would contrast only the unbelieving segment with the Gentiles. However, other elements of the text indicate not an antithesis but a neutral comparison indicating the sending of the message of salvation to Jews and Gentiles.

without specifying a positive response to the message heard.[1] Against this meaning in 28.28 it has been argued that the preceding quotation (vv. 26-27, quoting Isa. 6.9-10) uses ἀκούω with the connotation of a positive response.[2] But in fact the usage in the quotation is not decisive on this point. The first occurrence of ἀκούω in the quotation is neutral, affirming that the audience *does* hear, though without understanding (ἀκοῇ ἀκούσετε, v. 26). Only thereafter does the ironic play on words produce the declaration that although they hear, the audience is hard of hearing (τοῖς ὠσὶν βαρέως ἤκουσαν, v. 27a) and is prevented from hearing (μήποτε...τοῖς ὠσὶν ἀκούσωσιν). Thus, the quotation may suggest either meaning for the usage in v. 28.[3] Earlier in the context, moreover, Paul's audience indicates their willingness to 'hear' (v. 22).[4] A deliberate comparison between the opportunity of both Paul's Jewish

1.   The significance of the ambiguity is well noted by J.A. Darr (*On Character Building: The Reader and the Rhetoric of Characterization in Luke–Acts* [Louisville, KY: Westminster Press/John Knox, 1992], pp. 55-56). Stolle suggests the neutral meaning for ἀκούσονται because the outcome of the narrative is still in doubt, Paul's hearing before Caesar not yet having been decided (*Zeuge*, p. 86). But it is unlikely that Luke regards the decision of the emperor to be the decisive judgment of the Gentiles concerning the gospel. Tiede suggests the neutral meaning but offers no arguments in its favor (*Prophecy and History*, p. 122). Dupont notes the importance Luke attaches to 'hearing' in the Gospel, but his examples include instances where ἀκούω apparently carries a neutral meaning (e.g. Lk. 5.21; 6.18, 47 [cf. v. 49]; 8.18, 21; 'La conclusion des Actes', pp. 374-75). Hauser summarizes the Lukan usage more accurately (*Apg 28*, pp. 79-80).

2.   Dupont, 'La conclusion des Actes', pp. 372-73; Hauser, *Apg 28*, pp. 40, 79.

3.   Dupont indicates that by the time v. 28 is reached, the meaning of ἀκούω has been colored by the last two uses in the quotation ('La conclusion des Actes', pp. 372-73). But given the sharply ironic usage of ἀκούω in the quotation, it is not unlikely that Luke could reach back to the meaning employed in the first usage in the quote, which in fact forms the basis for the latter two.

4.   Hauser argues that 28.22 indicates that the Jews really did not listen to Paul because the 'Jewish' judgment of Paul's message is that it belongs to a 'sect' and is 'everywhere spoken against' (*Apg 28*, pp. 41-42). But such an interpretation does not appear to be warranted. Paul's audience reports a common opinion about the Christian gospel which stands in contrast with Paul's own view expressed in v. 20. But it also contrasts with their own desire to hear the gospel from Paul for themselves: μέν indicates the contrast in v. 22b. Cf. Dupont, 'La conclusion des Actes', pp. 367-69.

audience and the Gentiles to hear the gospel may be suggested by this earlier usage.[1]

Furthermore, adverbial καί appears frequently in the Cornelius episode and its retelling to emphasize that the gift of salvation and the Spirit are available to Gentiles as well as Jews (Acts 10.45 [καὶ ἐπὶ τὰ ἔθνη ἡ δωρεὰ τοῦ ἁγίου πνεύματος ἐκκέχυται], 47 [οἵτινες τὸ πνεῦμα τὸ ἅγιον ἔλαβον ὡς καὶ ἡμεῖς]; 11.1 [καὶ τὰ ἔθνη ἐδέξαντο τὸν λόγον τοῦ θεοῦ], 15 [ὥσπερ καὶ ἐφ᾽ ἡμᾶς ἐν ἀρχῇ], 17 [τὴν ἴσην δωρεὰν ἔδωκεν αὐτοῖς ὁ θεὸς ὡς καὶ ἡμῖν], 18 [ἄρα καὶ τοῖς ἔθνεσιν ὁ θεὸς τὴν μετάνοιαν εἰς ζωὴν ἔδωκεν], 20 [ἐλάλουν καὶ πρὸς τοὺς Ἑλληνιστάς]; 15.8 [δοὺς τὸ πνεῦμα τὸ ἅγιον καθὼς καὶ ἡμῖν]).[2] The consistency of this usage and the similarity of the subject matter in the Cornelius episode and in Acts 28 suggest that καί may well indicate the same continuity here. In other words, because in other statements concerning Jews and Gentiles using adverbial καί Luke stresses the access to salvation for both groups, the same may well be the case in Acts 28.28.

Such an interpretation is also suggested by the particular language employed in the earlier part of v. 28. The clause τοῖς ἔθνεσιν ἀπεστάλη τοῦτο τὸ σωτήριον τοῦ θεοῦ bears striking resemblance to Acts 13.26—ἡμῖν ὁ λόγος τῆς σωτηρίας ταύτης ἐξαπεστάλη—where the audience is composed of Jews and 'God-fearers'.[3] The similarity between the two clauses could suggest either a correspondence between the two groups ('Salvation is sent to the Gentiles as well as the Jews') or a contrast ('Having once been sent to the Jews and refused by

---

1.   Dupont suggests that the double use of ἀκούω indicates that v. 28 is Paul's response to the Jewish opinion of the gospel expressed in v. 22 ('La conclusion des Actes', pp. 368-69). On this view he regards the intervening material as preparation for the definitive response of v. 28. Against this view again is the fact that the hearsay of v. 22 stands in contrast to the audience's willingness to hear for themselves (see previous note). The Jewish audience *does hear* in v. 23; the Gentiles' hearing the gospel parallels the Jews' hearing it. Nevertheless, Dupont is correct insofar as the recalcitrant portion of the audience finally rejects Paul's view (v. 24b).

2.   Hauser notes the repeated assertion of Luke–Acts that salvation is sent to Jews and Gentiles and that Paul's ministry embraces both (*Apg 28*, p. 104). He does not, however, note the particular use of the postpositive καί construction, nor does he allow the general observation to influence his understanding of Acts 28.28.

3.   The similarity is noted by Gnilka (*Verstockung*, pp. 148-49) and Dupont ('La conclusion des Actes', p. 385).

them, salvation is now sent to the Gentiles, who will accept').[1] What decides in favor of the former view is Luke's insistence that salvation for the Gentiles has always been included in God's design and does not depend on Jewish rejection.[2] This idea is suggested in 28.28 by the use of σωτήριον. Elsewhere in Luke–Acts this neuter form appears only twice. In Lk. 2.30 it appears in a context which stresses both the universality of salvation (v. 32) and division in Israel (v. 34). In Lk. 3.6 it appears in the quotation of Isa. 40.3-5, where universality (v. 6) and division in Israel (vv. 7-14) are again stressed. The obvious congruence of these themes with the pronouncement of Paul in Acts 28.28 indicates an allusion to these earlier texts. The Isaianic setting common to Lk. 3.6 and Acts 28.28 reinforces this judgment.[3] Additionally, the aorist ἀπεστάλη indicates that the refusal of the Jewish audience does not cause the sending of the gospel to the Gentiles.[4] Rather, that sending is already an accomplished fact, announced by the risen Jesus and validated by the thrice-told Cornelius episode (10.1-48; 11.1-18; 15.6-11).[5]

1.   The latter is suggested by Maddox (*Purpose*, p. 44) following Stählin (*Apostelgeschichte*, p. 328). Cf. also Gnilka, *Verstockung*, p. 149.

2.   Johnson rightly notes that the aorist passive indicates that 'The salvation of the Gentiles was always part of God's plan' (*Possessions*, p. 58).

3.   Hauser's objection that an allusion to such a distant text appears strained overlooks both the importance of the two texts at the beginning and end of Luke's narrative and the striking use of a term (σωτήριον) for which Luke elsewhere consistently employs a synonym (σωτηρία; *Apg 28*, pp. 39-40). Cf. Dupont, 'La conclusion des Actes', p. 403.

4.   Jervell, *People of God*, pp. 60-63; Dupont, 'La conclusion des Actes', p. 403; O'Fearghail, 'Israel', p. 35. Hauser asserts that the rejection of the Jews does not cause the salvation of the Gentiles, though it does cause the message of salvation to be available to them (*Apg 28*, pp. 76-78). Beyond the incongruity of this view with Luke's earlier material on the Gentile mission, Hauser's position on this point implies that ἀκούσονται carries a neutral meaning, an implication which he explicitly rejects.

5.   Cf. O'Neill, *Theology*, p. 76 n. 1; S. Stowers, 'The Synagogue in the Theology of Acts', *ResQ* 17 (1974), p. 138; Brawley, *Luke–Acts and the Jews*, pp. 71-72. The relationship is causal in 13.46, as indicated by ἐπειδή, as Wilson (*Gentiles*, pp. 222-24) and Maddox (*Purpose*, p. 62 n. 95) rightly note. But what is caused in that instance is not the actual making available of salvation to the Gentiles but the immediate redirection of the Pauline mission in Pisidian Antioch (στρεφόμεθα). The divine intention to save Gentiles is affirmed in the quotation from Isaiah which follows in v. 47, just as it is more succinctly expressed with the aorist ἀπεστάλη in 28.28. Hence, Esler is wrong in his assertion that 13.46 implies

The particle οὖν in 28.28 does suggest a causal relationship, but the result is not the sending of the gospel to the Gentiles but the *declaration* that it has already been sent to them: οὖν appears in the main clause γνωστὸν οὖν ἔστω ὑμῖν, not in the dependent clause that follows. In 28.28 the gospel therefore does not go to the Gentiles because the Jews refuse it but because God has sent it to the Gentiles just as he did to the Jews.[1] Jewish refusal only causes the announcement that salvation is available to the Gentiles.

Furthermore, this body of data suggests that what might be called the Gentiles' characteristic receptivity to the gospel is not a concern in this context. If Jewish refusal causes the gospel to be sent to the Gentiles, then the Gentiles' receptivity is obviously relevant: the Jews forfeit salvation because of their stubbornness; the Gentiles obtain it because of their receptivity. But what is in fact affirmed is that salvation has already been sent to the Gentiles as it was to the Jews; the divine will, not the relative receptivity of the two groups, is the impetus in both cases. The concluding clause—αὐτοὶ καὶ ἀκούσονται—may still mean 'and they will listen', but in that case its relationship to the preceding material is less clear.

The cumulative force of this evidence suggests that ἀκούσονται in Acts 28.28 should be understood neutrally. What is affirmed is that the Gentiles will 'hear' the gospel according to divine intention. The clause τοῖς ἔθνεσιν ἀπεστάλη τοῦτο τὸ σωτήριον τοῦ θεοῦ indicates that God has commanded that salvation go to the Gentiles; αὐτοὶ καὶ ἀκούσονται affirms that through Paul the divine purpose will be realized. Thus, καί serves to introduce ἀκούσονται as the word which indicates that the purpose implied in the previous clause will indeed be fulfilled ('salvation is sent to them...they will indeed hear'). In this case ἀκούσονται in 28.28 is consistent with Luke's earlier usage in Acts 19.10, where all in Asia, explicitly Ἰουδαίους τε καὶ Ἕλληνας, 'hear' (ἀκοῦσαι) the word of the Lord.

Against this view it has been argued that elsewhere Luke deliberately represents the Gentiles as more receptive to the gospel than the Jews, so

---

that the gospel formerly was only for the Jews (*Community and Gospel*, pp. 39-40). To understand the verse in this way, one must entirely ignore Acts 10–11 as well as 13.47.

1.   Buss notes that the introductory particle οὖν does not demand the understanding that the Gentile mission comes as a result of Jewish rejection (*Missionspredigt*, p. 123).

that such a comparison is to be expected in 28.28.[1] Such relative judgments are difficult to disprove. However, Luke hardly represents the Gentiles as monolithically receptive. Paul's experience in Philippi (16.14-24), Athens (17.32-33) and Ephesus (19.23-40) all indicate the potential for Gentile rejection of the gospel.[2] Paul recounts a promise to be delivered both from ὁ λαός and from τὰ ἔθνη as a part of his Damascus Road vision (26.17), implying a hostile response from both. Conversely, Luke's editorial summaries concerning the Gentile mission (Acts 11.24; 16.5) do not include the striking enumeration of converts characteristic of the summaries of the mission among Palestinian Jews (Acts 2.41; 4.4; 5.14-16; 6.1, 7; 9.31; 21.20).[3] Likewise, on certain occasions the positive responses of diaspora Jews and Gentiles appear to be deliberately paralleled (14.1; 18.4; 19.17; cf. 19.10; 20.21).[4] Luke does place Gentile conversions in contrast to Jewish refusal (for example in Acts 13.48), but that contrast is between rejection by *some* Jews and acceptance by *some* Gentiles (for example, Acts 13.43, 50). What appears to be important for Luke is the ironic fact that although the gospel is Jewish in origin, some Jews rejected it while some non-Jews, who were not even understood by many Jews to be the objects of God's saving action, accepted it. He does not, however, characterize all Jews as stubborn and all Gentiles as receptive. The gospel is proclaimed to both, and both are divided in their response to it. But because the gospel is the fulfillment of *Israel's* hope, the receptivity of a segment of the Gentiles contrasts sharply with the refusal of a segment of Jews. Because the contrast is between segments of each group, not the groups as a whole, it cannot suggest a transfer of salvation from Israel as an entity to the Gentiles as an entity.

Furthermore, in Acts 13 Luke indicates in the narrative, not in the statement of Paul, that some Gentiles receive the gospel. Paul's words (13.46; cf. 18.6) express only the fact that salvation is available to the Gentiles, not that they are more receptive to it. Paul contrasts the refusal of salvation by a segment of the Jewish audience with the availability of that same salvation to the Gentiles. That some Gentiles do actually believe is revealed only as the narrative develops. Moreover, salvation is

1. Maddox, *Purpose*, pp. 55-56; cf. Franklin, *Christ the Lord*, pp. 110-11.

2. Eltester, 'Israel', p. 113.

3. These summaries lead Eltester ('Israel', pp. 114-15) to conclude that Luke understands that a sizable minority, if not a majority, of the Jewish people are Christians.

4. Cf. Moessner, *Banquet*, p. 310.

available to the Gentiles because of neither their receptivity nor Jewish refusal but because of the will of God expressed in Scripture (13.47, quoting Isa. 49.6).[1] Such appears also to be the case in Acts 28.28-30. If, as suggested above, αὐτοὶ καὶ ἀκούσονται is best understood as 'they will indeed hear', then the availability of the message of salvation to the Gentiles is the emphasis. Whether some actually accept can only be revealed in the narrative that follows. But the possibility that salvation will be realized among the Gentiles is used by the Lukan Paul as a final goad to conversion for the unbelieving segment of the Jews; hence, it 'must be known' to them that salvation goes to the Gentiles.[2] The use of the Gentiles to provoke Israel's repentance is a common theme in Jewish literature and not necessarily indicative of anti-Judaism, as D.L. Tiede has noted.[3]

Definitive Condemnation. But does the final episode in Acts 28 nevertheless indicate that a definitive judgment has been delivered against the entire Jewish nation? Does this scene mark the end of the epoch of Jewish salvation,[4] or is it another in a series of local 'turnings' which indicate that the rejection of the gospel by some Jews does not interfere with ongoing proclamation to the Gentiles?

Some have suggested that Luke identifies Paul's audience as τοὺς

1.   Cf. the discussions in Moessner, *Banquet*, p. 310; Koet, *Five Studies*, p. 118; and Evans, *Isaiah 6.9-10*, pp. 121-26.

2.   Tannehill ('Rejection by Jews', p. 98) and O'Fearghail ('Israel', p. 35) note that the announcement of v. 28 serves to provoke repentance but wrongly see it as a comparison of Jewish stubbornness to Gentile receptivity. D.L. Tiede suggests that Acts 28.28 alludes to the mission of Israel to be a light to the nations in Isa. 49.6 ('The Exaltation of Jesus and the Restoration of Israel in Acts 1', in G.W.E. Nickelsburg with G.W. MacRae [eds.], *Christians among Jews and Gentiles: Essays in Honor of Krister Stendahl on his Sixty-Fifth Birthday* [Philadelphia: Fortress Press, 1986], p. 285; also in *HTR* 79 [1986], p. 285). The allusion is admittedly vague here, although it is obvious in the parallel context of Acts 13.47. Hence, Paul's Jewish audience must know that Paul will preach to the Gentiles because thereby Israel's vocation as a light to the Gentiles is fulfilled and the claim that the gospel is the realization of the promises to Israel is vindicated. This interpretation is intriguing, but the difficulty of seeing an allusion to Isa. 49.6 in Acts 28.28 suggests that the explanation offered here should be accepted.

3.   Tiede, 'Glory', pp. 30-32. He cites *Jub.* 1.9-17; *4 Ezra* 2.33-35; 4.23; *2 Bar.* 83.5; *T. Sim.* 7.1-2; *T. Levi* 4.3-4.

4.   So, for example, Gnilka, *Verstockung*, pp. 149-50; Maddox, *Purpose*, p. 44.

ὄντας τῶν Ἰουδαίων πρώτους (28.17) so that they serve as representatives of the entire Jewish people.[1] In this way the condemnation of
vv. 26-28 serves as a condemnation of the whole nation. Such a
conclusion stands on little evidence apart from supposition, however.
Similar expressions in Josephus (Ἰουδαίων οἱ δυνατοί, *War* 1.242; οἱ
γνώριμοι τῶν Ἰουδαίων, *War* 2.240, 243) suggest that the phrase is
not exceptional but designates a sort of diplomatic delegation which
meets with visiting dignitaries. At most Luke's point may be that these
represent the Jewish community of Rome in an official capacity. However, the inclusion of this detail may serve no function beyond indicating
the importance with which Paul's arrival is treated by the Roman Jews.
Given Luke's evident interest in distinguishing leaders from people in
the passion narrative, any suggestion that he allows the former to represent the latter here requires more conclusive evidence.

The expression τοὺς πατέρας ὑμῶν (v. 25) could also suggest a
generalized condemnation of the Jews.[2] But the shift from Paul's earlier
terminology, which indicates his solidarity with Israel (ἀδελφοί, τοῖς
ἔθεσι τοῖς πατρῴοις, v. 17; τοῦ ἔθνους μου, v. 19; τῆς ἐλπίδος τοῦ
Ἰσραήλ, v. 20), to this second-person reference probably indicates
Luke's design for this latter expression.[3] Although the shift could conceivably be taken as an implicit renunciation of Paul's Jewishness and
condemnation of the entire nation, another possibility appears to be
more likely. Luke's stress on Paul's faithfulness to Judaism in the trial
narratives does not suggest that he intended for Paul finally to renounce
his Jewish identity. Instead, the point appears to be to identify the unbelieving portion of Paul's audience with those in Israel's past who failed
to heed the message of God through the prophets. 'Your fathers' is thus
a partitive expression, indicating the solidarity of a part of Paul's audience with a part of Israel's history. The implication is that their rejection,

---

1. For example O'Neill, *Theology*, p. 76 n. 1; Hauser, *Apg 28*, pp. 82-83.
Hauser suggests that the Jerusalem leaders represented all Jerusalem in the
crucifixion as indicated by the indictment of the people of Jerusalem in Acts 3.17;
13.27. But the Lukan crucifixion includes an emphasis on popular involvement as
well (Lk. 23.13ff.).

2. So argues Tyson ('Jewish Rejection', p. 129). Cf. the brief discussion in
Jervell, *Unknown Paul*, p. 134; and Brawley, *Luke–Acts and the Jews*, pp. 142-
43. Cf. also Hauser, *Apg 28*, p. 100.

3. Hauser rightly notes that the expression distances Paul from his hearers, but
he does not contrast it with the earlier expressions of solidarity (*Apg 28*, p. 99).

152   *Jewish Responsibility for the Death of Jesus in Luke–Acts*

far from negating the claim that Paul makes to hold to 'the hope of Israel' in the gospel, is in fact consistent with the biblical witness to the unbelief of a portion of Israel in the time of the prophets.[1]

Thus, the expression τοὺς πατέρας ὑμῶν in 28.25 serves to specify the intended application of the quotation of Isa. 6.9-10 in vv. 26-27. This citation, like the earlier excerpt from Hab. 1.5 (13.41) and the allusion to Ezek. 33.4 (18.6),[2] specifies the consequences of rejecting Paul's gospel.[3] Implicit on each occasion is the division of the audience into believing and unbelieving camps. A nonverbal equivalent is found in Acts 13.51, where Paul and Barnabas's shaking the dust from their feet (against the city, not just the synagogue) obviously does not serve as a token of judgment against the believers in Pisidian Antioch, only against the unbelievers. In these cases the warning or condemnation can be logically applied only to those who reject the message.[4] The absolute

---

1.   Similar conclusions likewise apply to the corresponding shift in expression in the Stephen speech (Acts 7.1-53); cf. the discussion above.

2.   Sanders indicates that the 'blood' of Acts 18.6 is either the blood of Jesus (*Jews in Luke–Acts*, pp. xvii, 53), the blood of the prophets (pp. 57-58, 187-88), or the blood of the Jews shed in their own violent judgment (p. 276). The last view appears to be closest to the truth; but in failing to acknowledge the allusion to Ezek. 33, Sanders misconstrues the expression as a condemnation of all Jews. Cf. the similar discussions in Wilson, *Gentiles*, pp. 225-26; Sandmel, *Anti-Semitism*, p. 91; Tannehill, 'Rejection by Jews', p. 90. Esler's view that καθαρός in 18.6 refers to Paul's ceremonial purity despite his moving to a Gentile's house (*Community and Gospel*, p. 100) entirely ignores the allusion to Ezek. 33. Paul's assertion that he is 'innocent of the blood of all' (Acts 20.26), which comes in a context that includes typical stress on Paul's ministry to Jews and Greeks (20.21), indicates that Luke regards the same judgment as falling on both Jews and Gentiles who reject Paul's gospel.

3.   Maddox correctly notes that the quotation in 28.26-27 is longer than any other in Luke–Acts save Acts 2.17-21 (*Purpose*, p. 44). To infer from this detail that Luke intends the quotation to serve as a definitive condemnation of the entire Jewish nation is, however, a non sequitur. It may just as well serve as the definitive condemnation of the unbelieving segment of the nation, as other elements of the text suggest. Sanders similarly asserts that the quotation applied 'this way' must refer to all Jews, though he fails to specify what he means by 'this way' and how it makes the generalized reference clear (*Jews in Luke–Acts*, p. 298).

4.   Dupont observes this in regard to 13.41 ('La conclusion des Actes', p. 384). M. Salmon makes the same observation about Luke's statement of condemnation in general ('Insider or Outsider? Luke's Relationship with Judaism', in Tyson [ed.], *Luke–Acts and the Jewish People*, pp. 80-82).

character of the condemnation is characteristic of prophetic expression; it does not reflect a tendency to ignore Jewish belief in the gospel and paint all Jews with the same judgmental brush.[1]

Likewise, Paul's use of 'this people' (v. 17), 'my nation' (v. 19) and 'the hope of Israel' does not indicate that the entire nation is addressed in condemnation.[2] Such language is typical of all the speeches to Jews in Acts (2.14, 22, 29, 36; 3.12, 17, 23, 25; 4.10; 5.31; 7.1, 11, 12, 15, 19, 38, 39, 45; 13.16, 26; 22.1; 23.1; 26.6-7; cf. 21.28), establishing the speaker's affinity with his Jewish audience and the gospel's continuity with Judaism.

In this case, nothing suggests that Paul's 'turning to the Gentiles' in Rome is different from his earlier 'turnings', both of which were followed by further preaching and conversions among Jews.[3] This understanding explains the reason for the declaration of 28.28. In Pisidian

---

1. Tiede stresses the typically absolute mode of expression for prophetic oracles (*Prophecy and History*, pp. 121-22). Dupont rightly observes that 'Le peuple de Dieu ne se confond pas avec ceux que désigne l'appellation "ce peuple". Il faut en prendre son parti: Luc fait des distinctions que son vocabulaire traduit fort imparfaitement' ('Conclusion', pp. 377-78). This is the very characteristic of Luke's use of λαός observed earlier by Dahl ('People', p. 326) and ignored by Stolle, who bases his view that Acts 28.26-27 condemns the Jews 'auf ihr Volksein' on the use of λαός (*Zeuge*, pp. 84-85). The failure to allow for such flexibility of language is what prompts questions like Hauser's (*Apg 28*, p. 67): 'Wie können alle unter das Urteil der Verstockung fallen, obwohl ein teil der Juden (und nicht nur in Rom) sich der Botschaft geneigt zeigte?' His answer (*Apg 28*, p. 69), that the division of Israel brings about its entire condemnation, neglects the repeated Lukan emphasis on the salvation of the believing segment (e.g. Acts 2.40). Cf. similar remarks in Maddox, *Purpose*, pp. 43, 62 (n. 95); Tannehill, 'Rejection by Jews', pp. 96-97; Cook, 'Mission to the Jews', p. 106; Tyson, 'Jewish Rejection', p. 126.

2. *Contra* Dupont, 'La conclusion des Actes', p. 376.

3. So Brawley, *Luke–Acts and the Jews*, pp. 75-77; Chance, *Jerusalem*, pp. 129-30; and even Hauser, *Apg 28*, pp. 108-109. The view of Haenchen (*Acts*, pp. 417-18, 724; 'Judentum und Christentum', p. 185), followed by O'Neill (*Theology*, pp. 86-87) and Wilson (*Gentiles*, pp. 226-27)—that the three turning episodes indicate that in a geographical schema Paul decisively forsook the Jews for the Gentiles in Asia Minor, Greece and Italy—is contradicted by Paul's return to the synagogue in Asia Minor (14.1; 18.28; 19.8-10). Sanders argues that a cyclical understanding of the turning episodes is incongruous with the intended progression of the narrative reflected in Acts 1.8 (*Jews in Luke–Acts*, pp. 263-64, 299). But a progression 'to the ends of the earth' does not in itself demand a forsaking of the Jewish mission in favor of the Gentile mission.

Antioch and in Corinth, Paul announces that he 'turns' (13.46) or 'will go' (18.6) to the Gentiles. As has already been noted, the subsequent narratives in those cases indicate that Paul's 'turning' or 'going' means giving up the synagogue as his venue and preaching in a setting not distinctly Jewish.[1] This view is confirmed in 18.7, where Paul leaves the synagogue for the house of Titius Justus, and in 19.9, where Paul leaves for the school of Tyrannus in response to Jewish refusal.[2] In these instances, as has been noted, the 'turning to the Gentiles' does not spell the end of the Jewish mission in those cities; Paul still preaches to Jews in the course of his universal ministry, and Jews are still converted. But in Acts 28, the situation is different. Paul is a prisoner; he cannot 'turn' or 'go' anywhere. His audience must come to him, as the Jewish audience already has. Therefore, Luke's lexical choice in Acts 28.28 is limited by the setting of the statement. The first part of Paul's declaration, τοῖς ἔθνεσιν ἀπεστάλη τὸ σωτήριον τοῦ θεοῦ, is the equivalent of quotation of Isa. 49.6 in Acts 13.47: it expresses the divine will to save the Gentiles. The second part, αὐτοὶ καὶ ἀκούσονται, expresses Paul's determination to preach to the Gentiles despite the refusal of his Jewish audience. It is the equivalent of the earlier statements ἰδοὺ στρεφόμεθα εἰς τὰ ἔθνη (13.46) and ἀπὸ τοῦ νῦν εἰς τὰ ἔθνη πορεύσομαι (18.6), offered now from the lips of a prisoner under house arrest. Verse 30 then corresponds to 18.8 and 19.10: it indicates the success of Paul's preaching among 'all', that is, both Jews and Gentiles.[3] Luke's πᾶς elsewhere in such expressions indicates the

---

1. Rightly observed by Tannehill ('Rejection by Jews', pp. 89-91). Cf. the conclusion of Esler that Luke depicts Paul's ministry in this way because the Lukan community is composed of Jews and Gentiles but is institutionally separated from the synagogue (*Community and Gospel*, pp. 45, 55-58). Previous to Esler, P. Grech had suggested that the best explanation of Luke's extensive justification of the Gentile mission is that a considerable Jewish-Christian contingent was at least in contact with, if not a part of, his community ('Jewish Christianity and the Purpose of Acts', *SE* 7 [= TU 26 (1982)], pp. 224-46).

2. Cf. Esler who sees in these texts Paul's establishing of table fellowship between Jews and Gentiles (*Community and Gospel*, pp. 40-41). Although the idea of table fellowship is probably less clear in the text than Esler makes it out to be, he rightly notes the Lukan emphasis on ongoing mission to Jews after the 'turning to the Gentiles'.

3. Dupont, 'La conclusion des Actes', pp. 377-78, 386. As a consequence he notes that the Western insertion in v. 30 is 'maladroite' but appears to represent the true intention of Luke. Moessner suggests that the imperfect ἀπεδέχετο implies that

propagation of the gospel to Jews and Gentiles without discrimination (Acts 17.30; 19.17; 20.26 [cf. 20.21]; 22.15 [cf. 9.15; 26.17, 23]); in Ephesus it appears *after* Paul has left the synagogue (19.10).[1] The narrative thus ends not with Jewish rejection and condemnation but with the free dissemination of the gospel despite Paul's imprisonment and the rejection by part of the Jewish community.[2]

Paul's Trial Defense

The views of Tyson, Sanders and Tannehill about Luke's narrative structure all imply a shift in orientation from Jews to Gentiles which is fully realized at the end of the narrative. The analysis above of the closing scene of Acts has demonstrated that such a shift is not in evidence there. But it might well be argued that other material near the end of Acts indicates such a reorientation. From Acts 21 onwards Paul is con-

---

Paul continued to receive Jews without interruption or cessation after the events previously narrated (*Banquet*, p. 311).

1. Löning notes that in Acts 22.15 Paul is God's witness to πάντας ἀνθρώπους, whereas the twelve are witnesses to τὸν λαόν (*Saulustradition*, p. 142). In this light, it is interesting to consider Luke's preoccupation with Paul's work among Jews. It suggests that in Luke's view a call to preach to πάντας ἀνθρώπους includes Jews as well as Gentiles. Because it is unlikely that Luke regarded Paul's call as having been revoked or changed in its essential object at the end of Acts, the conclusion follows that Luke's Paul continued to preach to Jews as well as Gentiles (cf. Tannehill, 'Rejection by Jews', p. 96, who comes to similar conclusions because in Acts 20.18-35 Paul is presented as a model for the church to follow, witnessing to Jews and Greeks, v. 21). Löning misses this implication; he insists that the turning to the Gentiles is necessarily the forsaking of the Jews and that Acts 28.28 marks the end of missionary efforts among the Jews (*Saulustradition*, pp. 160-61, 193).

2. F. Bovon suggests that the last clause of v. 27, expressed in the future indicative, indicates Luke's expectation that the Jews will accept the gospel in the end ('"Schön hat der heilige Geist durch den Propheten Jesaja zu euren Vätern gesprochen" [Apg 28.25]', *ZNW* 75 [1984], pp. 229-30). However, not only does Luke merely follow the LXX at this point, but the future indicative in such final clauses is not an uncommon way to indicate a further consequence (cf. BDF § 369 [3]). Furthermore, Bovon's suggestion assumes that Luke levels the condemnation of Isa. 6.9-10 against the entire nation, an assumption which is, of course, contradicted by the evidence cited above. A. Vanhoye offers the more accurate observation that the quotation of Isaiah offers an explanation of Israel's divided response to the gospel: this paradoxical situation is entirely conformed to the words of the prophets ('Les juifs selon les Actes des Apôtres et les Epîtres du Nouveau Testament', *Bib* 72 [1991], p. 77).

fronted by Jewish accusers. Indeed, all the Jews who appear in these chapters are opponents of Paul, or so it seems.[1] Does this indicate that Luke regards Judaism as monolithically opposed to Christianity?

Juxtaposed to the Jewish opposition of Acts 21–28 is the repeated insistence, both in narrative and in discourse, that the Christian Paul is a faithful Jew. Indeed, Paul's faithfulness to Judaism is a thread which runs throughout the final chapters of Acts.[2] The variety of means by which Paul's Jewish fidelity is presented and the frequency with which it appears suggests that Luke has deliberately emphasized it in the narrative.[3]

Paul's imprisonment is, of course, precipitated by his entering the temple to complete a vow (21.26-27). He takes this step specifically to demonstrate his Jewish fidelity against false charges that he seeks to undermine the law (21.20-24).[4] These charges become the basis for the chapters that follow. Whatever specific charges Paul faces, all relate to his faithfulness to the law in general. Hence, even though Paul's speeches may superficially appear not to address the immediate charges leveled against him, they all address this larger issue which stands behind

---

1.   Paul's nephew (Acts 23.16) might be an exception. His Jewishness is not stressed, but neither is it denied: his use of οἱ Ἰουδαῖοι (23.20) is consistent with his speaking as a Jew to the Roman centurion.

2.   Cf. the remarks of E. Trocmé, 'The Jews as Seen by Paul and Luke', in J. Neusner and E.S. Frerichs (eds.), *'To See Ourselves as Others See Us': Christians, Jews, 'Others' in Late Antiquity* (Chico, CA: Scholars Press, 1985), p. 146; of F.F. Bruce, 'Paul's Apologetic and the Purpose of Acts', *BJRL* 69 (1986–87), p. 389; of Moessner, *Banquet*, p. 309; and of J.A. Fitzmyer, *Luke the Theologian: Aspects of his Teaching* (London: Chapman, 1989), pp. 185-86. Harnack not only noted this important theme but argued for its essential historicity (*Acts*, pp. 235-38).

3.   Tiede perceptively notes that although Paul appears before Roman judges, Luke makes no attempt to present the charges against Paul in terms that interest the Romans but stresses that the charges against Paul concern his Jewishness ('Restoration of Israel', pp. 281-82).

4.   O'Neill offers the imaginative suggestion that Paul is apprehended just before he completes the vow so that Luke can represent him as faithful to the law while at the same time God drives Paul and other Jewish Christians away from legal observance and toward the Gentiles (*Theology*, p. 81). One difficulty with this view is that it requires Paul's persecutors to be unwitting agents of the divine will. But Luke does not offer any direct indication that such is his view; if anything, he stresses that Paul's opponents are disobedient to the divine will.

the specific charges: whether Paul the Christian is still a faithful Jew.[1]

As the scene is set for Paul's taking the vow, Luke reiterates the terms of the apostolic decree on the lips of James (21.25). The repetition comes not because Luke has forgotten Paul's presence at the conference of Acts 15 but because the decree stresses the unity of Gentiles and legally observant Jews in the church.[2] Paul's acceptance of the decree and of James's advice concerning the vow demonstrate his commitment to legal observance within the context of Christian universalism. It thereby demonstrates the falsehood of the charge that Paul has abandoned his Jewish heritage and taught others to do the same.[3]

After the disturbance in the temple begins, Paul's first words are an emphatic affirmation of his Jewishness (ἐγὼ ἄνθρωπος μέν εἰμι Ἰουδαῖος, 21.39). He speaks to the crowd τῇ Ἑβραΐδι διαλέκτῳ (21.40), a point which Luke repeats verbatim as he notes the effect on the crowd (22.2). Paul addresses the crowd in familial terms (ἄνδρες ἀδελφοὶ καὶ πατέρες, 22.1; cf. 22.5; 23.1, 6; 28.17). Again he emphatically affirms his Jewishness (ἐγώ εἰμι ἀνὴρ Ἰουδαῖος, 22.3a),[4]

---

1. Stolle asserts that the speech of Acts 22 does not directly address the charge of temple profanation but does establish that Paul is a faithful Jew who, by implication, would never profane the temple (*Zeuge*, p. 110; *contra* Löning, *Saulustradition*, p. 173-75, 181).

2. Stolle, *Zeuge*, p. 79.

3. Bruce suggests that the closing of the temple doors in Acts 21.30 signals the final doom of the temple ('Church of Jerusalem', pp. 647-48, 659). Chance suggests that it parallels the rending of the temple veil at the death of Jesus (Lk. 23.45b; *Jerusalem*, pp. 121-22). Although there is no verbal similarity between the two texts (for instance, Lk. 23.45b uses ναός; Acts 21.30 uses ἱερόν), a parallel is still possible. Chance also offers parallels in Josephus and the Babylonian Talmud, though he himself admits that they are remote. This explanation is intriguing, explaining as it does an otherwise enigmatic statement. But because little can be found to corroborate it, this interpretation cannot be deemed conclusive. In either case, however, it does not affect the point argued here: that for Luke, Paul was faithful to Judaism, demonstrating as much in completing a vow in the temple.

4. A chiasmus appears in 21.39–22.3:

A:	ἐγὼ ἄνθρωπος μέν εἰμι Ἰουδαῖος, 21.39
B:	τῇ Ἑβραΐδι διαλέκτῳ, 21.40
C:	ἄνδρες ἀδελφοὶ καὶ πατέρες, 22.1
B':	τῇ Ἑβραΐδι διαλέκτῳ, 22.2
A':	ἐγώ εἰμι ἀνὴρ Ἰουδαῖος, 22.3a

Whether the structure is deliberate or accidental is difficult to determine. If it was deliberate, it evinces a conscious emphasis on Paul's Jewishness. If not, the very adding to the earlier assertion that he was reared in Jerusalem and trained in the law under a distinguished teacher (22.3c-d).[1] He is, in fact, a ζηλωτὴς...τοῦ θεοῦ, just like his opponents (22.3e; cf. 21.20).[2] Although these declarations might be understood to apply only to Paul's life before his conversion, the fact that they are expressed in the present (εἰμι, ὑπάρχων) and perfect (ἀνατεθραμμένος, πεπαιδευμένος) tenses, in contrast to the aorist (ἐδίωξα, 22.4) and imperfect (ἐπορευόμην, 22.5) used in the recounting of Paul's persecution of the church, clearly indicates that for Luke Paul is still a Jew.[3]

Paul's first defense speech also indicates that Luke does not regard Paul's 'conversion' as in any way a departure from Judaism. Ananias, who baptizes Paul, is legally scrupulous and respected by the Damascene Jews (22.12; diff. Acts 9.10).[4] Furthermore, in his address to Paul Ananias begins by affirming that Paul's commission comes from ὁ θεὸς τῶν πατέρων ἡμῶν (22.14; diff. 9.17). Having become a Christian, Paul continues to pray in the Jerusalem temple, where he receives yet another divine message (22.17).[5] The content of this second message stresses Paul's relationship to Gentiles, the very issue which has led to his apprehension. Paul the faithful Jew is thus brought into the Christian community through a faithful Jewish intermediary and at the command of the God worshiped by the Jews. His missionary work among the Gentiles is

repetition of ideas also suggests as much, though perhaps not so decisively. Stolle also finds a chiasmus in 22.3 with παρὰ τοὺς πόδας Γαμαλιὴλ πεπαιδευμένος as the middle term (*Zeuge*, pp. 104-105).

1.   Stolle notes that the implication of Paul's earlier life in Jerusalem is that he was familiar with the temple and its regulations and would not have violated them (*Zeuge*, pp. 106-106). R.F. O'Toole notes that the charge of profaning the temple is also implicitly answered in 21.28-29: the Asian Jews were mistaken about Paul's having taken Trophimus into the temple (*Acts 26: The Christological Climax of Paul's Defense [Ac 22.1–26.32]* [AnBib, 78; Rome: Biblical Institute Press, 1978], p. 39).

2.   This expression may be intended to contrast with ζηλωταὶ τοῦ νόμου in Acts 21.20. If so, the distinction can only be a subtle one. The fact that Paul in the speech following 22.3 stresses his obedience to the divine voice as opposed to the law as such probably explains the difference. Stolle rightly notes that the expression also encompasses Paul's life before and after his conversion (*Zeuge*, pp. 105-106).

3.   Cf. the observation of Stolle, *Zeuge*, p. 104.

4.   F. Veltman, 'The Defense Speeches of Paul in Acts', in C.H. Talbert (ed.), *Perspectives on Luke–Acts* (Edinburgh: T. & T. Clark, 1978), pp. 253-54.

5.   Veltman, 'Defense Speeches', pp. 253-54.

also the result of a divine message.[1] His life as a Christian—even as a missionary to Gentiles—is therefore entirely consistent with his fidelity to Judaism.[2] Indeed, if Paul had not become a Christian, thereby disobeying the direct call of the God of Israel, only then would he have been unfaithful as a Jew (cf. 26.19).

The content of Paul's temple vision in Acts 22.18-21 proves offensive to his Jewish audience: in the temple itself he is called to go to the Gentiles. But does Luke intend this material to be understood as deliberately provocative? Has the speech, as Löning asserts, gone from a self-defense to a missionary speech to a harsh accusation?[3] That appears unlikely. Instead, Luke emphasizes that Paul's call to go to the Gentiles is received in the temple to show its essential compatibility with Paul's Jewish fidelity. Elsewhere he has stressed the fulfillment of Israel's vocation as a light to the Gentiles in Paul's missionary work (Acts 13.47; cf. 3.25; Lk. 2.32). Although it has the opposite effect, Paul's appeal to the temple vision is intended to persuade his audience that his association with Gentiles is consistent with his Jewish piety.[4]

---

1. O'Neill asserts that the claim of Paul to have been called to preach to the Gentiles is inconsistent with Luke's emphasis on his work among the Jews (*Theology*, p. 120). But Luke allows for Paul's work among both; the stress on the Gentiles in 22.21 stems from the charge of 21.29. Koet rightly observes that because Luke regards the Gentile mission as fulfillment of the law, only those Jews who support the Gentile mission are truly obedient to the law (*Five Studies*, pp. 92-94).

2. Stolle expresses the point aptly (*Zeuge*, p. 107): 'Die Zugehörigkeit zur Gemeinde bestimmt das Leben des Paulus nun ebenso wie seine Zugehörigkeit zum Judentum. Das Christsein tritt neben das Judesein, aus dem die Verfolgertätigkeit jedoch inzwischen grundsätzlich ausgeschlossen ist.' K. Stendahl stresses that Paul in his epistles does not indicate that he regarded the Damascus road experience as a conversion from Judaism to something else (*Paul among Jews and Gentiles* [Philadelphia: Fortress Press, 1976]). Luke's presentation of Paul's conversion indicates that he shares Paul's perspective on this aspect of it. Hence, Löning is wrong when he asserts that Paul's persecution of Christians indicates that for Luke the persecution of Christians is typical of the Jews (*Saulustradition*, pp. 118-20, 172-76). Only a segment of the Jews—not even all those who are not believers (Acts 2.47; 5.13, 26)—persecute Christians in Luke's view.

3. Löning, *Saulustradition*, p. 176.

4. Although Esler is correct that Paul's association with Gentiles would have been regarded as a violation of the law by some Jews (*Community and Gospel*, p. 128), it is not entirely clear that such behavior would have been so perceived by all—or even most—of Paul's Jewish contemporaries. Due weight must be given to the diversity of Jewish opinion and practice in the pre-Tannaitic period.

Paul's Jewish fidelity is again the emphasis in his appearance before the Sanhedrin. Again addressing his audience in familial terms (ἄνδρες ἀδελφοί), he asserts that he has served God with a good conscience ἄχρι ταύτης τῆς ἡμέρας (23.1). Once more the indication is that Paul's life as a Christian is consistent with his life as a Jew. Whatever the historical likelihood of his exchange with the high priest, Paul's knowledge and observance of the law—and his opponents' violation of the law—are stressed by it. He appeals to the law in his reproof after being struck (23.3c) and subsequently corrects his own action with a reference to the law (23.5c). Introduced with another familial address (ἄνδρες ἀδελφοί), his assertion of his Pharisaism and hope for the resurrection provide the basis for much of the defense of the following chapters (23.6; cf. 24.14-15, 21; 26.6-8). The resurrection of Jesus, presented in the early chapters of Acts as Jesus' vindication in the face of the opposition of the leaders of Jerusalem, now vindicates Paul as a faithful Jew. It fulfills the common hope of Israel, exemplified in the faith of the 'best party' of Judaism (cf. 26.5). Thus, those who oppose Paul are by implication in violation of the hope of Israel, just as the high priest violates the law by ordering that Paul be struck (23.3). The Pharisees' pronouncement of Paul's innocence (23.9), inadequate in Luke's view, nevertheless gives further testimony to the truth of Paul's claims. From this exchange Claudius Lysias concludes that the case against Paul is entirely a Jewish legal matter (23.29).

Before Felix Paul again asserts his Jewish fidelity. It is again the God of the fathers whom Paul serves, in keeping with the law and the prophets (24.14). His hope in the resurrection, for which he says he is on trial, in fact establishes his fidelity to Judaism (24.15). Moreover, this intimate connection between Paul's belief in 'all that is written in the law and the prophets' and the fulfillment of Israel's hope in the resurrection implies what Luke states explicitly elsewhere: Jesus' resurrection is the fulfillment of 'all' of the Jewish Scriptures (Lk. 24.25-26; Acts 3.18ff.; 26.22-23). Paul's Jewish fidelity is therefore demonstrated in his Christian belief. That fidelity is demonstrated in his purpose in coming to Jerusalem: far from intending to profane the temple, Paul came to bring alms for his people (24.17-18a). His opponents, misunderstanding his purpose, created the disturbance which led to his apprehension (24.18b-19). Hence, only his belief in the resurrection can be at issue; he is manifestly innocent of the specific charges brought against him (24.20-21).

Only the indecision and corruption of Felix prevent Paul's release (24.22-26).

Before Festus the narrator indicates that the charges against Paul cannot be proved (25.7). Paul himself again declares that he has not broken the law or violated the temple (25.8). His innocence is well known to Festus; Paul fears only the mendacity of his accusers (25.9-10). Therefore, he can appeal to Caesar in complete confidence of his vindication (25.11). Festus is depicted as grasping the essence of Paul's situation: he indicates, in language appropriate for a Gentile unbeliever, that Paul's case has to do with his unbelief in the resurrection of Jesus, a matter of Jewish doctrine (25.19).

This explanation of Paul's case serves as the backdrop for his speech before Agrippa.[1] Paul repeats once more his life-long devotion to the chief elements of Judaism (26.4-5). The congruence of his belief in the resurrection with Jewish faith is stressed with a series of expressions: it is a promise made to the fathers by God (26.6), the object of hope for all the twelve tribes throughout their constant service (26.7). Indeed, Paul's entire gospel is congruent with the law and the prophets (26.22). Hence, the charge that Paul is unfaithful to Moses (21.21), the law (21.28; 23.29; 25.8), circumcision (21.21), Jewish customs (21.21; 28.17), or the Jewish people (21.28) is refuted by his steadfast belief in the resurrection, the fulfillment of Israel's biblical hope (26.22-23).[2] Moreover, his association with Gentiles is consistent with his Jewish piety: it is the response to a divine vision (26.19) and is matched by his work among his own people (26.17, 20; cf. v. 23). Thus, it is sharply ironic that Paul is accused by Jewish brothers because of his very faithfulness to their common Jewish heritage (26.7). Löning and O'Toole note that the response of Agrippa is crucial for Luke: he is both competent, being familiar with the Jewish law (26.2-3, 26-27), and objective, not associated with Paul's accusers.[3] That response is short of the one Paul desires (26.28-29), but

---

1.   O'Toole argues that Luke deliberately omitted the charges from the speech because he addresses the reader, who knows that the charges have already been refuted (*Christological Climax*, pp. 19, 37-39). However, the more general issue of Paul's Jewish fidelity is still in view and is Luke's primary concern from the point of Paul's arrival in Jerusalem. As O'Toole notes, the 'specific' charges made against Paul, except for profanation of the temple, are hardly specific at all (*Christological Climax*, pp. 38-39).

2.   Cf. O'Toole, *Christological Climax*, p. 39.

3.   Löning, *Saulustradition*, p. 177; O'Toole, *Christological Climax*, pp. 136-37.

it nevertheless affirms Paul's innocence (26.31-32). Thus, 'Any conscientious Jew who knows his Scriptures, customs, and controversies will take Christianity seriously. It is not "madness" but what the prophets spoke about in their writings.'[1]

The same affirmations are stressed in the final scene in Rome. Again using familial address (ἄνδρες ἀδελφοί), Paul claims complete innocence before the people and the customs of the fathers (28.17).[2] His imprisonment stems not from his infidelity to Judaism but from his steadfast adherence to Israel's hope (28.20). His appeal is based on Moses and the prophets (28.23).

These elements of the text urge two conclusions relevant to the questions addressed here. One is that Luke makes no attempt to represent all Jews as opposed to Christianity at the end of his narrative. Instead, his repeated insistence on Paul's faithfulness to Judaism indicates a deliberate contrast with the accusations of his opponents. Paul the Christian is still and always the Jew. The Jews as a nation are not opposed to the gospel; instead they are divided between those who, like Paul, believe and those who, like his opponents, do not.[3]

Why, then, do other Jewish Christians disappear from the closing chapters of Acts? Does Luke deliberately suppress them in order to suggest monolithic Jewish opposition? Has the Jerusalem church lost its relevance, as Tyson suggests?[4] Is Paul the last of the Jewish Christians for Luke? Such suggestions appear unlikely. The remark of Acts 21.20 is entirely incongruous if such is the case. The absence of other Jewish Christians in the narrative is more likely explained on one or both of two counts. First of all, the unrelenting focus of these final chapters is on Paul. The setting changes, the opponents change, the judges change, but the defendant Paul is ever in view. Secondly, F.F. Bruce has recently offered a historical reconstruction which may explain the absence of Jewish Christian support for Paul at the end of the narrative. He

---

1. O'Toole, *Christological Climax*, p. 145.
2. Wilson has demonstrated that Luke's use of ἔθος for the Torah is consistent with the usage of Josephus and Philo in presenting the law to a Hellenistic audience (*Law*, pp. 7-11). It therefore does not indicate a loss of status or disparagement of the law, *contra* George, 'Israël', pp. 516-19. Wilson's observations are also consistent with the conclusions reached above concerning Ἰουδαῖος.
3. In Rom. 11.1 Paul likewise presents himself as an example of a Jew who believes the gospel in contrast to those who do not.
4. Tyson, 'Jewish Rejection', pp. 136-37.

suggests that the Jewish-Christian church of Jerusalem was under pressure to distance itself from Paul because of his activity among the Gentiles. The church's good relations with the non-Christian populace of Jerusalem had been maintained under the leadership of James, who had no direct involvement with the Gentile mission, unlike Peter. James had suggested that Paul take the vow in the temple to satisfy Jerusalem of his legal fidelity, but the result of that plan was the disaster narrated by Luke. As a result, the Jerusalem church was unable to associate itself with Paul without falling under the same violent threat.[1] Luke may or may not have been aware of such circumstances, but the absence in the narrative of support for Paul from the Jerusalem church may simply reflect its absence in his sources, absence which may betoken events like those that Bruce proposes. Furthermore, Jewish Christians have not necessarily disappeared from the narrative. Paul meets with Italian Christians on his way to Rome (28.13-15), and Luke has indicated earlier that Italian believers have Jews among their numbers (18.2). Luke does not state explicitly that these believers are Jewish, but neither does he deny it. Whether they were Jews or Gentiles is apparently not of interest to him. And that lack of interest itself suggests that Luke does not consciously suppress evidence of Jewish Christianity at the end of Acts.[2] Thus, contrary to the view of Tyson, the end of Acts gives no evidence that the Jews as a nation have finally and entirely rejected the gospel.

The cumulative force of this evidence is particularly difficult to square with Sanders's thesis. He insists that the discourses of Luke–Acts are uniformly hostile to Judaism, while the narrative only becomes so at the end. Yet here in the closing section of Acts is found a consistent, ringing affirmation of Paul's Jewish fidelity, largely included in the speeches.[3]

1. Bruce, 'Paul's Apologetic', pp. 385-86.
2. It is possible that Luke regards all Jewish Christians as having left Rome, never to return, because of the edict of Claudius. However, that view is most unlikely in light of the presence of non-Christian Jews in Rome (28.17).
3. The data likewise contradict Sanders's assertion that for Luke Paul is not a Jewish Christian because he does not associate himself with the Jerusalem elders who are 'zealots of the Law' (*Jews in Luke–Acts*, pp. 283-84). But in fact Paul does submit without protest to James's instructions concerning the vow. He does not do so merely in response to overwhelming pressure from Jerusalem (as Tyson, 'Jewish Rejection', pp. 134-36, suggests with Sanders); Luke indicates that Paul has taken a similar vow before (Acts 18.18; cf. 1 Cor. 9.20). The repeated stress on Paul's *ongoing* faithfulness to Judaism is difficult to square with any conclusion

Moreover, Tannehill's position appears to be inconsistent with this material. His proposal that the promises to Israel go unfulfilled at the end of the narrative is difficult to square with Paul's repeated affirmation that his own hope—fulfilled in the resurrection of Jesus—is taken from Scripture and held in common by the Jewish people.[1] It is particularly important that what is first identified as ἐλπὶς ἀναστάσεως νεκρῶν (Acts 23.6) is later named as ἐλπὶς...εἰς θεόν (24.15), ἐλπὶς τῆς εἰς τοὺς πατέρας ἡμῶν ἐπαγγελίας γενομένης ὑπὸ τοῦ θεοῦ (26.6), and finally simply as ἐλπὶς τοῦ Ἰσραήλ (28.20). This hope is held by the Pharisees (23.7), Paul's accusers (24.15), and all twelve tribes of Israel (26.7). This language hardly suggests that Israel's promises have gone unfulfilled. Rather, Israel's hope of redemption is firmly located in the resurrection, already realized in part in the resurrection of Jesus. Thus, the promises to Israel set forth in the infancy narrative find their fulfillment in the salvation at work among the people of Israel who believe the gospel.

For Luke, the fact that many of the Jews do not accept the gospel does not indicate that the promise to Israel goes unfulfilled. As has been repeatedly indicated in the preceding discussion, Luke regards Israel's division in response to the gospel to be in complete accord with the promises to Israel. It is first of all consistent with the Scriptures which establish Israel's hope (Acts 3.23; 7.39-43; 13.40-41; 18.6; 28.26-27). Moreover, the prophecies of Israel's salvation associated with Jesus' birth, so important in setting forth the fulfillment of Israel's hope as a key Lukan concern, speak of the division of Israel in the same breath as the redemption of Israel (Lk. 2.28-35).[2] Jesus' teaching about the arrival of the kingdom of God also indicates the division of Israel (Lk. 8.4-15). Furthermore, the divided response of Israel does not frustrate the fulfillment of Israel's divine vocation to be a light to the Gentiles (cf. Acts 3.25). That vocation is fulfilled through Jewish Christians like Paul who preach to the Gentiles despite the unbelief and opposition of their Jewish compatriots (Acts 13.44-52; 15.16-18). For Luke, the hope of Israel is fulfilled in the gospel and its reception by some Jews; the fact

---

other than that Luke regarded him as a 'Jewish Christian'.

    1. Tannehill has noted this fact himself ('Rejection by Jews', pp. 94-95).
    2. Cf. Johnson, *Possessions*, pp. 89-90; Esler, *Community and Gospel*, pp. 113-14; Tiede, 'Glory', pp. 25-29; Chance, *Jerusalem*, pp. 55-56.

that Israel is divided in its response to that gospel comes as no surprise to those familiar with the Scriptures.[1]

Conclusions and Implications

The previous analysis of key Lukan texts indicates that crucial elements of the narrative do not signal that Israel as a whole rejects Jesus and the gospel. Instead, another idea emerges: Luke sees Israel divided into believing and unbelieving portions.[2] Many respond to Jesus and the gospel with genuine faith. For these the promises made to the fathers are fulfilled. Others respond with hostility. In a manner consistent with Scripture, they are excluded from the promises and cut off from the people (Acts 3.23).

Correspondingly there is no 'blanket condemnation' of the Jews in these portions of Luke–Acts. Those phrases which could suggest it bear some affinity to the absolute language employed by the Hebrew prophets. At key points details of the text indicate that the author understood such expressions of judgment to apply only to the unbelieving portion of the nation. Furthermore, nowhere in these texts does Luke indicate that because of the rejection of some, the gospel is unavailable to all.

Likewise, Luke does not indicate a failure of the promises to Israel. At the end of the narrative the promises are intact. Although they are

1. It is this observation that weighs decisively against the position of Tyson that Luke views Jews as a whole in one way and individual Jews in another ('Jewish Rejection', pp. 126-27). From every perspective, Luke views Israel as divided; in this sense he has no view of the Jews as a whole. The pervasiveness of Luke's view of Israel divided is stressed by J. Schreiber, who notes that the appearance of Joseph of Arimathea, which Luke glosses as a 'city of the Jews' (Lk. 23.51), stresses division even within the Sanhedrin ('Die Bestattung Jesu: Redaktionsgeschichtliche Beobachtungen zu Mk 15.42-47 par', *ZNW* 72 [1981], pp. 141-77). Likewise, Tannehill is incorrect when he says that the tension between the promises to Israel and Israel's rejection of the gospel is never resolved in Acts ('Rejection by Jews', p. 88); Luke finds the resolution in the scriptural witness to the division of Israel.

2. On division of Israel in Luke–Acts, in addition to those cited at relevant points above, see Lohfink, *Sammlung*, p. 62; Jervell, *People of God*, pp. 41-49; Johnson, *Possessions*, pp. 121-22; Hare, 'Rejection', pp. 36-38; Talbert, 'Martyrdom', pp. 100-101; Lowe, 'Anti-Jewish Elements', p. 270; Tiede, 'Restoration of Israel', p. 283; Trocmé, 'The Jews', pp. 157-60; O'Fearghail, 'Israel', pp. 27-34; Chance, *Jerusalem*, p. 71; and Fitzmyer, *Luke the Theologian*, pp. 189-91.

understood by Luke in a distinctly Christian sense, he gives no hint of discontinuity with the original heritage of Israel. Nor does he see the rejection of the Christian gospel by a segment of Judaism as inconsistent with those promises. Israel's history, in Luke's view, has always been characterized by a division between the faithful and the unfaithful. The promises are realized only for the former, but such a limitation was always the intention of God as expressed in Scripture (Acts 3.22-24).[1]

The absence of Israel's definitive rejection of the gospel, of blanket condemnation of Israel, and of a final turning of the Christian mission from the Jews to the Gentiles suggests another important conclusion. The so-called epochal scheme of Luke, in which a period of Jewish salvation is followed by a period of Gentile salvation, appears to be groundless in the narrative of Acts. Although the periods of both Jewish salvation and Gentile salvation have beginnings, they overlap each other, and neither appears to end. This observation indicates that those exegetes are correct who see in Lk. 21.24 an indication not that salvation passes for a period from Jews to Gentiles but that Jerusalem will be controlled by Gentiles instead of Jews.[2] Without the development of distinct salvation-historical epochs for Jews and Gentiles in Acts, nothing in the text indicates that in Lk. 21.24 the subject matter has shifted from the destruction of Jerusalem.

These conclusions from the pivotal sections of the narrative likewise indicate that other texts probably are not intended as condemnations of Israel entire. The absence elsewhere of a clear condemnation of all Israel suggests that the parable of the fig tree (Lk. 13.6-9) does not identify the

---

1. Cf. D.P. Moessner, 'The Ironic Fulfillment of Israel's Glory', in Tyson (ed.), *Luke–Acts and the Jewish People*, pp. 47-48. This is the answer to the observation of Hauser that the disunity of the Jews contrasts with the unity of the biblical witness to Jesus (*Apg 28*, pp. 67-68): the Scriptures anticipate such a division in Israel.

2. For example Gnilka, *Verstockung*, p. 140; Giblin, *Destruction*, pp. 90-91; Brawley, *Luke–Acts and the Jews*, pp. 125-26, 132 (who notes that the end of the period of Gentile domination implies a restoration of mercy); Sanders, *Jews in Luke–Acts*, pp. 218-29; Chance, *Jerusalem*, pp. 134-35; *contra* O'Neill, *Theology*, p. 87 n. 1 (who nevertheless sees in Luke a softening of the emphasis on Israel's return); Keck, *Öffentliche Abschiedsrede*, pp. 224-31; I.H. Marshall, *Luke: Historian and Theologian* (Grand Rapids: Zondervan, 1978), p. 187; *idem*, *Gospel of Luke*, pp. 773-74; Maddox, *Purpose*, p. 120. Tiede observes that Luke's apparent omission of Mk 13.10 suggests that he had no particular interest in the salvation of the Gentiles in this context (*Prophecy and History*, pp. 92-93).

nation of Israel with the unfruitful tree.[1] Because 'Israel' as an entity is not subsequently rejected, although many are excluded from it because of their unbelief (Acts 3.23), the parable would more likely address the judgment which falls on such unbelievers. Furthermore, the emphasis of the immediate context on repentance (13.1-5) and entry through the narrow door (vv. 24ff.) implies not a national but an individual application: those who repent and bear fruit will escape destruction; those who do not will suffer it.[2]

Similarly, if elsewhere Luke does not insinuate that all Jews reject the gospel or that the mission turns to the Gentiles primarily as a result of Jewish rejection, then little remains to commend the view of the parable of the banquet (Lk. 14.16-24) which understands those who refuse the invitation as the Jews and those who receive it as the Gentiles.[3] At most, one could argue that those who reject are the recalcitrant of Israel and that the two accepting groups are the repentant Jews and Gentiles respectively. But the entire allegorical interpretation appears to be ill-founded.[4] The contrast between those who accept and those who reject, consistent with Luke's emphasis on division elsewhere, may well be the emphasis of the repeated invitation and the coming of two different groups.

Similarly, the rebellious people of the parable of the pounds (Lk. 19.14, 27) can hardly be identified with the Jews as a whole.[5] Instead, their presence appears to provide additional contrast with the two faithful servants.[6] The elaborate allegory necessary to support the

1. *Contra* Sanders, *Jews in Luke–Acts*, p. 189; cf. Hare, 'Rejection', p. 37.

2. Johnson notes that in the travel narrative Jesus' mode of address to the crowds differs from that to his opponents (*Possessions*, pp. 107-109). The former receive warnings and calls to repentance, as in 12.54–13.30; the latter are attacked, condemned and rejected (cf. 13.31–14.24). The disciples form a third group and are given 'essentially a positive catechesis'. This juxtaposition of material serves to underline the division in Israel provoked by Jesus and the gospel: 'Those who are going to reject are rejecting, those who are going to convert are being called; those who are following are being instructed' (*Possessions*, p. 112).

3. For example Sanders, *Jews in Luke–Acts*, pp. 58-60, 135-36.

4. Evans notes the difficulty of allegorizing the parable to indicate rejection of the Jews and acceptance of the Gentiles because of the three groups to whom the invitation is extended ('Luke's View', pp. 31-32).

5. Egelkraut, *Mission to Jerusalem*, pp. 188-89; Sanders, 'Parable of the Pounds', pp. 660-68; *idem*, *Jews in Luke–Acts*, pp. 61-62, 208.

6. Cf. Brawley, *Luke–Acts and the Jews*, pp. 147-48. He follows Eltester

anti-Jewish view of the parable is not supported by the subsequent development of the narrative.[1]

The condemnation of the Galilean cities (Lk. 10.13-15) provides another case in point. These sayings are taken by some as an indication that Luke condemns the Jews with little regard for that segment that responds favorably.[2] But the context of the sayings preserves the framework of division; it anticipates that the messengers will meet both acceptance and rejection (vv. 5-12, 16). This suggests that Luke intends the words of condemnation not to apply to the Galileans indiscriminately but to indicate, in contrast to the earlier notes of success in Galilee, the reality of rejection by some in Galilee and the consequences for those who reject.[3] Thus, even if the opportunity for Galilee to repent is past, the positive response of some in Galilee, suggested earlier in the narrative (4.14, 23, 36-37, 42; 5.1, 15, 26; 7.11, 29; 8.1-3, 4, 8; 9.11, 37, 43) is not thereby denied.

Another implication is that while Luke understands Jerusalem's leaders to have authority over the entire Jewish nation, as Bachmann has demonstrated, he does not use that authority as a means of indicting the entire nation for the death of Jesus. Insofar as Jerusalem acted in the crucifixion, it did not act as the representative of the nation of Israel. Luke's consistent restriction of condemnation to Jerusalem will allow no other understanding.

The Jerusalem Oracles

Confirmation of the hypothesis advanced above is to be found in Luke's handling of the Jerusalem oracles in the Gospel. These include indications that Luke did not intend the fate of Jerusalem to be understood as a judgment on the entire nation without exception. In the oracles he confined the attribution of responsibility for the death of Jesus to Jerusalem alone. And while recognizing that the destruction of Jerusalem

---

('Israel', pp. 84-85) in noting that the setting of the parable after the Zacchaeus episode with its statement about the 'son of Abraham' (19.9) also suggests a divided fate for Israel. Johnson argues that the context implies that the rebellious citizens are the Pharisees (19.38), whose rejection of Jesus is the counterpoint for his acceptance by the crowds in the travel narrative (*Possessions*, p. 170).

1.   Cf. the comments of Evans, 'Luke's View', p. 32.
2.   Sanders, *Jews in Luke–Acts*, pp. 181-82.
3.   Cf. the brief remarks of George, 'Israël', pp. 496-98.

had dire implications for the people as a whole, Luke nevertheless maintained a perspective which allowed for escape from that fate. Thus, this material exhibits the same emphasis on Jerusalem's unique role in the crucifixion and on the division which Jesus and the gospel brought to Israel as a whole.

The first such indication is found in Lk. 13.33, which introduces the first of the Jerusalem oracles. This saying comes in response to the warning of the Pharisees that Herod is seeking to kill Jesus. Not only does it provide the *Stichwort* to which the oracle of vv. 34-35 is connected, it also reflects the consistent emphasis on the role of Jerusalem in the death of Jesus.[1] Faced with another mortal threat, Luke's Jesus affirms that as a prophet he can die only in Jerusalem.[2] The oracle which follows then asserts Jerusalem's unique role as the killer of prophets and connects its coming fate to that role.[3] The killing of the prophets is, of course, associated elsewhere with people other than Jerusalemites (Lk. 11.49-51).[4] But in that case no specific connection is made between the killing of the prophets and the death of Jesus, and the language employed clearly refers only to a group of Jesus' opponents. The expression is, moreover, apparently taken by Luke from a source. If Luke found the saying in a context of the passion (cf. Mt. 23.34-36), then its removal to this earlier context suggests a further separation from

1. Miller misses both the *Stichwort* connection and the emphasis on Jerusalem when he asserts that Lk. 13.33-34 is inappropriately located by Luke because Jesus is not in Jerusalem ('Rejection of the Prophets', pp. 237-38).

2. Giblin does not take this factor into consideration when he asserts that Jerusalem is condemned in this passage only for its past treatment of the prophets (*Destruction*, p. 41). But he rightly observes that while judgment is threatened in 13.34-35, it is not realized and remains escapable (*Destruction*, p. 43). The early speeches of Acts clearly regard Jerusalem's sin as forgivable (e.g. Acts 2.38, 40; cf. 2.23, 36). Cf. George who connects the opportunity for repentance to the motif of ignorance ('Israël', pp. 505-506); and Tannehill, who sees hope for Israel's restoration in the Jerusalem oracles (*Narrative Unity*, I, pp. 164ff.).

3. Büchele asserts that οἶκος in v. 35 signifies the nation of Israel as a whole, but he cites no evidence for the view (*Tod*, p. 155). Giblin is on firmer ground when he suggests that the 'house' of Jerusalem is the Jerusalem leadership; that much is at least suggested by Luke's emphasis on their role in the crucifixion (*Destruction*, pp. 41-42).

4. Egelkraut notes the clear verbal connection between 13.34 and 11.49 but characteristically he ignores the evidence of a limited application of both sayings to maintain his view of an indictment of all Israel (*Mission to Jerusalem*, p. 178). A similar approach is taken by Moessner ('Leaven', p. 33).

the death of Jesus. It thus appears that while Luke compared all persecution of the faithful to the persecution and killing of the prophets (cf. Lk. 6.23), he nevertheless confined the direct comparison with the death of Jesus to settings which implicated Jerusalem alone.

Similar observations can be made for Lk. 19.41-44. Here the text emphasizes that only as Jesus draws near to Jerusalem (ἤγγισεν, cf. 19.29, 37) does he pronounce woe upon the city. The language of the oracle, furthermore, is emphatic in its second-person address; the second-person singular pronoun appears twelve times in vv. 42-44. The connection between Jesus' death and the fate to befall the city is implicit but nonetheless clear.[1] Jerusalem fails to recognize the time of its visitation, which is presumably contained in Jesus' presence. The failure is apparently manifested in the call for Jesus' death that is to come.[2] Hence, the intimate connection between Jerusalem, the crucifixion and its aftermath is maintained.

If Luke connects the fate of Jerusalem prophesied in 21.5-38 with the death of Jesus, that connection is even less obvious than in 19.41-44.[3] Nevertheless, some such connection cannot be ruled out, especially because of the proximity of the discourse to the passion events.[4] Particularly in light of the earlier oracles, it is difficult not to see some

1.   George notes that the position of the Jerusalem oracles in the passion narrative implies the connection between Jesus' death and the city's fate ('Israël', p. 504).

2.   The view that Luke restricts the acclamation of the crowd to ex-Jerusalem disciples and so indicates the failure to recognize the visitation in the triumphal entry is undermined by Luke's apparent motive in inserting μαθητῶν in 19.37 to prepare for the saying of v. 39; cf. the discussion in Chapter 2.

3.   Marshall, *Commentary on Luke*, p. 770.

4.   Giblin, *Destruction*, pp. 88-89; Chance, *Jerusalem*, pp. 116-17. Zmijewski argues that Lk. 22.1 is a deliberately less specific link of the eschatological discourse to the passion narrative than is Mk 14.1 (*Eschatologiereden*, p. 50). However, it is difficult to see in what way it is less specific, save for the omission of Mark's μετὰ δύο ἡμέρας. That omission, if indeed the phrase was present in Luke's source, may stem from Luke's omission of all notes about the passing of days in the Jerusalem narrative. Likewise, Zmijewski suggests that the omission of the anointing at Bethany has the same motive (*Eschatologiereden*, p. 50). But as has often been noted, Luke may omit the Bethany anointing because of his insertion of another anointing (Lk. 7.36-50). Nevertheless, the eschatological discourse itself makes no explicit reference to the death of Jesus. If the rending of the temple veil (Lk. 23.45) signifies the destruction of the temple for Luke (so Marshall, *Gospel of Luke*, pp. 873-75; Chance, *Jerusalem*, pp. 118-20), then the connection can be more confidently assumed in the eschatological discourse.

connection between Jerusalem's rejection of Jesus and its fate. This passage includes various features which have been taken as an indication that the destruction of Jerusalem is a judgment on all Israel and that behind that judgment lies an indictment of all Israel for Jesus' death. J.T. Sanders argues that Luke's insertion of φυλακάς in 21.12 sharpens the emphasis on Jewish opposition.[1] However, it is difficult to see how the term has a specifically Jewish reference. Furthermore, if Luke's source included the συνέδρια of Mk 13.9, then its omission may indicate a softening of the emphasis on Jewish opposition. J. Zmijewski has argued that this term is omitted because (1) Luke uses συνέδριον only in the singular for the supreme council of Judaism; and (2) his readers are Gentiles.[2] But in the first case, Luke could have used the singular, especially in light of the appearances of the apostles before the Sanhedrin in Acts; and in the second case the inclusion of συναγώγας is not accounted for. Furthermore, C.H. Giblin notes that because the testimony in vv. 12-19 is delivered before Jews and Gentiles, the opposition cannot be confined to Israel.[3] All in all, then, the description of the persecution of Jesus' followers does not suggest a special emphasis on Jewish persecution.

More critical is the expression τῷ λαῷ τούτῳ in v. 23. The phrase may indicate that Israel as a whole is the object of divine wrath manifested in the destruction of Jerusalem.[4] But the context of this expression suggests that Luke does not understand it as including all Israel. Several factors can be noted.

First of all, Luke apparently inserts into the discourse a specific reference to Jerusalem (21.20). Whether these are matters of *ex eventu* interpretation of the tradition or not, the specification is consistent with Luke's tendency elsewhere to locate both responsibility for the death of Jesus and the consequent disaster in Jerusalem. The insertion may therefore be explained at least in part by that tendency.[5] The insertion has the

---

1. Sanders, *Jews in Luke–Acts*, p. 217.
2. Zmijewski, *Eschatologiereden*, p. 131.
3. Giblin, *Destruction*, pp. 88-89.
4. Sanders, *Jews in Luke–Acts*, p. 218.
5. This explanation could tend to weaken the case for a post-70 CE date for Luke–Acts, since Jerusalem is named specifically because of Luke's interest in the city, not necessarily because of his knowledge of its actual destruction. Luke's interest in Jerusalem does not, of course, exclude his knowledge of its destruction, and it

effect of directing this section of the discourse more specifically to Jerusalem, making more difficult any interpretation which sees a general condemnation of Judaism.

Secondly, Luke preserves in the preceding context the command to flee the city. Zmijewski has argued at length that Luke, like Mark, understands this command to mean fleeing from Judaism and, unlike Mark, launching the Gentile mission.[1] Zmijewski bases much of this interpretation, however, on the assumptions that the responsibility for the death of Jesus in Acts is placed on all Jews and that the expression οἱ Ἰουδαῖοι in Acts implies a hardening of Judaism, both of which have been refuted earlier in the present discussion. Without these assumptions, it is very difficult to see how fleeing Judea for the mountains—which, as Zmijewski himself observes, means never actually leaving Judea—can stand for fleeing from Judaism for the Gentile mission. Likewise, the addition of 'those in the country must not enter into her' (v. 21c) hardly suggests a permanent departure, as Zmijewski asserts; it is instead the converse of the earlier instruction. The weakness of Zmijewski's argument leaves little to contradict the plain implication that those who heed Jesus' words escape the judgment about to come on the city. This factor suggests that Luke once again uses an inclusive term, λαός, with a partitive meaning in context.

Thirdly, the use of the demonstrative with ὁ λαός is striking.[2] The influence of a source cannot be ruled out as an explanation for this usage. But even if the expression was taken by Luke from a source, it contrasts with the expression πᾶς ὁ λαὸς Ἰσραήλ (Acts 4.10) by which Luke specifies the entire nation elsewhere. Thus, it is at least possible that Luke understands this expression in its immediate context as including only *this* people, the people of Jerusalem. The sudden and conspicuous introduction of the λαός in the trial narrative (23.13) makes such an understanding more likely.

Fourthly, the specification of τῆς γῆς as the object of distress parallel to τῷ λαῷ τούτῳ may not be entirely consonant with a judgment on all Jews. The expression clearly refers to 'the land' (i.e., Palestine), not to

---

could even be argued that the latter was the cause of the former (cf. Zmijewski, *Eschatologiereden*, pp. 204-206).

1. Zmijewski, *Eschatologiereden*, pp. 199-200, 208-11.

2. It occurs again in Acts 28.26, where it is taken directly from the LXX of Isa. 6.9.

'the earth' as a whole.[1] Luke, of course, is very much aware of the existence of the Jewish diaspora. Although distress in 'the land' could well signify a tragedy for the entire nation, including the diaspora, the conspicuous use of the expression, not found in the parallels, suggests more a particular concentration on Palestine than a concern for the Jewish nation as a whole. Like the specification of Jerusalem in v. 24, it probably reflects either the expectation of or the knowledge of bitter warfare in Palestine, not an interest in the condemnation of all Jews.

Fifthly, the use of τὰ ἔθνη does not require a contrast with Israel as a whole.[2] As J.B. Chance notes, the Gentiles are regularly the instruments of Jerusalem's destruction in Jewish literature (Zech. 12.3; Isa. 63.18; Ps. 79.1; Dan. 8.13-14; 1 Macc. 3.45, 51; 2 Macc. 8.2; *Ps. Sol.* 17.23-27).[3] Indeed, only the Gentiles could serve as the instrument of Jerusalem's destruction, since Jews could not be expected to destroy Jerusalem themselves.

Sixthly, it is unlikely that the use of καιροί is intended to contrast a period of Gentile salvation with the period of Jewish salvation presented with καιρός in 19.44.[4] In 19.44 the καιρός is linked to salvation with the genitive τῆς ἐπισκοπῆς. In 21.24 such a genitive is lacking, but the preceding clause makes clear what the καιροὶ ἐθνῶν are: the period of Jerusalem's desolation by the Gentiles. In both cases, as in 21.8, καιρός refers to some eschatological or apocalyptic event, but the nature of that event is determined by the context of the expression.

Finally, following the destruction of Jerusalem 'your redemption' will appear (21.28). Jesus' audience, the 'you' that will be redeemed, appears to be composed not just of his disciples but of the λαός which has heard his teaching in the temple (cf. 20.45; 21.5-7, 37-38).[5] As was argued

1. Zmijewski, *Eschatologiereden*, pp. 187-89, 214-15.
2. *Contra* Zmijewski, *Eschatologiereden*, pp. 189, 215-16.
3. Chance, *Jerusalem*, pp. 134-35.
4. *Contra* Zmijewski, *Eschatologiereden*, pp. 218-19. He argues that the plural καιροί in 21.24 indicates that the period of Gentile salvation is unlimited, whereas the singular in 19.44 indicates that the period of Jewish salvation is circumscribed.
5. Zmijewski, *Eschatologiereden*, p. 96; Chance, *Jerusalem*, pp. 135-36; Evans, 'Prophecy and Polemic', pp. 181-82. Chance argues further that because Luke exhibits a 'consistent pattern of viewing Jerusalem as the literal city', the redemption of 21.28 should be understood as a restoration of literal Jerusalem (*Jerusalem*, p. 137). This judgment depends on the strength of Chance's argument that Luke is indeed concerned with literal Jerusalem in contrast to other writers of the New Testament, an evaluation of which is irrelevant for the purposes here. However,

above, Luke understands this λαός to be Jerusalemite. This observation suggests two significant points. One is that among those who suffer in the coming destruction of Jerusalem are those who are subsequently redeemed. Whatever judgment they have received is therefore not final. Secondly, the fact that this subsequent redemption is redemption of the Jerusalemite audience ('you' in the discourse) again indicates that the catastrophe is viewed primarily as a catastrophe for Jerusalem and its inhabitants. The cumulative force of all the arguments above is inescapable: Luke does not condemn all Israel with τῷ λαῷ τούτῳ.

Zmijewski has argued at length that Luke has changed the address of the apocalyptic discourse from the disciples to the people so that it concerns not the fate of the Christian community but that of 'condemned Jewry'.[1] Several difficulties adhere to this view, however. One is that it depends on the assumption that Luke's only source for the apocalyptic discourse was Mark. Hence, Luke 'omits' Mk 13.18, 20 because they suggest too much sympathy with the objects of the disaster.[2] Aside from the possibility that Luke follows another source, the difficulty of this interpretation lies in the fact that the instruction to flee the city is included (v. 21), as is the promise of coming redemption (v. 28). More important, however, is the larger observation that Jesus' audience is composed of Jerusalemites who elsewhere do not function as representatives of all Israel for Luke. At most, then, Luke orients the apocalyptic discourse toward 'condemned Jerusalem'.

The same restricted application is to be found in the oracle to the women in Lk. 23.27-31. The vocative θυγατέρες Ἰερουσαλήμ (v. 28) serves to specify the object of the suffering that follows. It is unlikely that the reference to unborn children serves to draw all Judaism into the circle of destruction; more likely it serves to emphasize the helplessness of mothers and children facing a siege.[3] Here the connection between the death of Jesus and the fate of Jerusalem is more overt: although the

Moessner ('Ironic Fulfillment', pp. 37-46) observes that a number of details suggest that Luke believed the fulfillment of Israel's promises to be found in Christ, specifically (and ironically) in his death, not in a literal, political restoration in the future.

1. Zmijewski, *Eschatologiereden*, pp. 83-84, 89-90, 96, 189-90, 192, 204-206, 222-23, 428.

2. Zmijewski, *Eschatologiereden*, pp. 186, 189.

3. *Contra* Zmijewski, *Eschatologiereden*, p. 214.

saying of v. 31 is enigmatic, it at least connects the impending execution of Jesus with the future doom of the city.

Conclusions

The analysis above indicates that the conclusions of the previous chapter are justified. Luke–Acts gives no indication that its author regarded the entire nation of Israel as having rejected Jesus and the gospel. Nor does it indicate that the entire nation stands under judgment. Instead, it presents a nation divided in its response and divided in its fate. This negative conclusion in turn confirms the earlier positive conclusion: Luke confines responsibility for the death of Jesus among the Jews to the people of Jerusalem and their leaders.

This observation suggests another line of inquiry. What is Luke's theological purpose in presenting the response of the Jews in this way? If he portrays an Israel divided, then hypotheses which suggest an anti-Jewish tendency may be ill-founded. What alternative can be offered? Furthermore, what is the relationship between Luke's portrayal of Israel's response in general and the involvement of Jerusalem in the crucifixion in particular? How can Luke on the one hand portray Israel as divided in its response while on the other hand portraying Jerusalem as united in calling for Jesus' death? Partial answers to these questions lie in Luke's use of traditions concerning responsibility for Jesus' death, the subject of the second part of this study.

Chapter 4

RESPONSIBILITY FOR THE DEATH OF JESUS IN PAUL:
1 THESSALONIANS 2.14-16

What was the origin of Luke's portrayal of responsibility for the crucifixion of Jesus? Was it based on a tradition that Luke received, or was it his own creation? The search for the answer to that question naturally follows two paths: toward Paul, whose epistles predate Luke–Acts, and toward the other Gospels, especially the Synoptics, with whom Luke shares common traditions. This chapter considers the former path. Its concern is to determine whether Paul's epistles suggest that he knew of any traditions regarding who was responsible for Jesus' death, and, if so, what the relationship of those traditions was to Luke's material.

Most of what Paul writes about the crucifixion of Jesus suggests nothing about human agencies. Rom. 8.32 is typical in this respect. In it Paul emphasizes that the crucifixion of Jesus is God's giving of his own Son; the involvement of any people is simply passed over. 1 Cor. 2.8 indicates another agency, τῶν ἀρχόντων τοῦ αἰῶνος τούτου, a phrase which could refer to political figures or demonic beings.

In 1 Thess. 2.14-16, however, Paul does apparently make a statement about those involved in the death of Jesus.[1] Furthermore, this text may indeed have a basis in pre-Pauline tradition.[2] If so, the tradition was necessarily early, since 1 Thessalonians was written no more than two

1.   Elsewhere I have argued that the evidence favors the authenticity of this text (J.A. Weatherly, 'The Authenticity of 1 Thessalonians 2.13-16: Additional Evidence', *JSNT* 42 [1991], pp. 79-98).

2.   The text may have a basis in pre-Lukan or pre-Pauline tradition even if it is not authentic. W.O. Walker has observed that an interpolation in a Pauline epistle may be interpolated Pauline material ('Text Critical Evidence for Interpolations in the Letters of Paul', *CBQ* 50 [1988], p. 631); likewise, a non-Pauline interpolation may be based on pre-Pauline tradition.

decades or so after the passion events.[1] Consequently, a fresh consideration of the evidence that 1 Thess. 2.14-16 depends on a piece of pre-
Pauline tradition about the death of Jesus is in order.[2]

The Traditional Basis of 1 Thessalonians 2.14-16

For this discussion E.E. Ellis's definition of 'tradition' is useful:

> As it is used here, 'tradition' means more than a prior idea or story
> floating in the memory of the Apostle, of his co-traditioners or of the
> amanuenses and co-senders of the letters. It is, more concretely, a specific
> item in a traditioning process that was formed in oral or written usage
> before Paul incorporated it into his letter.[3]

In order to establish the appropriate burden of proof, Paul's use of
passion traditions in general will be considered first. Then the specific
indications of a tradition lying behind 1 Thess. 2.14-16 will be discussed.
Finally, a tentative reconstruction of the tradition which may lie behind
the text will be offered, as will a hypothesis as to the *Sitz im Leben* in
which the tradition may have arisen.

---

1.   The importance of 1 Thess. 2.14-16 in this respect is demonstrated in the
way it figures in two recent publications. Ruether accepts its authenticity and argues
from its early provenance that anti-Semitism is inherent in Christology (*Faith and
Fratricide*, pp. 92, 94). Wilson, on the other hand, concedes that Luke's treatment
of Jewish responsibility may be less his own creation if it can be found in a source
other than Mark—i.e., a source such as 1 Thess. 2.14-16, if it is indeed authentic
and traditional ('Jews and the Death of Jesus in Acts', p. 160).
2.   A traditional basis for the passage would further weaken objections to its
authenticity based on the apparent conflict with Rom. 9–11; cf. O.H. Steck, *Israel
und das gewaltsame Geschick der Propheten: Untersuchungen zur Überlieferung des
deuteronomistischen Geschichtsbildes im Alten Testament, Spätjudentum und
Urchristentum* (WMANT, 33; Neukirchen–Vluyn: Neukirchener Verlag, 1967),
pp. 275-76; T. Holtz, *Der erste Brief an die Thessalonicher* (EKKNT, 13;
Neukirchen–Vluyn: Neukirchener Verlag, 1986), pp. 27, 104; I. Broer,
'"Antisemitismus" und Judenpolemik im Neuen Testament: Ein Beitrag zum bessern
Verständnis von 1 Thess. 2,14-16', *Biblische Notizen* 29 (1983), pp. 70-71. This
point must not be exaggerated, however, since Paul presumably agreed with
whatever traditions he used (cf. W.O. Walker, 'I Corinthians 11.2-16 and Paul's
View of Women', *JBL* 94 [1975], pp. 108-109 n. 55; W. Munro, *Authority in Paul
and Peter: The Identification of a Pastoral Stratum in the Pauline Corpus and 1 Peter*
[SNTSMS, 45; Cambridge: Cambridge University Press, 1983], pp. 21-22).
3.   E.E. Ellis, 'Traditions in 1 Corinthians', *NTS* 32 (1986), p. 481.

Paul's Use of Passion Traditions

Paul's possible knowledge of and transmission of material about the life of Jesus is a controversial issue.[1] Although debate continues on several aspects of this question, considerable evidence indicates that Paul knew and passed on traditions about the death of Jesus.

First of all, Paul's possible use of traditions about the passion must be considered in light of his insistence on the independence of his gospel. That Paul believed that his gospel had authority independent of the Jerusalem church is clear from his autobiographical account in Galatians 1–2. But exactly how Paul understood this independence can only be inferred from a wider selection of texts. Elsewhere Paul insists that his gospel is essentially the same as that of the other apostles (1 Cor. 9.1-27), particularly with regard to the passion and resurrection of Jesus (1 Cor. 15.3-7).[2] It would therefore be illegitimate to assume that Paul's independence precluded his use of any pre-formed material about the death of Jesus.[3]

Likewise, Paul's interest in the transcendent Christ does not necessarily exclude his interest in the historical Jesus and traditions about him.[4] Clear examples of Paul's use of Jesus traditions indicate that Paul's perspective on the historical Jesus and the transcendent Christ was one of continuity.[5] To insist on exclusive interest in one or the other is to force

---

1.   Typical of the opinion that Paul knew or used few traditions about Jesus are V.P. Furnish (*Theology and Ethics in Paul* [Nashville: Abingdon Press, 1968], p. 55) and P. Richardson and P. Gooch ('Logia of Jesus in 1 Corinthians', in D. Wenham [ed.], *The Jesus Tradition Outside the Gospels* [Gospel Perspectives, 5; Sheffield: JSOT Press, 1985], p. 55). Representative opinions on the other side of the debate are cited in the discussion below.

2.   P. Stuhlmacher, 'Das paulinische Evangelium', in *idem* (ed.), *Das Evangelium und die Evangelien* (WUNT, 2.28; Tübingen: Mohr [Paul Siebeck], 1983), pp. 165-69; Wenham, 'Samples', pp. 29-30.

3.   Cf. the discussion in B. Gerhardsson, *Memory and Manuscript: Oral Tradition and Written Transmission in Rabbinic Judaism and Early Christianity* (ET; ASNU, 22; Lund: Gleerup; Copenhagen: Munksgaard, 1961), pp. 295-96.

4.   As is assumed by E.L. Ehrlich ('Paulus und das Schuldproblem, erläutert an Römer 5 und 8', in W.P. Eckert, N.P. Levinson and M. Stöhr [eds.], *Antijudaismus im Neuen Testament? Exegetische und systematische Beiträge* [Abhandlungen zum christlich-jüdischen Dialog, 2; Munich: Chr. Kaiser Verlag, 1967], p. 46), who therefore argues that the ascription of responsibility for the death of Jesus to Jews in 1 Thess. 2.14 is Paul's reading back of his own experience into the life of Jesus.

5.   This widely debated point has recently been persuasively argued by C.F.D. Moule ('The Gravamen against Jesus', in E.P. Sanders [ed.], *Jesus, the*

a false choice. Moreover, Paul's interest in the salvific aspect of the passion is probably connected to his use of passion traditions: P. Stuhlmacher notes that the tradition of the Last Supper would have interested Paul because in it Jesus speaks of his death as an offering for sin.[1] Therefore, the evidence for Paul's use of tradition can be allowed to stand on its own.

Paul's interest in traditions about Jesus is exemplified in his account of the Last Supper (1 Cor. 11.23-27), which is almost universally recognized as Paul's use of a pre-formed passion tradition.[2] D.C. Allison notes, moreover, that the phrase ἐν τῇ νυκτὶ ᾗ παρεδίδετο in v. 23 assumes knowledge of other details of the passion, both the fact of the betrayal (παρεδίδετο) and at least a general chronology (ἐν τῇ νυκτί).[3] In other words, this introduction to the Last Supper account makes little sense apart from a knowledge not only of the fact of Jesus' death but also of some of the events surrounding it. Thus, it cannot be concluded from the brief notice of Jesus' death in 1 Cor. 15.3 that Paul had not transmitted to the Corinthians a passion account as such. In the case of the Corinthian church, at least, it appears that the relative lack of allusions to the passion events bespeaks not a lack of interest in them but the assumption that they are well known and do not need repeating.[4] This conclusion is corroborated by the use of technical terms for the transmission of tradition in v. 23 (παραλαμβάνω, παραδίδωμι; cf.

Gospels and the Church: Essays in Honor of William R. Farmer [Macon, GA: Mercer University Press, 1987], pp. 189-90).

1.   Stuhlmacher, 'Paulinische Evangelium', pp. 166-67.

2.   This point is affirmed even by many who are highly skeptical about Paul's use of other traditions about Jesus: for example, Richardson and Gooch, 'Logia', p. 41.

3.   D.C. Allison, 'The Pauline Epistles and the Synoptic Gospels: The Pattern of the Parallels', *NTS* 28 (1982), p. 16.

4.   Allison, 'Pattern', p. 16. This type of argument has been widely employed concerning Paul's knowledge of the life and teachings of Jesus in general; cf. D.L. Dungan, *The Sayings of Jesus in the Churches of Paul: The Use of the Synoptic Tradition in the Regulation of Early Church Life* (Oxford: Basil Blackwell, 1971), pp. 147-49; D. Wenham, 'Paul and the Synoptic Apocalypse', in *idem* and R.T. France (eds.), *Studies of History and Tradition in the Four Gospels* (Gospel Perspectives, 2; Sheffield: JSOT Press, 1981), p. 365; Ellis, 'Traditions in 1 Corinthians', p. 486; W. Marxsen, *Der erste Brief an die Thessalonicher* (Züricher Bibelkommentare, NT, 11.1; Zürich: Theologischer Verlag, 1979), p. 17; B. Gerhardsson, 'Der Weg der Evangelientradition', in P. Stuhlmacher (ed.), *Das Evangelium und die Evangelien* (WUNT, 2.28; Tübingen: Mohr [Paul Siebeck], 1983), p. 81.

1 Cor. 11.2; 15.3; Rom. 6.17; 16.17; Gal. 1.9; Phil. 4.9; 1 Thess. 2.13; 4.1; 2 Thess. 3.6). Further corroboration is found in the judgment of the early form-critics that the passion narratives of the Synoptics, though consisting of self-contained units, nevertheless are characterized by a continuity which indicates that a passion narrative existed from an early date.[1] Thus, the Corinthians' knowledge of a version of the passion narrative can be inferred from Paul's allusion to the Last Supper.

Other Pauline texts include apparent allusions to material about the passion or material that was closely associated with the passion. Such allusions have been identified in Rom. 13.7 (cf. Mk 12.13-17); 2 Cor. 5.1 (cf. Mk 14.58); 2 Cor. 5.7; Gal. 3.1; Col. 4.2 (cf. Mk 14.38); and 1 Thess. 4.2-4 (cf. Mt. 24.34).[2] These references are not weighty in themselves. But given the occasional nature of Paul's epistles and the cumulative force of these allusions, it appears likely that Paul knew traditions of the passion and passed some of them on to his congregations. Furthermore, the presence of one such allusion elsewhere in 1 Thessalonians (i.e., 4.2-4) indicates that the Thessalonian church was not an exception to Paul's usual practice of transmitting traditions about Jesus, including passion traditions.

Evidence for Tradition in 1 Thessalonians 2.14-16

Several converging lines of evidence suggest that 1 Thess. 2.14-16 is based on a pre-Pauline tradition which Paul modified for use in the Thessalonian epistle. No one argument is decisive in itself, but taken together, the case is compelling. The following discussion of the evidence arranges it in several convenient categories.

Structural and Syntactical Evidence. Divisibility of a text into lines of nearly equal length, especially with balanced parallelism, is an important criterion for the identification of fragments of tradition.[3] This

---

1. Cf. the useful survey of the discussion in Gerhardsson, 'Weg', p. 97.

2. Allison, 'Pattern', pp. 16-17; p. 30 n. 93; Ellis, 'Traditions in 1 Corinthians', pp. 489-90; A.M. Hunter, *Paul and his Predecessors* (London: SCM Press, rev. edn, 1961), p. 11; Wenham, 'Synoptic Apocalypse', p. 347; J.B. Green, *The Death of Jesus: Tradition and Interpretation in the Passion Narrative* (WUNT, 2.33; Tübingen: Mohr [Paul Siebeck], 1988), pp. 185-86.

3. M. Barth, 'Traditions in Ephesians', *NTS* 30 (1984), pp. 8-9; Ellis, 'Traditions in 1 Corinthians', p. 494. E. Best (*A Commentary on the First and Second Epistles to the Thessalonians* [BNTC; London: A. & C. Black, 1972],

characteristic is readily evident in several lines of 1 Thess. 2.14-16. The most obvious example of balanced parallelisms is to be found in v. 15 with its series of parallel participial phrases. Interestingly, if the division of lines is made between Ἰησοῦν and καί, then the first two lines of this verse have an equal number of syllables, that is, thirteen. The same number of syllables also occurs in v. 16c. Furthermore, a certain degree of editing, all of which is plausible given the use to which Paul could have put a tradition, yields thirteen syllables in two other lines. If the closing phrase of v. 14, καθὼς καὶ αὐτοὶ ὑπὸ τῶν Ἰουδαίων, was based on tradition, that tradition may well have read ἐπάθομεν καὶ ἡμεῖς ὑπὸ τῶν Ἰουδαίων, a line with thirteen syllables. Likewise, if in v. 16b the prefix ἀνα- is dropped from ἀναπληρῶσαι and αὐτῶν is omitted, then this line also includes thirteen syllables. Further justification for the admittedly conjectural reconstruction of these lines is offered below. For the present it is necessary only to note that two lines of the text are parallel and of equal length and that at least one and possibly three lines are also of the same length.

The repeated use of aorist participles has also been employed as a criterion for the identification of traditions.[1] Again, the aorist participles in the two parallel lines of v. 15 (ἀποκτεινάντων, ἐκδιωξάντων) are noteworthy, as is the shift from the aorist to the present with ἀρεσκόντων.[2]

The use of infinitives as an expression of purpose or result is another criterion for identifying traditions.[3] In v. 16b ἀναπληρῶσαι is just such an infinitive. In itself, such an infinitive is unexceptional, but in concert with other elements which might suggest the presence of a tradition, it carries corroborative weight.

Introductory formulae are also telltale signs of traditional material. καθὼς καί is one such formula.[4] In v. 14 this phrase may be an

---

p. 123) refers generally to a liturgical or creedal structure in 1 Thess. 2.15-16.

1. Barth, 'Traditions', pp. 8-9; G. Lüdeman, *Paulus und das Judentum* (Theologische Existenz Heute, 215; Munich: Chr. Kaiser Verlag, 1983), p. 22.

2. Wenham, *Eschatological Discourse*, p. 352. If ἐκδιωξάντων is based on tradition, then there is no need to see in the aorist a reference to a specific experience of Paul as do Best (*Thessalonians*, p. 116), I.H. Marshall (*1 and 2 Thessalonians* [NCB; London: Marshall, Morgan & Scott, 1983], p. 79) and K.P. Donfried ('Paul and Judaism: 1 Thessalonians 2.13-16 as a Test Case', *Int* 38 [1984], p. 249).

3. Barth, 'Traditions', pp. 8-9.

4. Barth, 'Traditions', pp. 8-9.

ordinary means of introducing the comparison between the Thessalonians and their Judean counterparts. On the other hand, the length of the material in the second member of the comparison, which entirely overbalances the first member, lends plausibility to the assumption that καθὼς καί introduces not just a comparison but a citation of a pre-formed tradition which is quoted at length and perhaps embellished.

A text that is relatively self-contained may also be suspected of having a basis in tradition.[1] The material of vv. 15-16, with the addition of an introductory statement like the one suggested above, would easily stand independently, comparing the experience of the recent past (ἐπάθομεν) with the experience of God's representatives in the past ('Ιησοῦν, τοὺς προφήτας) interpreting that experience (εἰς τὸ [ἀνα]πλρῶσαι...), and anticipating its ultimate outcome (ἔφθασεν...ἡ ὀργὴ εἰς τέλος).

Lexical Evidence. The presence of words or phrases uncharacteristic of a writer is commonly regarded as an indication that tradition may underlie a text.[2] Several such terms appear in 1 Thess. 2.14-16, as has been widely noted. Elsewhere Paul uses ἀποκτείνω only three times, and never of the death of Christ. With the exception of Tit. 2.8, ἐναντίος appears only here in the Pauline corpus, and ἐκδιώκω is not found elsewhere in Paul. G. Lüdemann has also argued that ἀναπληρῶσαι ἁμαρτίας and φθάνειν ἐπί τινα are un-Pauline phrases, as is the negative phrase θεῷ μὴ ἀρέσκειν.[3]

A certain degree of caution is necessary in evaluating this evidence. The verb ἀποκτείνω is in itself unexceptional; its use may have to do with the constraints of the context, as noted above. Nevertheless, the connection of the death of Jesus to the killing of the prophets is unique in Paul, so the use of ἀποκτείνω may still point to an un-Pauline, traditional element. Likewise, although exact lexical parallels to ἀναπληρῶσαι ἁμαρτίας and φθάνειν ἐπί τινα are lacking, similar

---

1. Ellis, 'Traditions in 1 Corinthians', p. 485.
2. Steck, *Geschick*, p. 274; G.E. Cannon, *The Use of Traditional Material in Colossians* (Macon, GA: Mercer University Press, 1983), pp. 14ff.; Ellis, 'Traditions in 1 Corinthians', p. 485; R. Schippers, 'The Pre-Synoptic Tradition in I Thessalonians II 13-16', *NovT* 8 (1966), pp. 232-33; Broer, 'Antisemitismus', p. 71.
3. Lüdemann, *Paulus und das Judentum*, p. 22.

concepts are to be found elsewhere in Paul, as I. Broer has noted.[1] Furthermore, Paul does express the negative of θεῷ ἀρέσκειν indirectly elsewhere (Rom. 8.8), and the positive occurs later in 1 Thess. 4.1; so the use of the negative in 2.15 may be Pauline.[2] Nevertheless, the presence of terms which are at least unusual, if corroborated by other evidence, can be taken as an indication of the use of tradition.

Literary Parallels. When a document roughly contemporary to the text in question includes similar material and direct literary dependence is unlikely, the use of common tradition can explain the similarities.[3] In the case of 1 Thess. 2.14-16, the parallels are to be found in Mt. 23.29-38; 24.2b and Lk. 11.49-40. There are several correspondences: the terms ἀποκτείνω, προφῆται (ἐκ)διώκω, (ἀνα)πληρόω; references to the killing of the prophets, to the filling of sins/the measure of the fathers, and to a coming judgment.

The weight of these parallels can only be judged when their differences are noted. First of all, the order of the common elements is different in Matthew; there, filling up the measure of the fathers precedes the killing of the prophets. Secondly, the differences between simple and compound terms are noteworthy. Although the compound ἐκδιώκω does appear in some MSS of Lk. 11.49, the simple form διώκω, used by Paul elsewhere, appears in Mt. 23.34 and in the best MSS of Luke. Moreover, neither of the parallels has the compound ἀναπληρόω, although this compound is found elsewhere in Paul. Thirdly, the poetic structure found in 1 Thess. 2.14-16 is entirely lacking in the Synoptic parallels.

At least two different hypotheses would explain these similarities: (1) Paul and the synoptics depended on a common source, which Paul

1. Broer, 'Antisemitismus', p. 71.

2. The positive phrase θεῷ ἀρέσκειν is common in Paul; cf. the discussion in P.T. O'Brien, *Introductory Thanksgivings in the Letters of Paul* (NovTSup, 49; Leiden: Brill, 1977), p. 88.

3. Schippers, 'Pre-Synoptic Tradition', pp. 232-33; Ellis, 'Traditions in 1 Corinthians', p. 485. Although J.B. Orchard ('Thessalonians and the Synoptic Gospels', *Bib* 19 [1938], pp. 21-23) has argued for Paul's dependence on Matthew at 1 Thess. 2.14-16, and M.D. Goulder (*The Evangelists' Calendar: A Lectionary Explanation of the Development of Scripture* [London: SPCK, 1978], pp. 237-38) has argued the opposite, few scholars have followed either of them, adopting instead the hypothesis of a common tradition. Cf. Wenham, 'Synoptic Apocalypse', p. 364.

edited into the present form of 1 Thess. 2.14-16;[1] (2) Paul did not depend directly on such a source but drew on similar ideas;[2] (3) Paul depended on a tradition related to but distinct from the pre-synoptic source of Mt. 23.29-38; 24.2b and Lk. 11.49-50. Though the second alternative cannot be dismissed entirely, it does not explain the particular cluster of ideas found both in 1 Thessalonians and in the Synoptics. In some respects the first hypothesis is the simpler one, since it eliminates the additional hypothetical source. On the other hand, the third accounts more readily for the presence of non-Pauline elements not found in the synoptic parallels, notably the compound verb ἐκδιώκω, and for some of the poetic features. Other factors must be considered before a judgment is reached.

Other Evidence. Various features of 1 Thess. 2.14-16 are consistent with the hypothesis that it is based on tradition. These are not decisive in themselves; indeed, some are quite tenuous. But they do tend to corroborate the cumulative case already made.

One is the presence of a technical term for the transmission of tradition, παραλαμβάνω, in v. 13. Although the verb does not refer directly to the passing on of the tradition of vv. 14-16, it does indicate that the wider context has some orientation to the transmission of tradition in general.[3] This impression is strengthened when it is noted that in 1.6, where a similar statement is made (cp. δεξάμενοι to ἐδέξασθε in 2.13), such tradition language does not appear. It would not be surprising if, having alluded to the transmission of tradition to the

1. This is a commonly held view: C.H. Dodd, 'Matthew and Paul', in *New Testament Studies* (Manchester: Manchester University Press, 1953), p. 65; U.B. Müller, *Prophetie und Predigt im Neuen Testament: Formgeschichtliche Unterschungen zur urchristlichen Prophetie* (SNT, 10; Gütersloh: Gerd Mohn, 1975), p. 177; Schippers, 'Pre-Synoptic Tradition', pp. 232-33; F.F. Bruce, *1 & 2 Thessalonians* (WBC, 45; Waco, TX: Word Books, 1982), p. 43; Wenham, *Eschatological Discourse*, p. 284; Donfried, 'Paul and Judaism', pp. 248-49.

2. So B. Rigaux, *Saint Paul: Les épîtres aux Thessaloniciens* (EBib; Paris: Gabalda, 1956), pp. 103, 445; F. Hahn, *Mission in the New Testament* (ET; SBT, 47; London: SCM Press, 1965), pp. 105-106; Steck, *Geschick*, p. 274; R.F. Collins, 'Apropos the Integrity of 1 Thess', in *Studies on the First Letter to the Thessalonians* (BETL, 66; Leuven: Leuven University Press, 1984), p. 131.

3. Wenham rightly notes that the use of language referring to the transmission of tradition is a weakness in Goulder's hypothesis that Matthew depends on 1 Thessalonians ('Synoptic Apocalypse', p. 364).

Thessalonians, Paul then quoted or paraphrased a relevant portion of that tradition in the following section.[1] This observation obviously does not prove that the passage is traditional, but it does suggest that a traditional basis is possible.

A second indication is the fact that vv. 15-16 tend to interrupt the context. The initial focus of v. 14 is on the Thessalonians (ὑμεῖς), who are compared to their Judean counterparts. But then the focus shifts immediately to the persecutors of the Judean Christians, who are discussed at length in vv. 15-16. The emphatic ἡμεῖς of v. 17 serves to resume the original focus after the long digression. Each step follows in turn, so that it is impossible to 'restore' an 'authentic' text by excising any one portion. But the length of the digression in vv. 15-16 is congruent with the hypothesis that Paul here incorporates traditional material.

Thirdly, the relative brevity with which the death of Jesus is discussed suggests that Paul was alluding to something that his readers already knew. If the Thessalonians were not already acquainted with the notion that Jesus' own people instigated his death, such a passing allusion would be most surprising. If, on the other hand, that idea was part of the tradition that they had received from Paul, then a brief mention of the fact as a part of a wider discourse is entirely consonant.[2] This observation tends to confirm that the idea of Jewish involvement in the crucifixion was a part of the tradition that Paul transmitted, even if the precise form in v. 15 was not.

Fourthly, the presence of tradition in this text is consistent with the apparent use of tradition elsewhere in 1 Thessalonians. D.C. Allison has noted that allusions to dominical tradition tend to be clustered in specific contexts in Paul's epistles, and 1 Thessalonians 4–5 is one such context.[3] The connection is all the more striking since the Synoptic parallels to 1 Thessalonians 4–5 are found in Matthew 24, not far from the parallels to 1 Thess. 2.14-16.[4] Again, this observation cannot be said to prove

---

1. W.D. Davies cites 1 Thess. 2.13 as an example of one kind of tradition which Paul incorporated into his epistles, namely, 'That which deals with Christian preaching where the tradition is identified with the Gospel or the Apostolic message itself' (*The Setting of the Sermon on the Mount* [Cambridge: Cambridge University Press, 1964], pp. 354-55). Cf. also the discussion of Paul's use of technical terms for the transmission of tradition in Gerhardsson, *Memory*, pp. 265, 290.

2. Cf. Gerhardsson, *Memory*, pp. 290-91.

3. Allison, 'Pattern', pp. 10-11; cf. Wenham, 'Synoptic Apocalypse', p. 347.

4. Cf. Orchard, 'Thessalonians', pp. 21-42.

that a tradition lies behind the passage, but it does indicate that the use of a tradition here would be consistent with Paul's practice elsewhere in the epistle.

Non-Traditional Elements in 1 Thessalonians 2.14-16
Various features of 1 Thess. 2.14-16 do not appear to be traditional. Some distinctly Pauline elements appear in the text, suggesting either Pauline composition or editorial work. Furthermore, the presence of statements which resemble the anti-Jewish calumnies of pagans could also suggest the incorporation of material that did not originate in Jewish-Christian circles. These factors can be surveyed briefly.

Pauline Elements. R.F. Collins notes several words, phrases and concepts in 1 Thess. 2.14-16 which appear to be Pauline:[1] (1) μή negating a participle; (2) ἵνα to express purpose after λαλεῖν (cf. 1 Cor. 14.9);[2] (3) the use of κύριος for Jesus; (4) the phrase 'churches of God which are in Christ Jesus';[3] (5) the use of ὀργή in an eschatological sense;[4] (6) the emphasis on preaching to the Gentiles, which is opposed by Jews.[5] Additionally, the verb ἀναπληρόω appears to be Pauline; in the New Testament it occurs only once outside of the undisputed Pauline epistles (Mt. 13.14). And as has been noted above, the phrase θεῷ ἀρέσκειν is also Pauline.

These elements have varying claims to being distinctively Pauline. The particle μή with the participle, although characteristic of Paul, is hardly distinctive (cf. BDF § 430); the same may be said for use of κύριος and ὀργή. Nevertheless, Paul's compositional or editorial hand can probably be detected in the other elements listed.

---

1. Collins, 'Integrity', pp. 131-32.
2. Cf. J. Coppens, 'Miscellanées bibliques. LXXX. Une diatribe antijuive dans I Thess., II, 13-16', *ETL* 51 (1975), p. 91.
3. Cf. Weatherly, 'Authenticity', pp. 95-97.
4. Cf. Weatherly, 'Authenticity', pp. 90-91.
5. Cf. Hahn, *Mission*, pp. 105-106 n. 3; O. Michel, 'Fragen zu 1 Thessalonicher 2, 14-16: Antijüdische Polemik bei Paulus', in Eckert, Levinson and Stöhr (eds.), *Antijudaismus im Neuen Testament?*, p. 55; K. Haacker, 'Elemente des heidnischen Antijudaismus im Neuen Testament', *EvT* 48 (1988), p. 109. Wenham's connection of this theme to a pre-Synoptic eschatological discourse is interesting (*Eschatological Discourse*, pp. 283-84), but given Paul's interest in the Gentile mission, his conclusions are not compelling.

Elements of Pagan Anti-Judaism. It has been widely observed that the phrases 'not pleasing God' and 'opposing all men' in v. 15 resemble various anti-Jewish statements found in Hellenistic literature.[1] Of importance here is the fact that this material is connected to some of the apparently Pauline elements in the text. The participle ἀρεσκόντων occurs in this block,[2] and the phrase πᾶσιν ἀνθρώποις ἐναντίων is explicated with the note which alludes to the Gentile mission. Furthermore, although these phrases resemble a number of Hellenistic texts, they do not appear to depend on any extant text. These factors suggest that these phrases are the result of Paul's borrowing from some common Hellenistic *topoi* to make a point consistent with his theological interpretation of Jewish rejection of the Gospel.[3] It is unlikely, then, that they belonged to a tradition as Paul received it; rather, they are part of his adaptation of the tradition.

Tentative Reconstruction of the Pre-Pauline Tradition

The reconstruction of the sources or traditions which lie behind extant documents is notoriously subjective.[4] Ultimately, one can never know whether a given reconstruction is correct without direct access to the sources or traditions themselves. Such reconstructions are not, however, entirely worthless. If a reasonable reconstruction can be effected, then the probability is increased that some tradition resembling the reconstruction lay behind the passage. Furthermore, such a reconstruction will

---

1.   References to such statements are listed in M. Dibelius, *An die Thessalonischer I–II: An die Philippier* (HNT, 3.2; Tübingen: Mohr [Paul Siebeck], 1911), pp. 40-42; Haacker, 'Heidnischen Antijudaismus', pp. 406-408, 413-16.

2.   Cf. Broer, 'Antisemitismus', pp. 79-80.

3.   So Rigaux, *Thessaloniciens*, p. 448; Michel, 'Antijüdische Polemik', pp. 56-57; Best, *Thessalonians*, p. 117; Holtz, *Thessalonicher*, pp. 105-106; Haacker, 'Heidnischen Antijudaismus', pp. 408-11; Broer, 'Antisemitismus', pp. 81-83. In this regard it is important to note that Paul adapts the Hellenistic *topoi* for application to only a portion of the Jewish nation, namely, those in Judea who rejected Jesus; cf. Weatherly, 'Authenticity', pp. 86-87. This observation weakens the argument against the authenticity of the passage that a Jew like Paul would not make use of Hellenistic anti-Jewish material (so B.A. Pearson, 'I Thessalonians 2.13-16: A Deutero-Pauline Interpolation', *HTR* 64 [1971], pp. 83-85; Bruce, *Thessalonians*, pp. 47, 51; Beck, *Mature Christianity*, pp. 42-44). Paul's adaptation of Hellenistic material is in this respect no more surprising than the Jewish-Christian adaptation of the killing-of-the-prophets motif.

4.   Cf. the warnings of Barth, 'Traditions', pp. 11-12.

demonstrate whether the conclusions reached about individual parts of the passage are consistent with each other. If the individual parts can be fitted together into a harmonious whole, then at least the parts have been shown not to be inconsistent. If on the other hand no consistent reconstruction is possible, doubt may be cast on the hypothesis of a tradition lying behind a passage. Thus, it is helpful to consider whether such a reconstruction is possible in the case of 1 Thess. 2.13-16. Of course, it cannot be claimed that any hypothetically reconstructed tradition ever actually existed in the form proposed, though the possibility cannot be positively excluded either. But if a coherent tradition can be reconstructed, then the probability is greater that some tradition lies behind a passage in question.

The evidence reviewed above suggests that the following reconstruction is at least plausible:

> ἐπάθομεν καὶ ἡμεῖς ὑπὸ τῶν Ἰουδαίων
> τῶν καὶ τὸν κύριον ἀποκτεινάντων Ἰησοῦν
> καὶ τοὺς προφήτας καὶ ἡμᾶς ἐκδιωξάντων
> εἰς τὸ πληρῶσαι τὰς ἁμαρτίας πάντοτε.
> ἔφθασεν δὲ ἐπ᾽ αὐτοὺς ἡ ὀργὴ εἰς τέλος.

The reconstruction is based on the following considerations.

1. Everything before the introductory formula καθὼς καί is omitted. The legitimacy of this omission is confirmed by the evidently Pauline diction of the phrases modifying ἐκκλησιῶν in v. 14.

2. The aorist of πάσχω is inserted into the elliptical clause καὶ αὐτοὶ ὑπὸ τῶν Ἰουδαίων. The first person plural is used on the assumption that the tradition was originally circulated among Christians experiencing persecution. The phrase καὶ ἡμεῖς, altered from καὶ αὐτοί to reflect the change in person, is retained to explicate the connection between the experience of those presently under persecution and that of Jesus and the prophets ('we ourselves have also suffered'). Ἰουδαίων is retained, though some other term may have been original (for example ἱερέων, ἀρχόντων, Φαρισαίων).

3. Lines two and three are retained without change from the text of v. 15. These lines contain elements that are unattested elsewhere in Paul (ἀποκτείνω for the death of Jesus, ἐκδιώκω) and material paralleled in the Synoptics (including the killing or persecution of the prophets). They also form a balanced parallelism involving two aorist participles.

4. The next two phrases καὶ θεῷ μὴ ἀρεσκόντων καὶ πᾶσιν ἀνθρώποις ἐναντίων are omitted because of elements that indicate the

hand of Paul. Pleasing God is a characteristically Pauline expression, and the idea of opposing all people is tied to the Gentile mission in the following phrase, a characteristically Pauline concept.[1] Moreover, as was argued above, it is at least plausible that Paul used Hellenistic anti-Jewish *topoi*, particularly since they are connected to Pauline elements.

5. The line κωλυόντων ἡμᾶς τοῖς ἔθνεσιν λαλεῖν σώθωσιν is omitted because of its evident reflection of Paul's evangelistic work among the Gentiles and the Jewish response to it.[2]

6. The line εἰς τὸ πληρῶσαι τὰς ἁμαρτίας πάντοτε is retained because of its connection to the Synoptic parallels.[3] The prefix ἀνα- is dropped from ἀναπληρῶσαι because (1) ἀναπληρόω is characteristic of Paul; (b) the simple form is found in the Synoptic parallels. The genitive αὐτῶν is omitted because it derives its importance from the insertion of the material about speaking to the Gentiles. As the text stands in 1 Thessalonians, αὐτῶν serves to resume the reference to the Jewish opponents after the digression about the Gentiles. The omission of the Gentile material renders the pronoun superfluous.

7. The concluding line is retained because it supplies a plausible ending for a self-contained tradition. As is characteristic of apocalyptically oriented responses to persecution, it remarks on the fate of the persecutors in the eschaton. Furthermore, it is the expected conclusion to the filling up of sins in the preceding line.

8. The reconstruction yields five lines of thirteen syllables each, resulting in a decidedly poetic composition. This outcome tends to confirm the previous conclusions.

Admittedly, varying degrees of probability attach to this reconstruction. Most likely to have been part of a pre-Pauline tradition are lines

1.   That κωλυόντων is subordinate to πᾶσιν ἀνθρώποις ἐναντίων is commonly noted; cf. J.E. Frame, *A Critical and Exegetical Commentary on the Epistles of St Paul to the Thessalonians* (ICC; Edinburgh: T. & T. Clark, 1912), p. 111. Steck argues that the absence of καί ties this phrase to the previous one and so indicates that the phrase was included in the tradition (*Geschick*, p. 275); on the other hand Lüdemann argues that the omission of καί indicates an insertion at the end of the tradition (*Paulus und das Judentum*, p. 23). Neither considers the possibility that the previous phrase is Paul's insertion.

2.   On the relationship of this statement to Paul's mission and experience, see Vanhoye, 'Les juifs', p. 79.

3.   The expression is also similar to various Jewish texts (for references see Rigaux, *Thessaloniciens*, pp. 450-51), a fact which further suggests an origin in a Jewish-Christian circle.

two and three, where a large number of indications converge and no editing of the text is presupposed. And indeed, for the purposes of the present argument, this is the most crucial element of the text, as it contains the direct statement about responsibility for the death of Jesus. Nevertheless, the rest of the reconstruction deserves consideration, integrating as it does a wide variety of observations about the text. While it must be repeated that the entire reconstruction is conjectural and may not represent the precise form of an actual pre-Pauline tradition, its coherence increases the probability that something like it lay behind the text of 1 Thess. 2.14-16.

Origin of the Tradition

As was noted above, the points of contact between 1 Thess. 2.14-16 and Synoptic material may indicate varying degrees of connection between them. The tentative reconstruction of the tradition behind the Thessalonian text now allows a judgment about that relationship to be made. While it is entirely possible that both Paul and Matthew/Luke depend on a common pre-Synoptic source, that relationship does not explain the poetic features discerned in the pre-Thessalonian text. If Paul composed the piece, the presence of ἐκδιωξάντων, which is found neither elsewhere in Paul nor in the Synoptic parallels, is without explanation. It therefore appears more likely that Paul adapted a ready-to-hand poetic tradition which was related in some way to the pre-Synoptic tradition.

Is poetic or hymnic structure consistent with the content of the tradition? Primitive Christian hymns have generally been understood to have been composed for worship and to reflect the distinctive Christology of the early believers. However, the New Testament witness to the Christians' rejoicing in the face of persecution (Acts 5.41; Rom. 5.3; Jas 1.2-3; 1 Pet. 4.13-14) would suggest that Christians could have sung about more than their Christology. In Jewish circles examples of lamentations of persecution combined with cries for divine retribution on the persecutors are not lacking: Psalm 137, especially vv. 7-9, is a well-known case. Luke's account of Paul's and Silas's singing in the Philippian jail (Acts 16.25) suggests that hymnic responses to persecution were not unknown among early Christians. It is therefore entirely possible that persecuted Christians composed and sang hymns in response to persecution to express the ironic joy that they associated with persecution, to voice their confidence in divine judgment, and to bolster one another's spirits. In this respect it may be significant that the notion of rejoicing in persecution is grounded in the experience of the prophets in Mt. 5.12//Lk. 6.23.

Is it possible to conceive of a specific setting in which such a tradition could have been composed? The use of Jewish themes (the killing of the prophets, the filling up of sins, the coming of wrath) all suggest a Jewish-Christian origin, and the absence of pagan anti-Judaism is consistent with that hypothesis. Two Jewish-Christian settings commend themselves as possibilities.

E.E. Ellis has recently proposed that the Pauline entourage was itself a tradition-producing body and that Paul frequently incorporated traditions composed by his associates into his epistles.[1] It is possible that one of Paul's associates composed this tradition. Certainly Paul and his circle had experienced persecution. Moreover, it would appear that ἐκδιωξάντων carries the nuance of pursuit or expulsion, since the more common διώκω would otherwise be expected.[2] If so, it is congruent with the experience of Paul. In 2 Cor. 11.23-33 Paul recounts several experiences (beatings, stonings, fleeing Damascus) which could be understood as expulsion. The Judaizers in Galatia, who may have deliberately traveled from Palestine to Galatia to 'pursue' Paul and undermine his work (Gal. 1.7), could also fit the description, though Paul himself appears to have been absent when they arrived.[3] Likewise, Acts specifically portrays Paul's opponents, particularly those from Thessalonica, as pursuing him from city to city (Acts 17.13).[4]

However, it was observed above that the text of 1 Thess. 2.14-16 is markedly oriented to Judea. Although it is possible that such an orientation arises more or less accidentally as Paul incorporates the tradition into the Thessalonian epistle, it may be that the Judean orientation was original because the persecutors of the Pauline circle were Judeans. R. Jewett's proposal that the persecution of these verses was instigated by Zealots of Palestinian origin has the virtue of integrating a variety of

---

1. Ellis, 'Traditions in 1 Corinthians', pp. 495-96.

2. In the LXX, ἐκδιώκω can signify either persecution or affliction in a general sense (Ps. 68.5; 118.157; Sir. 30.19; 1 Macc. 9.26), pursuit (1 Kgdms 30.10 [A]; Ps. 100.5; Sir. 39.30) or expulsion (Deut. 6.19; 1 Chron. 8.13; 12.16; Joel 2.20; Jer. 27.44; Dan [Theodotion] 4.22, 29, 30). Cf. the discussion in Holtz, *Thessalonicher*, p. 104 n. 486.

3. If Galatians is judged to be later than 1 Thessalonians, then this situation is probably not the referent.

4. Cf. Bruce, *Thessalonians*, p. 47.

historical details into a comprehensive hypothesis.[1] Whether this hypothesis is correct cannot be determined with any certainty with the evidence available. But it does demonstrate the plausibility of the tradition's having been composed in the Pauline circle with reference to a Judean-based persecution.

There is, on the other hand, another plausible setting for the composition of this tradition. Acts 8.1 indicates that the persecution which followed the death of Stephen resulted effectively in the expulsion of believers from Jerusalem. The account of Stephen's speech includes the same link between the persecution of the prophets, the killing of Jesus and the persecution of believers (7.51-52) as do 1 Thess. 2.15 and the reconstructed tradition. Moreover, the situation is firmly located in Judea, originating in Jerusalem.[2] If this was indeed the setting for the composition of the tradition, Paul may even have learned it not as a Christian but as an oppressor of Christians, perhaps overhearing it as he persecuted Christians himself.[3]

What would such an origin suggest about the relationship between the pre-Thessalonian tradition and the Synoptic parallels and their antecedents? Although it is possible that the Synoptic material represents the elaboration of a hymnic tradition, such a process appears to be inherently unlikely. If the Matthean parallel is in fact a composition of the church and not based on authentic material, it appears more likely that it was the result of reflection on common Christian experience rather than an expansion of an existing hymn. The points of contact may in this case be the result either of the use of common themes or of the influence of the hymnic tradition on the selection of certain words and phrases.[4] On the other hand, if the Matthean passage is based on

1.   R. Jewett, 'The Agitators and the Galatian Congregation', *NTS* 17 (1970–71), pp. 204-206.

2.   In this case, the more general reference to Judea in the text of 1 Thessalonians is a consequence of the parallelism with the situation of the Thessalonians; cf. the observation of Holtz, *Thessalonicher*, pp. 99-100.

3.   D.M. Stanley offers the same *Sitz im Leben* but on a different basis ('"Become Imitators of Me": The Pauline Conception of Apostolic Tradition', *Bib* 40 [1959], pp. 868-69; cf. *idem*, 'Imitation in Paul's Letters: Its Significance for his Relationship to Jesus and to his Own Christian Foundations', in P. Richardson and J.C. Hurd (eds.), *From Jesus to Paul: Studies in Honour of Francis Wright Beare* [Waterlo, Ont.: Wilfrid Laurier University Press, 1984], p. 136); and Gaston unites the two, but without offering evidence (*No Stone*, p. 456).

4.   If the hymnic tradition continued to exist independently, then its influence

authentic dominical sayings, then it does appear likely that such sayings would influence the composition of a hymnic tradition, or even be consciously adapted into such a tradition. Final judgments on this issue depend on a wide variety of considerations that cannot be undertaken here. The significant point for the immediate purpose is to observe that the existence of Synoptic parallels is no objection to the hypothesis offered here for the origin of the pre-Thessalonian tradition.

Not only is a hymnic response to persecution plausible in itself; specific *Sitze im Leben* can also be offered for the composition of this particular hymnic tradition. Although the tradition may in fact have been composed in another setting unknown to us, the two proposed above demonstrate that there can be no historical objection to the hypothesis that a tradition underlies 1 Thess. 2.14-16.

Conclusion: 1 Thessalonians 2.14-16 and Responsibility for the Death of Jesus in Luke–Acts

The conclusions reached in this chapter are of signal importance for understanding Luke's presentation of responsibility for the death of Jesus. These conclusions are summarized below.

1. Because 1 Thess. 2.14-16 is authentic, it confirms that the assertion of some Jewish responsibility for the death of Jesus arose before 50 CE. It cannot be assumed, therefore, that this assertion was created only as the result of post-70 conflict between Christians and Jews;[1] nor can it be asserted that it was the creation of any of the Synoptic Evangelists, including Luke.

2. The passage's apparent basis in tradition indicates that Jewish responsibility for the death of Jesus was a part of the preaching or teaching of at least some Christians before 50 CE. Because Christians in this period were almost certainly predominantly Jewish, it is likely that the assertion of Jewish responsibility for the death of Jesus arose among Jewish Christians. The presence of the assertion cannot in itself, therefore, indicate that a text arose among Gentile Christians in conflict with Jews.[2]

3. The assertion of Jewish responsibility for the death of Jesus was

---

may explain the variant ἐκδιώξουσιν at Lk. 11.49. On the other hand, such influence may also have come from the text of 1 Thess. 2.15.

1. *Contra*, for example, Beck, *Mature Christianity*, p. 47.

2. *Contra*, for example, P. Lapide, *Wer war schuld an Jesu Tod?* (Gütersloh: Gerd Mohn, 1987), p. 45.

transmitted in the context of the Christian response to persecution. It was linked to the traditional Jewish motif of the killing of the prophets and served to connect Christian experience to that of God's people in the past. Whether it was also transmitted in other settings remains to be determined.

4. As Paul uses the motif in this passage, it asserts that only a portion of the Jewish people are responsible for the death of Jesus. The assertion is limited to Judea and is further limited to a faction that rejects Jesus and opposes the gospel in contrast to Jewish Christians in Palestine, who continue to suffer persecution from their compatriots.

5. This same geographical orientation and partitive reference may have been part of the specific tradition to which Paul alludes. If the tradition was formulated in Paul's circle in response to persecution instigated by Jews associated with Zealot elements in Palestine, then it likely had an orientation to Judea in general. If the tradition was formulated in response to the persecution of Hellenistic Jewish Christians in Jerusalem, then it had a more specific geographical orientation toward Jerusalem.

The implications for Luke's presentation of responsibility for the death of Jesus are clear. It is not likely that in his treatment of Jewish responsibility for the death of Jesus Luke depended on 1 Thess. 2.14-16 or on the specific tradition on which it is based. But it is clear that at the very least Luke transmits a part of accepted Christian teaching; he does not himself invent the idea of Jewish involvement. Furthermore, although Luke's precise depiction of responsibility as confined to Jerusalem is not matched by 1 Thess. 2.14-16, it is closely paralleled by that passage's implicit restriction of responsibility to Palestine. Furthermore, if the tradition behind this text was indeed formed in response to the persecution of Hellenistic Jewish Christians in Jerusalem, then Luke's restriction of responsibility to Jerusalem may be related to this tradition or similar material.

Careful analysis of 1 Thess. 2.14-16 has demonstrated a strong possibility, if not the likelihood, that Luke reflects primitive Christian tradition in presenting Jerusalem's involvement in the death of Jesus. Further clues to his use of such tradition may be found in the other Synoptics. Therefore, attention must now turn to Matthew and Mark.

Chapter 5

RESPONSIBILITY FOR THE DEATH OF JESUS IN
PRE-SYNOPTIC TRADITION

The previous chapter's discussion has brought to light strong evidence
to suggest that a tradition ascribing responsibility for the death of Jesus
to Palestinian Jews—possibly even Jerusalemite Jews—was in circulation
before 50 CE. But were such traditions available to Luke? The most
obvious place to turn for an answer to that question is the other
Synoptics, Matthew and Mark, from whose texts pre-Synoptic passion
traditions may be inferred.[1] If it can be established from these that
responsibility for the death of Jesus was ascribed to Jerusalem Jews in
pre-Synoptic tradition, then Luke may be regarded as developing a
motif already present in the traditions that he used.

Of course, such an inquiry is fraught with difficulties. Successive generations of criticism of the Gospels have yielded a plethora of reconstructions of the pre-Synoptic tradition.[2] Furthermore, the erosion of

---

1. In the discussion that follows, most examples are taken from Matthew and
Mark, since it has already been established that Luke has a particular redactional
emphasis on the responsibility of Jerusalem. In certain instances, recourse to the
Lukan text remains useful in ascertaining the history of the tradition.

2. Scholars representing a wide spectrum of methods and opinions have agreed
that a connected passion narrative lay behind the Synoptic Gospels, although they
disagree as to the exact content of that narrative: R. Bultmann, *The History of the
Synoptic Tradition* (ET; Oxford: Basil Blackwell, 1968), pp. 275-79, 370-71;
M. Dibelius, *From Tradition to Gospel* (ET; London: James Clarke, 1971), pp. 178-
80; V. Taylor, *The Formation of the Gospel Tradition* (London: Macmillan, 2nd edn,
1949), pp. 44-47, 59-60; *idem, The Gospel according to St Mark* (London:
Macmillan, 1952), pp. 524, 658; J. Jeremias, *The Eucharistic Words of Jesus* (ET;
London: SCM Press, 1966), pp. 89-96; R. Pesch, *Das Markusevangelium* (2 vols.;
HTKNT, 2; Freiburg: Herder, 1976), II, pp. 1-25; *idem, Das Evangelium der
Urgemeinde* (Freiburg: Herder, 1979), *passim*. More skeptical is W.H. Kebler,
'Conclusion: From Passion Narrative to Gospel', in *idem* (ed.), *The Passion in
Mark: Studies on Mark 14–16* (Philadelphia: Fortress Press, 1976), pp. 156-59.

confidence in the two-document hypothesis casts additional doubt on many tradition-critical studies which have assumed Markan priority.[1] Nevertheless, the situation is not hopeless. In the present case, a wide variety of materials in the Gospels can be brought to bear on the issue. Therefore, the conclusions can be drawn not with a single method but with an accumulation of evidence from a wide range of materials and methods of criticism. What this chapter will show is that Jerusalem's responsibility for the death of Jesus is expressed or implied in a multiplicity of texts and types of texts, many with excellent claims to a basis in primitive tradition. The relevance of these lines of evidence (Jesus' lament over Jerusalem [Mt. 23.37-39//Lk. 13.34-35], the designation of Jesus' opponents, Jesus' journey to Jerusalem, and various incidental references to Jerusalem) is treated under the appropriate headings. The cumulative force of these data indicates that the pre-Synoptic tradition limited Jewish responsibility for the death of Jesus to Jerusalem.

The Lament over Jerusalem

Mt. 23.37-39//Lk. 13.34-35 is clearly a traditional text on either the two-document or multi-stage theories of Synoptic relationships.[2] In the former case, it is taken from Q; in the latter, it belongs to some unspecified pre-Synoptic tradition. The question is somewhat more difficult on the Griesbach theory, according to which Matthew may have composed the passage. There is, however, a clear indication that Matthew did not create this text. Contrary to his universal practice elsewhere, Matthew here uses the Semitic spelling for Jerusalem ('Ιερουσαλήμ).[3] No theological explanation for this spelling is forthcoming,[4] but the

---

1. The possibility that Luke's passion source is different from Mark's and Matthew's (cf. D.R. Catchpole, *The Trial of Jesus: A Study in the Gospels and Jewish Historiography from 1770 to the Present Day* [SPB, 12; Leiden: Brill, 1971], pp. 153-220) is an additional complication. But it does not rule out this investigation a priori, since it is clear that an independent Lukan source is closely related to the Markan/Matthean source.

2. H.F. Bayer has argued that this text is an authentic saying of Jesus (*Jesus' Predictions of Vindication and Resurrection: The Provenance, Meaning and Correlation of the Synoptic Predictions* [WUNT, 2.20; Tübingen: Mohr (Paul Siebeck), 1986], pp. 45-48). If his argument is correct, then the passage is obviously also part of the pre-Synoptic tradition.

3. Cf. Sand, *Matthäus*, p. 475.

4. J. Gnilka is among those who assert that Matthew uses 'Ιεροσόλυμα

assumption that the pre-Matthean tradition used the Semitic form adequately accounts for the anomaly.

Most commentators regard the vocative 'Jerusalem, Jerusalem' in Mt. 23.37 as a synecdoche referring to all Israel.[1] This interpretation depends largely on judgments about Matthew's theology based on other texts.[2] At the level of pre-Synoptic tradition, however, what is important to note is that Jerusalem is specified as the killer of the prophets despite the fact that it is not so identified in other materials which draw on the killing-of-the-prophets motif.[3] Although the vocative 'Jerusalem, Jerusalem' could have functioned in the tradition as a poetic figure for all Israel, it must be asked why such a figure would be used in this context. It could reflect the prophetic usage of Jerusalem as a figure for Israel (e.g., Isa. 51.17; Jer. 6.8).[4] The phrase 'who kills the prophets'

because of its 'secular' association in order to convey God's abandonment of Judaism (*Das Matthäusevangelium* [HTKNT, 1; 2 vols.; Freiburg: Herder, 1986–88], I, pp. 67-68). But because Matthew uses that spelling exclusively except for 23.37 (nowhere in Matthew is Jerusalem more 'abandoned' than here), and because Mark also uses it exclusively, it is difficult to see any basis for discerning a theological motive for the spelling. Matthew may have used it simply because it was used in his sources or among his circle.

1. For example, Gnilka, *Matthäusevangelium*, II, p. 304; Sand, *Matthäus*, p. 475.

2. Hare understands the tension in the transition from the scribes and Pharisees stoning the prophets (Mt. 23.29-35) to the pronouncement of judgment on 'this generation' (v. 36) to the Jerusalem oracle (vv. 37-39) as an indication that 'Jerusalem' stands for all Israel ('Rejection', p. 39; cf. Sand, *Matthäus*, p. 475). However, three considerations circumscribe the difficulty for the issue at hand. The first is the uncertainty that vv. 37-39 were found in the Matthean context in the tradition. The second is the characteristic Synoptic use of 'this generation', discussed above with respect to Luke. The third is the observation that in any case Matthew preserves the traditional exclusion of the Pharisees from the passion narrative (see discussion below). Thus, although the Pharisees' rejection of the prophets is linked to the killing of the prophets, the discourse ends with the reference to the killer of the prophets *par excellence*, introducing the discussion of Jerusalem's fate (Mt. 24) which in turn precedes the passion events (Mt. 26–27).

3. Cf. the definitive analysis of the killing of the prophets, namely Steck, *Geschick, passim*. It must be stressed that in the saying, 'Jerusalem', not 'your children', is identified as the one who kills the prophets. Hence, even if Jerusalem's children are all Israel and not just the city's inhabitants (so Gnilka, *Matthäusevangelium*, p. 303), the saying implies only the involvement of Jerusalem in the death of Jesus.

4. Steck notes that Jerusalem sometimes stands for all Israel by means of

could even mark the vocative 'Jerusalem' as referring to all Israel, since traditionally it is Israel and not merely Jerusalem that kills the prophets.[1] On the other hand, other terms with unambiguously wider denotations were available, and these too have antecedents in the prophetic literature (e.g., 'Israel', 'house of Jacob', Jer. 2.4). Thus, the juxtaposition of Jerusalem with the killing of the prophets may have been a deliberate variation on the usual killing-of-the-prophets motif in order to call attention to Jerusalem's distinctive role in the death of Jesus.

Thus, there are good arguments for understanding 'Jerusalem' to refer specifically to Jerusalem in the pre-Matthean/Lukan tradition. But at this point, the arguments cannot be regarded as decisive. A conclusion can only be drawn when the wider case is considered. If Mt. 23.27// Lk. 13.34 is an isolated instance in the pre-Synoptic tradition, then 'Jerusalem' can be taken as a figure for all Israel. But if there are indications elsewhere that Jerusalem was traditionally specified as the agent of the crucifixion, then the reference to Jerusalem in the lament is probably another such specification.[2] At this point the text does provide a preliminary indication that Jerusalem was isolated in at least part of the pre-Synoptic tradition. Therefore, other texts can be considered in that light.

The Opponents of Jesus

The opponents of Jesus are variously named in the Synoptic Gospels: scribes, Pharisees, Herodians, Sadducees, high priests, elders, even

---

synecdoche, but never in connection with the deaths of the prophets (*Geschick*, pp. 88-89, 227-29). Moessner's recent observations merely reinforce Steck's earlier observations, since his citations from the Qumran literature do not allude to the deaths of the prophets either (*Banquet*, p. 235 n. 133).

1.   Steck (*Geschick*, pp. 227-29) and Moessner (*Banquet*, p. 235 n. 133) both insist that the common synecdoche of Jerusalem for Israel and the common association of all Israel with the deaths of the prophets demands that Jerusalem be understood to stand for all Israel in this logion; however, Luke's restriction of responsibility to Jerusalem elsewhere indicates that he, at least, understood the reference to be restricted (cf. discussion above, Chapter 2).

2.   U. Luz remarks that Jerusalem is in Q 'die (an Jesu Tod) schuldige Stadt' (*Das Evangelium nach Matthäus* [EKKNT, 1.1; Zürich: Benziger Verlag; Neukirchen–Vluyn: Neukirchener Verlag, 1985], I, p. 71 n. 170). However, he exaggerates the degree to which Matthew stresses this idea, for it is countered by Matthew's retention of texts like Mt. 3.5; 4.25 and omission of references to Jerusalem in 12.24//Mk 3.22 and his unique use of the phrase ἡ ἁγία πόλις (4.5; 27.53).

disciples of John the Baptist. This sometimes bewildering profusion of antagonists has led to a variety of hypotheses about exactly who the opponents were and how the Evangelists understood them.[1] Nevertheless, concerning the opponents who bring Jesus to the cross, a distinct, consistent pattern emerges from the Synoptic materials. Although Jesus is opposed by a variety of groups, those who instigate his death are indigenous to Jerusalem. This identification is implied in several different ways, as the following discussion of the different groups implicated in the Synoptic materials will show.

The High Priests

Among the striking features of the Synoptic presentation of the passion is the consistent identification of the 'high priests' as the opponents of Jesus who instigate his death.[2] Although linked to others, namely

1. For example, M.J. Cook, *Mark's Treatment of the Jewish Leaders* (NovTSup, 51; Leiden: Brill, 1978), pp. 4-5 and *passim*; S. van Tilborg, *The Jewish Leaders in Matthew* (Leiden: Brill, 1972), p. 1 and *passim*.

2. That such an identification is historically correct has been affirmed by many critics, including A.N. Sherwin-White ('The Trial of Jesus', in D.E. Nineham [ed.], *Historicity and Chronology in the New Testament* [Theological Collections, 6; London: SPCK, 1965], pp. 97-116), J. Blinzler (*Der Prozess Jesu* [Regensburg: Pustet, 4th edn, 1969], p. 448), D.R. Catchpole ('The Problem of the Historicity of the Sanhedrin Trial', in E. Bammel [ed.], *The Trial of Jesus: Cambridge Studies in Honour of C.F.D. Moule* [SBT, 2.13; London: SCM Press, 1970], pp. 59-63), G.S. Sloyan (*Jesus on Trial: The Development of the Passion Narratives and their Historical and Ecumenical Implications* [ed. J. Reumann; Philadelphia: Fortress Press, 1973], pp. 16, 45-46, 68-72, 128-29), O. Betz ('Probleme des Prozesses Jesu', *ANRW* II.25.1, pp. 594-96), K. Kertelge ('Einführung', in *idem* [ed.], *Der Prozess gegen Jesus: Historische Rückfrage und theologische Deutung* [QD, 112; Freiburg: Herder, 1989], pp. 7-8), K. Müller ('Möglichkeit und Vollzug jüdischer Kapitalgerichtsbarkeit im Prozess gegen Jesus von Nazaret', in Kertelge [ed.], *Prozess*, pp. 41-83), and J. Gnilka (*Das Evangelium nach Markus* [EKKNT, 2; 2 vols.; Zürich: Benziger Verlag; Neukirchen–Vluyn: Neukirchener Verlag, 1978–79], II, p. 272, 286-88; 'Der Prozess Jesu nach den Berichten des Markus und Matthäus mit einer Rekonstruktion des historischen Verlaufs', in Kertelge, *Prozess*, pp. 26-31). Even if the highly skeptical arguments of Paul Winter are accepted, the Sanhedrin under priestly leadership still plays a leading role in the passion events (*On the Trial of Jesus* [ed. T.A. Burkill and G. Vermes; SJ, 1; Berlin: de Gruyter, 2nd edn, 1974], *passim*; cf. Betz, 'Probleme', p. 620; and the comments of J. Neusner in *A History of the Mishnaic Law of Damages* [5 vols.; Leiden: Brill, 1983–85], V, p. 131). For the present purpose, the central issue is not simply whether the high priests were involved in the actual crucifixion of Jesus but whether traditions of the

'scribes' and 'elders', the high priests figure most prominently in the final plot.[1] Indeed, nowhere within the Synoptic passion narratives is that plot reported without reference to the high priests (Mk 11.18; 12.12; 14.1-2, 10, 43, 53; 15.1-3, 10-11, 31 and parallels; Mt. 27.3-6, 62; 28.11; Lk. 23.4, 10, 13; 24.20).

Furthermore, the identification of the high priests as Jesus' opponents is commonly accepted as part of the pre-Synoptic tradition by a wide range of critics. Although opinions on specific texts differ, there is a broad consensus that at least some of the references to the high priests are traditional. Any redactional references to the high priests are generally taken as the Evangelist's specification of opponents where the tradition left the opponents unnamed. That specification, however, involves no real innovation on the part of the Evangelist, since the high priests are named as the opponents elsewhere in the tradition.[2] Hence, though many of the Synoptic references to the high priests may be redactional,

---

passion preserved a distinct place for them, though obviously if the former is true, the latter is likely.

1. E.S. Malbon offers the observation that in Mark the high priests appear by themselves, as members of a tripartite group with the scribes and elders, and in the two-part group with the scribes, so that the reader comes to regard them as the leaders in the plot ('The Jewish Leaders in the Gospel of Mark: A Literary Study of Marcan Characterization', *JBL* 108 [1989], p. 268).

2. For example, E. Best (*The Temptation and the Passion: The Marcan Soteriology* [SNTSMS, 2; London: Cambridge University Press, 1965], p. 90), E. Linnemann (*Studien zur Passionsgeschichte* [FRLANT, 102; Göttingen: Vandenhoeck & Ruprecht, 1970], pp. 46-49), and W. Schenk (*Der Passionsbericht nach Markus: Untersuchungen zur Überlieferungsgeschichte der Passionstraditionen* [Gütersloh: Gerd Mohn, 1974], pp. 144-48) regard the reference to the high priests in Mk 14.1 as traditional. Gnilka takes it as redactional but regards the references in 11.18 and 14.43 to be traditional (*Markus*, II, pp. 127, 219, 228, 267). T.A. Mohr regards Mk 14.1-2 as tendentious and Jn 11.47ff. as more reliable, though the reference to the priests in both is a part of the primitive passion narrative on which both ultimately depend (*Markus- und Johannespassion: Redaktions- und traditionsgeschichtliche Untersuchung der Markinischen und Johanneischen Passionstradition* [ATANT, 70; Zürich: Theologischer Verlag, 1982], pp. 79, 127). F. Lentzen-Deis regards texts which tend to implicate a wider circle (e.g. Mk 9.31) as indicating the Evangelist's interest in implicating the hearers/readers of the gospel, so that references to specific opponents like the high priests are traditional ('Passionsbericht als Handlungsmodell? Überlegungen zu Anstössen aus der "pragmatischen" Sprachwissenschaft für die exegetischen Methoden', in Kertelge [ed.], *Prozess*, pp. 212-13).

there remains a core of references in the tradition such that the high priests still appear as the leading opponents in the final plot against Jesus.

The identification of the high priests as the opponents of Jesus extends to the Synoptic passion predictions, though not to all of them.[1] The high priests are named in Mk 8.31; 10.33 and parallels, but not in Mk 9.31 or Mt. 26.1-2. Some have theorized that these latter texts represent the more original form of the passion predictions, in which the opponents were referred to only generally, if at all.[2] However, it is not at all clear that this is the case. The combination of similarities and differences in Mt. 16.21//Mk 8.31//Lk. 9.22 is difficult to explain on any hypothesis other than the varying influences of pre-Synoptic traditions on the different Evangelists. Matthew and Luke show significant agreement against Mark at this point: both use ἀπό in the place of Mark's ὑπό, both omit the articles before ἀρχιερέων and γραμματέων, and both have ἐγερθῆναι in the place of Mark's ἀναστῆναι. But Luke's use of Matthew does not in itself easily explain the differences between them. Although Luke's ἀποδοκιμασθῆναι could be taken as an allusion to Ps. 118.22 in order to sharpen the identification of the 'builders' with the Jerusalem leadership (Lk. 20.17), it is difficult to understand why Luke would omit Matthew's direct reference to Jerusalem in light of Luke's own heightening of emphasis on Jerusalem and its leaders elsewhere. Thus, unless the agreements of Matthew and Luke are merely coincidental, independent recourse to tradition best explains the texts, whatever the general literary relationship of the Synoptics. The fact that all three Synoptics name the elders, high priests and scribes would therefore indicate that the identification is traditional.

Moreover, it is not entirely clear that the more general expressions are

---

1. Evaluations of the tradition history of the passion predictions are numerous. Among those arguing for authenticity are V. Taylor, 'The Origin of the Markan Passion Sayings', *NTS* 1 (1954–55), pp. 159-67; Mann, *Mark*, pp. 344-45; and Bayer, *Predictions*, pp. 150-51, 213-15 and *passim*. Arguments for a traditional setting in the church are offered by Dibelius, *Tradition*, pp. 225-27; W. Grundmann, *Das Evangelium nach Markus* (THKNT, 2; Berlin: Evangelische Verlagsanstalt, 3rd edn, 1968), p. 215; R. McKinnis, 'An Analysis of Mark 10.32-34', *NovT* 18 (1976), pp. 90-99.

2. For example, McKinnis, 'Mark 10.32-34', p. 98; Gnilka, *Markus*, II, pp. 12, 15. A contrary opinion is offered by Pesch, *Markusevangelium*, II, pp. 50, 170. Interestingly, both suggest that the naming of the officials in Mk 8.31 is in accord with the tradition of the suffering righteous one, but from that observation they draw different conclusions about the tradition history of the verse.

remnants of primitive tradition that did not name the opponents. The expression 'hands of men' in Mk 9.31 is clearly intended to contrast with 'Son of Man'.[1] That this contrast, and not a lack of interest in the specific identity of the opponents, is the salient factor is suggested by the similar expressions 'hands of sinners' in Mk 14.41 and 'hands of sinful men' in Lk. 24.7. In those cases the innocence of Jesus is stressed through a contrast with the sinfulness of his opponents.[2] Specific identification of the opponents may be downplayed to express this contrast, but it is not necessarily excluded by it: Mark's narrative, for example, implicitly identifies the opponents named in 14.43 with the sinners of v. 41. Whether this sequence was part of the pre-Synoptic tradition can remain an open question; what can be said with certainty is that generalized references to Jesus' opponents do not *ipso facto* exclude specific identifications of them in the same strata of tradition.

However, if the original form of the passion predictions did not name the opponents, the insertion of specific groups still appears to be based on other passion traditions. The conclusion that at least portions of the pre-Synoptic tradition identified the high priests as the final opponents of Jesus appears to be secure.

Two factors about this identification make it especially pertinent to the question under consideration here. The first is that the high priests were obviously indigenous to Jerusalem. Thus, a traditional identification of the opponents of Jesus with the high priests is consistent with the hypothesis that the tradition restricted Jewish responsibility for the death of Jesus to people associated with Jerusalem. Secondly, the Jerusalem locus of the high priests appears to have been distinctly maintained in the tradition: the high priests are named only in the Jerusalem narrative and in predictions of the passion which anticipate events in Jerusalem. That this exclusion of the high priests from material associated with Galilee was traditional appears to be incontrovertible; there is no evidence whatever to suggest that a redactor removed them from traditions located outside of Jerusalem.

The Associates of the High Priests

But does the consistent association of the high priests with other groups indicate that the tradition either obscured the association of Jesus'

---

1. This contrast is commonly noted: see for example Pesch, *Urgemeinde*, p. 118.

2. It is therefore gratuitous to identify the 'men' of Mk 9.31 as the nation Israel, as does Pesch (*Urgemeinde*, p. 118).

opponents with Jerusalem or maintained no such association at all? Different evaluations have been given as to the origin of the references to 'elders' and 'scribes' as among those who instigate Jesus' death.[1] But less important than their origin in tradition or redaction is the significance of these references. In particular, the fact that 'scribes' are prominent among Jesus' opponents in Galilee might suggest that the Synoptic tradition tended to obscure the association of Jesus' death with Jerusalemite opponents.[2]

However, several factors suggest that these other groups did not serve to dilute the distinctive role of Jerusalem. One is the apparent function of the tripartite list 'high priests, scribes and elders'. In all of the Synoptics these three groups appear to compose the Sanhedrin in its entirety. Explicit references to 'the whole Sanhedrin' appear in close proximity to the tripartite list. In Mk 15.1 ὅλον τὸ συνέδριον appears at the end of the tripartite list, apparently to emphasize that the involvement of the three groups constitutes the entire Sanhedrin. τὸ συνέδριον ὅλον in Mk 14.55//Mt. 26.59 is preceded by reference to the gathering of the scribes and elders in Mk 14.53//Mt. 26.57; Matthew's reference there to τὸν ἀρχιερέα (singular) probably reflects a stylistic decision not to refer to the 'high priests' in the plural immediately after the mention of

---

1. For example, Mohr regards the combination of high priests and scribes to be redactional in Mk 11.18; 14.2 and 15.31 but traditional in 10.33 (*Markuspassion*, p. 120). Schenk similarly regards the reference to scribes in Mk 11.18 as redactional, reflecting the antithesis between the teaching of Jesus and that of the scribes, although he takes all references to elders as traditional (*Passionsbericht*, pp. 152, 207). L. Schenke regards all references to scribes or elders to be redactional except for the elders in Mk 8.31 (*Studien zur Passionsgeschichte des Markus: Tradition und Redaktion in 14.1-42* [FB, 4; Würzburg: Echter Verlag, 1971], pp. 39-42). D. Dormeyer regards all references to opponents other than the high priests to be Mark's redactional projection of the pre-passion opponents into the passion narrative (*Die Passion Jesu als Verhaltensmodell: Literarische und theologische Analyse der Traditions- und Redaktionsgeschichte der Markuspassion* [NTAbh NS, 11; Münster: Aschendorff, 1974], pp. 68-71). Pesch is more cautious, suggesting that the influence of oral tradition explains the variations in the enumeration of opponents (*Markusevangelium*, II, p. 51). If the high priests alone appeared in Mark's sources, then his motives for inserting 'scribes' and 'elders' but not 'Pharisees' or 'Herodians' remain unclear, unless he sought thereby to preserve a distinctive role for the Jerusalemite opposition.

2. Mohr regards references to the scribes in Mark's passion narrative as the Evangelist's insertion of the opponents identified with venues outside Jerusalem (*Markuspassion*, p. 79). Cf. also Dormeyer, *Passion*, pp. 69-71.

the one 'high priest' *par excellence*, not an exclusion of the 'high priests' from the proceedings.[1] In both cases, then, the tripartite list appears to stress the unanimity of the Sanhedrin in its opposition against Jesus. Although the high priests may take the lead in the plot, the rest of the Sanhedrin gives its consent. Thus, although 'scribes' appear both within and outside the passion events and both within and outside Jerusalem, those associated with the high priests appear to be identified with the Sanhedrin and are therefore characteristically Jerusalemite scribes.[2]

On several occasions, of course, one of the three members of the tripartite list is not mentioned. However, this factor does not alter the significance of the groups. The high priests are consistently named in such fractional lists. Phrases like 'high priests and scribes' or 'high priests and elders' may represent the Evangelists' abbreviating of sources, or they may be the result of the insertion of only one additional group to a source that named a single group of opponents. In either case, the purpose could be either to refer to the entire Sanhedrin with less verbosity or to suggest a segment of the Sanhedrin. Still, the coming together of the three groups in the trial of Jesus and the constant presence of the high priests indicates that a plot of the supreme council under priestly leadership is in view.

Whether the tripartite list was primitive or secondary is irrelevant for the purpose of this investigation.[3] The significant factor is that in either

---

1. Lentzen-Deis has suggested that πάντες in Mk 14.53 also stresses the role of the entire Sanhedrin ('Passionsbericht', pp. 222, 228). However, it may merely indicate Mark's grappling with the awkward juxtaposition of the singular τὸν ἀρχιερέα and the plural οἱ ἀρχιερεῖς, so that 'all the high priests' are distinct from 'the [one] high priest [*par excellence*]'. This interpretation is corroborated by the observation that the article is repeated with πρεσβύτεροι and γραμματεῖς, so that it is not clear that πάντες refers to all three groups. Nevertheless, the interest of Mark or his sources in the entire Sanhedrin is assured by the other, unambiguous references.

2. Cf. the discussion in D. Lührmann, 'Die Pharisäer und die Schriftgelehrten im Markusevangelium', *ZNW* 78 (1980), p. 172; and R.L. Mowery 'Pharisees and Scribes, Galilee and Jerusalem', *ZNW* 80 (1989), p. 267.

3. Gnilka asserts that the emphasis on the entire Sanhedrin is Mark's own (*Markusevangelium*, II, pp. 220, 268; 'Prozess', pp. 19-21; cf. Sloyan, *Trial*, pp. 130-31). Schenk understands that πρεσβύτεροι is the most primitive term for the final opponents of Jesus but suggests that this term alone would have referred to the members of the Sanhedrin in particular (*Passionsbericht*, p. 207).

case it does not represent a dilution of emphasis on the distinctive role of Jerusalem. The Sanhedrin is as distinctively Jerusalemite as the priesthood: although it is indeed the supreme council for the entire nation, it is intimately associated with Jerusalem. Although 'scribes' appear outside Jerusalem, they are connected to the other Sanhedrin members—and to the plot against Jesus—only in Jerusalem. Again, the fact that the Sanhedrin and the tripartite list are mentioned in the Synoptics only in close association with Jerusalem is coherent with the hypothesis of a distinct role for Jerusalem in the pre-Synoptic tradition. If the tripartite list is redactional, it does not indicate the Evangelists' broadening of responsibility beyond Jerusalem. If it is traditional, it is consistent with the restriction of responsibility to Jerusalem.

Matthew's appellation πρεσβύτεροι τοῦ λαοῦ has been widely understood as indicating a broadening of responsibility for the death of Jesus to all Israel. The genitive 'of the people' is understood to stress the representative function of the elders and their associates. Thus, when Jesus dies at the instigation of οἱ πρεσβύτεροι τοῦ λαοῦ, all Israel is implicated.[1] Two observations are relevant in this respect. One is that the congruence of this phrase with Matthew's distinct use of λαός elsewhere in his Gospel suggests that it is indeed redactional. The second concerns its significance. The genitive τοῦ λαοῦ is associated not just with πρεσβύτεροι but also with γραμματεῖς in Mt. 2.4. Significantly, this is the only occasion in Matthew where the phrase is dependent on γραμματεῖς, despite the fact that the latter occurs in Matthew some 17 times. The 'scribes' of 2.4 and the 'elders' of 21.23; 26.3, 47 share a common feature: both are found in Jerusalem. It may be that Matthew or his sources employ τοῦ λαοῦ to distinguish these scribes and elders from their provincial counterparts: these are the supreme scholars and officials associated with Jerusalem, not those with lesser, local authority from the outlying regions. Thus, it is not self-evident that a representative function is intended even at the level of Matthean redaction. In fact, the association of πρεσβύτεροι τοῦ λαοῦ with the death of Jesus may be another indication that Jerusalem has a distinct role in the passion tradition.

---

1.   Van Tilborg, *Jewish Leaders*, p. 5; D. Senior, *The Passion Narrative according to Matthew* (BETL, 39; Leuven: Leuven University Press, 1975), p. 25; Gnilka, *Matthäusevangelium*, I, p. 38; II, p. 384; *idem*, 'Prozess', p. 21; Sand, *Matthäus*, pp. 50-51, 428.

The Pharisees, Herodians and Sadducees

High priests, scribes and elders are not the only opponents of Jesus in the Synoptic tradition. Other groups appear in opposition to Jesus, both outside and inside Jerusalem. These groups have no clear association with Jerusalem, and so their opposition could indicate that Jerusalem's role is not distinct. But on closer examination, the treatment of these opponents tends to confirm the hypothesis that Jerusalem has a particular function in the passion tradition: opponents without a firm connection to Jerusalem are not implicated in the final plot against Jesus.[1]

Pharisees and Herodians are credited with a plot to do away with Jesus in Mk 3.6. Opinion is divided on whether this verse is traditional or redactional. Because it serves as a climax to the controversy pericopae of Mk 2.1–3.5, those who regard this section as the result of Markan editing take the verse as redactional.[2] If, on the other hand, the controversy section in Mark is based on an earlier collection of pericopae, then it is entirely possible that the verse is traditional.[3] Again, however, the significance of this verse for the issue at hand is seen in its relationship to other materials, not simply in hypotheses about its origin. Although the

1.   The absence of the Pharisees from the Synoptic passion narratives has been widely noted and variously interpreted: cf. Winter, *Trial*, p. 174; P. Richardson, 'The Israel-Idea in the Passion Narratives', in Bammel (ed.), *Trial*, pp. 3-4; Pesch, *Markusevangelium*, I, p. 180; L.W. Hurtado, *Mark* (Good News Commentaries; London: Harper & Row, 1983), p. 123; Cook, *Jewish Leaders*, p. 94; Malbon, 'Leaders', pp. 272-75. Recently Lührmann ('Pharisäer', p. 172) and Mowery ('Pharisees and Scribes', p. 266) have stressed the Markan association of the Pharisees with Galilee.

2.   For example, Bultmann, *Tradition*, pp. 52-53; Dibelius, *Tradition*, pp. 44-45; Gnilka, *Markus*, I, p. 126. Pesch regards the controversies as belonging to a pre-Markan collection but 3.6 as redactional, although the naming of opponents is based on other traditions (*Markusevangelium*, I, pp. 149-50, 177, 196).

3.   Although W.H. Kebler writes of a 'virtual consensus' that the verse is redactional (*The Kingdom in Mark: A New Place and a New Time* [Philadelphia: Fortress Press, 1974], p. 21), some do argue that it has a traditional basis. R.A. Guelich argues that the verse is traditional, and though he agrees that the identification of the opponents is redactional, he nevertheless argues that Mark has inserted the identification of Jesus' opponents found in his sources for 2.15-28 and 12.13 (*Mark 1–8.26* (WBC, 34a: Dallas: Word Books, 1989], pp. 132, 138-39; cf. Taylor, *Mark*, p. 224; Pesch, *Markusevangelium*, I, pp. 149-50, 196; Gnilka, *Markus*, II, p. 151). Green offers a compelling argument that the very fact that the Pharisees and Herodians are not included in the Markan passion narrative suggests that the reference to them in 3.6 is traditional (*Death*, pp. 141-42, 185).

plot of Mk 3.6 has Jesus' death as its object, that object is not realized by these plotters, who are absent from the Markan passion narrative. Furthermore, the issues which give rise to the plot in Mk 3.6—Jesus' forgiveness of sins and association with sinners, his neglect of fasting and the Sabbath—play no explicit part in the passion tradition. The Evangelist and/or his sources appear to present a different scheme: Jesus meets deadly opposition from the very beginning of his ministry onwards, but he meets his death only in Jerusalem through the intrigues of the Jewish leaders of Jerusalem.[1]

The coupling of Pharisees and Herodians has been the subject of considerable critical speculation. A common opinion is that at this point Mark brings together religious and political leaders in a plot against Jesus, just as the two come together, in different form, in the passion narrative.[2] However, it is not clear that for Mark the categories 'religious leaders' and 'political leaders' were important; nor is it clear whether he would regard Pharisees as strictly religious and Herodians as strictly political. Indeed, little can be known of Mark's 'Herodians' apart from their opposition to Jesus.[3] Similarly, it has been suggested that the two groups represent the convergence of the friends and enemies of the Romans in opposition to Jesus.[4] This hypothesis may have some slender

1. This scheme is exactly the one noted in Lk. 4.16-30 and 13.31-35. Cf. the discussion above; Taylor, *Mark*, p. 224; Mann, *Mark*, pp. 101-102, 243.

2. Taylor, *Mark*, pp. 130-31, 224; Gnilka, *Markus*, I, p. 129; Guelich, *Mark 1–8.26*, pp. 138-39, 141.

3. Commonly the Markan 'Herodians' are understood to reflect the memory of the persecution of the church under Herod Agrippa I (cf. Gnilka, *Markus*, I, p. 129). There is, of course, no positive evidence for this hypothesis, and Jürgen Roloff has offered a compelling argument against it (*Das Kerygma und der irdische Jesus: Historische Motive in den Jesus-Erzählungen der Evangelien* [Göttingen: Vandenhoeck & Ruprecht, 1970], p. 64 n. 45). If there was a traditional connection between the death of John the Baptist at Herod's instigation and the death of Jesus (Mk 1.14 and parallels; 6.14-16 and parallels; cf. Best, *Temptation and Passion*, p. 120 n. 1), no extension of responsibility beyond Jerusalem appears to be implied. The Synoptic foreshadowing of Jesus' fate with John's stresses that both die according to God's will and despite their popularity (cf. Pesch, *Markusevangelium*, I, p. 101; Gnilka, *Markus*, I, p. 65; *idem*, *Matthäusevangelium*, I, p. 95; II, p. 217; Guelich, *Mark 1.1–8.26*, p. 42); any connection between their opponents is latent and undeveloped (Sand, *Matthäus*, p. 303). The absence of any apparent theological motive for their presence in the text of Mark does suggest that the Herodians appeared in Mark's sources.

4. Gnilka, *Markus*, II, p. 151.

support in the text: Mark or his sources may have understood the Pharisees and Herodians as taking different sides of the tribute issue in 12.13, though only the Pharisees are mentioned explicitly. But if such a convergence is intended to be connected to the death of Jesus, the connection is unclear. Although their intentions may be deadly, the Pharisees and Herodians do not appear among those who realize their deadly intentions.[1]

The appearance of the two groups in Mk 12.13 is instructive in other ways, however. Here it has been suggested that the appearance of the Pharisees and Herodians owes to a traditional collection of controversies which successively present all the opponents of Jesus.[2] Whatever their origin at this point, Mark indicates that the Pharisees and Herodians are sent by others to challenge Jesus (ἀποστέλλουσιν), those others apparently being the chief Jerusalemite opponents, the high priests, scribes and elders (11.27).[3] With the final plot already in motion (11.18), the

---

1.   Certain hypotheses that link the early opponents of Jesus to the passion may be dealt with briefly. Taylor hypothesizes that the controversies of Mk 2.1–3.6; 11.15-17, 27-33; 12.13-40 belonged to a pre-Markan collection that introduced the passion narrative (*Mark*, pp. 130-31). But if this is the case, the difference in the identity of the opponents in the pre-passion and passion materials is all the more mysterious. This observation suggests a more likely alternative: there were two streams of tradition about Jesus in conflict, only one of which was connected to his passion. A.B. Kolenkow has argued that Mark and John depend on a source which identified Jesus' healing ministry as the cause of the plot against him ('Healing Controversy as a Tie between Miracle and Passion Material for a Proto-Gospel', *JBL* 95 [1976], pp. 623-38). But Kolenkow himself indicates that Mark has not picked up the connection to healing (*Healing Controversy*, pp. 628-29), and significantly in the Fourth Gospel the connection between healing and the passion is realized through the agency of the Jerusalem Sanhedrin, among whom John reckons 'Pharisees' (Jn. 11.47-53). Thus, even if Kolenkow's hypothesis is correct, the Jerusalem connection still appears to be vital. Malbon has suggested that the Pharisees are linked to the passion by their association in Mk 2.16 with the 'scribes' who appear in both pre-passion and passion pericopae ('Leaders', p. 226). Such a connection is highly tenuous, however; it ignores the question of the conspicuous absence of 'Pharisees' from the Markan passion. Gnilka is probably right to link the 'leaven of the Pharisees and Herod' to their rejection of Jesus at 3.6 (*Markus*, I, p. 311), though the simple fact of rejection is adequate to explain the warning and no connection to the passion events is implied.

2.   Schenke, *Passionsgeschichte*, p. 40 n. 1.

3.   Cf. Gnilka, *Markus*, II, p. 151. Matthew's indication that the opponents are sent by the Pharisees (22.16) is apparently part of his own emphasis on the vigor of

initiative of the opposition is firmly in the hands of the Jerusalem Sanhedrin. Whether this note is a matter of tradition or redaction is unclear. If it is traditional, then it indicates again the tendency to implicate the tripartite opposition. If it is redactional, it indicates the Evangelist's reinforcement of the tendency already in the tradition.

Moreover, if, as Gnilka purposes, Mark found the Pharisees and Herodians in his source for 12.13 and inserted them into 3.6,[1] their exclusion from the passion events is all the more remarkable. If 12.13 was associated with Jerusalem in Mark's source, it is striking that Mark would insert the Pharisees and Herodians into an ex-Jerusalem controversy but not into the passion narrative.

Matthew presents a different pairing, Pharisees and Sadducees (16.1; cf. 3.7). Again, it is typically assumed that for the Evangelist the two groups represent the Jews united in opposition against Jesus.[2] But even if this is the case, Matthew does not directly implicate either 'Pharisees' or 'Sadducees' in the decisive plot. In 27.62 the Pharisees are named with the high priests as part of the delegation which requests a guard at Jesus' tomb. But this is the only instance in which Matthew associates them with the leading opponents of the passion. It may indeed be the Evangelists' intention to suggest that the Pharisees, although opposed to Jesus, were not involved in the final plot against him but did seek to squelch rumors of his resurrection once his execution had been carried out. It may also be that a particular Matthean interest in the Pharisees motivated his associating them with the high priests and indirectly with the final plot. If this is the case, the fact that the association is indirect is all the more striking. The identity of the passion opponents appears to be inviolable; Matthew can only implicate the Pharisees in the aftermath of the passion.[3] Nor are the Pharisees directly indicted in Mt. 23.34. As D.A. Carson has noted, those who are crucified here are sent by the

the Pharisees' opposition to Jesus (cf. Mt. 12.14, where Pharisees alone appear; diff. Mk 3.6).

1. Gnilka, *Markus*, II, p. 151.

2. For example, P. Bonnard, *L'évangile selon Saint Matthieu* (CNT, 1; Neuchâtel: Delachaux & Niestlé, 1963), pp. 237-38; Luz, *Matthäus*, I, p. 148; Gnilka, *Matthäusevangelium*, II, p. 40.

3. Bonnard suggests that because 27.62 associates the Pharisees with the high priests and 28.11 the elders with the high priests, the three groups compose the Sanhedrin for Matthew (*Matthieu*, p. 485). If this is the case, then the schema appears to be Matthew's own, perhaps owing to his interest in the Pharisees and association of them with the scribes (Mt. 23.1-36).

speaker, and for Matthew the speaker is Jesus.[1] In Matthew's presentation those persecuted by the Pharisees would appear to be Christians, those 'sent' (ἀποστέλλω) by Jesus (cf. Mt. 10.5, 16; 28.19), not Jesus himself. Thus, any indictment of the Pharisees for the death of Jesus is ruled out by the structure of the discourse.

But should those who are directly implicated be identified with the Pharisees or Sadducees? Are the 'elders' Pharisees and the 'high priests' Sadducees, for example? Such may well have been the case historically. But the terms used in the Synoptics indicate that any such identification was not of interest in the tradition or to the Evangelists. The opponents in the passion narrative appear to have been named so as to identify them as members of the Sanhedrin. In the tradition 'scribes' and 'elders', when associated with 'high priests', appear to have implied 'Sanhedrin members'. 'Pharisee' and 'Sadducee' are used outside the passion narrative, apparently with a different emphasis. In the case of the Sadducees, the stress seems to have fallen on their distinct theology, as in Mk 12.18 and parallels. Reasons for the naming of 'Pharisees' are less obvious; a connection with the opponents of the Evangelists' communities is often suggested but remains a speculative hypothesis. But the clear difference in usage within and without the passion narrative reinforces the impression that the passion tradition distinctly and deliberately implicated only persons associated with Jerusalem and that the Synoptists recognized and preserved that distinction.

The Crowds
The treatment of the crowds in the Synoptic material is consistent with the other data about the final opponents of Jesus in the pre-Synoptic passion tradition. In particular, the division between people and leaders, though probably less attenuated than in the text of Luke, appears to have been traditional and reinforces the impression of a unique role for Jerusalem's leaders in the passion.

Once again, opinions differ as to whether specific texts which set forth this division are traditional or redactional. But that the division was present in the tradition, at least implicitly, is extremely likely. Two types of material obviously existed side-by-side in the pre-Synoptic tradition. One is material in which Jesus is confronted with opposition from Jewish leaders. All of the controversy pericopae assume such conflict. The

---

1.   Carson, *Matthew*, p. 485.

other type of material is pericopae which assume the presence of large crowds of followers. Several of the miracle accounts (the feeding miracles [Mk 6.30-44 and parallels; 8.1-10 and parallels], the healing of the paralytic [Mk 2.1-12 and parallels],[1] the healing of the woman with hemorrhage [Mk 5.25-34 and parallels]), as well as Jesus' teaching from a boat (Mk 3.9; 4.1), assume that Jesus is surrounded by large numbers of people. Unless these pericopae are all entirely redactional creations, they indicate that the pre-Synoptic tradition presented Jesus as, on the one hand, opposed by Jewish leaders and, on the other hand, surrounded by large crowds of followers. It is therefore likely that the contrast between Jesus' popularity and the opposition of Jewish leaders was explicated at the pre-literary stage. Thus, even if texts like Mk 1.22 or 14.2 are redactional, they amount to the Evangelists' development of what was, at the very least, implicit in the tradition.[2]

Jesus' popularity with the crowds takes a fateful turn, of course, in the Barabbas episode.[3] But it is here that the vital connection to Jerusalem is made. It is not at all clear whether the crowd before Pilate was identified in the tradition as indigenous to Jerusalem or not. None of the Synoptics indicates as much in its narration of the episode; only retrospective summaries make the identification clear in Luke–Acts (Acts 13.27; cf. 2.5, 14, 23, 36). However, the cry for Barabbas's release and Jesus' crucifixion comes at the prompting of the Jerusalemite high priests

---

1.   Gnilka objects that the large crowd is Markan redaction, since its inability to enter the house (Mk 2.2) is in tension with Jesus' speaking to it (*Markus*, I, p. 97). This tension is more imagined than real, however: Jesus may speak to the crowd which has squeezed into the house while those forced to remain outside strain at the door and windows to hear. This understanding appears more likely than Gnilka's explanation of the pericope without the crowds: the demon which besets the paralytic did not know the correct way into the house (*Markus*, I, p. 97). But was the man then not a paralytic in the original account, so that he was able to come in through the roof himself? And how was an exorcism transformed into a healing? Pesch's judgment that the crowds are original is more satisfactory (*Markusevangelium*, I, p. 154).

2.   For example, Gnilka judges 1.22 to be redactional (*Markus*, I, p. 77). Pesch agrees but suggests that it is based on the tradition behind 1.27 (*Markusevangelium*, I, pp. 120-21). Mohr argues that the contrast in 14.2 is traditional, though originally with an emphasis more like that in Jn 11.47-53 than Mark (*Markuspassion*, pp. 120-22).

3.   In regard to the status of this pericope in the tradition, Green argues that it is attested in three independent sources and so must be traditional (*Death*, pp. 287-88).

(Mk 15.11) and elders (Mt. 27.20). Again, their initiative is stressed; and again, even if the note is secondary, it amounts to an augmentation of a tendency already present in the tradition.

But does the cry of an anonymous, implicitly Jewish crowd indicate a broadening of responsibility that indicts an ex-Jerusalem element, or even all Israel? And is such an understanding reinforced by the parable of the vineyard, which could imply that Israel as a nation has rejected the 'son' and so forfeited its elect status? There is little that suggests such an interpretation in Mark. The Markan parable of the vineyard is unambiguously directed against the leaders in contrast to the crowds (12.12; cf. 11.27), and the 'builders' of Ps. 118.22 are identified with those leaders.[1] In Mark's Barabbas episode the crowd is apparently identified as a group that went to the governor specifically to ask for a prisoner's release (15.8),[2] and nothing suggests that they have a wider significance. Although others in Mark do reject Jesus or aspects of his ministry, nothing serves to connect them to his death.[3] In Matthew, however, the situation is more complex: the vineyard is to be given to

---

1.   Bayer has offered cogent reasons for regarding the parable of the vineyard and the application of Ps. 118.22 to the leaders in connection with the parable as authentic teachings of Jesus (*Predictions*, pp. 90-106; *contra* Gnilka, *Markus*, II, p. 148).

2.   Blinzler, *Prozess*, pp. 305-307. Mohr (*Markuspassion*, pp. 292, 294) and Gnilka (*Markus*, II, pp. 297-98) both argue that Mk 15.8 is redactional, though the cry of the crowd for Barabbas's release and Jesus' death is traditional. Schenk's dismissal of the entire scene as secondary because of its incongruity with Roman jurisprudence ignores the difficulties of explaining the origin of the details if it is not based in historical events (*Passionsbericht*, pp. 247-48; cf. Gnilka, 'Prozess', pp. 19, 35-36). A. Strobel notes both the congruity of the scene with what is known of Roman practices and a basis in rabbinic legal tradition (*t. Sanh.* 11.7; *m. Sanh.* 11.3) for bringing a false prophet before the people of Israel at the time of a festival (*Die Stunde der Wahrheit: Untersuchungen zum Strafverfahren gegen Jesus* [WUNT, 21; Tübingen: Mohr (Paul Siebeck), 1980], pp. 124-27, 145).

3.   Lentzen-Deis confuses the Markan interest in the failures of Jesus' associates with responsibility for his death ('Passionsbericht', pp. 212-13). The restriction of the latter to specific groups suggests that while Mark may stress the failure of all around Jesus in his hour of distress, those who instigate his death nevertheless have a distinct role. The same caveat applies to Gnilka's connection between the hardening of Israel (Mk 4.12), the critique of the purity code (7.1-23), the temple protest and the cursing of the fig tree (11.12-19): Israel's failure (if it can rightly be termed that) may still be distinct from involvement in the death of Jesus (*Markus*, I, p. 25).

another ἔθνος (21.43), and the crowd before Pilate is climactically identified as πᾶς ὁ λαός (27.25).

However, the very convergence of these two factors in Matthew suggests that they represent a particular emphasis of the Evangelist and are not traditional elements. Matthew retains 21.46 along with 21.43 despite the tension between the reference to another ἔθνος and the specific application of the parable to the leaders. But this tension does have a point of resolution: Matthew apparently regards the Jerusalem leaders as the instigators of the rejection which leads to the giving of the vineyard to another ἔθνος. Likewise, the retention of the leaders' fomenting the crowd in 27.20 alongside the cry of πᾶς ὁ λαός in 27.25 indicates the same understanding: the crowd rejects Jesus, but only with the leaders' prompting. Furthermore, the use of the phrase πᾶς ὁ λαός in the LXX raises several interesting possibilities for the referent of πᾶς ὁ λαός in Mt. 27.25.[1] It appears unlikely that the Evangelist envisages an actual assembly of the entire nation before Pilate. At most, he could regard the crowd as having a representative function: those assembled effectively speak for the entire nation. However, it is also possible that he uses πᾶς ὁ λαός merely to indicate the crowd's unanimity.[2] It may even be

1. In the LXX, the phrase can be used in different contexts with a variety of emphases. In the Pentateuch it is used for the assembly of Israel (e.g. Exod. 18.21, 23; 20.18; 34.10; Num. 11.11-12; 15.26; Deut. 27.15-26). This reference is recognized in the translation of כל העם with πάσῃ τῇ συναγωγῇ in Lev. 10.3. However, a more limited referent is often implied. In the Deuteronomic instructions on executions, πᾶς ὁ λαός is to follow the witnesses in stoning an idolater (Deut. 13.10; 17.7). Obviously, the text does not envisage an assembly of the entire nation to perform an execution (aside, perhaps, from the idealized situation of the assembly of Israel in the wilderness) but stresses the responsibility of all Israelites within a community to participate. The interpretation of these texts in *m. Sanh.* 6.4 reflects an even more attenuated example of this pattern of usage: 'stoning him is [the duty] of all Israelites' (*The Mishnah: A New Translation* [ed. J. Neusner; London: Yale University Press, 1988]). The phrase πᾶς ὁ λαός refers to a subset of all Israelites elsewhere in the LXX as well. In Josh. 7.3 and Judg. 20.2 it refers to Israel's military forces, in the latter case excluding the tribe of Benjamin. In 2 Esd. 18.3-6 an assembly like those of all Israel in the wilderness is suggested, but those assembled implicitly consist only of the community returned from the exile. Thus, judgments, like Gnilka's, that πᾶς ὁ λαός refers to all Israel because Matthew only uses the phrase in 27.25 are premature (*Matthäus*, p. 458).

2. Frequently in the LXX the specific force of πᾶς in such contexts is to imply the unanimity of Israel's response (e.g., Exod. 19.8, 16; 24.3; 32.3; 33.8, 10; Lev. 9.23-24; cf. 2 Esd. 18.5-6).

intended to distinguish the people from the priests and could implicitly suggest that the crowd is indigenous to Jerusalem.[1] More plausible is the background provided by Deut. 17.7. This text sets forth the protocol of execution: πᾶς ὁ λαός is to join in stoning the convict after the witnesses have begun the process. Thus, in Mt. 27.25, πᾶς ὁ λαός participates in Jesus' execution after the witnesses, who also act at the behest of the Sanhedrin leadership (26.59-61). Alternately, the phrase may be the Evangelist's adoption of the traditional λαός from 26.5 in order to contrast the leaders' earlier concern for a θόρυβος ἐν τῷ λαῷ with the present acquiescence of πᾶς ὁ λαός. If, however, the marked shift from ὄχλος to λαός does indicate that a representative function is in view,[2] then it is at this point that the particular Matthean significance appears to work itself out. The crowd assembled effectively rejects Jesus on behalf of the nation. But it does so at the instigation of the leaders, who elsewhere are carefully distinguished from the crowds.[3] This turn of events engenders what the parable of the vineyard anticipates: the replacement of Israel with a new ἔθνος (i.e., the church composed of Jews and Gentiles)[4] because of the insidious, corrupting influence of the Jerusalem leadership.[5] The fact that this emphasis is made by the convergence of two uniquely Matthean texts in different settings, one of which is in

1. In Jer. 35.5 πᾶς ὁ λαός is distinguished from the priests and apparently refers to those assembled in the temple. In Jer. 43.9 πᾶς ὁ λαός ἐν Ἰερουσαλήμ is distinguished from [ὁ] οἶκος Ἰουδά, and in v. 10 πᾶς ὁ λαός refers to those assembled in the temple. However, such limited referents are demanded by the contexts; there is no evidence that the referent of the phrase was limited to the people of Jerusalem or the temple congregation apart from such contextual markers.

2. The reference to τὰ τέκνα ἡμῶν may underscore the representative function of the crowd (so Senior, *Passion Narrative*, p. 258, who says this is the opinion of nearly all commentators), but it may also serve to connect the rejection of Jesus with the destruction of Jerusalem (so Bonnard, *Matthieu*, p. 398; followed by France, *Matthew*, pp. 392-93).

3. Cf. van Tilborg, *Jewish Leaders*, p. 142.

4. That Matthew's church is largely Jewish is affirmed by commentators who give full weight to his 'replacement theology'; Bonnard, *Matthieu*, pp. 317, 369; J. Fitzmyer, 'Anti-Semitism and the Cry of "All the People"', *TS* 26 (1965), pp. 670-71; Hare, 'Rejection', pp. 38-39; Luz, *Matthäus*, pp. 66-67; France, *Matthew*, p. 310; I. Broer, 'Der Prozess gegen Jesus nach Matthäus', in Kertelge (ed.), *Prozess*, pp. 109-10.

5. Cf. France, *Matthew*, p. 52; Broer, 'Prozess nach Matthäus', pp. 103-104. Matthew's abiding interest in the leadership is overlooked in the judgments of commentators like Sand (*Matthäus*, pp. 435-36).

tension with its context, suggests that this particular emphasis is the result of Matthew's own combination and redaction of traditional material—particularly the insertion of πᾶς ὁ λαός in 27.25.[1] Indeed, this understanding is confirmed by two additional Matthean texts. In 27.64 the high priests and Pharisees' request for a guard at the tomb is intended to prevent deception of the λαός by reports of a resurrection, and in 28.11-15 the leaders' bribing of the soldiers leads to a false story circulating παρὰ 'Ιουδαίοις μέχρι τῆς σήμερον.[2] In both the role of the leaders in perpetuating the rejection of Jesus by the Jewish people is stressed.

The role of the crowds in the pre-Synoptic tradition of responsibility for Jesus' death may now be summarized: (1) the traditional division between people and leaders tends to underscore the role of the Jerusalem leadership in the passion; (2) the outcry of the crowd is instigated by the leaders and further stresses their responsibility; (3) the crowd itself is not identified with all Israel, although neither is it explicitly identified with Jerusalem; (4) the representative function of the crowd appears to be a peculiar Matthean emphasis and therefore is probably secondary. Thus, the presentation of the crowds is consistent with the view that the tradition restricted responsibility to Jerusalem, even reinforcing it at some points.

The Journey to Jerusalem

It is widely recognized that Luke is not the only Evangelist to present a fateful journey of Jesus to Jerusalem. A similar, if somewhat less prominent, journey is also found in Matthew and Mark. Scholarship is

---

1. Blinzler argues that Matthew here preserves tradition that the other Evangelists omit because only he is interested in the primitive tradition that all Israel shared in responsibility for Jesus' death (*Prozess*, pp. 315-17). Although it is granted that Matthew's peculiar interest is at work here, evidence that the primitive view was as Blinzler characterizes it is not forthcoming. The tradition of Pilate's hand-washing, for example, could have existed apart from emphasis on responsibility of all Israel: it underscores the responsibility of the leaders and crowds but does not equate them with all Israel.

2. Bonnard notes that in 28.11-15 the 'Jews' are still victims of their leaders (*Matthieu*, p. 415). The fact that Matthew apparently regards the λαός as subject to 'deception' (from the perspective of the leaders) about the resurrection reinforces the view that 27.25 does not close the door to Jewish participation in the new ἔθνος but serves as the fulcrum between the old and the new.

deeply divided, however, as to whether the journey is traditional or redactional. Much redaction-critical work has proceeded on the assumption that Mark is almost entirely responsible for the order of pericopae in the pre-passion section of his Gospel. Thus, any 'journey' spanning several pericopae is a Markan creation. Consequently, the journey is taken as a strong indication of Mark's distinctive theology or of the *Sitz im Leben* of the Markan community.[1] The position has been forcefully challenged by R. Pesch, who argues from converging lines of evidence that Mark employed a passion source in which the journey to Jerusalem was integral.[2] Particularly because the geographical and chronological notes that are characteristic of the journey material are not found in the earlier part of the Gospel, Pesch insists that those notes cannot ipso facto be ascribed to Markan redaction.[3]

Several points indicate that Pesch's argument may well be correct, at least in its broad outlines. One is the inadequacy of theological explanations for the Galilee-Jerusalem structure of Mark. It is not true that for Mark Galilee is a place of acceptance and Judea/Jerusalem a place of rejection: Jesus meets with significant controversy and rejection in Galilee as well, even in his hometown (2.1–3.6; 6.1-6a).[4] Likewise, it is

---

1.   Leading exponents of the view that Markan geography is theologically motivated are summarized in E.S. Malbon, 'Galilee and Jerusalem: History and Literature in Marcan Interpretation', *CBQ* 44 (1983), pp. 242-47; and McKinnis, 'Mark 10.32-34', p. 84. An extensive critique is supplied by Best, *Temptation and Passion*, pp. 125-33. Gnilka offers a fundamentally different explanation of the Markan geography as indicating the shutting of the door of salvation to Israel (*Markus*, I, p. 25; II, p. 107).

2.   R. Pesch, 'Der Schluss der vormarkinischen Passionsgeschichte und des Markusevangeliums: Mk, 15,42–16,8', in M. Sabbe (ed.), *L'Evangile selon Marc: Tradition et rédaction* (BETL, 34; Gembloux: Duculot, 1974), pp. 365-409; *idem*, 'Die Überlieferung der Passion Jesu', in K. Kertelge (ed.), *Rückfrage nach Jesus* (QD, 63; Freiburg: Herder, 1974), pp. 148-73; *idem*, 'Die Passion des Menschensohnes: Eine Studie zu den Menschensohnworten der vormarkinischen Passionsgeschichte', in *idem*, R. Schnackenburg and O. Kaiser (eds.), *Jesus und der Menschensohn: Für Anton Vögtle* (Freiburg: Herder, 1975), pp. 166-95; *idem*, *Markusevangelium*, II, pp. 1-25; *idem*, *Urgemeinde, passim*; *idem*, 'Das Evangelium in Jerusalem', in P. Stuhlmacher (ed.), *Das Evangelium und die Evangelien* (WUNT, 2.28; Tübingen: Mohr [Paul Siebeck], 1983), pp. 113-55; *et al.*

3.   Pesch, *Markusevangelium*, II, pp. 12, 16-18; *Urgemeinde*, pp. 58, 64-69.

4.   The presence of significant controversy outside Jerusalem suggests that the journey to Jerusalem is not entirely explained on Gnilka's theory of a decisive

not at all clear that Mark challenges the leadership of the Jerusalem church identified with Peter and the Lord's brothers: Peter is explicitly identified as a Galilean, even while in Jerusalem (14.70).[1] Nor is Galilee the exclusive place of miracles: the blind man is healed at Jericho (10.46-52). At most, then, it may be argued that Mark arranged material as he did because of his knowledge that Jesus ministered in Galilee before traveling to Jerusalem, where he died. Hence, at the very least the Evangelists were constrained in their arrangement of material by a broad framework in which Jerusalem stood prominently as the place of Jesus' death.

Nevertheless, there are indications that more than merely a broad framework may have been part of the pre-Synoptic tradition. The healing of the blind man (Mk 10.46-52 and parallels) is linked to a journey of Jesus not only at the seams (vv. 46, 52) but also in the middle of the pericope (v. 49: 'and he followed him on the way').[2] Although such a note may simply have reflected the itinerant nature of Jesus' ministry, the prominent and unusual geographical note in the pericope (v. 46) suggests more. The association of the healing with Jericho is widely regarded to be traditional, even by those who regard the journey to Jerusalem as a Markan creation.[3] But the very existence in the tradition of such a geographical note, relatively rare in Mark's Gospel and combined with the note about journeying in v. 49, begs for explanation. A pre-Markan journey to Jerusalem to which the pericope was attached supplies just such an explanation.

Significant for the present concern is the fact that many of the notes in both Mark and Matthew which provide the foundation for the journey to Jerusalem either explicitly or implicitly connect it to the death of Jesus. The first Matthean passion prediction (16.21) is precise in this regard: εἰς Ἱεροσόλυμα ἀπελθεῖν explicitly states what is implicit in

confrontation with Judaism (*Markus*, II, p. 107). If Jesus engages opponents in Galilee with no less vigor than in Jerusalem, Mark's reason for reserving decisive confrontation in Jerusalem is unclear. This observation is even more true for Matthew (*contra* Gnilka, *Matthäusevangelium*, II, p. 81), who includes the denunciation of the Galilean cities (11.20-24), though Sand incorrectly identifies this as a contrast to Mark's more favorable view of Galilee (*Matthäus*, p. 91).

1.   Schenk argues that the verse is redactional (*Passionsbericht*, pp. 222-23).

2.   Pesch, *Urgemeinde*, p. 53.

3.   For example, Kebler, *Kingdom*, pp. 69-70; Gnilka, *Markus*, II, p. 108.

Mk 8.31 and Lk. 9.22.[1] Moreover, the introductory ἀπὸ τότε in this verse signals the beginning of a new section of Matthew and suggests that such intimations are habitual from this point in the narrative.[2] The journey to Jerusalem is also connected to the second passion prediction in Matthew and Mark. Both Mt. 17.22 and Mk 9.30 suggest that Jesus is traveling south through Galilee with Jerusalem as his destination.[3] Thus, even though the saying which follows makes no connection to Jerusalem, in the context of both Evangelists the clear implication is that Jesus' death will occur in Jerusalem. The third prediction is, of course, most explicit in this regard. In Mark the saying is preceded with a relatively elaborate introduction which begins with a reiteration of the ongoing journey to Jerusalem (10.32) such that the mention of the journey in the saying itself (v. 33) appears redundant.[4] Matthew's shorter introduction simply contains the phrase ἐν τῇ ὁδῷ, which, while less explicit than the Markan phrase, nevertheless connects with earlier explicit Matthean expressions so that the reader understands that the way leads ultimately to Jerusalem. In both Gospels, when the goal of the journey is reached, Jerusalem is mentioned at the beginning and the end of the entry pericope (Mk 11.1//Mt. 21.1; Mk 11.11//Mt. 21.10) in a manner that suggests an emphasis on the culmination of the journey.[5] In Mark the immediate upshot of the arrival in Jerusalem is the fomenting of the plot against Jesus (11.18).

In Mark, the 'journey itself' does not disappear with Jesus' arrival in the city. It is recapitulated in 15.41, at the end of the passion events. The reference to Jerusalem here is widely regarded as redactional.[6] There is

---

1.   Van Tilborg rightly notes that although this phrase may be Matthew's insertion, it is based on tradition in the wider sense (*Leaders*, p. 75).

2.   Gnilka, *Matthäusevangelium*, II, p. 81.

3.   Cf. Grundmann, *Markus*, p. 192.

4.   Opposite views of the origin of v. 32 are taken by McKinnis ('Mark 10.32-34', p. 83) and Gnilka (*Markus*, II, p. 95) on the one hand and Pesch ('Menschensohn', p. 181) on the other. Bayer has offered evidence that the reference to Jerusalem in v. 33 is Markan (*Predictions*, p. 174); and the reference to high priests in the verse is widely regarded as traditional (cf. Sand, *Matthäus*, p. 404). If either element is traditional, then v. 32 is merely an expansion of the traditional material even if it is redactional.

5.   Mohr has argued that both these references are traditional (*Markuspassion*, pp. 46, 64).

6.   Schenk, *Passionsbericht*, p. 24; T.J. Weeden, Sr, 'The Cross as Power in Weakness (Mark 15.20b-41)', in Kebler (ed.), *Passion*, p. 120; Mohr,

some reason, however, to question that consensus. Green notes that the presence of the women in both the Synoptic and Johannine narratives suggests at least a traditional basis for the verse.[1] Both R. Pesch and C.S. Mann have offered evidence from the language of the verse which suggests tradition.[2] Beyond their evidence, it would appear that if the verse is editorial, it amounts to the explication of what was already implicit in the tradition. The women are generally conceded to be traditional figures: the Evangelists would not have invented female witnesses, who would be regarded as less reliable than men.[3] If it was traditional that they were not just women but followers of Jesus from Galilee, as appears likely, then the phrase αἱ συναναβᾶσαι αὐτῷ εἰς Ἱεροσόλυμα is nothing more than an outgrowth of that identification. In particular, the nature of the reference to Jerusalem is instructive, certainly about Mark's narrative and possibly about the nature of the tradition that he used. An apologetic motive is usually ascribed to vv. 40-41: Mark's purpose is to establish the women as witnesses of the burial and so establish the truth of the empty tomb narrative that follows.[4] If this is the case, then those identified as αἱ συναναβᾶσαι αὐτῷ εἰς Ἱεροσόλυμα are effectively those who accompany Jesus at the time of his death. At this point in the development of Mark's narrative, Jesus' going to Jerusalem and his passion are sufficiently identified that the former can stand for the latter.

Beyond specific details of the text, it is also significant that the Synoptics narrate only one journey of Jesus to Jerusalem (as an adult). Whether traditions of other journeys were available cannot be determined with certainty: Mt. 23.37//Lk. 13.34 (ποσάκις) and the Johannine tradition raise the possibility that they could have been. If indeed they were available, then the deliberate choice to narrate only one such journey may again stress the distinct role of Jerusalem in Jesus' death.

All of this evidence is, of course, qualified by the evaluation given to the references to the journey to Jerusalem. If Pesch is in any way correct, then the journey is a pre-Synoptic tradition. If the more

---

Markuspassion, pp. 331-35; Gnilka, *Markus*, II, p. 313.

   1.   Green, *Death*, pp. 309-10.

   2.   Pesch, 'Mk 15,42–16,8', p. 384; Mann, *Mark*, p. 655. Mann's evidence is based, of course, on the Griesbach hypothesis and is less compelling apart from that view.

   3.   For example, Schenk, *Passionsbericht*, p. 24.

   4.   Dibelius, *Tradition*, pp. 189-91.

conventional form- and redaction-critical position is correct, then it is Markan. But even if the latter is true, the Markan journey to Jerusalem would appear to be an explication or elaboration of what was already present in the tradition: the consciousness that Jesus died in Jerusalem at the instigation of people distinctly associated with the city. In this respect, the journey motif could involve little creative redaction and suggests that the distinct role of Jerusalem in the tradition was recognized by the Evangelists.

Incidental References to Jerusalem

Directly or indirectly, Jerusalem appears in passing in the texts of Matthew and Mark. Some of these references may have little to do with the role of Jerusalem in the passion, but others are more intimately connected. These latter are sufficiently numerous and sufficiently subtle as to be highly suggestive for the concerns of this study. They indicate that there was sufficient consciousness in the Synoptic tradition of the distinct place of Jerusalem in the passion for it to be integrated into the tradition even at the most incidental level. This observation puts great strain on the hypothesis that the distinct role of Jerusalem was redactional, for it requires that the Evangelists insinuated the motif into the tradition in an obscure and intricate manner. These references therefore provide strong corroboration for the hypothesis that Jerusalem's role was already distinct in the pre-Synoptic tradition.

References Outside the Passion Narrative

Early references to Jerusalem in Mark have no clear connection to the passion events. In 1.5 'all Judea and Jerusalem' hear John's message and are baptized. The emphasis appears to be on the wide impact of John's message. There is no suggestion that his Jerusalemite audience is connected either to John's arrest and death or to Jesus'. A similar observation applies to the reference in Mk 3.8: the powerful impression made by Jesus' ministry is in view, in this case furnishing a contrast with the opposition of 3.6.[1] This verse seems to prepare the way for the first reference to opposition from Jerusalem in 3.22. The 'scribes from Jerusalem' appear as a delegation sent to investigate Jesus after his

---

1.   L.E. Keck, 'Mark 3.7-12 and Mark's Christology', *JBL* 84 (1965), pp. 346-47; Guelich, *Mark 1–8.26*, pp. 142-43, 146, 150.

preaching and healing become known in the metropolis.[1] Their appearance may serve to foreshadow the passion,[2] but if this is the case, Mark leaves the issue undeveloped. Clearer is the contrast of opposition from Jerusalem with the great crowds present (3.20), presumably with Jerusalemites in their number (3.8). Similar observations apply to the reference in Mk 7.1. There the contrast between opponents from Jerusalem and large crowds of Jesus' followers (6.53-56) is again clear, but little if anything connects the reference to the passion.

The situation may be different for the Matthean parallels, however. In Matthew, Jerusalem may take on a sinister aspect from its first appearance in 2.3. The fact that 'all Jerusalem' is troubled with Herod, who intends to have Jesus killed, could well foreshadow the passion.[3] However, it is far from clear that Matthew carries this theme throughout his narrative. In 3.5-7 the people who respond favorably to John are explicitly identified with Jerusalem, while the leaders warned to bring forth the fruit of repentance are not.[4] Although Jerusalem is mentioned in 15.1 (//Mk 7.1), Matthew has no reference to Jerusalem in 12.24 (//Mk 3.22); thus, he exhibits no particular interest in exploiting the possibilities of foreshadowing the passion with references to Jerusalem until the first passion prediction (16.21). Likewise, he includes a reference to Jesus' early popularity among Jerusalemites (4.25//Mk 3.7-8). Moreover, Matthew is unique among the Synoptics in referring to Jerusalem as the 'holy city' (4.5; 27.53) and 'city of the great king' (5.35). Again, no consistent effort to exploit the usefulness of Jerusalem as a symbol or foreshadowing device is in evidence.

These references indicate that whereas both Matthew and Mark evince a certain tendency to align Jerusalem with the passion, the

---

1. Grundmann, *Markus*, p. 83; Pesch, *Markusevangelium*, I, p. 213.
2. J.R. Donahue, 'Temple, Trial and Royal Christology', in Kebler (ed.), *Passion*, pp. 68-69; Malbon, 'Galilee and Jerusalem', pp. 249-50; *idem*, 'Leaders', p. 265; Gnilka, *Markus*, I, p. 148. Guelich connects these scribes to the ones who charge Jesus with blasphemy (cf. 3.28-29), a capital crime, in 2.6 to find a foreshadowing of the passion (*Mark 1–8.26*, pp. 173-74, 185-86). Such a connection appears overly subtle and remote. Gnilka (*Markus*, I, p. 148) and Guelich (*Mark 1–8.26*, p. 174) both rightly dismiss the interpretation of those such as Kebler (*Kingdom*, p. 26) who see here a Markan polemical allegory against the Jerusalem church.
3. Luz, *Matthäus*, I, pp. 119-20; Gnilka, *Matthäusevangelium*, I, p. 38.
4. *Contra* Luz, *Matthäus*, I, p. 146.

tendency is in check. The Evangelists have not rendered every mention of the city into a forecast of Jesus' death.

References within the Passion Narrative

However, the situation is very different once the narrative reaches Jerusalem. Thereafter a variety of details indicate that the distinct role of Jerusalem in the passion is thoroughly integrated into the passion materials.

Among these details is Jesus' lodging in Bethany during his Jerusalem ministry (Mt. 21.17; 26.6; Mk 11.11, 12; 14.3). It has been suggested that Bethany is a part of Mark's intra-church, anti-Jerusalemite polemic.[1] However, the general weaknesses of the anti-Jerusalemite hypothesis are compounded at this point by the fact that Bethany does nothing to suggest a positive view of Galilee. But seen from the perspective that the Evangelists and their sources understood that Jesus met singular hostility in Jerusalem, the retreat to Bethany is entirely coherent: Jesus lodges in Bethany because Jerusalem is unsafe. The same may be said for the preparation for the Passover (Mk 14.12-16//Mt. 26.17-19), the intrigues of which would serve to keep knowledge of Jesus' whereabouts during the private festivities from opponents who sought to arrest him away from the crowds (Mk 14.2//Mt. 26.5). In neither case do the Evangelists emphasize the connection to opposition in Jerusalem, but in both cases the details are coherent within such a setting. One is left with the impression that the identification of Jesus' opponents with Jerusalem was taken for granted by the Evangelists and by the traditions they employed.

Jesus' opponents are indirectly identified with the Jerusalem leadership in the narrative of his arrest. The identification of the high priest's slave (Mk 14.47//Mt. 26.51) is again coherent only in a narrative that identifies the opponents with the high priest and his associates. The same is true of the saying of Mk. 14.49a//Mt. 26.54c: Jesus was accessible to his enemies in the temple because they are officials associated with the temple. Likewise, the identifications of Jesus as a Nazarene (Mk 14.67; Mt. 26.71) or Galilean (Mt. 26.69) and Peter as a Galilean (Mk 14.70) during Peter's denials assume that Jesus and his disciples are provincials in the hostile capital.

---

1. Mohr, *Markuspassion*, p. 416.

These details within the Jerusalem narrative contrast with the incidental references to the city in the earlier sections of Matthew and Mark. The contrast is itself instructive. Both Evangelists are apparently interested in supplying hints about the death of Jesus early in their narratives. But Mark does not appear to have used references to Jerusalem to supply those hints, preferring instead to use parallels with the Baptist's fate (1.14) or abortive conspiracies (3.6). Matthew may use such an allusion in 2.3, but he clearly passes up other opportunities to do the same elsewhere. Nevertheless, when the passion is announced by Jesus, the focus of the narrative changes. The hostility of the Jerusalem leadership is unmistakable. Although Jesus is confronted with hostile leaders elsewhere in his ministry, only in Jerusalem is the hostility so thoroughly woven into the fabric of the narrative. The reader is left with the firm impression that in Jerusalem Jesus is continually surrounded by the threat of death.

Again, it is possible to ascribe all such allusions to redactional activity. But to posit so thorough a redaction in one section of a Gospel when similar redaction is lacking in another puts strain on the hypothesis. It is inherently more likely that many of these elements were indeed traditional. The passion materials, both the passion narrative and the predictions, appear to have emphasized that those who instigated Jesus' crucifixion were indigenous to Jerusalem.

Conclusions

The previous discussion has offered a number of lines of argument which converge at a particular point. That convergence can now be summarized.

1. Mt. 23.37-39//Lk. 13.34-35 is not alone in suggesting a distinct role for Jerusalem. The prima facie case that it provided is corroborated by other materials; therefore, 'Jerusalem' can be understood as referring at the pre-literary stage of the saying to Jerusalem specifically, not to Israel in general.

2. The materials that indicate a distinct role for Jerusalem come from a wide variety of materials. These include Markan or triple-tradition materials (Mk 10.32 and parallels) as well as Q or double-tradition materials (Mt. 23.37-39; Lk. 13.34-35), material within pericopae (Mk 8.31 and parallels) as well as material in editorial 'seams' (Mk 10.31), explicit statements (Mt. 16.21; Mk 10.32 and parallels) as

well as indirect allusions (Mk 14.70). These materials have been variously evaluated as to their status in the tradition. Most definitely traditional appear to be the Jerusalem oracle and the identification of the high priests. But taken as a whole, the multiple attestation of the motif suggests a high probability that Jerusalem's distinct role was traditional and that whatever redactional activity there was merely emphasized or reiterated what was already present in the tradition.

3. The corollary to this observation is that little, if anything, obscures the impression that Jerusalem's role is distinct. Jesus encounters many opponents, some who plot his death (Mk 3.6 and parallels), but only persons with intrinsic connections to Jerusalem are implicated in the plot that is realized, despite the proximity of other opponents (Mk 12.13, 18 and parallels).

4. Apparent Matthean redactional activity corroborates this hypothesis. Matthew emphasizes the opposition of the Pharisees; but although their hostility to Jesus is linked to the plotters (27.62), it does not encroach on the plot or its denouement. Likewise, Matthew apparently presents the rejection of Jesus in Jerusalem as decisive for the nation of Israel (21.41-43; 27.25). However, he maintains, despite the consequent tension, an emphasis on the instigation of that rejection by the Jerusalem leadership (21.45-46; 27.20) and implicitly allows that many repudiate the leaders' position to side with Jesus and his followers.

5. Nothing in the Synoptics explicitly identifies the crowds who call for Jesus' crucifixion as Jerusalemite. But the cry of the crowd is explicitly instigated by the leaders of Jerusalem (Mk 15.11; Mt. 27.20), and other elements associating the crucifixion with Jerusalem could indicate that the identification of the crowd as Jerusalemite is implicit.

Thus, this chapter has answered one question and raised another. It appears from the evidence of Matthew and Mark that Luke depended on tradition in ascribing responsibility for the death of Jesus to Jerusalemites. That the tradition of Palestinian Jewish—possibly even Jerusalemite—involvement was primitive is clear from Paul. That such traditions were available to Luke is clear from Matthew and Mark. What is not yet clear is whether in Acts the identification of the crowd as indigenous to Jerusalem is traditional or is the product of Luke's augmenting of the Synoptic tradition. This question will occupy our attention in the following chapter.

Chapter 6

ORIGINS OF JERUSALEM'S RESPONSIBILITY FOR THE DEATH OF JESUS IN ACTS

Clearly Luke did not innovate in identifying Jerusalem as the agent of Jesus' death. That identification was a part of the gospel tradition that he received. A survey of the Synoptic material shows a consistent attribution of responsibility for the death of Jesus to Jerusalem, particularly the leaders of Jerusalem. Moreover, the Synoptic tradition included a tradition of a popular outcry for Jesus' death, although the identity of the crowd is not specified. Luke in his Gospel followed this tradition, perhaps with some redactional emphasis on the role of Jerusalem. So much is clear from the preceding discussion. In Acts, however, the question is more complicated. Certain texts in Acts, like the Synoptics, attribute responsibility to the Sanhedrin leadership (4.10-11; 5.28b, 30-31; 7.52; 13.27-29). Others could ascribe responsibility to Jews generally (4.27; 10.39), but in light of the specific attribution elsewhere of popular responsibility to the people of Jerusalem (2.23, 36; 3.13-15; 13.27-29), they are probably restricted in focus to the people of Jerusalem.[1] This emphasis on the people of Jerusalem, while perhaps implicit in Luke's Gospel (cf. Lk. 23.28), is uniquely precise in Acts. How, then, can the specific, explicit attribution of responsibility to the *people* of Jerusalem in Acts be explained?

This chapter will address this issue. The discussion that follows will assess the merits of different hypotheses about the origin of the ascription of responsibility for the death of Jesus in Acts. The inquiry will proceed in two stages. The first will explore a prima facie case: if texts in Acts ascribing responsibility for the death of Jesus to Jerusalem are found in the midst of material which appears to be traditional, the possibility is opened that the texts in question may also be traditional. Of

---

1. Cf. the extensive discussion of these texts in Chapter 2 above.

course, because Luke's method of composition in Acts, especially the speeches, is complex, the mere proximity of traditional material to the texts in question is not decisive. Therefore, the second stage of the inquiry will consider how best to account for the attribution of responsibility for the death of Jesus in Acts. Consideration will be given to three hypotheses: (1) that Luke extrapolated his attribution of responsibility from the Synoptic material; (2) that Luke followed his theological *Tendenz* in his attribution of responsibility; (3) that Luke followed a source unique to Acts for his attribution of responsibility.

The Question of Traditions in the Speeches

Modern study of the speeches of Acts has been, to say the least, controversial.[1] Nevertheless, a consensus does exist on two points: (1) the speeches contain at least some traditional elements; (2) whatever the traditions or sources that Luke used in the speeches, he worked the material over thoroughly, so that it largely reflects his literary style and theological interests.[2] These points in turn must inform the method used to distinguish traditional material in the speeches. It implies that material which reflects Lukan style, vocabulary or theology may nevertheless be based on tradition, though it cannot be proved to be so.[3] This observation in turn suggests that when material exhibiting Lukan features appears in a context that contains several apparently traditional elements,[4] the critic may suspect that the Lukan material represents editing of a tradition or source, not creative activity. That is, the presence of traditional elements in its immediate context provides a prima facie case

---

1.   The methodological difficulties in the tradition-criticism of the speeches were succinctly set forth by H.J. Cadbury ('The Speeches in Acts', in Foakes-Jackson and Lake [eds.], *Beginnings*, IV, p. 416).

2.   Statements to this effect can be found both among those who credit Luke with a high degree of historical accuracy (for example I.H. Marshall, 'The Resurrection in the Acts of the Apostles', in W.W. Gasque and R.P. Martin [eds.], *Apostolic History and the Gospels* [Exeter: Paternoster Press, 1970], p. 95; F.F. Bruce, 'The Acts of the Apostles: Historical Record or Theological Reconstruction?', *ANRW* II.25.3, p. 2582) and those who regard Luke as having created much of the material of Acts (for example Weiser, *Apostelgeschichte*, p. 100). Cf. the summary statements in Schneider (*Apostelgeschichte*, I, p. 83) and Pesch (*Apostelgeschichte*, I, p. 43).

3.   Cf. Marshall, 'Resurrection', p. 94; Wilcox, 'Study of the Speeches', p. 212.

4.   Wilcox provides a useful summary of criteria for identifying traditional elements in the speeches of Acts ('Study of the Speeches', p. 224).

that a statement may be based on tradition.

Ascription of responsibility for the death of Jesus appears in various texts in Acts, always in direct discourse and largely in the so-called missionary speeches (Acts 2.22-24, 36; 3.13-15; 4.10-11, 27-28; 5.28b, 30-31; 7.52; 10.38-40; 13.27-30). The question at hand is whether these texts appear in contexts where traditional elements have been identified and whether the texts themselves include such elements.

The Contribution of Studies of Translation Greek and Semitisms

The identification of Semitisms in the speeches of Acts—and the evaluation of those Semitisms identified—remains a disputed matter. Nevertheless, careful study of the issue does suggest that expressions reflecting Semitic syntax can be legitimately identified in the speeches of Acts.[1] Several such expressions occur within or near texts ascribing responsibility for the death of Jesus in Acts.

R.A. Martin's groundbreaking study of 'translation Greek' in Acts has the merit of a broad base of empirical data supporting its method. Martin concludes that among those texts of Acts which reflect Semitic sources are 4.23-31; 5.27-32; and 13.26-41, and among those which probably reflect Semitic sources is 2.29-36.[2] Martin's methods, of course, are not suitable for determining whether any individual element of a speech has a Semitic source: they are most accurate when applied to large blocks of material and cannot rule out the interpolation of foreign material into those large blocks. Nevertheless, his conclusions raise the possibility that Luke had sources for at least some of the texts which ascribe responsibility for the death of Jesus.

---

1.   The hypothesis of H.F.D. Sparks that the Semitisms of Acts are in fact Septuagintalisms, Luke's conscious imitation of the LXX, was aimed at the earlier hypothesis of Torrey that Acts 1–15 was a translation of an Aramaic original ('The Semitisms of the Acts', *JTS* NS 1 [1950], pp. 16-28). Sparks's hypothesis has since been effectively countered by the more cautious and methodologically refined work of Wilcox (cf. *Semitisms of Acts*, pp. 4, 52-54, 59-61, 81, 111, 154; 'Study of the Speeches', p. 225; 'Semitisms in the New Testament', *ANRW* II.25.2, pp. 983-86, 994) and R.A. Martin (*Syntactical Evidence of Semitic Sources in Greek Documents* [SBLSCS, 3; Cambridge, MA: SBL, 1974], *passim*). The relatively recent hypothesis of F.L. Horton that the use of the LXX in the synagogue influenced Luke does not explain the absence of Semitic elements for the portion of Acts set in the diaspora ('Reflections of the Semitisms of Luke–Acts', in C.H. Talbert [ed.], *Perspectives on Luke–Acts* [Edinburgh: T. & T. Clark, 1978], pp. 1-23).

2.   Martin, *Syntactical Evidence*, pp. 2-3, 87-104.

More specific is the approach of M. Black and M. Wilcox. Both identify possible Semitisms in close proximity to several texts ascribing responsibility for the death of Jesus. Black identified *casus pendens* in Acts 2.22-23 ('Jesus of Nazareth, a man...this one') and 4.10 ('Jesus Christ the Nazarene whom...whom...in him').[1] Likewise, Black notes asyndeton in 3.13 ('The God of Abraham...'); 5.30 ('The God of our fathers...'); and 7.52 ('Which of the prophets...'). Wilcox suggests that the phrase γνωστὸν ἔστω in 4.10 could be a trace of an older Semitic tradition, either Hebrew or Aramaic.[2] Both scholars consider that the verbs ἠτήσαντο in 13.28 and ἔθηκαν in v. 29 may reflect the Semitic impersonal third person plural verb.[3]

Particularly interesting are Black's and Wilcox's observations about the Western text of Acts. In 3.14; 7.52; 10.38-40; and 13.28 they offer explanations for variants in D which suggest that a Semitic substratum, either in documentary or oral form, may have influenced the Western text.[4] Such examples are particularly suggestive, since they raise the possibility that Luke depended on traditions or sources which continued to circulate after the writing of Acts and influenced the Western variants.

The value of Black's and Wilcox's studies for the present issue is qualified by two considerations. One is the methodological problem of distinguishing a true Semitism from an accidental irregularity in a writer's Greek. Because of this difficulty, one can never be sure that an alleged Semitism does reflect an earlier layer of tradition. The second consideration is more specific: only one of the Semitisms identified by Black or Wilcox is directly part of a phrase or clause which ascribes responsibility for the death of Jesus, namely ἠτήσαντο in 13.28, for

1. M. Black, *An Aramaic Approach to the Gospels and Acts* (London: Oxford University Press, 3rd edn, 1967), p. 53.

2. Wilcox, *Semitisms of Acts*, pp. 89-91, 110.

3. Black argues for the Semitic origin of the former expression (*Aramaic Approach*, p. 127), but Wilcox notes that the subject of this verb is probably 'the people of Jerusalem and their leaders' (*Semitisms of Acts*, p. 128). Wilcox allows that the latter example is more likely a Semitism, since a change of subject would be expected for the burial of Jesus (*Semitisms of Acts*, p. 128).

4. Black, *Aramaic Approach*, pp. 99-100 (on 7.52); Wilcox, *Semitisms of Acts*, pp. 116-18 (on 10.38), pp. 118-21 (on 13.28), 139-41 (on 3.14). Concerning 10.38-40 cf. the alternate hypothesis of H. Riesenfeld ('The Text of Acts x.36', in E. Best and R.McL. Wilson [eds.], *Text and Interpretation: Studies in the New Testament Presented to Matthew Black* [Cambridge: Cambridge University Press, 1979], pp. 191-94).

which an alternative explanation, offered by Wilcox himself, appears to be more satisfactory.[1] Therefore, these observations can be regarded as only preliminary and suggestive, not in any way definitive.

Lukan and Non-Lukan Elements

Various words, phrases or concepts uncommon in Luke–Acts appear in some of the texts under discussion. These appear side by side with other expressions and concepts which are more decidedly Lukan, so that Luke's redaction of traditional material is again indicated. As before, these features can be briefly summarized.

In Acts 2.23, the verb προσπήγνυμι is a biblical *hapax legomenon* and may (in connection with other factors) suggest the use of a source.[2] Likewise, the reference to the Romans as ἄνομοι in the same verse would appear to run counter to Luke's universalistic interests and so may also be traditional.[3] Similarly, in v. 36 language which suggests that Jesus is installed as Lord and Christ at his ascension may reflect primitive theology.[4] The presence of Lukan stylistic elements in vv. 22-24, such as the resumptive construction,[5] and theological themes, such as the divine 'must' of Jesus' death,[6] therefore appear to be the consequence of Luke's redaction of traditional material.

Acts 3.13-15 is widely regarded as reflecting the passion narrative of Luke's Gospel.[7] Nevertheless, it is just as widely conceded that the text incorporates christological titles that are primitive.[8] And even

1. Wilcox, *Semitisms of Acts*, p. 128.
2. For a recent discussion see Green, *Death*, pp. 184-85.
3. Green assumes the common view that Luke has a pro-Roman tendency in attributing the term to tradition (*Death*, p. 185). Evidence against that view has been offered above in Chapters 2–3, *passim*.
4. E. Schweizer, *Erniederung und Erhöhung bei Jesus und seinen Nachfolgern* (ATANT, 28; Zürich: Zwingli-Verlag, 1962), p. 59.
5. E. Richard, 'Jesus' Passion and Death in Acts', in D.D. Sylva (ed.), *Reimaging the Death of the Lukan Jesus* (BBB, 73; Frankfurt: Hain, 1990), p. 141. Richard's reference to the repetition of αὐτός in this text should read οὗτος.
6. Roloff, *Apostelgeschichte*, p. 56; G. Lüdeman, *Early Christianity according to the Traditions in Acts: A Commentary* (ET; London: SCM Press, 1989), p. 46.
7. Cf. Wilckens, *Missionsreden*, pp. 128-31; Roloff, *Apostelgeschichte*, pp. 74-75; Weiser, *Apostelgeschichte*, p. 113; Pesch, *Apostelgeschichte*, I, p. 153.
8. Cf. B. Lindars, *New Testament Apologetic: The Doctrinal Significance of the Old Testament Quotations* (London: SCM Press, 1961), p. 79; Schweizer, *Erniederung*, pp. 55-57; Roloff, *Apostelgeschichte*, p. 71; Pesch, *Apostelgeschichte*,

U. Wilckens notes that the verb ἀρνέομαι in v. 13 appears to be traditional.[1] Again, the mixture of Lukan and non-Lukan elements renders
the separation of tradition and redaction difficult.[2]

The question of tradition and redaction in Acts 4.27-28 has been thoroughly worked over in recent critical literature, and with widely differing
conclusions.[3] The use of language in these verses from Psalm 2 has been
ascribed both to pre-Lukan exegesis and to Luke himself.[4] Likewise,
apparently traditional terms such as 'servant' have been ascribed both to
a particular tradition which lies behind these verses and Luke's adaptation of language from other speeches in Acts.[5] But at the very least it is
generally conceded that the text has been influenced by traditional material, though the tradition is often regarded as relatively late in origin.[6]

The speech of Stephen, including Acts 7.52, has been regarded by
many scholars as having a basis in pre-Lukan tradition.[7] Recently, however, A. Weiser has challenged this consensus, arguing that much of
vv. 51-53 is distinctively Lukan.[8] But Weiser exaggerates when he
identifies the Deuteronomic killing-of-the-prophets theme as distinctively
Lukan: it is clearly traditional elsewhere (Lk. 11.47-51; 13.33-35;
1 Thess. 2.14-16 [cf. Chapter 4 above]). As in other cases, tradition-
critical judgments about this text depend on determining whether Luke
simply incorporates language found elsewhere in his work or depends
on a distinct source or tradition. Weiser opts for the latter alternative but
does so without offering evidence against the former. The question should

---

I, p. 150. J.A.T. Robinson's theory that Luke presents a revision of a primitive
Christology in which Jesus has not yet 'come' as Christ ('The Most Primitive
Christology of All?', *JTS* NS 7 [1956], pp. 180-89) has been convincingly refuted
by C.F.D. Moule ('The Christology of Acts', in L.E. Keck and J.L. Martyn [eds.],
Studies in Luke–Acts [Nashville: Abingdon Press, 1966], p. 168).

1. Wilckens, *Missionsreden*, pp. 129-30.

2. Cf. the observations of Roloff, *Apostelgeschichte*, p. 71.

3. Green offers compelling arguments against the view that Luke created
Lk. 23.6-12 to accommodate the interpretation of Ps. 2 in Acts 4.27 (*Death*, p. 81).

4. For the former view, cf. Roloff, *Apostelgeschichte*, p. 85; for the latter, cf.
Weiser, *Apostelgeschichte*, pp. 131-32.

5. Again, for the former view, cf. Roloff, *Apostelgeschichte*, pp. 85-86; for the
latter, cf. Weiser, *Apostelgeschichte*, p. 132.

6. Cf. Robinson, 'Primitive Christology', p. 179; and the thorough discussion
in Lüdemann, *Early Christianity*, pp. 58-59.

7. For example, Steck, *Geschick*, pp. 266-67.

8. Weiser, *Apostelgeschichte*, pp. 182, 188.

therefore be left open until other evidence is brought to bear on it.

The issue of pre-Lukan tradition in Acts 10.38-40 has been thoroughly discussed by G.N. Stanton and by R.A. Guelich. Both note in the text and its immediate context a concentration of apparently non-Lukan expressions (for example 'peace through Jesus Christ', 'Jesus, the one from Nazareth', 'doing good', 'healing those oppressed by the devil') and non-Lukan themes (prominence of John the Baptist, emphasis on miracles).[1] Stanton adds to these observations the hypothesis that from v. 36 the text is more coherent if Ps. 107.19-20 appeared before it, so that Luke's editing of a source or tradition may be indicated.[2] The grammatical difficulties of vv. 36-38 have been discussed extensively;[3] these may also owe to the condensation of traditional material. Moreover, R. Pesch has recently noted the inherent likelihood that any narrative of Cornelius's reception of the Spirit or of his baptism would be preceded by preaching of some kind.[4] Therefore, even though Lukan elements are present,[5]

---

1. G.N. Stanton, *Jesus of Nazareth in New Testament Preaching* (SNTSMS, 27; Cambridge: Cambridge University Press, 1974), pp. 78-79; R. Guelich, 'The Gospel Genre', in P. Stuhlmacher (ed.), *Das Evangelium und die Evangelien* (WUNT, 2.28; Tübingen: Mohr [Paul Siebeck], 1983), p. 211.

2. Stanton, *Preaching*, pp. 71-77.

3. Cf. the summary in Schneider, *Apostelgeschichte*, II, p. 75.

4. Pesch, *Apostelgeschichte*, I, p. 333. Weiser observes that the narrative does exist without preaching in Acts 11 (*Apostelgeschichte*, p. 258). But the narrative of ch. 11 in its present form obviously assumes that of ch. 10 and even alludes to the speech (vv. 14-15). Weiser's inference is therefore unfounded, since it cannot be known from the present text whether the account of 11.5-18 ever existed apart from some tradition of Peter's speech.

5. Cf. the enumeration in Weiser, *Apostelgeschichte*, p. 258; Guelich, 'Genre', p. 211 n. 190; Lüdemann, *Early Christianity*, p. 128. M.M.B. Turner has suggested that Acts 10.35-40 is a Lukan composition modeled on Lk. 4.16-30: many of the elements which Stanton and Guelich identify as non-Lukan Turner correlates with the Nazareth pericope ('Jesus and the Spirit in Lucan Perspective', *TynBul* 32 [1981], pp. 22-25). If Turner's hypothesis is correct, then Luke's dependence on tradition for the passage must have been considerably less than has been otherwise understood. However, the possibility that Luke draws on independent tradition for both Lk. 4.16-30 and Acts 10.35-40, particularly in light of the number of expressions which occur only in those two passages, cannot be entirely dismissed. Moreover, the similarities between the discussion of Jesus' death in Acts 10.38-40 and other 'kerygmatic' passages in Acts suggests the influence of other material. Additionally, the fact that Lk. 4.16-30 and Acts 10.38-40 specify different groups as Jesus' opponents (i.e. Nazarenes and Jerusalemites; cf. discussion above) could also

Luke's use of some traditional material in the text must be allowed.[1]

Acts 13.27-30 includes many expressions and ideas which appear elsewhere in the Lukan corpus.[2] Nevertheless, the text gives evidence of a traditional basis in v. 29: the absence of a change of subject for the verb ἔθηκαν suggests that Luke has condensed a source or tradition.[3] Such a tradition would probably have included a longer version of the entire passion summary of these verses, though Luke may also have inserted other material.

Once again, these observations do not assure that sources or traditions on which the speeches depend ascribe responsibility for the death of Jesus to Jerusalem. But they do raise the distinct possibility of such a traditional ascription.

Traditional Exegesis of Scripture

Traces of traditional Jewish exegetical procedures are in evidence in many of the speeches of Acts.[4] For instance, J.W. Bowker has suggested that the speeches of Acts 2, 7 and 13 are all based on the proem homily form.[5] Bowker's analysis is largely inferential, as he admits;[6] furthermore, it obviously does not rule out Luke's insertion of his own material. Nevertheless, it again suggests the possibility that the ascription of responsibility for the death of Jesus in the speeches is based on tradition.

indicate the influence of other traditional material on the latter text.

1.   Roloff argues that the entire speech is Lukan but concedes that traditional elements are incorporated in vv. 38-40 (*Apostelgeschichte*, pp. 167-68, 173).

2.   Cf. the enumeration in Lüdemann, *Early Christianity*, p. 153.

3.   This alternative is more likely than the suggestion that the text depends on a tradition which ascribed the burial of Jesus to those who brought about his death (cf. Schweizer, *Erniederung*, pp. 53-54 n. 208; Green, *Death*, p. 185). If Luke incorporated such a divergent tradition here, it is likely that he would have altered it to conform to his passion account. Even less likely is the argument of Wilckens that the ascription of the burial to Jewish agency is Luke's own sharpening of Jewish responsibility (*Missionsreden*, pp. 135-36). Cf. the discussion above.

4.   Summaries of this issue are given in E.E. Ellis, 'Midrashic Features in the Speeches of Acts', in A. Descamps and A. de Halleux (eds.), *Mélanges bibliques en homage au R.P. Béda Rigaux* (Gembloux: Duculot, 1970), pp. 307-309; and J.I.H. McDonald, *Kerygma and Didache: The Articulation and Structure of the Earliest Christian Message* (SNTSMS, 37; Cambridge: Cambridge University Press, 1980), pp. 51-53.

5.   J.W. Bowker, 'Speeches in Acts: A Study in Proem and Yelamedenu Form', *NTS* 14 (1967–68), pp. 104-107.

6.   Bowker, 'Speeches', p. 111.

This is even more the case since Bowker identifies Acts 2.36 as a key stage in the exegesis of the texts on which the homily is based.

Similar conclusions can be drawn from B. Lindars's work on the use of Scripture in the speeches of Acts. He regards the speeches of Acts 2 as reflecting traditional exegesis of Joel 2 and Psalm 110 and the speech of Acts 13 as reflecting traditional exegesis of Psalm 16.[1] Likewise, he finds traditional use of Ps. 68.19 in Acts 2 and, consequently, in 5.30-32.[2] Once more, however, Lukan redaction is also in evidence,[3] so again the evidence is only suggestive, not conclusive.

Particularly interesting for the question at hand is the use in the speeches of two texts, Ps. 118.22 (LXX 117.22) and Deut. 21.22. Because these texts are used prominently outside the Lukan corpus, they may connect Luke's exegesis to a larger traditional sphere. Moreover, because both are applied by Luke to the issue of responsibility for the death of Jesus, they have a direct bearing on the issue at stake here.

Psalm 118.22. Several features in the use of this verse in Acts 4.11 deserve attention. One is the use of midrashic language: οὗτός ἐστιν as the introduction to the citation, and the insertion of ὑφ' ὑμῶν within the citation.[4] Unless Luke is consciously imitating *pesher* language here, these terms suggest that the text is based on a Jewish-Christian exegetical tradition. Likewise, the use of ἐξουθενέω instead of ἀποδοκιμάζω (LXX) indicates either the use of an alternate version or the influence of Isa. 52.14–53.3.[5] In the former case, it represents a departure from Luke's ordinary pattern, which in turn suggests the influence of tradition.[6] In the latter case, Luke appears to be unaware of the Isaianic allusion, so that tradition is again indicated.

In either case, though, the insertion of ἐξουθενέω has an important bearing on another significant question: the relationship of Acts 4.11 to

1. Lindars, *Apologetic*, pp. 37-47.

2. Lindars, *Apologetic*, p. 54.

3. Cf. Lindars, *Apologetic*, p. 54.

4. Ellis, 'Midrashic Features', p. 311.

5. J. Dupont, 'L'utilisation apologétique de l'Ancien Testament dans les discours des Actes', in *Etudes sur les Actes des Apôtres* (LD, 45; Paris: Cerf, 1967), pp. 260-61.

6. Schneider, *Apostelgeschichte*, I, p. 348.

Mk 12.10-11 par.[1] In both texts the builders are identified with the Jerusalem leaders.[2] This raises the possibility that in Acts 4 Luke simply reapplied the text from his Synoptic sources. However, this hypothesis does not satisfactorily explain the differences in the two citations. The use in Acts emphasizes the passion and exaltation of Jesus, whereas the Synoptic use, especially in Lk. 20.17-18, emphasizes the fate of the leaders.[3] The different setting could explain the shift, although the apparent Lukan redaction in Lk. 20.18 makes this explanation less likely. Acts 4.11 also omits Ps. 118.23, which is included in Mk 12.11 par. This difference could be accounted for by Luke's condensation of the reference in Acts, although the clause παρὰ κυρίου ἐγένετο αὕτη would appear to have applied nicely to the last clause of Acts 4.10 (ὃν ὁ θεὸς ἤγειρεν ἐκ νεκρῶν). But there seems to be no accounting for the substitution of ἐξουθενέω if Luke simply extrapolated the reference from the Synoptic material. Thus, not only is it apparent that Acts 4.11 reflects traditional exegesis,[4] the tradition would also appear to be independent of Mk 12.10-11 par.[5]

Deuteronomy 21.22. Allusions to this text appear in the phrase κρεμάσαντες ἐπὶ ξύλου in Acts 5.30; 10.39 and the corresponding καθελόντες ἀπὸ τοῦ ξύλου in 13.29. The unique προσπήξαντες in 2.23 may also serve as an oblique allusion to Deut. 21.22.[6] As was the case with Ps. 118.22, the importance of these citations lies in their relationship to other New Testament quotation of the scriptural text. First of all, because Luke's Gospel makes no reference to Deut. 21.22, it appears to be unlikely that Luke created these allusions.[7] Likewise, it appears unlikely that he employed the text under the influence of Paul's usage

1.   Ps. 118.22 is also cited in 1 Pet. 2.4, and a similar text, Isa. 28.16, in Rom. 9.33. There is nothing to suggest that either of these texts influenced Luke, either directly or indirectly.

2.   F.F. Bruce, 'New Wine in Old Wine Skins: The Corner Stone', *ExpTim* 84 (1973), p. 233.

3.   Ellis, 'Midrashic Features', p. 311.

4.   So Lindars, *Apologetic*, p. 170; Roloff, *Apostelgeschichte*, p. 82; Pesch, *Apostelgeschichte*, I, pp. 166-67. Weiser characteristically ascribes the entire scene to Lukan composition (*Apostelgeschichte*, pp. 122-23).

5.   *Contra* Lüdemann, *Early Christianity*, p. 59.

6.   J.A. Fitzmyer, 'Crucifixion in Ancient Palestine, Qumran Literature, and the New Testament', *CBQ* 40 (1978), p. 508; Wilckens, *Missionsreden*, p. 126.

7.   Green, *Death*, p. 185.

(Gal. 3.13; cf. 1 Pet. 2.24). The Pauline citation stresses the placing of the curse on the one crucified; Luke's usage neglects this point entirely. While it may be that Luke deliberately omitted this emphasis to avoid a substitutionary view of the crucifixion, the presence of passing allusions to such a view elsewhere (Lk. 22.19-20; Acts 20.28) does not suggest that such was his practice.

Instead, either of two other explanations appears more likely. One is the common hypothesis that Deut. 21.22 was first applied to the crucifixion of Jesus by Jews to refute Christian claims about Jesus and was subsequently taken up by Christians as part of the contrast-scheme of the kerygma.[1] In this case the emphasis on the curse and substitution is understood as a Pauline innovation; consequently, the traditions on which Luke depends would be pre-Pauline.[2] An alternative to this view can be offered on the basis of the conjecture of O. Betz that Deut. 21.22 actually formed a part of the rationale for the Sanhedrin's demand for Jesus' death.[3] If, as Betz proposes, the Sanhedrin sought not just Jesus' execution but specifically his crucifixion because he was regarded as a blasphemer and traitor, then the Christian use of Deut. 21.22 may have

---

1. So Lindars, *Apologetic*, pp. 233-36; F.F. Bruce, 'The Speeches in Acts—Thirty Years After', in R.J. Banks (ed.), *Reconciliation and Hope: New Testament Essays on Atonement and Eschatology Presented to L.L. Morris* (Grand Rapids: Eerdmans, 1974), p. 61; C. Dietzfelbinger, *Die Berufung des Paulus als Ursprung seiner Theologie* (WMANT, 58; Neukirchen–Vluyn: Neukirchener Verlag, 1985), pp. 36-37; Lüdemann, *Early Christianity*, pp. 71-72.

2. At the pre-Pauline stage, the answer to the objection that crucifixion indicated that Jesus was accursed would be in the contrasting assertion of God's vindication of Jesus through the resurrection. Dietzfelbinger's summary is apt: 'Gott hat den Gekreuzigten und mit Fluch Belegten durch die Auferweckung rehabilitert' (*Berufung*, p. 37). The objections of G. Friedrich to the origin of the allusion in Jewish anti-Christian polemic fail to account for the use of Deut. 21.22 in Acts without a substitutionary interpretation (*Die Verkündigung des Todes Jesu im Neuen Testament* [Biblisch-Theologische Studien, 6; Neukirchen–Vluyn: Neukirchener Verlag, 1982], pp. 125-30). Similar objections apply to Max Wilcox's conjecture that a midrashic combination of Deut. 21.22 and Gen. 22 lies behind all New Testament use of the 'tree' motif ('"Upon the Tree"—Deut. 21.22f.', *JBL* 96 [1977], pp. 96-99): it fails to account for the absence of allusion to the Abrahamic promise apart from Gal. 3.13.

3. Betz, 'Probleme', pp. 606-11. On the understanding of Deut. 21.22 in Jewish legal practice cf. J.M. Ford, '"Crucify him, Crucify him", and the Temple Scroll', *ExpTim* 87 (1976), p. 277; Fitzmyer, 'Crucifixion', pp. 498-510; Wilcox, 'Tree', pp. 88-90.

originated as an allusion to the actual circumstances of the passion. On this hypothesis the tradition behind the citation in Acts of Deut. 21.22 must likewise be primitive. Moreover, it would suggest that the attribution of the deed to the Sanhedrin is traditional, since on Betz's proposal it is the Sanhedrin which sought Jesus' crucifixion on the basis of Deut. 21.22.

Taken with the other evidence already cited, these texts suggest intriguing possibilities about the traditions of responsibility for the death of Jesus which lie behind the speeches of Acts. But they remain mere possibilities apart from corroboration. The possibility that the attribution of responsibility for the death of Jesus in Acts is the product of sources unique to Acts must be weighed against other possible origins for the motif.

Evaluating Hypotheses for the Origin of the Motif

To establish the tradition history of the attribution of responsibility for the death of Jesus in Acts, one must weigh the relative merits of different hypotheses about its origin. There appear to be three possible ways that popular Jerusalemite responsibility could have found its way into the speeches of Acts: (1) through Luke's extension of Synoptic passion traditions; (2) through Luke's own theological creation; (3) through tradition independent of the Synoptic tradition. What follows is an evaluation of each of these hypotheses in broad terms. Consideration will be given to the adequacy of each to account for the data and the likelihood of each in light of other factors known about Luke's composition.

Luke's Extension of Synoptic Tradition

Particularly since the publication of U. Wilckens's *Die Missionsreden der Apostelgeschichte* it has become a critical commonplace to assert that the 'kerygmatic' sections of the missionary speeches of Acts are Luke's own summaries of his passion narrative.[1] Indeed, in regard to responsibility for the death of Jesus, it has already been argued above that the speeches of Acts are consistent with the Lukan passion narrative.[2] However, to assert that the passion narrative is consistent with the

---

1. Wilckens, *Missionsreden*, pp. 112-31, 207; Roloff, *Apostelgeschichte*, pp. 74-75; Schneider, *Apostelgeschichte*, II, p. 129; Weiser, *Apostelgeschichte*, p. 113; Rese, 'Aussagen', pp. 344-45; Lüdemann, *Early Christianity*, p. 51.

2. Cf. Chapter 2 above.

speeches is one thing, but to assert that in itself it is sufficient to account for the content of the speeches is another. The question remains whether extension of Synoptic tradition alone can adequately account for Luke's assessment of responsibility for the death of Jesus in the speeches of Acts.

The analysis of the Synoptic passion traditions in Chapter 5 above identified three relevant strands of tradition: (1) the Q or double tradition which personified Jerusalem as the one who killed Jesus (Mt. 23.37-39//Lk. 13.34-35); (2) the Markan or triple tradition which indicted the Jerusalem leadership; (3) the Markan or triple tradition which included the popular cry for Jesus' death in the Barabbas narrative. It was noted that the Synoptics, Luke's Gospel included, do not explicitly identify the crowd in the Barabbas narrative as Jerusalemite, though such an identification is not excluded either. It is conceivable, then, that Luke integrated these traditional elements into the speeches of Acts with the result that the crowd that called for Jesus' death was identified as Jerusalemite, as is presupposed in some texts of Acts (2.23, 36; 3.13-15) and explicitly stated in others (13.27).

But if Luke depended solely on Synoptic passion traditions, was attribution of responsibility to the people of Jerusalem the only possible outcome? Clearly it would not be. The identification of Jerusalem with the passion (Q material) could have been entirely integrated with the emphasis on the Jerusalem leadership (Markan material): in Acts Jerusalem *through its leaders alone* could have been indicted for the crucifixion, and the Synoptic material would have been sufficiently accounted for. Indeed, that same emphasis could also be used to explain the cry of the people for Jesus' death (Markan material). Matthew and Mark both emphasize the role of the high priests in inciting the mob (Mt. 27.20//Mk 15.11), and Luke could well have followed a similar procedure in Acts. Luke's Gospel, of course, omits the statement of the priests' provocation of the outcry, but such an omission hardly excluded such activity, which could have been made explicit in Acts without contradiction of the first volume. In such a case popular responsibility could even have been ascribed to a segment of the people beholden to the priestly aristocracy instead of the people of Jerusalem in general. Thus, using only Synoptic passion material, Luke could have composed speeches which attributed responsibility for the death of Jesus to the Jerusalem leaders, explaining the popular outcry as the result of their provocation.

This observation is no less true if, as R. Pesch implies, Luke follows not the Markan passion account but his own passion source, used in his Gospel, as the basis for the kerygma of Acts.[1] There is nothing unique to the Lukan passion narrative in itself that suggests that the crowd in the Barabbas episode is Jerusalemite. The consistently recurring attribution of responsibility to the *people* of Jerusalem is therefore still not accounted for merely on the basis of the passion traditions employed in Luke's Gospel.

Obviously, there may be other ways in which an author, attempting to summarize the Lukan passion narrative in kerygmatic speeches, might reconcile the different elements in apportioning responsibility. But for our purposes it is only necessary to show that there is one other alternative. That alternative shows that the Lukan passion narrative is not sufficient *in itself* to account for the allocation of responsibility in the speeches. Some element beyond Luke's intention to be consistent with his passion narrative must also have played a role in the composition of the speeches.

Theologically Motivated Creation

The ascription of responsibility for the death of Jesus in Acts to Jerusalemites could conceivably be the result of various Lukan theological interests, the product of the author's own creative activity. It is therefore necessary to examine the possible theological motives for such a creation and to evaluate the possibility that any one of them accounts for the attribution of responsibility to the people of Jerusalem. These motives must also be judged in light of what has been determined about Luke's theological program in previous discussion.

First of all, it is clear that a particular hostility to Jerusalem cannot account for Luke's attribution of responsibility. Even if hypotheses about Mark's pro-Galilee, anti-Jerusalem tendency are correct, there can be no question of Luke sharing a similar perspective. As is well known, Luke differs from Mark in locating the resurrection appearances in and around Jerusalem, omitting all reference to appearances in Galilee. Moreover, the very positive response of Jerusalem to the gospel in the early chapters of Acts appears to be inconsistent with anti-Jerusalem tendencies. Likewise, Jerusalem is not the chief seat of Jewish anti-Christian hostility for Luke: in the arrest of Paul in Jerusalem, Asian

---

1. Pesch, *Apostelgeschichte*, I, pp. 121, 150, 153; II, p. 37.

Jews are singled out as the instigators (Acts 21.27; 24.18).[1] As was discussed at length in Chapter 3 above, Luke–Acts as a whole gives no indication that Jerusalem represents for the author a special object of antipathy. There is no grand narrative structure in which Jerusalem is transformed from the center of Jewish-Christian continuity to the font of anti-Christian animosity.

In his seminal work on the speeches of Acts, U. Wilckens argued that Luke emphasized Jewish responsibility for the death of Jesus in order to accommodate his transfer of the Hellenistic-Christian scheme of repentance preaching: responsibility for the death of Jesus is the concrete sin for which the Jews must repent, just as the Gentiles must repent of their idolatry.[2] But, as J. Dupont pointed out after the publication of Wilckens's first edition, this point flounders on the restriction of responsibility to Jerusalem.[3] Thus, Wilckens's hypothesis fails to account for the data of the text.

Luke's interest in connecting the death of Jesus to the killing-of-the-prophets motif is well known and has been discussed elsewhere in this work. Although that motif is sometimes connected to his presentation of responsibility for the death of Jesus,[4] the evidence does not support the hypothesis that this motif motivated Luke's restriction of responsibility for the death of Jesus to Jerusalem. In his definitive study of the killing of the prophets, O. Steck notes emphatically that nothing in Jewish tradition—indeed, nothing apart from Mt. 23.37-39//Lk. 13.34-35—identifies Jerusalem in particular as the murderer of the prophets. Rather, Israel as a whole is charged with the crime.[5] Far from explaining

---

1. This observation also rules out Lukan interest in parallels between Jesus and Paul as the motivation for the restriction of popular responsibility to Jerusalem Jews: although both are arrested in Jerusalem, Paul's antagonists are not all Jerusalemites.

2. Wilckens, *Missionsreden*, p. 182.

3. Dupont, 'Les discours missionaires', pp. 45-50.

4. For example, Bruce writes, 'Jerusalem is traditionally the prophet-killing city; it would never do for a prophet to be killed anywhere else' ('Stephen's Apologia', p. 48).

5. 'Jerusalem ist im spätjüdischer Tradition sonst nicht Subjekt des Ungehorsams und auch mit dem gewaltsamen Prophetengeschick nie betont verbunden' (Steck, *Geschick*, pp. 227-28). Steck cites *Pes. R.* 146a, which asserts that 'Zion' knows its evil deeds, including the killing of the prophets, but notes that Zion here stands as the representative of Israel (*Geschick*, pp. 88-89). He notes further that the Babylonian destruction of Jerusalem is commonly connected to the killing of the prophets but recognizes that rabbinic traditions view Jerusalem's

the origin of Luke's attribution of responsibility, the killing-of-the-prophets motif makes it all the more puzzling.

The analysis offered above in Chapter 3 of Luke's presentation of Israel's response to the gospel found repeated emphasis on the division of Israel. That theme emerged in the various patterns of division evident in different portions of Luke–Acts: (1) in the pre-Jerusalem section of Luke's Gospel, the people are generally positive and the leaders (largely scribes and Pharisees) negative; (2) in the Jerusalem narrative of the Gospel of Acts, the people are positive and the leaders (now the high priests and their associates) negative; (3) in the diaspora, Jews are divided in their response without reference to their status (e.g. in Acts 17.4-5). But the emphasis on the responsibility of the people of Jerusalem for Jesus' death disturbs this largely consistent literary pattern. Had Luke emphasized the priests' manipulation of the crowd, or had he explicitly identified the crowd with a specific segment of Jerusalem's populace, or had he explicitly contrasted the people of Jerusalem with other Jews, his own literary-theological pattern would have been preserved with greater uniformity. Thus, Luke's distinctive theological interests do not account for his assessment of responsibility for the death of Jesus in Acts.

Independent Tradition

Indeed, there are significant positive implications in the observation that attributing responsibility to the people of Jerusalem does not advance Lukan theological interests. It is a widely accepted method to identify elements of the speeches of Acts which are incongruous with Lukan theology as elements of pre-Lukan tradition.[1] Thus, the variance

---

destruction as the consequence of the entire nation's sin (*Geschick*, pp. 88-89). He calls attention to certain midrashic texts which name Jerusalem as the place of the murders of certain individual prophets but judges this insufficient to connect the killing of the prophets in general to Jerusalem (*Geschick*, p. 228 n. 1). And he mentions the Old Testament connection of Jerusalem to sin and judgment, but finds again no connection to the fate of the prophets (*Geschick*, p. 228 n. 8). The Jewish texts which even remotely connect Jerusalem to the killing of the prophets are generally later rabbinic works. Steck accounts for the anomaly of Mt. 23.37-39//Lk. 13.34-35 as the *ex eventu* reading back of the punishment (the Roman destruction of Jerusalem) to the criminal (Jerusalem personified, which nevertheless still represents all Israel) on analogy with a similar pattern in Jewish texts (*Geschick*, pp. 228-29).

1.   Representative statements of this principle are made by Robinson ('Primitive Christology', p. 180), Wilcox ('Study of the Speeches', pp. 213-14), Schneider

between the attribution of responsibility for the death of Jesus to the people of Jerusalem and Luke's presentation of Israel divided suggests that the attribution was part of Luke's sources. The attribution of responsibility for the death of Jesus in Acts is consistent with the attribution of responsibility in Luke's Gospel, but it is relatively inconsistent with his presentation of Israel divided. This inconsistency suggests the use of an independent tradition.

Moreover, this hypothesis has none of the inadequacies or difficulties of the others. It requires no further motivation than the author's desire to represent his sources faithfully, even at the cost of obscuring a literary or theological emphasis. Indeed, it accounts for the difficulties of the other hypotheses. On this hypothesis, Luke's sources for the speeches of Acts were simply more specific than his Gospel sources in attributing popular responsibility. Thus, whereas the Gospel stresses Jerusalem's role generally and the leaders' role specifically, the designation of the people of Jerusalem in Acts is the consequence of a source or tradition other than those used by Luke in his Gospel, one more specific in this respect than his Gospel traditions but nevertheless broadly consistent with those traditions. The different focus in the traditions used in Acts explains the shift in the attribution of responsibility; the consistency of the different strands of tradition accounts for the consistency of Luke's emphasis on Jerusalem's responsibility across the two volumes of his narrative.

If there is a weakness to this hypothesis, it is its appeal to something that is inherently conjectural. Luke's sources for his Gospel can be at least broadly inferred through Synoptic analysis. Likewise, his theological interests can be known through exegesis. But his sources in Acts, particularly for the speeches, are not so accessible; they inevitably remain inferential. However, it is the very fact that the 'known' factors fail to account for the phenomena that requires recourse to the 'unknown'. Furthermore, the hypothetical nature of the sources of Acts should not be exaggerated: though few would insist that they can be reconstructed in any detail, few would deny that Luke employed sources of some kind in the speeches of Acts.[1] Thus, whereas this hypothesis calls for recourse to something 'unknown', it does so on the basis of that which can be 'known'. And what is 'unknown' is not the existence of the sources or traditions but their specific characteristics. The

(*Apostelgeschichte*, I, p. 83) and Bruce ('Historical Record', p. 2582).

1. This point was amply demonstrated in the discussion above.

difference between this hypothesis and the others is therefore one of degree, not of kind.

Conclusions

This discussion has demonstrated that Luke's use of traditions independent of his sources for the Gospel accounts best for the ascription of responsibility for Jesus' death to the people of Jerusalem in Acts. An initial case for such a tradition emerges from Luke's apparent use of traditional material in the context of key statements about responsibility for the death of Jesus. It is indicated negatively by the failure of other hypotheses to account for the data and positively by its divergence from Luke's literary-theological presentation of Israel divided.

To assert that Luke had such traditions raises another question: in what setting were they transmitted? The following chapter will offer a hypothesis as to the *Sitz im Leben* of traditions about Jerusalem's responsibility for the death of Jesus.

Chapter 7

TRANSMISSION OF TRADITIONS OF RESPONSIBILITY FOR THE DEATH OF JESUS

Evidence from Paul and the Synoptics indicates that traditions about responsibility for the death of Jesus were transmitted among Christians in the early years of the church. Moreover, the evidence of the book of Acts suggests the existence of an additional strand of such tradition, one independent of the Synoptics. But under what circumstances were such traditions circulated? For what reason, or in what *Sitz im Leben*, did early Christians pass on traditions about who instigated the death of Jesus? The answer to this question may in turn reveal more about the nature of primitive Christianity and shed further light on the texts which incorporate those traditions.

In Acts, material about responsibility for the death of Jesus is found in two settings. In Acts 4.27-28 and 7.52 it appears in the course of Christian response to persecution. In the first text, the Jerusalem community alludes to those responsible in the course of a prayer offered in thanksgiving for deliverance from persecution. In the second, Stephen equates his audience's violent rejection of Jesus with their ancestors' murder of the prophets and implicitly with their continuing rejection of Christian preachers like Stephen. That the response to persecution was one setting for the transmission of traditions about responsibility for the death of Jesus is further suggested by 1 Thess. 2.13-16, where the Thessalonian Christians' suffering is compared to Judean Christians' and ultimately to Jesus'. Since a similar application appears to have been a part of the pre-Pauline tradition underlying this text, the primitive Christian use of such material in response to persecution appears likely.[1]

The other setting in Acts for statements about responsibility for Jesus' death is proclamation of the crucifixion and resurrection of Jesus, that is, the kerygma. Such texts represent the bulk of those which address the

---

1. Cf. the discussion above in Chapter 4.

subject in Acts (2.22-24, 36; 3.13-15; 4.10-11; 5.30-31; 10.38-40; 13.27-30; cf. 5.28b, which reflects the accounts of Peter's preaching earlier in Acts). But determining whether such a setting is not merely Luke's own creation is not as simple as in the other case. The so-called kerygmatic summary in 1 Cor. 15.3ff. says nothing about responsibility for the death of Jesus. Does this fact indicate that Luke has inserted statements about responsibility for the death of Jesus into his kerygmatic sections, having extrapolated the statements from other traditions dealing with persecution of the church? Such a conclusion has been drawn,[1] but it may be unwarranted. Obviously, although 1 Cor. 15.3ff. is a summary of Paul's kerygma, it can hardly be thought to contain everything that Paul or others 'preached'.[2] Whereas phrases such as 'for our sins' (v. 3) serve parts of the subsequent argument (v. 17: 'you are still in your sins'), a statement about who put Christ to death would appear to have contributed nothing to Paul's immediate purpose. Moreover, Paul assumes some knowledge of traditions about responsibility for the death of Jesus earlier in 1 Cor. 2.8, though in what setting the information had originally been transmitted to the Corinthians cannot be known. In any case, then, the absence in 1 Cor. 15.3ff. of ascription of responsibility does not indicate ipso facto that such ascription was not a part of primitive Christian kerygma, at least in some circles.

Once again, then, the relative lack of direct evidence necessitates a degree of conjecture. It may be that a reasonable judgment on this issue can be made through a comparison with other ancient literature which deals with the persecution—and especially the judicial execution—of innocent victims. Examples of such literature are not lacking; they are found in both eras and in Jewish and non-Jewish cultural contexts. Therefore, what is offered here is a consideration of a broad, representative selection of such literature, giving special attention to the portrayal of the opponents of the innocent victim(s). The question for which an answer is sought is threefold.[3] With what degree of specificity do such texts identify the opponents of the innocent sufferer? How do such

---

1.   Wilckens, *Missionsreden*, p. 207.

2.   Cf. Gerhardsson's observation that the citation of tradition in 1 Cor. 15.3ff. is abbreviated to stress the resurrection (*Memory*, pp. 295-96).

3.   A similar method is employed to address a different question in J. Pobee, 'The Cry of the Centurion—A Cry of Defeat', in E. Bammel (ed.), *The Trial of Jesus: Cambridge Studies in Honour of C.F.D. Moule* (SBT, 2.13; London: SCM Press, 1970), pp. 91-102.

identifications relate to other elements in the portrayal of opponents? And what do such portrayals suggest about the kinds of constraints which govern the telling of such a story? The first two questions will be addressed as the literature is analyzed; the third after the results are summarized. Then the effect of the constraints in the circumstances of the primitive church will be considered.

Jewish Literature

A variety of Jewish works touch on the theme of the innocent sufferer. Those considered here represent some of the most widely circulated of those materials.[1] These texts can be loosely divided into two categories: (1) poetic materials regarding oppression, and (2) accounts of specific persecution or martyrdom. These will be considered in turn.

Poetic Materials regarding Oppression

Various poetic texts in the Psalms, Prophets and Wisdom books present the theme of the suffering righteous one. Significant for this discussion is the fact that in all such texts both the victim and the tormentors are anonymous. Such anonymity serves the purpose for which these texts were composed, allowing their continued use in the worshiping community. The prayers and laments of the righteous leave the victim and the opponents unnamed, so that the text can readily be applied to the suffering of the righteous in different circumstances. Similarly, proverbial statements about the oppression of the righteous serve as broad generalizations about a common experience.[2]

Nevertheless, these texts do portray the opponents in certain characteristic ways. Commonly, the innocence of the victim is reinforced by explicit statements about the wickedness of the oppressors. In Ps. 7.9; 14.4; 18.20-27; 34.21; 35.12; 94.3-6, 21-23; 97.10; and Hab. 1.4, 13 the wickedness of the opponents is contrasted directly with the righteousness of those oppressed. In the Psalms and elsewhere the opponents of the righteous are particularly characterized as slanderers and liars

---

1. Qumran literature has been omitted from this survey because of the interpretive difficulties involved in the material about the suffering of the Teacher of Righteousness.

2. Cf. the statement of G.W.E. Nickelsburg concerning Wis. 2, 4–5: 'The deletion of proper names is characteristic not only of the story, but of Wisdom as a whole' (*Resurrection, Immortality, and Eternal Life in Intertestamental Judaism* [HTS, 26; London: Oxford University Press, 1972], p. 67).

(Ps. 4.2; 5.6, 9; 7.14; 27.12; 31.13, 18; 35.11, 20; 41.4-6; 43.1; 55.10, 23; 56.5; 59.9-15; 63.11; 64.3, 8; 109.2, 20; 116.11; 119.69; 120.2-3; 140.3, 9, 11; Jer. 20.10; Lam. 3.62; Ezek. 13.22; Sir. 51.2, 5-6).[1] The falsehood of the opponents' charges contrasts with the innocence and righteousness of the victim. Hence, the Psalmist insists that he is persecuted without cause (Ps. 35.19; 38.19; 69.4; 109.2-3; 129.4).[2] The victim seeks God's assistance as the righteous judge who vindicates the faithful and punishes the wicked.

In his landmark study of the suffering righteous one in Jewish literature, L. Ruppert has proposed that the oppressors in such literature were first identified as the enemies of Yahweh because of their opposition to Yahweh's anointed, the Davidic king. Later this relatively neutral characterization of the enemies was replaced with a morally and religiously determined enemy-terminology: the enemies of the righteous appear as God-forsaking, impious, twisted and underhanded persecutors and tormentors, motivated by demonic forces.[3] Clearly underlying every stage of the development, however, is a particular moral outlook: those who oppress the righteous are, merely by virtue of that oppression, wicked and deserving of punishment. Those who persecute the righteous are patently evil, and their evil is seen in the persecution itself. It is for this reason that at every stage such texts call for judgment on the oppressors as well as deliverance of the oppressed. The two are inseparable.[4]

The traditional headings of many of the Psalms of righteous suffering are also relevant. As is well known, several of these headings offer a historical setting for the particular psalm in the life of David. Relevant here is the fact that some of these include explicit identification of the opponent or opponents (cf. Pss. 3, 7, 18, 54, 56, 59). These suggest that a part of the motivation in assigning these psalms to events in David's career may have been interest in identifying who the wicked oppressors

---

1. Cf. L. Ruppert, *Der leidende Gerechte: Eine motivgeschichtliche Untersuchung zum Alten Testament und zwischentestamentlichen Judentum* (FB, 5; Würzburg: Echter Verlag, 1972), pp. 37, 48, 205.

2. Ruppert, *Leidende Gerechte: Motivgeschichtliche Untersuchung*, p. 30-33.

3. L. Ruppert, *Der leidende Gerechte und seine Feinde: Eine Wortfelduntersuchung* (FB, 6; Würzburg: Echter Verlag, 1973), pp. 6-109, 270-71.

4. Ruppert identifies Pss. 7 and 35 as representatives of the earliest stage of development (*Leidende Gerechte: Motivgeschichtliche Untersuchung*, pp. 25-27). Both couple the deliverance of the sufferer with judgment on his persecutors (Ps. 7.16-17; 35.1-8).

were. While not a part of the Psalms themselves, such interest arose in the course of their transmission.

Accounts of Specific Persecutions or Martyrdoms

Various Jewish works, encompassing a wide range of genres, narrate or summarize specific instances in which the righteous are persecuted or killed. Some describe the opponents of the righteous only in general terms, but most are specific about their identity.

Danielic Literature. Daniel 3 and 6 are examples of such narratives from within the Hebrew canon. In these accounts the three youths and Daniel respectively are accused because of their Jewish piety, subjected to an ordeal which is expected to result in their death, miraculously delivered from that ordeal, and thereby vindicated. In both accounts, the identity of the persecutors is quite vague: the three youths are accused before Nebuchadnezzar by 'certain Chaldeans' (3.8), and Daniel is accused by 'commissioners and satraps' (6.4-8, 12-13). In the latter case the reader is told that the accusers meet the end intended for the accused (6.24). In Daniel 3 the fate of the accusers is not indicated, though Nebuchadnezzar issues a decree which demands execution for anyone offering offense to the God of the three youths, perhaps implying that the accusers are to be so executed. At any rate, the narrative is more concerned with the deliverance of the victims and the vindication of the God of Israel than with either the identity or the fate of the accusers. Furthermore, little is said which impugns the character of the accusers. At most, it is implied that Daniel's adversaries act out of jealousy at his preeminence (Dan. 6.3-4). The writer appears to be more concerned to show the power of God to deliver the faithful and so vindicate himself and his people before the Gentiles than to characterize the identity or nature of the opposition.

Similar observations may be made about the story of Daniel and Susanna. Here the accusers—Jews, in contrast to the Gentile opponents of the canonical stories—are merely identified as 'two elders', even though the other principals, including even the husband of Susanna who takes no part in the action, are named (Sus. 1-2, 45). But like Daniel's own accusers in Daniel 6, they too suffer the fate intended for the innocent victim (Sus. 62).

Esther. The vague designation of opponents in the Danielic literature is unusual when compared to other texts. Other Jewish accounts of persecution and martyrdom are considerably more specific about the identity of the persecutors. Many also go to some length to explicate the evil character of the persecutors, and some include accounts of divine retribution. Among these is the book of Esther. This text, of course, names its persecutor as 'Haman, son of Hammedatha, the Agagite' (Esth. 3.1). His motivation is clear: resentment of the Jew Mordecai's lack of obeisance (3.2-6). Like Daniel's rivals in the imperial court, Haman too meets the end he intended for his victim (7.9-10).

2 Maccabees. The leading adversary in 2 Maccabees is 'the king' (ὁ βασιλεύς), that is, Antiochus Epiphanes.[1] His underlings appear in the narrative, but little attention is given to them. Indeed, their submission to the insidious purposes of Antiochus serves to emphasize all the more the king's role as the chief persecutor. For example, in 2 Macc. 6.1 'the king' sends an anonymous 'elderly Athenian' (γέροντα ᾿Αθηναῖον) to compel 'the Jews' (τοὺς ᾿Ιουδαίους) to forsake the law. As the account of the persecution begins, it is first 'the Gentiles' (τῶν ἐθνῶν) who defile the temple (6.4). When the actual persecution of individual Jews begins in 6.10-11, passive and third person plural active verbs without expressed subjects are employed, focusing attention on the victims and the acts of persecution rather than the persecutors. The same syntax appears in 6.18. But in 6.21 the persecutors are referred to as 'those appointed over the illegal eating of entrails' (οἱ δὲ πρὸς τῷ παρανόμῳ σπλαγγχνισμῷ τεταγμένοι), a phrase which emphasizes that their authority is delegated from Antiochus. These figures appear in a somewhat more sympathetic light when they suggest to Eleazar a ruse to allow his escape (6.21-22). But Eleazar righteously refuses their plan, and as a result their goodwill (εὐμένεια) is transformed to ill will (δυσμένεια) because they regard Eleazar as mad (6.29).

The account of Eleazar's death introduces the climax of the account of persecution in 2 Maccabees: the story of the seven brothers (2 Macc. 7), in which Antiochus himself appears as the chairman of the proceedings. In fact, the account begins by asserting that the torture is performed ὑπὸ τοῦ βασιλέως (7.1, cf. vv. 3, 12, 25, 30, 39). Antiochus is

---

1. All references to the Greek text of 2 Maccabees–*4 Maccabees* are from A. Rahlfs's edition of the LXX (Stuttgart: Deutsche Bibelgesellschaft, 1935). The translations are my own. In this survey 1 Maccabees is omitted from consideration because it contains no material directly relevant to the issue at hand; *4 Maccabees* is treated before *3 Maccabees* because of the former's affinity to 2 Maccabees.

addressed by the brothers in the second person and is contrasted with ὁ τοῦ κόσμου βασιλεύς in v. 9; similar direct address of the king recurs throughout the account (vv. 14, 16-19, 31, 34). 'The king' is specified as Antiochus in 7.24. Additionally, his character is impugned with expressions like τὸν ὠμὸν τύραννον ('this cruel tyrant', v. 27) and ἀνόσιε καὶ πάντων ἀνθρώπων μιαρώτατε ('impious and foulest of all people', v. 34).

This expression in the speech of the last of the seven brothers begins his assertion that God will punish Antiochus for his persecution. That judgment comes to fruition in 2 Macc. 9.4-29. Antiochus dies a painful and humiliating death, comparable to the deaths he inflicted on his victims (v. 28), so that the brothers and the other faithful sufferers are vindicated.

4 Maccabees. The tendency of 2 Maccabees to focus attention on Antiochus Epiphanes as the persecutor of the Jews is also evident in *4 Maccabees*. Here Antiochus personally orders 'each one of the Hebrews' (ἕνα ἕκαστον Ἑβραῖον) to eat pork and meat offered to idols (*4 Macc.* 5.1). In the course of this episode, Eleazar appears; thus, Antiochus himself becomes the interrogator and persecutor of Eleazar (5.6) as well as of the seven brothers (8.2ff.). Attention is focused on Antiochus's role as persecutor through repeated reference to his character: he is 'arrogant and terrible' (ὑπερήφανος καὶ δεινός, 4.15), 'most abominable tyrant, enemy of heaven's justice and bent on slaughter' (τύραννε μιαρώτατε καὶ τῆς οὐρανίου δίκης ἐχθρὲ καὶ ὠμόφρων, 9.15), 'most bloodthirsty of tyrants' (πάντων ὠμότατε τύραννε, 9.30), 'most vile tyrant' (μιαρώτατε τύραννε, 9.32; 10.10), 'bloodthirsty and murderous and most abominable' (ὁ αἱμοβόρος καὶ φονώδης καὶ παμμιαρώτατος Ἀντίοχος, 10.17), and 'impious and of all the wicked the most ungodly tyrant' (ἀνόσιε...καὶ πάντων πονηρῶν ἀσεβέστατε τύραννε, 12.11). Repeatedly he is told that his actions mark him out for divine judgment (9.32; 10.11, 15; 12.12-14) as one who disregards the justice of heaven (9.15). As in 2 Maccabees, Antiochus's underlings are anonymous; unlike their moderate and sympathetic counterparts in the other account, they are characterized as 'cruel' (πικρός, 6.8).

3 Maccabees. In *3 Maccabees*, the persecutor is again a Hellenistic ruler: Ptolemy IV Philopator. His desire to enter the temple marks him in the

text as 'rash and impure' (θρασὺς καὶ βέβηλος, 2.14) and characterized by 'insolence' (ὕβρις, 2.21). His experience of God's punishment
results in an increase in his wickedness (κακία, 2.25), and later setbacks
further enrage him (3.1). He is characterized by an 'ungodly heart'
(δυσσεβῆ φρένα, 5.47). Once again, he has associates who encourage
his persecution. They are identified as Philopator's 'drinking buddies
and comrades' (συμποτῶν καὶ ἑταίρων) who are 'severed from
everything just' (τοῦ παντὸς δικαίου κεχωρισμένων, *3 Macc.* 2.25;
cf. 7.3). Although these companions are unnamed in the present text,
either in an earlier version or in the source of *3 Maccabees* some other
characterization of them must have been included, for in the present text
of 2.25 they are 'aforementioned' (προαποδεδειγμένων).[1] Likewise,
Philopator is supported by elements of the populace hostile to the Jews
(4.1; cf. 5.24), though some are shamed by the spectacle of Jewish
misery (4.5). The sum of the opponents are characterized as 'arrogant
Gentiles' (ἔθνεσιν ὑπερηφάνοις, 5.13) and 'abominable and lawless
Gentiles' (ἐβδελυγμένων ἀνόμων ἐθνῶν, 6.9). After the deliverance is
effected, these persecutors do not suffer the fate intended for their
victims, but they do experience profound humiliation (6.34).

Traditions of the Deaths of the Prophets. A different kind of material is
encountered in literature which incorporates Jewish traditions about the
deaths of the prophets.[2] These traditions are preserved in a variety of
sources, including rabbinic and patristic materials as well as texts classed
among the pseudepigrapha of both testaments.[3] Here we will consider
only four of the most prominent of those sources: the *Martyrdom and
Ascension of Isaiah*, the Babylonian Talmud, the *Lives of the Prophets*,
and the *Apocalypse of Paul*. Because all of these works include accounts

---

1.   Cf. the remark of H. Anderson in Charlesworth (ed.), *Old Testament
Pseudepigrapha*, II, p. 519 n. e.

2.   But cf. the remarks of M.A. Knibb on the similarities of *Mart. Isa.* 1.1–3.12;
5.1-16 to *2 Macc.* 6.18–7.42 (in Charlesworth [ed.], *Old Testament
Pseudepigrapha*, II, p. 150). The source of *Mart. Isa.* 1.1–3.12; 5.1-16 is widely
regarded as having been composed at about the same time as the legends of Eleazar
and the seven brothers, i.e., under Antiochus Epiphanes or immediately after his
death; cf. O. Eissfeldt, *The Old Testament: An Introduction* (ET; Oxford: Basil
Blackwell, 1965), p. 609.

3.   Cf. H.J. Schoeps, 'Die jüdischen Prophetenmorde', in *Aus früchristlicher
Zeit* (Tübingen: Mohr [Paul Siebeck], 1950), pp. 135-37; B.H. Amaru, 'The Killing
of the Prophets: Unraveling a Midrash', *HUCA* 54 (1983), pp. 153-80.

of the death of Isaiah, they particularly illustrate the kinds of features which tend to remain constant in the transmission of such accounts.

As it stands, the *Martyrdom and Ascension of Isaiah* is a Christian work. Nevertheless, it is generally understood that the basic material of 1.1–3.12 and 5.1-16 is the oldest material in the work and is Jewish in origin. Although Christian reworking of these sections cannot be excluded, the essence of the Jewish account about Isaiah's death contained in these sections appears to have been preserved without significant alteration, and the portrayal of Isaiah's enemies in particular belongs to the Jewish stratum.[1] Of course, the adversarial figure of Manasseh looms large in the account. His instigation is the leading cause of the prophet's death. A variety of details focus attention on Manasseh. Isaiah warns Hezekiah that his fatherly words of instruction will have no effect on his wicked son, who will cause the prophet to 'depart' (*Mart. Isa.* 1.7).[2] Later, Manasseh's evils are catalogued; their consequence is that Beliar or Belkira, a shadowy figure who sometimes appears to be human but elsewhere is demonic, rejoices 'over Jerusalem because of Manasseh...and in the iniquity which was disseminated in Jerusalem' (2.1-6).[3] Isaiah sees 'the great iniquity which was being committed in Jerusalem, and the service of Satan, and his wantonness' and so withdraws to Bethlehem (2.7). But the iniquity has reached even there, so Isaiah and his contemporaries (Micah, Joel and Habakkuk [*sic*]) retreat to the wilderness to lament the 'going astray of Israel' (2.8-10). The human manifestation of Beliar/Belkira then figures prominently. His lineage is connected to the prophets of Baal under Ahab, suggesting his antipathy for the true prophets (2.12-16). He proposes the arrest of Isaiah to Manasseh (3.1-12). As the death of Isaiah is related, Beliar/Belkira again is prominent: he 'dwells in the heart of Manasseh' as Isaiah is sawn in half and mocks Isaiah as he is executed.[4] Thus,

1. Knibb notes that 1.2b-6a, 7, 13; 2.9; and 5.15-16 show the hand of a Christian editor (Charlesworth [ed.], *Old Testament Pseudepigrapha*, II, pp. 143, 148).

2. The verse includes a trinitarian formula which betrays the hand of a Christian interpolator (cf. Knibb in Charlesworth [ed.], *Old Testament Pseudepigrapha*, II, p. 157). But the interpolation appears to be confined to the formula itself; the statement about Manasseh is probably Jewish.

3. On the alternation of the names 'Beliar' and 'Belkira', cf. Knibb, in Charlesworth [ed.], *Old Testament Pseudepigrapha*, II, pp. 151-52.

4. The extant text of *Mart. Isa.* 5.1-16 is unclear as to who actually saws Isaiah in half. 5.1 could suggest either Beliar or Manasseh ('Beliar dwelt in the heart of Manasseh, and he sawed Isaiah in half...'); some of this ambiguity may be the result

throughout the narrative the prophet's opponents are conspicuous.

The prominence of Manasseh as Isaiah's enemy does not appear to have been unique to the account preserved in the *Martyrdom and Ascension of Isaiah*. The longest talmudic reference to Isaiah's death, *b. Yeb*. 49b, though characteristically using the story to discuss apparent contradictions between the book of Isaiah and the Pentateuch, uses the figure of Manasseh to voice these problems as Isaiah's adversary. Furthermore, the text includes the interesting note that Rabbi Simeon ben 'Azzai had discovered genealogical records in which was written 'Manasseh slew Isaiah'. It would appear, therefore, that the traditional account which stood behind the talmudic text was concerned not just to relate that Isaiah had been killed but that he was killed by a specific individual.

The same kind of specificity is in evidence in the *Lives of the Prophets*. This collection of traditions about the prophets, evidently independent of the *Martyrdom and Ascension of Isaiah*,[1] is apparently of Jewish origin and may be as early as the first century.[2] Part of its more or less uniform pattern in presenting each prophet includes the account of the prophet's death.[3] Six of the prophets are said to have been killed: Isaiah (1.1), Jeremiah (2.1), Ezekiel (3.2, 17b-19), Micah (6.2),

---

of Christian redaction of the Jewish material (5.1 resumes the Jewish material after a Christian interpolation of some length). But in 5.12 Manasseh, Belkira, the false prophets, the princes and the people stand by and watch as Isaiah is killed. It may be that the original Jewish text conceived of Manasseh and Beliar as having ordered the execution and so informally spoke of their having performed the act itself. Cf. the ambiguity of Lk. 23.24-25.

1. D.R.A. Hare, in Charlesworth (ed.), *Old Testament Pseudepigrapha*, II, p. 380.

2. The consensus is that the *Lives of the Prophets* contains little overtly Christian interpolation, and none that impinges on the interests of this volume (cf. C.C. Torrey [ed.], *The Lives of the Prophets: Greek Text and Translation* [JBLMS, 1; Philadelphia: Society of Biblical Literature and Exegesis, 1946], p. 9-10; Hare, in Charlesworth [ed.], *Old Testament Pseudepigrapha*, p. 380; Schoeps, 'Prophetenmorde', pp. 131-32). Torrey (*Lives*, p. 1) and Hare (in Charlesworth [ed.], *Old Testament Pseudepigrapha*, II, pp. 380-81) agree on the likelihood of a first-century date, influenced in part by the possible dependence of Heb. 11.37 on the accounts of the deaths of Isaiah, Jeremiah and Ezekiel. Schoeps demurs at specifying the first century for the present text of the *Lives* but allows that the traditions behind the work must have originated no later than the early part of the first century ('Prophetenmorde', pp. 131-32).

3. Torrey, *Lives*, p. 3.

Amos (7.2), and Zechariah ben Jehoiada (23.1). With the exception of Jeremiah, all of these deaths are ascribed to specific individuals. Most of the killers are Israelite political rulers: Manasseh (Isaiah), Joram (Micah), Joash (Zechariah) and 'the leader of the Israelite exiles' (ὁ ἡγούμενος τοῦ λαοῦ 'Ισραὴλ ἐκεῖ; Ezekiel). Amos is slain by the son of Amaziah, priest of Bethel. Although Jeremiah's death is ascribed to τοῦ λαοῦ, he dies in Egypt after the exile and so implicitly at the hands of a specific group of his countrymen. In two cases the motivation of the killers is also related; in both the motive is opposition to the prophet's message. The resentment of the exile leader for Ezekiel's denunciation of idolatry is noted twice (3.2, 17b-19), and similar resentment is also noted in the cases of Micah. Such a motivation is probably implicit in ascribing the death of Amos to the priestly line associated with the renegade cult of Bethel. In any case, the specific interest in the persons responsible for the death of the prophets is interesting in the context of the *Lives*. The common opinion is that the accounts of the prophets' deaths in the document reflect interest not in their exemplary nature but in veneration of their graves. Relating exactly who killed the prophets would appear to be of little interest in such a setting; the fact that the information is nevertheless transmitted suggests that it was an integral part of the traditions employed.

The influence of these traditions is also apparent in the *Apocalypse of Paul* 49.[1] Here the three major prophets Isaiah, Jeremiah and Ezekiel appear and relate the circumstances of their deaths. Isaiah's and Jeremiah's conform to the accounts in the *Lives*, but Ezekiel is said to have been slain when 'the children of Israel' dragged him 'by the feet over the rocks on the mountain' until his brains were dashed out. It is possible that an alternate tradition is employed here, but the interest of the context in developing the theme of Israel's rejection of God's messengers (cf. ch. 48) suggests that Christian anti-Judaism may have provoked some alteration of the tradition as well.[2] If this is the case, the ascription of Isaiah's death to Manasseh alone, in contrast to the other two prophets' deaths at the hands of a larger group of Israelites, could indicate that that aspect of the tradition was firmly ensconced.

---

1. References are from E. Hennecke and W. Schneemelcher (eds.), *New Testament Apocrypha* (2 vols.; ET; London: Lutterworth, 1964).

2. This generalizing of responsibility contrasts with the lack of interest in ascribing the death of the prophets to 'Israel' in the *Lives*; cf. Hare, in Charlesworth (ed.), *Old Testament Pseudepigrapha*, II, p. 382.

Conclusion. The sum of this evidence suggests a certain proclivity in the Jewish sources to ascribe the death of martyrs and the persecution of the righteous to specific individuals or groups. Usually those opponents are explicitly portrayed as evil; often, specific motives are supplied for their persecution. Occasionally their own deaths are narrated to illustrate divine retribution, thus further reinforcing the moral contrast between persecutor and victim. Only in certain texts, especially those used in worship as the supplication of the community, are persecutors unnamed.

Pagan Literature

Non-Jewish, non-Christian material provides several texts which are interesting for the purpose at hand. Exhaustive consideration of such literature is, of course, impossible in the limitations of a study such as this one. Therefore, attention will be given to a representative sample. *Ahiqar* is considered because of its dissemination in Jewish circles. Accounts of the death of Socrates are treated because of their influence on the development of the martyr ideal in the ancient world. The *Acts of the Pagan Martyrs* receives attention as an example of the outworking of the martyr ideal in Hellenistic literature. Philostratus's *Life of Apollonius of Tyana* is examined because of the parallels often drawn between it and the Gospels. Finally, a nonliterary work, a letter of Mara ben Serapion, will be considered because of the parallels that it draws among several martyrdoms, including an apparent reference to the death of Jesus.

Ahiqar

Although transmitted in Jewish circles and associated with the Old Testament Pseudepigrapha, the tractate *Ahiqar* is in fact of Assyrian origin.[1] In the first part of the text, the sage Ahiqar is betrayed by his nephew and heir, Nadin (or Nadan), and nearly killed by the Assyrian king (*Ahiqar* 18-31). Ahiqar is saved through a ruse he plans with the executioner, who happens to be an old friend, but in the oldest extant version the end of the story is lost. Later versions include both the vindication of Ahiqar and the reproaching and execution of his opponent, Nadin.[2]

---

1.   J.M. Lindenberger, in Charlesworth (ed.), *Old Testament Pseudepigrapha*, II, pp. 479-81.

2.   Cf. the discussion in Lindenberger's translation in Charlesworth (ed.), *Old Testament Pseudepigrapha*, II, p. 498.

Socrates

The various accounts of the trial of Socrates and its aftermath were highly influential in forming attitudes toward martyrdom in the Hellenistic world.[1] Of interest here is their inclusion of several significant features in the portrayal of Socrates' three accusers—Meletus, Anytus and Lycon—and of the jury that convicts him. As will be seen, these accounts are all the more interesting since it appears that for some time after Socrates' death the controversy about him continued in Athens.[2]

The Accounts of Plato. In Plato's version of the trial of Socrates, Meletus is the key opponent.[3] Even in a dialogue set before the trial begins, Meletus is characterized negatively: a 'young and unknown person...with long hair and only a little beard, but with a hooked nose (*Euthyphro* 2B).[4] Meletus's charges against Socrates are treated with sarcasm and ridicule, with the implication that Meletus is arrogant and foolish (*Euthyphro* 2C-3A). Finally, the charges are said to be 'absurd' and to amount to 'slander' (*Euthyphro* 16A); the implications for the character of a person already so unsympathetically portrayed are unmistakable. In the *Apology* itself, Meletus and his associates are again treated with contempt and ridicule as Socrates makes his defense. The accusers are said to be persuasive, but their speeches contain little truth; indeed, they 'lied' in characterizing Socrates as a clever speaker (*Apology* 17A). The accusations themselves are false (*Apology* 18A) and spring from a false prejudice in which Meletus trusts (*Apology* 19A-B).

1.   On the influence of the story of Socrates, see A.D. Nock, *Conversion: The Old and the New in Religion from Alexander the Great to Augustine of Hippo* (Oxford: Clarendon Press, 1933), p. 194; M. Hengel, *The Atonement: The Origins of the Doctrine in the New Testament* (London: SCM Press, 1981), p. 16. A general bibliography of studies of Socrates' trial is provided by T.G. West, *Plato's Apology of Socrates: An Interpretation, with a New Translation* (London: Cornell University Press, 1979), p. 71 n. 1. On the so-called Socratic problem, cf. the discussion in W.K.C. Guthrie, *A History of Greek Philosophy* (6 vols.; Cambridge: Cambridge University Press, 1962–81), III, pp. 325-77.

2.   Cf. R. Hackforth, *The Composition of Plato's* Apology (Cambridge: Cambridge University Press, 1933), pp. 49, 71.

3.   Hackforth notes: 'Every time Meletus is referred to there is some word of disparagement' (*Composition*, p. 108).

4.   Textual references and translations of Plato's *Euthyphro* and *Apology* are from the edition of H.N. Fowler and W.R.M. Lamb (LCL; London: Heinemann, 1913).

In fact, all three accusers are said to follow such 'vehement slanders' in reaction against Socrates' insistence that those regarded as wise are in fact foolish (*Apology* 23E-24A). Because the charges are so manifestly false that they cannot be taken seriously, Meletus is a 'wrongdoer' who makes light of solemn matters (*Apology* 24C). Meletus is 'careless': he himself shows no concern for the youth of Athens with whose corruption he charges Socrates (*Apology* 25C, 26B). Meletus is not to be believed (even by himself), having brought the charges in 'a spirit of violence and unrestraint and rashness'. The charge of atheism is so patently false that Meletus is said to have brought it simply because he could find no better charge (*Apology* 27E). Thus, Socrates is a 'better man' who will not be injured by a 'worse', even if he is convicted and sentenced (*Apology* 30C-D). Responding to his conviction, Socrates asserts that it was the result of 'villainy and wrong' (*Apology* 39B). Thus, throughout the dialogues, the refutation of the charges against Socrates involves the denigration of those who bring the charges. If Socrates is innocent, then those who accuse him are themselves guilty.[1]

Plato's Socrates points out another sinister influence lurking behind the immediate charges. He speaks at length of the considerable prejudice against him in Athens, prejudice created and encouraged by a series of slanderers who have circulated rumors about him out of envy (*Apology* 18A-D). These opponents by the nature of the case must remain anonymous, says Socrates, 'except when one of them happens to be a writer of comedies' (*Apology* 18D), a transparent allusion to Aristophanes' disparaging portrayal of Socrates in the *Clouds*. In summing up his defense, Socrates indicates that if he is found guilty, his conviction will ultimately be the result of 'the prejudice and dislike of the many' created by such slander (*Apology* 28A-B). Likewise, when the verdict has been delivered, Socrates charges the jury, addressed as 'men of Athens' (*Apology* 38C), with blame for his death and responsibility for its consequences, especially the reproach that will come upon Athens (*Apology* 32A-C, 38C, 39C).[2] Indeed, all of Athens is included in

---

1.   Cf. also Plato, *Epistles* 7.325B-C, which cites the death of Socrates as an example of the duplicity of those with political power (from the edition of R.G. Bury [LCL; London: Heinemann, 1942]).

2.   Cf. Plato's *Gorgias* 521E, where Socrates says that if he is tried in Athens, 'I shall be like a doctor tried by a bunch of children on a charge brought by a cook'. Earlier, Socrates had suggested that cookery was a substitute for medicine, just as flattery can substitute for justice (*Gorgias* 521E); what Plato implies both about the

Socrates' accusations: as T.G. West has noted, Socrates redefines the charges against him and directs them against the entire city, denouncing its corruption and impiety (*Apology* 28B-31C).[1]

The sum of this evidence suggests that Plato was concerned in part to defend the reputation of Socrates by pointing out the falsehood of the charges against him and, as a corollary, the sinister motives of his accusers and judges.[2] Socrates could be rehabilitated only insofar as he is shown to be innocent. But if he died an innocent man, then those who brought about his death were themselves guilty of wrongdoing. Hence, for Plato the defense of Socrates went hand in hand with denunciation of his opponents.

The Accounts of Xenophon. Xenophon's two works dealing with the trial of Socrates follow a similar approach to Plato's in regard to Socrates' opponents, though with somewhat different emphases. The *Memorabilia* begins with the question of how those who drew up the indictment against Socrates (οἱ γραψάμενοι Σωκράτην) could persuade the Athenians that he should be executed (1.1.1).[3] The text refers repeatedly to 'the accuser' (ὁ κατήγορος: *Memorabilia* 1.2.9, 12, 26, 49, 58). However, the impression should not be gained from such terms that the accusers are unknown or remain anonymous for Xenophon. Without formal introduction Meletus is named as having written the indictment (*Memorabilia* 4.4.4; 4.8.4). If the commonly received critical opinion is correct, that Xenophon composed the *Memorabilia* in response to a speech written by the sophist Polycrates purporting to be the speech of Anytus,[4] then the vague expressions for Socrates'

accusers of Socrates and about his jury are clear (translations from the edition of W.R.M. Lamb [LCL; London: Heinemann, 1925]).

1. West, *Plato's Apology: An Interpretation*, p. 150.

2. West has argued that Socrates' arrogance toward his accusers and the jury account for his conviction and execution (*Plato's Apology: An Interpretation*, p. 76 and *passim*). A significant portion of the evidence West cites is the denigration of Meletus and of the jury (*Plato's Apology: An Interpretation*, pp. 76, 82-83, 136-43, 145, 150, 188). Plato's apparent disregard for the effect of Socrates' words in their original setting may reflect his interest in rehabilitating the master for a later audience. Cf. also the discussion of Hackforth on *Crito* 48C, a text which could allude to a later change of feeling toward Socrates in Athens (*Composition*, p. 49).

3. References to the text and translations of Xenophon's *Memorabilia* are taken from the edition of E.C. Marchant (LCL; London: Heinemann, 1923).

4. Cf. the discussion in Marchant, *Memorabilia*, pp. ix-x.

opponents may be deliberately ambiguous, referring both to the historical accuser Anytus and to the more recent adversary Polycrates.[1] Furthermore, the casual way in which Meletus is introduced suggests that Xenophon assumes the readers' knowledge of the accuser's identities. In any case, Xenophon's Socrates, despite his equanimity in the face of execution, appeals to the judgment of posterity and insists that those who bring about his death kill him unjustly and will bear shame for it (*Memorabilia* 4.8.9). Likewise, his refusal to flatter the jury stands in contrast with the accusers' manipulation of the jury (*Memorabilia* 4.4.4).

Xenophon's *Apology* is similar to his longer Socratic work in its approach to the accusers. Again, they are referred to with a general expression: 'his adversaries' (οἱ ἀντίδικοι; *Apology* 10). And again Meletus is named later and given no introduction (*Apology* 19). Addressed directly by Socrates, Meletus responds to his questions during the defense (*Apology* 20). Thus, the figure of Meletus is again relatively prominent. More striking about Xenophon's *Apology*, however, is the so-called 'Anytus episode'. Socrates is said to have remarked about Anytus that his enmity was motivated by Socrates' disapproval of his treatment of his son (*Apology* 29). He then goes on to utter a prophecy that Anytus's son will fall into disgrace (*Apology* 30). Xenophon then relates that the son did in fact become a drunkard, so that 'Anytus, even though dead, still enjoys an evil repute (κακοδοξίας) for his son's mischievous education and for his own hard-heartedness' (*Apology* 31). Thus, Anytus is seen to have been recompensed for his treachery. A.-H. Chroust has noted that similar 'slanderous literary persecution of Anytus' is found in later Socratic writers who wished to impugn the motives of Socrates' accusers.[2]

Later Accounts. The tendency to exonerate Socrates by implicating his accusers is reflected in later works which include accounts of his trial

---

1. This interpretation is offered by, among others, Hackforth (*Composition*, p. 71). A.-H. Chroust also notes that Diogenes Laertius (2.38-39) later confuses Anytus and Polycrates, perhaps as a result of the deliberate ambiguity of Xenophon (*Socrates, Man and Myth: The Two Socratic Apologies of Xenophon* [London: Routledge & Kegan Paul, 1957], p. 73).

2. Chroust, *Socrates, Man and Myth*, p. 36. Cf. also the discussion in Hackforth, who notes the pattern of contrasting Socrates' noble death with the ignoble death of Anytus (*Composition*, pp. 42-43).

and death. Diodorus Siculus relates that long before Socrates' trial Anytus was accused of treason and escaped conviction only by bribing the jury (13.64.6).[1] Similarly, Diogenes Laertius relates that Anytus was motivated by his envy and resentment of Socrates' ridicule. Therefore, he first stirs up τοὺς περὶ 'Αριστοφάνην (i.e. the shadowy 'first accusers' of Plato's *Apology*) and later organizes the indictment which brings him to trial (2.38).[2] Both historians relate a tradition, widely judged by modern historians to be false, that the Athenians later repented of the death of Socrates and punished the accusers. Diodorus Siculus indicates that 'the accusers' (τοὺς κατηγορήσαντας) were put to death without trial (14.37.7); Diogenes Laertius indicates that only Meletus was executed while the other two were exiled (2.43; 6.10). The tradition appears to have arisen in the same vein as Xenophon's initial question in the *Memorabilia*: how could Athens condemn one so righteous as Socrates? Thus, in the texts of both historians the tendency to bolster Socrates' reputation by maligning his opponents is clearly in evidence. If Socrates was innocent, then those who put him to death were guilty, a point sharpened all the more if the accusers are punished for their wrongdoing.

The Acta Alexandrinorum
The so-called *Acta Alexandrinorum* or *Acts of the Pagan Martyrs* includes a number of texts which appear to have depicted conflict between individual Hellenists in Egypt and their tyrannical rulers.[3] Most of the texts are simply too fragmentary to suggest anything of relevance to the concerns addressed here. But one, the *Acta Appiani* from P.Oxy. 33, is preserved in sufficient extent to allow consideration. The text is set around 190 CE and portrays the trial and execution of an Alexandrian named Appian by Commodus during the latter's 'reign of terror'.[4] In the extant text, Appian twice addresses Commodus with derogatory epithets. Asked by Commodus if he knows to whom he speaks, Appian

---

1.   References to Diodorus Siculus are from the text and translation of C.H. Oldfather (LCL; London: Heinemann, 1950).
2.   The text and translation of Diogenes Laertius employed is that of R.D. Hicks (LCL; London: Heinemann, 1925).
3.   The text and translation employed is H.A. Musurillo (ed.), *The Acts of the Pagan Martyrs: Acta Alexandrinorum* (Oxford: Clarendon Press, 1954). Musurillo provides succinct comments on the nature of the corpus (pp. 239-41).
4.   Musurillo, *Pagan Martyrs*, pp. 206-10.

tersely replies, ἐπίσταμαι, 'Ἀππιανὸς τυράννῳ ('I know: Appian speaks to a tyrant'; *Acta Appiani* 48 [P.Oxy. 33, 2.5]). Later, Appian calls the emperor ὁ λήσταρχος ('the bandit-chief'; *Acta Appiani* 81 [P.Oxy. 33, 4.8]). H.A. Musurillo understands that Appian stands trial for accusing the emperor of corruption.[1] If that is the case, then Appian's insulting words are to be understood not as negative instances of insolence but as the just accusations of a man falsely charged by a corrupt ruler. His innocence stands in bold relief against the background of his adversary's degeneracy.

Philostratus's Life of Apollonius of Tyana
Philostratus's account of the sophist Apollonius has been compared to the Gospels almost since its appearance.[2] Although it is considerably later than the Gospels, it purports to depend on sources from the late first century (*Apollonius* 1.2-3) and so provides a particularly interesting subject for consideration here. Apollonius is not executed in the course of the narrative, but on two occasions he faces judicial proceedings which threaten death. In both cases his adversaries are specifically named and extensively characterized.

Nero appears as Apollonius's first adversary. Philostratus prepares for Nero's trial of Apollonius by first indicating his opposition to all philosophers, illustrated by his imprisonment of Musonius (4.25).[3] With this background a certain Philolaus warns Apollonius not to enter Rome, implying that death awaits him if he does (4.26). Characteristically Apollonius meets the challenge head on: he states that in Nero's Rome 'a tyranny has been established...so harsh and cruel, that it does not suffer men to be wise', observes that οἱ πόλλοι call Nero τύραννος, compares him to a wild beast, and recounts his killing of his mother as typical of his character (4.28). Nero's designs on Apollonius are carried out by Tigellinus. Philostratus notes that Nero had given him capital authority and indicates his support for Nero's policy against philosophers by recounting his banishing of Demetrius, an associate of Apollonius (4.42). Thus, it is Nero's underling Tigellinus who imprisons

1.   Musurillo, *Pagan Martyrs*, p. 207.
2.   A historical survey of such comparisons is provided by E. Oldmeadow in his preface to F.W.G. Campbell, *Apollonius of Tyana: A Study of his Life and Times* (repr.; Chicago: Argonaut, 1968 [1908]), pp. 7-17.
3.   All references to *The Life of Apollonius of Tyana* are from the text and translation of F.C. Conybeare (2 vols.; LCL; London: Heinemann, 1912).

Apollonius for making a disrespectful remark about the emperor (4.44). Although Philostratus indicates that Tigellinus encouraged the cruelty of Nero, ultimately Tigellinus releases Apollonius because of his exceptional wisdom.

The pattern of introducing the persecuting emperor and his henchmen through their persecution of others recurs in the account of Domitian's imprisonment of Apollonius. Domitian first appears in the narrative when he issues a decree forbidding the making of eunuchs or the planting of vineyards. Apollonius treats the decree with contempt, offering a witticism which exposes the emperor's foolishness (6.42). Later, however, Domitian's cruelty is extensively catalogued by the narrator (7.4). Like other figures Domitian is called a τύραννος (7.4). Again, Apollonius's co-philosopher Demetrius appears in the narrative leading up to the hero's imprisonment. He offers a comparison of Domitian's persecution of philosophers to the charges of Anytus and Meletus against Socrates (7.11; cf. 8.2, 8.7.1) and compares Domitian unfavorably to Nero (7.12; cf. 7.4). Later, while Apollonius awaits trial, he meets a young man imprisoned for rejecting Domitian's sexual advances (7.42), a case which the narrator regards as typical of Domitian's behavior.

By various means the emperor's actions toward Apollonius are represented as dishonest. He twice sends an informer into Apollonius's prison cell (7.27, 36). While in prison Apollonius remarks repeatedly on the emperor's dishonesty and foolishness (7.32, 33; 8.2). Standing behind such accusations is the narrator's observation that Domitian imprisoned Apollonius because of his association with the emperor's rival Nerva (7.9, 36). After Apollonius is released, Domitian takes credit for not having him executed (8.5), despite his unwarranted cruelty toward him (7.34).

Two of Domitian's underlings figure in the plot. One is Euphrates, a sophist whose rivalry with Apollonius leads him to plot against the sage. He first appears in an earlier narrative in which he slanders Apollonius to the 'naked sages' of Egypt (6.7). It is Euphrates who reports an ambiguous but possibly defaming remark to Domitian, who consequently orders Apollonius's arrest (7.9). Later Euphrates supplies Domitian with information for charges against Apollonius (7.36). At the trial Euphrates sends his servant to give money to Apollonius's accuser and to report on the outcome to Euphrates (8.3). Apollonius himself refers to the 'slanders of Euphrates' in his defense speech (8.7.16). The second is Aelian, a former student of Apollonius who has capital authority from the emperor (7.16). His secret support of Apollonius serves as a foil to the actions of Domitian and Euphrates (7.16, 40).

Philostratus narrates Domitian's death in such a way as to suggest that it comes as retribution for his tyranny. While giving a speech in Ephesus, Apollonius receives a vision of Domitian's assassination while it takes place. As he sees the event, Apollonius shouts, 'Smite the tyrant', and then tells his lecture audience to 'take heart' because the tyrant has been killed (8.26). The contrast between the righteousness of the hero and his persecutor's wickedness is firmly underlined in this final episode.

A Letter of Mara bar Serapion
Written in the late first or early second century CE, this Syriac letter draws parallels between the deaths of Socrates, Pythagoras and the Jews' 'wise king', probably a reference to Jesus.[1] The focus in each case is on the fate of those responsible for their unjust deaths: the Athenians suffer 'famine and pestilence' and die of hunger, the inhabitants of Samos are 'overwhelmed by the sea' and have their island entirely covered with sand, and the Jews have 'their kingdom taken away' and 'live in complete dispersion'. In contrast, each of the victims attains a level of immortality: Socrates through the teaching of Plato, Pythagoras through the statue of hero, and the Jewish wise king through his teaching. The assumption of the writer is that the victims were innocent in each case: the reputations of Socrates and Pythagoras were by his time secure, and the appellation 'wise king' secures the verdict for Jesus. Consequently, whatever disasters befell their killers were matters of divine retribution: 'God justly avenged these three wise men'. Mara casts a wide net of responsibility as all Athens, all Samos and all the Jews are made to suffer for these deeds; this perspective may owe to his lack of proximity to the events. Certainly, though, his interest in the matter of responsibility for unjust deaths, expressed as it is in personal correspondence, reflects a widespread perspective of his time.

Accounts of the Persecution of Christians

Reports of the executions of Christians are obviously subject to influence from traditions of the passion of Jesus. An examination of such

---

1. The text of the letter is found in W. Cureton, *Spicilegium Syriacum: Containing Remains of Bardesan, Meliton, Ambrose and Mara bar Serapion* (London: Rivingtons, 1855), p. 73.

materials may show, however, a pattern of similarities which are too subtle or too integral to the telling of the story to be regarded as imitations of the passion narratives. Considered first will be the accounts of the death of James in Josephus and Eusebius.[1] Then the features of what can be distinctly referred to as Christian martyrological literature will be surveyed.

The Death of James

The different accounts of Josephus and Hegesippus about the death of James suggest the kinds of features which recur in such accounts. For Josephus the death of James is important because it supplies the reason for Agrippa's deposition of Ananus as high priest (*Ant.* 20.201). Hence, Ananus is the figure who is most prominent. Josephus indicates that he was 'rash' (θράσυς) and 'daring' (τολμητής) and a member of the Sadducees, the more cruel (ὠμοί) of the Jewish parties (20.200). Stress is also placed on his taking the opportunity between the death of Festus and the arrival of Albinus to put his plot into action. Ananus's actions are contrasted with the attitude of the 'most fair-minded' (ἐπιεικέστατοι) and 'observant of the law' (περὶ τοὺς νόμους ἀκριβεῖς), who were offended at James's execution (20.201).

The account of Hegesippus found in Eusebius is generally recognized as including a number of legendary elements. In this account τῶν Ἰουδαίων καὶ γραμματέων καὶ Φαρισαίων are said to have ordered James to restrain Christian preaching (*Eccl. Hist.* 2.23.10).[2] Then it is γραμματεῖς καὶ Φαρισαῖοι who push James from the pinnacle of the temple and stone him (2.23.12-15), and εἷς τῶν γναφέων ('one of the laundrymen') finally clubs him to death (2.23.18). Although the account obviously differs widely from Josephus's, it similarly indicates that τοὺς Ἰουδαίων ἔμφρονας thought that the death of James was the cause of the fall of Jerusalem (2.23.19). Indeed, this remark

1. Obviously the narratives of the death of Stephen and James bar Zebedee in Acts 7 and 12 could be relevant as well. These have been omitted because they are part of the narrative of Acts to which material in this section is ultimately being compared.

2. Since in its generic sense τῶν Ἰουδαίων would be inclusive of scribes and Pharisees, it appears that Hegesippus uses the term to refer to Jewish officials, perhaps the priests. Cf. Lowe's observation that national terms can be used without qualification to refer specifically to the authorities of a nation ('IOYΔAIOI', p. 107).

reveals Eusebius's interpretation of the event, for he then cites what he refers to as a quotation of Josephus (not in the present text of Josephus) to the same effect, here ascribing the death of James to οἱ Ἰουδαῖοι (2.23.20). Eusebius then cites Josephus's account from the *Antiquities* in full (2.23.21ff.), offering nothing by way of reconciliation of the two accounts. For him both give testimony to the righteousness of James and the wickedness of his Jewish opponents, wickedness which led ultimately to the destruction of Jerusalem.

Despite the different *Tendenzen* of the two accounts, their common elements are instructive. Both make some attempt at specifying those who brought about James's death: Ananus for Josephus and the scribes and Pharisees (and perhaps priests) for Hegesippus. Both explicitly contrast the actions of the persecutors with the judgment of the best citizens of the community. And both indicate that the persecutors were recompensed in some form: for Josephus, Ananus is deposed, and for Hegesippus, Jerusalem is destroyed.

Christian Martyrologies

Christian martyrological literature, such as the *Martyrdom of Polycarp* and the other works collected in the *Acts of the Christian Martyrs*, encompasses a wide range of stylistic orientations and includes texts in Greek and Latin. All such works are primarily concerned with setting forth the exemplary behavior of the martyrs and glorifying their deaths. But a number of significant features in the portrayal of the Christians' opponents recur frequently throughout the corpus. These can be delineated briefly.

Occasionally the presiding judge, usually the Roman prefect or proconsul, is a nameless figure (*Acts of the Christian Martyrs* 2.1; 5.8; 13.1.1; 14.2.4; 15.2.1).[1] More often, however, the adjudicator's personal name is given (3.12; 4.1.1; 6.1; 7.1; 8.6.3; 9.2; 10.19.2; 11.1.1; 11.3.1; 12.2.2; 16.3; 17.1.2; 18.1.1; 18.2.2; 20.1, 26; 21.6.1; 22.3.1; 23.2.1; 24.1; 25.1; 27.1). An interesting case is the *Martyrdom of Polycarp*, in which the governor is unnamed (*Mart. Pol.* 3.1; 4.1) until the very close of the book, where his name is given as a part of the synchrony which serves to date the martyrdom (*Mart. Pol.* 21.1).[2] Although the judge often acts

---

1. References are to H. Musurillo (ed.), *The Acts of the Christian Martyrs* (Oxford Early Christian Texts; Oxford: Clarendon Press, 1972).

2. References are from the edition of K. Lake (LCL; London: Heinemann, 1976).

in a stereotypical way, he is no mere cipher in most of these accounts.

Similarly, other adversarial figures are named. The police captain who arrests Polycarp, the reader is told, was named Herod (*Mart. Pol.* 6.1-2). The specification of his name is exploited for its obvious parallels with the Gospel traditions, but no such motive is in evidence when the captain's father, who urges Polycarp to recant, is named as Nicetes (*Mart. Pol.* 8.2-3; 17.2). Police and soldiers are also named in later works (*Acts of the Christian Martyrs* 10.15.4; 12.1.2 [a list of six soldiers' names]; 13.2.1; 18.2.2). Other opponents are also named specifically in the *Acts*. A slave owner who has her slave bound and abandoned on a mountain (10.9.3-4), the accusing verger of a pagan temple (10.3.1), a city father known by two names (13.2.1), an executioner (21.12.1) and a court clerk (22.3.1) all appear with personal names. Although the tendency to assign such names is not consistent throughout the corpus, it is frequent enough to suggest some interest in specifically identifying the Christians' opponents.

Occasionally, the leading opponents are supported by a crowd. Such a crowd is plainly in evidence in *Mart. Pol.* 12.2; 13.1. Similar crowds also appear elsewhere in the *Acts* (5.7; 8.21.7; 15.2.1). Accounts of the passion of Jesus may have influenced these portrayals. However, their relative infrequency in the corpus indicates that furious crowds were not a stock element in Christian martyrologies. Where they do appear, therefore, they could well reflect some reminiscence of the actual course of events.

Only rarely is the execution of the Christians explicitly declared to be unjust (*Acts of the Christian Martyrs* 2.45; 3.16). More often, the point is made by implication, specifically by maligning the character of the opponents (2.39; 2.4.2 [Latin recension]; 4.1.1; 5.9, 37; 7.38-41; 8.18.6; 8.21.7; 13.4.3; 13.5.2, 5; 14.2.4-5; 14.5.1; 14.10.1; 15.2.1; 21.1.1). At least once the denigration of the accuser is contrasted directly with the righteousness of the accused (13.6.6-7). The pronouncement of judgment on the opponents, so prominent in 2 Maccabees and *4 Maccabees*, is quite rare in the *Acts of the Christian Martyrs* (8.18.8). But all these elements suggest again the tendency to stress the righteousness of the victim by accentuating the wickedness of the victimizer.

Conclusions and Implications

As one would expect in such a broad survey, a variety of emphases in the portrayal of opponents is evident in the literature under discussion.

But several general trends do emerge. Most of the texts are specific about who persecutes the innocent victim. Some of those that are not, namely the Psalms of the suffering righteous, require such anonymity in order to allow for liturgical use. Others, such as Daniel, appear to neglect the opponents' identity simply because the writer is concerned with other issues. But specific identification is frequent, even predominant, despite the fact that none of the texts appears to be primarily concerned with identifying the persecutors.

Moreover, whether the opponents are identified or not, almost universally they are explicitly characterized as wicked. Such characterization is often made by direct statements, sometimes repeatedly and at great length. In other cases it is made by impugning the motives for bringing the charge against the victim. In still others, the opponent is threatened with retribution; sometimes that retribution is realized in the text. Frequently, the function of such characterizations appears to be to contrast the evil of the accuser with the innocence and positive righteousness of the accused.

Obviously, opponents may be identified for a variety of reasons. The storyteller may relish the vividness that such identifications give the narrative, or they may simply be less cumbersome than less specific designations. But the possible relationship between the identification of opponents and their characterization as evil and subject to judgment must be considered as well. The texts considered here come from a variety of cultures and eras, though all arise in the Mediterranean and Near East within the span of approximately 500 BCE to 300 CE. Within such a broad span it is impossible to posit any direct literary or philosophical influence that would account for the similarities noted above. Instead, what appears to be at work is a factor which inheres in the moral structure of accounts of innocent sufferers. The assumption of such stories, by the very nature of the case, is that those who cause the innocent to suffer and die unjustly have committed an evil act. The demands of justice, recognized by the cultures in which these stories arose,[1] could therefore compel the identification of those who instigated the unjust suffering. We may thus posit a 'moral constraint' which generally

---

1.   This sense of justice is patently obvious in the Jewish, Athenian and Roman contexts. It might be weaker in the case of *Ahiqar* (although the Assyrians were certainly not a lawless people), but there the kinship between Ahiqar and Nadin and the beneficence of the former for the latter reinforces the sense of injustice in Nadin's betrayal.

necessitates that an account of innocent suffering specify those responsible for the suffering.

This moral constraint would appear to be particularly compelling when the reputation of the victim is in question. Obviously, most would assume that someone executed by those in political power was in fact a wrongdoer. But if the victim's innocence were to be established, then the assumption would be that the opponents were the wrongdoers. The expectation that those responsible for the death of an innocent victim will be identified is thus inherent in any account which seeks to vindicate the victim. The identification, if not the condemnation, of the executioner is the reverse side of the vindication of the executed.

The relevance of this observation for the primitive kerygma is obvious.[1] If the kerygma proclaimed Jesus as the crucified one vindicated by the resurrection, the expectation that those responsible for his death would be identified in some way would be inherent.[2] Since Jesus' execution was a public event and was probably well known, some references to his opponents would therefore appear to be all the more likely. Apart from evidence to the contrary, therefore, it appears to be legitimate to assume that in addition to the response to persecution, the proclamation of Jesus as crucified and resurrected was also a *Sitz im*

1. The literature on the primitive kerygma is, of course, enormous, beginning with C.H. Dodd, *The Apostolic Preaching and its Developments* [London: Hodder & Stoughton, 1936). Because Dodd did not address the question of whether statements about responsibility for the death of Jesus were included in the kerygma, subsequent discussion neglected the issue until the work of Wilckens (*Missionsreden*, pp. 115-21). Further discussion of the issue is found in Rese, 'Tod', pp. 344-37; Roloff, *Apostelgeschichte*, pp. 74-75; Lüdemann, *Early Christianity*, p. 51.

2. On Jesus' resurrection as vindication in early Christian preaching, cf. Nickelsburg, *Resurrection, Immortality, and Eternal Life*, pp. 18, 33, 36, 58, 67, 94; and *idem*, 'The Genre and Function of the Markan Passion Narrative', *HTR* 73 (1980), p. 174-75; J. Roloff, 'Anfänge der soteriologischen Deutung des Todes Jesu (Mk. x.45 und Lk. xxii.27)', *NTS* 19 (1972–73), pp. 38-39; *idem*, *Apostelgeschichte*, p. 50-51; Green, *Death*, p. 323. This observation does not depend in any way on the hypothesis, championed by L. Ruppert, that primitive Christianity viewed Jesus primarily as a suffering righteous one (*Jesus als der leidende Gerechte? Der Weg Jesu im Licht eines alt- und zwischentestamentlichen Motivs* [SBS, 59; Stuttgart: Katholisches Bibelwerk, 1972]; followed by, *inter alia*, Roloff, 'Deutung', pp. 38-39; Green, *Death*, pp. 224-25, 316-17; cf. the critique in Hengel, *Atonement*, pp. 40-48). The evidence shows that the tendency to identify opponents is present in such literature but is also inherent in a wide variety of materials which do not strictly follow the theme.

Leben for traditions about responsibility for the death of Jesus. Primitive Christian preaching generally proclaimed not simply that Jesus was crucified but that he was crucified *by someone*.

But who was that someone? A reasonable conjecture can be drawn from what is known about the circumstances of the primitive church. Obviously the Romans could have been specified. But in the political climate of first-century Palestine it is likely that if such proclamation were widespread and forthright, in the eyes of the Roman government it would have implicated the Christian community in insurrection. As there is no evidence of any tension between the primitive church and the Romans, it appears that the specification of the Romans as the ones responsible for Jesus' death was not a prominent feature of Christian proclamation.

On the other hand, there is evidence of conflict between at least some elements of the primitive Jerusalem community with the temple hierarchy. Such tension accords with the hypothesis that the church did in fact proclaim that the leaders of Jerusalem instigated Jesus' death. Credence can therefore be attached to Luke's implication that such proclamation led the Sanhedrin to attempt to silence the apostles (Acts 5.28).[1] Thus, Luke's account of the apostles' proclamation of Jesus as crucified by the Sanhedrin followed by the Sanhedrin's persecution of the apostles is not only internally consistent; it also coheres with the expectation that those responsible for Jesus' death would be identified in Christian preaching.

But what of Luke's insistence that the people of Jerusalem were also implicated in Jesus' death? Here the question is more difficult. It might be expected that if primitive Christians implicated only the Sanhedrin, then their proclamation might have produced a degree of popular revolt

---

1.   Cf. Lüdemann, *Early Christianity*, p. 60. In this light, the assumption that Christian laxity about the temple was the sole impulse for the persecution of the Jerusalem church must be modified (*contra*, for example, Hengel, *Atonement*, pp. 55-57). Such conflict may have played its part. But the assumption that it was the sole motivation is unwarranted. Likewise, the assumption that Luke invented either the apostles' continuing temple piety or their conflict with the Sanhedrin (in contrast to the Hellenists') is also invalid. It would appear, however, that contrasting attitudes to the temple may have accounted for the differences in the severity of persecution of the Hellenists as compared to the apostles. Because of their lack of temple piety, the Hellenists may not have enjoyed the same popularity with non-Christian Jews in Jerusalem as the apostles, popularity which restrained the Sanhedrin's persecution of the apostles.

against the Sanhedrin. Such a rebellion associated with Christian circles is, of course, not in evidence,[1] although the paucity of sources warrants extreme caution in basing conclusions on silence. Likewise, ascription of popular responsibility could also explain why even occasional references to Roman responsibility did not fuel the fires of rebellion or incur the displeasure of the imperial authorities: if Rome acted with popular support, grounds for popular insurrection are hardly provided. On the other hand, the notion that such proclamation would have met with outright rejection among the Jerusalem populace is completely unwarranted. The entire tradition of prophecy in Israel is filled with instances of mass condemnation and consequent calls to repentance. It is gratuitous to assume in such circumstances that an appeal to repent of involvement in the crucifixion of Jesus would be rejected by the mass of Jerusalemites.[2] At the very least, therefore, it can be said that Luke's portrayal of the church's early success in Jerusalem does not rule out the possibility that the kerygma included reference to popular Jerusalemite responsibility.

But why are the people of Jerusalem specified and not a more inclusive group? The distinction would probably not have been significant until after the Christian mission left the confines of Jerusalem. Within Jerusalem, second person address, such as that in the speeches of Acts 2–7, would naturally have been employed in proclamation. Once the kerygma was taken beyond Jerusalem, several factors may have influenced the pattern of proclamation. The church's firm identification of the crucifixion with Jerusalem may have combined with the tradition of popular responsibility to yield such an outcome. It may simply have struck Christian preachers as impossible to implicate anyone not directly associated with Jerusalem in an event that took place in Jerusalem. Furthermore, some memory of the actual course of events may well lie behind the distinction. It may be that the crowd who called for Jesus' death was composed primarily of Jerusalemites whose livelihood depended on the temple and who were especially subject to the influence of the priesthood, not pilgrims, many of whom may still have been asleep in the hours just after dawn.

Like all such investigations, this one is conjectural. But to the degree that it allows a reconstruction of primitive Christian proclamation, it yields a coherent picture which in turn lends credibility to Luke's account in Acts. That Christians referred to those who crucified Jesus in

---

1. Cf. Roloff, *Apostelgeschichte*, p. 103.
2. *Contra* Sanders, *Jews in Luke–Acts*, pp. 234-35.

their response to their own persecution appears highly likely on the basis of 1 Thess. 2.13-16. That they made some reference to the crucifiers as a part of their proclamation of the crucified and risen Jesus appears highly likely from literary parallels. That the Romans were not prominent in such proclamation, though perhaps mentioned in passing, is probable. That those so named were primarily the Sanhedrin leadership is also probable. That the people of Jerusalem were also implicated is at least plausible, but ultimately the question defies the application of evidence independent of the book of Acts itself.

Chapter 8

CONCLUSIONS

This study began with certain specific questions posed by the current state of research on the Lukan corpus. On the basis of the data assembled and analyzed above, those questions can now be answered. In what follows, the conclusions of the previous chapters will be summarized.

Those conclusions have an immediate relevance to two larger issues: the value of Luke's work as history and the allegation of anti-Semitism in Luke–Acts. Following the summary, brief consideration will be given to the implications of this study for those concerns.

Summary of Results

Central to the entire study has been the conclusion reached in Chapter 2: among Jews Luke regards only the leaders of Jerusalem and the people of Jerusalem as responsible for the crucifixion of Jesus. The Gospel of Luke indicates that Jewish leaders associated with Jerusalem instigated Jesus' death and that they did so with popular assent. Acts indicates that the people who assented to Jesus' death were also associated specifically with Jerusalem. Moreover, both the Gospel and Acts affirm a measure of responsibility for various non-Jews, namely Pilate, Herod and the Roman soldiers. Neither book indicates any consistent attempt to ameliorate Gentile responsibility in order to accentuate Jewish responsibility.

Furthermore, the implication that the leaders and people of Jerusalem brought about Jesus' death does not appear to have been part of a larger Lukan aim of condemning or denigrating Jews generally. This is the conclusion of Chapter 3. Luke does not view Israel monolithically as evil or unbelieving. The evidence suggests, on the contrary, that he stresses the division of Israel in response to Jesus and the gospel, a division consistent with the response of Israel to God's overtures in the Scriptures. This understanding, which has been argued by several others, can be asserted more confidently in light of the analysis offered in this chapter. Hence, Luke's indictment of the Jerusalem Jews can be taken at face value: he does not use Jerusalem's involvement in the crucifixion as a figure for all Israel's rejection of the gospel.

Moreover, Luke's assessment of responsibility for the death of Jesus appears to have been based on the sources and traditions which underlie his two volumes. 1 Thess. 2.14-16 also points to 'Judeans' as those who crucified Jesus and gives evidence of having been based on traditional material, as Chapter 4 indicates. Chater 5 notes that Matthew and Mark present Jewish involvement in the crucifixion much as does Luke's Gospel. Both reserve responsibility for leaders associated with Jerusalem and for a crowd incited by those leaders. But neither identifies the crowd specifically. Thus, the hypothesis that the assertions in Acts of popular responsibility are based entirely on the passion material of the Synoptic tradition is inadequate, leaving unexplained the specification of the people involved as Jerusalemites. Nor can these statements be explained as Luke's own creations, since they disturb the clear pattern of division between the leaders and the people in Jerusalem. Thus, Luke's use in Acts of traditional material which specified the people of Jerusalem as responsible for the death of Jesus is the only hypothesis consistent with the data. This hypothesis is furthermore consistent with the observation that assertions of popular Jerusalemite responsibility are found in texts which give other indications of traditional origin. These are the conclusions of Chapter 6. Whether a plausible *Sitz im Leben* existed for the preservation and transmission of such material was considered in Chapter 7. The observation having been made that the response to persecution provides one such situation, this chapter notes that other literature dealing with the slaying of the innocent generally specifies those responsible for the unjust death. Such is required by the moral constraints of such an assertion: if an innocent has been killed, then the killer is culpable. Thus, the proclamation that Jesus was crucified unjustly, very likely a part of primitive Christian preaching, would appear to have been accompanied by a related statement of who was responsible. From what little can be known of the situation of the primitive church, it appears that such statements focused on the Jewish leaders of Jerusalem but also made reference to the involvement of the people of Jerusalem and of Roman officials.

Implications

Luke–Acts and History

The debate about the value of Luke and Acts as historical sources is familiar enough not to require introduction. Although this volume is not primarily concerned with that issue, it nevertheless offers conclusions germane to it. These may be summarized briefly.

One concerns Luke's use of sources. Works discussing the speeches of Acts have generally asserted that because what the speeches say about the passion is consistent with the passion material in Luke's Gospel, the latter served as the source for the former. This investigation, however, suggests otherwise. Although the speeches in Acts are consistent with the passion in Luke's Gospel, they are not adequately explained by it. Only the use of independent sources for the assertion of popular responsibility in Acts can fully account for the specification of the people of Jerusalem. The fact that the specification in Acts is consistent with the less definite presentation of popular involvement in the Gospel could indicate corroboration instead of dependence. Luke appears to have employed a sound historical method at this point. His work is based on two separate sources or traditions which are consistent with each other but which do not advance his evident theological interests.

Does Luke's assessment of responsibility for the death of Jesus reflect the actual course of events in Jesus' passion? To offer a complete answer to this question would involve lengthy discussion of another complicated debate. But the material examined here does suggest the probability that Jesus was killed by those whom Luke reports. If, as Chapter 7 concluded, Luke's assessment of responsibility for the death of Jesus had its origin in the primitive kerygma, the proximity of that proclamation to the actual events suggests that the assessment is accurate. A prima facie case has been made that those who brought about Jesus' death were those indicated in Luke–Acts. Whether that case can be sustained is a subject for others to consider.

Luke–Acts and Anti-Semitism

In light of the foregoing analysis, what can be said of the allegation, found in various recent works, that Luke–Acts is anti-Semitic? This question is complicated by the fact that no agreed-upon definition exists of what does and does not constitute anti-Semitism.[1] Therefore, consideration will be given in turn to some of the more prominent ways in which the term has been understood in critical literature on the New Testament.

J.T. Sanders has offered the most thorough assertion to date of Luke's anti-Semitic tendencies. His definition of anti-Semitism is 'a fundamental and systematic hostility toward Jews'.[2] More important than this definition, however, is the analysis of the Lukan text that Sanders offers. This study has shown, however, that Sanders's exegesis of Luke–Acts is mistaken at several crucial points. As a consequence, Luke appears considerably less hostile toward Jews than Sanders indicates. For Luke the crucial factor is not Jewish or Gentile origin but positive response to Jesus and the gospel. Whatever hostility is to be found in his narrative is directed not against Jews as such but against those who reject the message of salvation through Jesus, whether Jews or Gentiles.

It must be admitted, however, that Jewish rejection is what interests Luke most. But other factors besides anti-Semitism would appear to account for this interest. Luke's belief—in common with other early Christians—that in Christianity is the fulfillment of the Jewish Scriptures raises the problem of Jewish unbelief.[3] If Christian claims are true, why are they rejected by so many of those most familiar with the Jewish Scriptures, namely the Jews themselves? Luke's interest in Jewish rejection of the gospel would appear to stem from this very issue. He focuses on Jewish rejection in order to explain it. Although many Jews reject the Christian message, not all do. Israel is divided, not monolithic, in response to Jesus. And that division, far from being inconsistent with Christian claims about the fulfillment of the Jewish Scriptures, is in fact itself a fulfillment of the pattern of Israel's response found in them.

In this respect, Luke's approach to the Jews does not meet D.R.A. Hare's sociological definition of 'Gentilizing anti-Judaism' either. Hare suggests that insofar as a Christian writer maintains Jewish identity

---

1.   Cf. the discussion of the problem of definitions in my article, 'Anti-Semitism', in J.B. Green, S. McKnight and I.H. Marshall (eds.), *Dictionary of Jesus and the Gospels* (Downers Grove, IL: Inter-Varsity Press, 1992), pp. 13-17.

2.   Sanders, *Jews in Luke–Acts*, p. xvi. He apparently borrows the definition from Simon, *Verus Israel*, p. 395.

3.   Cf. Loisy's observation that Jewish unbelief was the great difficulty in early Christian apologetics (*Actes*, pp. 115-17). Evans has more recently noted this problem in connection with the Lukan corpus (*Isaiah* 6.9-10, p. 126).

and allows for Israel's repentance and salvation, the critique of Jews for their unbelief in Jesus belongs within the tradition of sectarian Judaism.[1] Only when Jewish identity is renounced and Israel is regarded as utterly hardened against the gospel and forsaken by God can Gentilizing anti-Judaism be affirmed. As noted above, the former is precisely Luke's position. His Jewish characters—especially Paul—are Jewish to the end of the narrative, and some Jews continue to respond to the gospel with faith at the end of the narrative. The mission to Jews does not appear to be over, and the church remains composed of both Jews and Gentiles.[2]

1. Hare, 'Rejection', pp. 28-32.
2. These observations also address the criteria advanced by Wilson ('Jews and the Death of Jesus in Acts', p. 164). Cf. the similar observations of Evans (*Isaiah* 6.9-10), p. 124; 'Faith and Polemic: The New Testament and First-Century Judaism', in *idem* and D.A. Hagner [eds.], *Anti-Semitism and Early Christianity* [Minneapolis: Fortress Press, 1993], pp. 1-17).

BIBLIOGRAPHY

Ackroyd, P.R., 'נצח—εἰς τέλος', *ExpTim* 80 (1968–69), p. 126.

Aletti, J.-N., 'Jésus à Nazareth (Lc 4, 16-30): Prophétie, écriture et typologie', in F. Refoulé (ed.), *A cause de l'évangile: Etudes sur les Synoptiques et les Actes offertes au P. Jaques Dupont, O.S.B. à l'occasion de son 70ᵉ anniversaire* (LD, 123; Paris: Cerf, 1985), pp. 431-51.

Allison, D.C., 'The Pauline Epistles and the Synoptic Gospels: The Pattern of the Parallels', *NTS* 28 (1982), pp. 1-31.

Amaru, B.H., 'The Killing of the Prophets: Unraveling a Midrash', *HUCA* 54 (1983), pp. 153-80.

Antoniadis, S., *L'évangile de Luc: Esquisse de grammaire et de style* (Collection de l'Institut Néo-hellénique, 7; Paris: Société d'édition 'Les belles lettres', 1930).

Ashton, J., 'The Identity and Function of the Ἰουδαῖοι in the Fourth Gospel', *NovT* 27 (1985), pp. 40-75.

Bachmann, M., *Jerusalem und der Tempel: Die geographisch-theologischen Elemente in der lukanischen Sicht des jüdischen Kultzentrums* (BWANT, 6.9; Stuttgart: Kohlhammer, 1980).

Bammel, E., 'Judenverfolgung und Naherwartung: Zur Eschatologie des Ersten Thessalonicherbriefs', *ZTK* 56 (1959), pp. 294-315.

Barrett, C.K., 'Old Testament History according to Stephen and Paul', in W. Schrage (ed.), *Studien zum Text und zur Ethik des Neuen Testaments: Festschrift zum 80. Geburtstag von Heinrich Greeven* (BZNW, 47; Berlin: de Gruyter, 1986), pp. 57-69.

Barth, M., 'Traditions in Ephesians', *NTS* 30 (1984), pp. 3-25.

—'Was Paul an Anti-Semite?', *JES* 5 (1968), pp. 78-104.

Baur, F.C., *Paulus, der Apostel Jesu Christi: Sein Leben und Wirken, seine Briefe und seine Lehre: Ein Beitrag zu einer kritischen Geschichte des Urchristentums* (ed. E. Zeller; 2 vols.; Leipzig: Fues [Reisland], 2nd edn, 1866–67).

Bayer, H.F., *Jesus' Predictions of Vindication and Resurrection: The Provenance, Meaning and Correlation of the Synoptic Predictions* (WUNT, 2.20; Tübingen: Mohr [Paul Siebeck], 1986).

Beck, N.A., *Mature Christianity: The Recognition and Repudiation of the Anti-Jewish Polemic of the New Testament* (London: Associated University Presses, 1985).

Bellinzoni, A.J. (ed.), *The Two-Source Hypothesis: A Critical Appraisal* (Macon, GA: Mercer University Press, 1985).

Best, E., *A Commentary on the First and Second Epistles to the Thessalonians* (BNTC; London: A. & C. Black, 1972).

—*The Temptation and the Passion: The Marcan Soteriology* (SNTSMS, 2; London: Cambridge University Press, 1965).

Betz, O., 'Probleme des Prozesses Jesu', *ANRW* II.25.1, pp. 565-647.

Bietenhard, H., 'People, Nation, Gentiles, Crowd, City', in C. Brown (ed.), *The New International Dictionary of New Testament Theology* (Grand Rapids: Zondervan, 1978), II, pp. 788-805.

Bihler, J., *Die Stephanusgeschichte im Zusammenhang der Apostelgeschichte* (Münchener theologische Studien, 1.16; Munich: Hueber, 1963).

Black, M., *An Aramaic Approach to the Gospels and Acts* (London: Oxford University Press, 3rd edn, 1967).

Blinzler, J., *Der Prozess Jesu* (Regensburg: Pustet, 4th edn, 1969).

Boers, H., 'The Form Critical Study of Paul's Letters: I Thessalonians as a Case Study', *NTS* 22 (1976), pp. 140-58.

Bovon, F., ' "Schön hat der heilige Geist durch den Propheten Jesaja zu euren Vätern gesprochen" (Apg 28.25)', *ZNW* 75 (1984), pp. 226-32.

Bonnard, P., *L'évangile selon Saint Matthieu* (CNT, 1; Neuchâtel: Delachaux & Niestlé, 1963).

Bowker, J.W., 'Speeches in Acts: A Study in Proem and Yelamedenu Form', *NTS* 14 (1967-68), pp. 96-111.

Brawley, R.L., *Luke-Acts and the Jews: Conflict, Apology and Conciliation* (SBLMS, 33; Atlanta: Scholars Press, 1987).

Broer, I., ' "Antisemitismus" und Judenpolemik im Neuen Testament: Ein Beitrag zum bessern Verständnis von 1 Thess. 2,14-16', *Biblische Notizen* 29 (1983), pp. 59-91.

—' "Der ganze Zorn ist schon über sie gekommen." Bemerkungen zur Interpolationshypothese und zur Interpretation von 1 Thess 2,14-16', in R.F. Collins (ed.), *The Thessalonian Correspondence* (BETL, 87; Leuven: Leuven University Press, 1990), pp. 136-59.

—'Der Prozess gegen Jesus nach Matthäus', in K. Kertelge (ed.), *Der Prozess gegen Jesus: Historische Rückfrage und theologische Deutung* (QD, 112; Freiburg: Herder, 1989), pp. 84-110.

Bruce, F.F., *The Acts of the Apostles: The Greek Text with Introduction and Commentary* (Grand Rapids: Eerdmans, 1951).

—'The Acts of the Apostles: Historical Record or Theological Reconstruction?', *ANRW* II.25.3, pp. 2569-2603.

—'The Church of Jerusalem in the Acts of the Apostles', *BJRL* 67 (1984–85), pp. 641-61.

—*1 & 2 Thessalonians* (WBC, 45; Waco, TX: Word Books, 1982).

—'New Wine in Old Wine Skins: The Corner Stone', *ExpTim* 84 (1973), pp. 231-35.

—'Paul's Apologetic and the Purpose of Acts', *BJRL* 69 (1986–87), pp. 379-93.

—'The Speeches in Acts—Thirty Years After', in R.J. Banks (ed.), *Reconciliation and Hope: New Testament Essays on Atonement and Eschatology Presented to L.L. Morris* (Grand Rapids: Eerdmans, 1974), pp. 53-68.

—'Stephen's Apologia', in B.P. Thompson (ed.), *Scripture: Meaning and Method: Essays Presented to Anthony Tyrrell Hanson for his Seventieth Birthday* (Hull: Hull University Press, 1987), pp. 37-50.

Buchanan, G.W., 'Has the Griesbach Hypothesis Been Falsified?', *JBL* 93 (1974), pp. 550-72.

Büchele, A., *Der Tod Jesu im Lukasevangelium: Eine redaktionsgeschichtliche Untersuchung zu Lk 23* (Frankfurter Theologische Studien, 26; Frankfurt: Knecht, 1978).

Büchsel, F., 'γενεά, κτλ', *TDNT*, I, pp. 662-65.

Bultmann, R., *The History of the Synoptic Tradition* (ET; Oxford: Basil Blackwell, 1968).

Buss, M.F.-J., *Die Missionspredigt des Apostels Paulus im Pisidischen Antiochien* (FB, 38; Stuttgart: Verlag Katholisches Bibelwerk, 1980).

Busse, U., *Das Nazareth-Manifest: Eine Einführung in das lukanische Jesusbild nach Lk 4, 16-30* (SBS, 91; Stuttgart: Katholisches Bibelwerk, 1978).

Butler, B.C., *The Originality of St Matthew* (Cambridge: Cambridge University Press, 1951).

Cadbury, H.J., *The Book of Acts in History* (New York: Harper & Brothers; London: A. & C. Black, 1955).

—*The Making of Luke–Acts* (London: SPCK, 2nd edn, 1958).

—'The Speeches in Acts', in F.J. Foakes-Jackson and K. Lake (eds.), *The Beginnings of Christianity*. I. *The Acts of the Apostles* (5 vols.; London: Macmillan, 1933), IV, pp. 402-27,

Campbell, F.W.G., *Apollonius of Tyana: A Study of his Life and Times* (repr.; Chicago: Argonaut, 1968 [1908]).

Cannon, G.E., *The Use of Traditional Material in Colossians* (Macon, GA: Mercer University Press, 1983).

Caragounis, C.C., 'Kingdom of God, Son of Man and Jesus' Self-Understanding (Part I)', *TynBul* 40 (1989), pp. 3-23.

Carroll, J.T., 'Luke's Crucifixion Scene', in D.D. Sylva (ed.), *Reimaging the Death of the Lukan Jesus* (BBB, 73; Frankfurt: Hain, 1990), pp. 108-24, 194-203.

Carson, D.A., *Matthew* (Expositor's Bible Commentary, 8; Grand Rapids: Zondervan, 1984).

Cassidy, R.J., 'Luke's Audience, the Chief Priests, and the Motive for Jesus' Death', in R.J. Cassidy and P.J. Scharper (eds.), *Political Issues in Luke–Acts* (Maryknoll, NY: Orbis Books, 1983), pp. 146-67.

Catchpole, D.R., 'The Problem of the Historicity of the Sanhedrin Trial', in E. Bammel (ed.), *The Trial of Jesus: Cambridge Studies in Honour of C.F.D. Moule* (SBT, 2.13; London: SCM Press, 1970), pp. 47-65.

—*The Trial of Jesus: A Study in the Gospels and Jewish Historiography from 1770 to the Present Day* (SPB, 12; Leiden: Brill, 1971).

Cerfaux, L., *La théologie de l'église suivant saint Paul* (Paris: Cerf, 2nd edn, 1948).

Chance, J.B., *Jerusalem, the Temple, and the New Age in Luke–Acts* (Macon, GA: Mercer University Press, 1989).

Chroust, A.-H., *Socrates, Man and Myth: The Two Socratic Apologies of Xenophon* (London: Routledge & Kegan Paul, 1957).

Clark, K.W., 'Realised Eschatology', *JBL* 59 (1940), pp. 367-83.

Collins, R.F., 'Apropos the Integrity of 1 Thess', in *Studies on the First Letter to the Thessalonians* (BETL, 66; Leuven: Leuven University Press, 1984), pp. 96-135. Reprinted from *ETL* 55 (1979), pp. 67-106.

Combrink, H.J.B., 'The Structure and Significance of Lk 4, 16-30', *Neot* 7 (1973), pp. 27-47.

Conzelmann, H., *The Theology of St Luke* (ET; New York: Harper & Brothers, 1960).

Cook, M.J., *Mark's Treatment of the Jewish Leaders* (NovTSup, 51; Leiden: Brill, 1978).

—'The Mission to the Jews in Acts: Unraveling Luke's "Myth of the "Myriads"', in

J.B. Tyson (ed.), *Luke–Acts and the Jewish People: Eight Critical Perspectives* (Minneapolis: Augsburg, 1988), pp. 102-23.

Coppens, J., 'Miscellanées bibliques. LXXX. Une diatribe antijuive dans I Thess., II, 13-16', *ETL* 51 (1975), pp. 90-95.

Creed, J.M., *The Gospel according to St Luke* (London: Macmillan, 1965).

Dahl, N.A., ' "A People for his Name" (Acts XV, 14)', *NTS* 4 (1957–58), pp. 319-27.

Darr, J.A., *On Character Building: The Reader and the Rhetoric of Characterization in Luke–Acts* (Louisville, KY: Westminster Press/John Knox, 1992).

Davies, W.D., 'Paul and the People of Israel', in *Jewish and Pauline Studies* (London: SPCK, 1984), pp. 123-52. Reprinted from *NTS* 24 (1977–78), pp. 4-39.

—*The Setting of the Sermon on the Mount* (Cambridge: Cambridge University Press, 1964).

Davies, W.D., and D.C. Allison, Jr, *A Critical and Exegetical Commentary on the Gospel according to Saint Matthew* (ICC; 3 vols.; Edinburgh: T. & T. Clark, 1988).

Dawsey, J.M., *The Lukan Voice: Confusion and Irony in the Gospel of Luke* (Macon, GA: Mercer University Press, 1986).

Delling, G., 'Die Jesusgeschichte in Acts', *NTS* 19 (1972–73), pp. 373-89.

Dibelius, M., *An die Thessalonicher I–II: An die Philippier* (HNT, 3.2; Tübingen: Mohr [Paul Siebeck], 1911).

—*From Tradition to Gospel* (ET; London: James Clarke, 1971).

—*Studies in the Acts of the Apostles* (ed. H. Greenven; London: SCM Press, 1956).

Dietzfelbinger, C., *Die Berufung des Paulus als Ursprung seiner Theologie* (WMANT, 58; Neukirchen–Vluyn: Neukirchener Verlag, 1985).

Dodd, C.H., *The Apostolic Preaching and its Developments* (London: Hodder & Stoughton, 1936).

—'Matthew and Paul', in *New Testament Studies* (Manchester: Manchester University Press, 1953), pp. 53-66.

Donahue, J.R., 'Temple, Trial and Royal Christology', in W.H. Kebler (ed.), *The Passion in Mark: Studies on Mark 14–16* (Philadelphia: Fortress Press, 1976), pp. 61-79.

Donaldson, T.L., 'Moses Typology and the Sectarian Nature of Early Christian Anti-Judaism', *JSNT* 12 (1981), pp. 27-52.

Donfried, K.P., 'Paul and Judaism: 1 Thessalonians 2.13-16 as a Test Case', *Int* 38 (1984), pp. 242-53.

Dormeyer, D., *Die Passion Jesu als Verhaltensmodell: Literarische und theologische Analyse der Traditions- und Redaktionsgeschichte der Markuspassion* (NTAbh NS, 11; Münster: Aschendorff, 1974).

Dumais, M., *Le langage de l'évangélisation: L'annonce missionnaire en milieu juif (Actes 13, 16-41)* (Recherches, 16, Théologie; Tournai: Desclée; Montreal: Bellarmin, 1976).

Dungan, D.L., 'Mark—The Abridgement of Matthew and Luke', in *Jesus and Man's Hope* (Pittsburg: Pittsburg Theological Seminary, 1970), pp. 51-97.

—*The Sayings of Jesus in the Churches of Paul: The Use of the Synoptic Tradition in the Regulation of Early Church Life* (Oxford: Basil Blackwell, 1971).

Dupont, J., 'La conclusion des Actes et son rapport à l'ensemble de l'ouvrage de Luc', in J. Kremer (ed.), *Les Actes des Apôtres: Traditions, rédaction, théologie* (BETL, 48; Gembloux: Duculot; Leuven: Leuven University Press, 1979), pp. 359-404.

—'Les discours de Pierre dans les Actes et le chapitre XXIV de l'évangile de Luc', in

F. Neirynck (ed.), *L'Evangile de Luc: Problèmes littéraires et théologiques: Mémorial Lucien Cerfaux* (BETL, 32; Gembloux: Duculot, 1973), pp. 329-74.

—'Les discours missionaires des Actes des Apôtres d'après un ouvrage récent', *RB* 69 (1962), pp. 37-60. Reprinted in *idem, Etudes sur les Acts des Apôtres* (LD, 45; Paris: Cerf, 1967), pp. 133-55 (ET: *The Salvation of the Gentiles: Essays on the Acts of the Apostles* [New York: Paulist Press, 1979]).

—'Un peuple d'entre les nations (Actes 15.14)', *NTS* 31 (1985), pp. 321-35.

—'Le salut des gentils et la signification théologique du livre des Actes', *NTS* 6 (1959-60), pp. 132-55. Reprinted in *idem, Etudes sur les Actes des Apôtres* (LD, 45; Paris: Cerf, 1967), pp. 393-419.

—'La structure oratoire du discours d'Etienne (Actes 7)', *Bib* 66 (1985), pp. 153-67.

—'L'utilisation apologétique de l'Ancien Testament dans les discours des Actes', in *Etudes sur les Actes des Apôtres* (LD, 45; Paris: Cerf, 1967), pp. 245-82.

Egelkraut, H.L., *Jesus' Mission to Jerusalem: A Redaction Critical Study of the Travel Narrative in the Gospel of Luke, Lk 9.51–19.48* (Europäische Hochschulschriften, Reihe 23, Theologie 80; Frankfurt: Peter Lang; Bern: Herbert Lang, 1976).

Ehrlich, E.L., 'Paulus und das Schuldproblem, erläutert an Römer 5 und 8', in W.P. Eckert, N.P. Levinson and M. Stöhr (eds.), *Antijudaismus im Neuen Testament? Exegetische und systematische Beiträge* (Abhandlung zum christlich-jüdischen Dialog, 2; Munich: Chr. Kaiser Verlag, 1967), pp. 44-49.

Eissfeldt, O., *The Old Testament: An Introduction* (ET; Oxford: Basil Blackwell, 1965).

Ellis, E.E., *The Gospel of Luke* (NCB; London: Nelson, 1966).

—'Gospels Criticism', in P. Stuhlmacher (ed.), *Das Evangelium und die Evangelien* (WUNT, 2.28; Tübingen: Mohr [Paul Siebeck], 1983), pp. 27-54.

—'Midrashic Features in the Speeches of Acts', in A. Descamps and A. de Halleux (eds.), *Mélanges bibliques en homage au R.P. Béda Rigaux* (Gembloux: Duculot, 1970), pp. 303-12.

—'Traditions in 1 Corinthians', *NTS* 32 (1986), pp. 481-502.

Eltester, W., 'Israel im lukanischen Werk und die Nazarethperikope', in *Jesus in Nazareth* (BZNW, 40; Berlin and New York: de Gruyter, 1972), pp. 76-147.

Esler, P.F., *Community and Gospel in Luke–Acts: The Social and Political Motivation of Lucan Theology* (SNTSMS, 57; Cambridge: Cambridge University Press, 1987).

Evans, C.A., 'Faith and Polemic: The New Testament and First-Century Judaism', in *idem* and D.A. Hagner (eds.), *Anti-Semitism and Early Christianity* (Minneapolis: Fortress Press, 1993), pp. 1-17.

—'Is Luke's View of the Jewish Rejection of Jesus Anti-Semitic?', in D.D. Sylva (ed.), *Reimaging the Death of the Lukan Jesus* (BBB, 73; Frankfurt: Hain, 1990), pp. 29-56, 174-83.

—'Prophecy and Polemic: Jews in Luke's Scriptural Apologetic', in *idem* and J.A. Sanders (eds.), *Luke and Scripture: The Function of Sacred Tradition in Luke–Acts* (Minneapolis: Fortress Press, 1993), pp. 171-211.

—*To See and Not Perceive: Isaiah 6.9-10 in Early Jewish and Christian Interpretation* (JSOTSup, 64; Sheffield: JSOT Press, 1989).

Evans, C.F., '"Speeches" in Acts', in A. Descamps and A. de Halleux (eds.), *Mélanges bibliques en homage au R.P. Béda Rigaux* (Gembloux: Duculot, 1970), pp. 287-302.

Farmer, W.R., *The Synoptic Problem: A Critical Analysis* (Dillsboro, NC: Western North Carolina Press; Macon, GA: Mercer University Press, rev. edn, 1976).

Farmer, W.R. (ed.), *New Synoptic Studies: The Cambridge Gospel Conference and Beyond* (Macon, GA: Mercer University Press, 1983).

Farrer, A.M., 'On Dispensing with Q', in D.E. Nineham (ed.), *Studies in the Gospels: Essays in Memory of R.H. Lightfoot* (Oxford: Basil Blackwell, 1955), pp. 55-88.

Fitzmyer, J., 'Anti-Semitism and the Cry of "All the People" ', *TS* 26 (1965), pp. 667-71.

—'Crucifixion in Ancient Palestine, Qumran Literature, and the New Testament', *CBQ* 40 (1978), pp. 493-513.

—*The Gospel according to Luke* (AB, 28a, 28b; 2 vols.; Garden City, NY: Doubleday, 1981, 1985).

—*Luke the Theologian: Aspects of his Teaching* (London: Chapman, 1989).

Flender, H., *St Luke: Theologian of Redemptive History* (London: SPCK, 1967).

Franklin, E., *Christ the Lord: A Study in the Purpose and Theology of Luke–Acts* (London: SPCK, 1975).

Foakes-Jackson, F.J., and K. Lake (eds.), *The Beginnings of Christianity*. Part I. *The Acts of the Apostles* (5 vols.; repr.; Grand Rapids: Baker, 1979 [1933]).

Ford, J.M., ' "Crucify him, Crucify him", and the Temple Scroll', *ExpTim* 87 (1976), pp. 275-78.

Frame, J.E., *A Critical and Exegetical Commentary on the Epistles of St Paul to the Thessalonians* (ICC; Edinburgh: T. & T. Clark, 1912).

France, R.T., *The Gospel according to Matthew* (TNTC; Leicester: Inter-Varsity Press, 1985).

Friedrich, G., *Die Verkündigung des Todes Jesu im Neuen Testament* (Biblisch-Theologische Studien, 6; Neukirchen–Vluyn: Neukirchener Verlag, 1982).

Furnish, V.P., *Theology and Ethics in Paul* (Nashville: Abingdon Press, 1968).

Gaston, L., 'Anti-Judaism and the Passion Narrative in Luke and Acts', in P. Richardson and D. Granskou (eds.), *Anti-Judaism in Early Christianity* (Studies in Christianity and Judaism, 2; Waterloo, Ontario: Wilfrid Laurier University Press, 1986), pp. 127-53.

—*No Stone on Another* (NovTSup, 23; Leiden: Brill, 1970).

George, A., 'Israël dans l'oeuvre de Luc', *RB* 75 (1968), pp. 481-525.

—'Le sens de la mort de Jésus pour Luc', *RB* 80 (1973), pp. 186-217.

Gerhardsson, B., *The Gospel Tradition* (ConBNT, 15; Malmö: Gleerup, 1986).

—*Memory and Manuscript: Oral Tradition and Written Transmission in Rabbinic Judaism and Early Christianity* (ET; ASNU, 22; Lund: Gleerup; Copenhagen: Munksgaard, 1961).

—'Der Weg der Evangelientradition', in P. Stuhlmacher (ed.), *Das Evangelium und die Evangelien* (WUNT, 2.28; Tübingen: Mohr [Paul Siebeck], 1983), pp. 79-102.

Giblin, C.H., *The Destruction of Jerusalem according to Luke's Gospel: A Historical-Typological Moral* (AnBib, 107; Rome: Biblical Institute, 1985).

Goulder, M.D., *The Evangelists' Calendar: A Lectionary Explanation of the Development of Scripture* (London: SPCK, 1978).

—'A House Built on Sand', in A.E. Harvey (ed.), *Alternative Approaches to New Testament Study* (London: SPCK, 1985), pp. 1-24.

Gnilka, J., *Das Evangelium nach Markus* (EKKNT, 2; 2 vols.; Zürich: Benzinger Verlag; Neukirchen–Vluyn: Neukirchener Verlag, 1978-79).

—*Das Matthäusevangelium* (HTKNT, 1; 2 vols.; Freiburg: Herder, 1986–88).

—'Der Prozess Jesu nach den Berichten des Markus und Matthäus mit einer Rekonstruktion des historischen Verlaufs', in K. Kertelge (ed.), *Der Prozess gegen Jesus: Historische Rückfrage und theologische Deutung* (QD, 112; Freiburg: Herder, 1989), pp. 11-40.

—*Die Verstockung Israels: Isaias 6, 9-10 in der Theologie der Synoptiker* (SANT, 3; Munich: Kösel, 1961).

Grech, P., 'Jewish Christianity and the Purpose of Acts', *SE* 7 (= TU 126 [1982]), pp. 223-26.

Green, J.B., *The Death of Jesus: Tradition and Interpretation in the Passion Narrative* (WUNT, 2.23; Tübingen: Mohr [Paul Siebeck], 1988).

Grundmann, W., *Das Evangelium nach Markus* (THKNT, 2; Berlin: Evangelische Verlagsanstalt, 3rd edn, 1968).

Guelich, R.A., 'The Gospel Genre', in P. Stuhlmacher (ed.), *Das Evangelium und die Evangelien* (WUNT, 2.28; Tübingen: Mohr [Paul Siebeck], 1983), pp. 183-219.

—*Mark 1–8.26* (WBC, 34a; Dallas: Word Books, 1989).

Guthrie, W.K.C., *A History of Greek Philosophy* (6 vols.; Cambridge: Cambridge University Press, 1962–81).

Haacker, K., 'Elemente des heidnischen Antijudaismus im Neuen Testament', *EvT* 48 (1988), pp. 404-18.

Hackforth, R., *The Composition of Plato's Apology* (Cambridge: Cambridge University Press, 1933).

Haenchen, E., *The Acts of the Apostles: A Commentary* (Oxford: Basil Blackwell; Philadelphia: Westminster Press, 1971).

—'Judentum und Christentum in der Apostelgeschichte', *ZNW* 54 (1963), pp. 155-89.

Hahn, F., *Mission in the New Testament* (ET; SBT, 47; London: SCM Press, 1965).

Hare, D.R.A., 'The Rejection of the Jews in the Synoptic Gospels and Acts', in A. Davies (ed.), *Antisemitism and the Foundations of Christianity* (New York: Paulist Press, 1979), pp. 27-47.

Harnack, A., *The Acts of the Apostles* (New Testament Studies, 3; Crown Theological Library, 27; New York: Putnam's, 1909).

Hauser, H.J., *Strukturen der Abschlusserzählung der Apostelgeschichte (Apg 28:16-31)* (AnBib, 86; Rome: Biblical Institute, 1979).

Heil, J.P., 'Reader-Response and the Irony of Jesus before the Sanhedrin in Luke 22.66-71', *CBQ* 51 (1989), pp. 271-84.

Hengel, M., *The Atonement: The Origins of the Doctrine in the New Testament* (London: SCM Press, 1981).

Holtz, T., *Der erste Brief an die Thessalonicher* (EKKNT, 13; Neukirchen–Vluyn: Neukirchener Verlag, 1986).

—'Traditionen im 1. Thessalonischerbrief', in U. Luz and H. Weder (eds.), *Die Mitte des Neuen Testaments: Einheit und Vielfalt neutestamentlicher Theologie: Festschrift für Eduard Schweizer zum siebzigsten Geburtstag* (Göttingen: Vandenhoeck & Ruprecht, 1983), pp. 55-78.

Horsley, G.H.R., 'Speeches and Dialogue in Acts', *NTS* 32 (1986), pp. 609-14.

Horton, F.L., 'Reflections of the Semitisms of Luke–Acts', in C.H. Talbert (ed.), *Perspectives on Luke–Acts* (Edinburgh: T. & T. Clark, 1978), pp. 1-23.

Hunter, A.M., *Paul and his Predecessors* (London: SCM Press, rev. edn, 1961).

Hurd, J.C., 'Paul Ahead of his Time: 1 Thess. 2.13-16', in P. Richardson and

D. Granskou (eds.), *Anti-Judaism in Early Christianity* (Studies in Christianity and Judaism, 2; Waterloo, Ontario: Wilfried Laurier University Press, 1986), pp. 21-36.

Hurtado, L.W., *Mark* (Good News Commentaries; London: Harper & Row, 1983).

Jeremias, J., *The Eucharistic Words of Jesus* (ET; London: SCM Press, 1966).

Jervell, J., *Luke and the People of God* (Minneapolis: Augsburg, 1972).

—'Paulus in der Apostelgeschichte und die Geschichte des Urchristentums', *NTS* 32 (1986), pp. 378-92.

—*The Unknown Paul* (Minneapolis: Augsburg, 1984).

Jewett, R., 'The Agitators and the Galatian Congregation', *NTS* 17 (1970–71), pp. 198-212.

—*The Thessalonian Correspondence: Pauline Rhetoric and Millenarian Piety* (Philadelphia: Fortress Press, 1986).

Johnson, L.T., *The Literary Function of Possessions in Luke–Acts* (SBLDS, 39; Missoula, MT: Scholars Press, 1977).

—'The New Testament's Anti-Jewish Slander and the Conventions of Ancient Polemic', *JBL* 108 (1989), pp. 419-41.

Kebler, W.H., *The Kingdom in Mark: A New Place and a New Time* (Philadelphia: Fortress Press, 1974).

—'Conclusion: From Passion Narrative to Gospel', in *idem* (ed.), *The Passion in Mark: Studies on Mark 14–16* (Philadelphia: Fortress Press, 1976), pp. 153-80.

Keck, F., *Die öffentliche Abschiedsrede Jesu in Lk 20, 45–21, 36* (Forschung zur Bibel, 25; Stuttgart: Katholisches Bibelwerk, 1976).

Keck, L.E., 'Mark 3.7-12 and Mark's Christology', *JBL* 84 (1965), pp. 341-58.

Kertelge, K., 'Einführung', in *idem* (ed.), *Der Prozess gegen Jesus: Historische Rückfrage und theologische Deutung* (QD, 112; Freiburg: Herder, 1989), pp. 7-10.

Kilgallen, J.J., 'The Function of Stephen's Speech (Acts 7, 2-53)', *Bib* 70 (1989), pp. 173-93.

Kodell, J., 'Luke's Use of *LAOS*, "People", Especially in the Jerusalem Narrative', *CBQ* 31 (1969), pp. 327-43.

Koenig, J., *Jews and Christians in Dialogue: New Testament Foundations* (Philadelphia: Westminster Press, 1979).

Koester, H., 'I Thessalonians—Experiment in Christian Writing', in F.F. Church and T. George (eds.), *Continuity and Discontinuity in Church History* (Leiden: Brill, 1979), pp. 33-44.

Koet, B.J., *Five Studies on Interpretation of Scripture in Luke–Acts* (Studiorum Novi Testamenti Auxilia, 14; Leuven: Leuven University Press, 1989).

Kolenkow, A.B., 'Healing Controversy as a Tie between Miracle and Passion Material for a Proto-Gospel', *JBL* 95 (1976), pp. 623-38.

Kränkl, E., *Jesus der Knecht Gottes: Die heilsgeschichtliche Stellung Jesu in den Reden der Apostelgeschichte* (Münchener Universitäts-Schriften, Katholisch-Theologische Fakultät; Regensburg: Pustet, 1972).

Kuhn, K.G., G. von Rad and W. Gutbrod, ''Ισραήλ, κτλ', *TDNT*, III, pp. 356-91.

Lapide, P., *Wer war schuld an Jesu Tod?* (Gütersloh: Gerd Mohn, 1987).

Leaney, A.R.C., *The Gospel according to St Luke* (BNTC; London: A. & C. Black, 1958).

Lentzen-Deis, F., 'Passionsbericht als Handlungsmodell? Überlegungen zu Anstössen aus der "pragmatischen" Sprachwissenschaft für die exegetischen Methoden', in

K. Kertelge (ed.), *Der Prozess gegen Jesus: Historische Rückfrage und theologische Deutung* (QD, 112; Freiburg: Herder, 1989), pp. 191-232.

Léon-Dufour, X., 'Redaktionsgeschichte of Matthew and Literary Criticism', in *Jesus and Man's Hope* (Pittsburgh: Pittsburgh Theological Seminary, 1970), pp. 9-35.

Levinson, S.H., *Textual Connections in Acts* (SBLMS, 31; Atlanta: Scholars Press, 1987).

Lindars, B., *New Testament Apologetic: The Doctrinal Significance of the Old Testament Quotations* (London: SCM Press, 1961).

Linnemann, E., *Studien zur Passionsgeschichte* (FRLANT, 102; Göttingen: Vandenhoeck & Ruprecht, 1970).

Lohfink, G., *Die Sammlung Israels: Eine Untersuchung zur lukanischen Ekklesiologie* (SANT, 39; Munich: Kösel, 1975).

Loisy, A., *Les Actes des Apôtres* (repr.; Frankfurt: Minerva, 1973 [1920]).

—*L'Evangile selon Luc* (repr.; Frankfurt: Minerva, 1971 [1924]).

—*Les Evangiles synoptiques* (2 vols.; Ceffonds, près Montier-en-Der [Haute-Marne]: pub. by author, 1907–1908).

Longenecker, B.W., 'Different Answers to Different Issues: Israel, the Gentiles and Salvation History in Romans 9–11', *JSNT* 36 (1989), pp. 95-123.

Longenecker, R.N., *The Acts of the Apostles* (Expositor's Bible Commentary, 9; Grand Rapids: Zondervan, 1981).

Löning, K., 'Lukas—Theologe der von Gott geführten Heilsgeschichte (Lk, Apg)', in J. Schreiner (ed.), *Gestalt und Anspruch des Neuen Testaments* (Würzburg: Echter Verlag, 1969), pp. 200-28.

—*Die Saulustradition in der Apostelgeschichte* (NTAbh, 9; Münster: Aschendorff, 1973).

Louw, J.P., *Semantics of New Testament Greek* (SBLSS; Philadelphia: Fortress Press, 1982).

Lövestam, E., 'Der Rettungsappel in Ag 2, 40', *ASTI* 12 (1983), pp. 84-92.

Lowe, M., 'The Demise of Arguments from Order for Markan Priority', *NovT* 24 (1982), pp. 27-36.

—'From the Parable of the Vineyard to a Pre-Synoptic Source', *NTS* 28 (1982), pp. 257-63.

—'Real and Imagined Anti-Jewish Elements in the Synoptic Gospels and Acts', *JES* 24 (1987), pp. 267-86.

—'Who Were the ΙΟΥΔΑΙΟΙ?', *NovT* 18 (1976), pp. 101-30.

Lüdemann, G., *Early Christianity according to the Traditions in Acts: A Commentary* (ET; London: SCM Press, 1989).

—*Paulus und das Judentum* (Theologische Existenz Heute, 215; Munich: Chr. Kaiser Verlag, 1983).

Lührmann, D., 'Die Pharisäer und die Schriftgelehrten im Markusevangelium', *ZNW* 78 (1980), pp. 169-85.

Luz, U., *Das Evangelium nach Matthäus* (EKKNT, 1.1; Zürich: Benziger Verlag: Neukirchen–Vluyn: Neukirchener Verlag, 1985).

McDonald, J.I.H., *Kerygma and Didache: The Articulation and Structure of the Earliest Christian Message* (SNTSMS, 37; Cambridge: Cambridge University Press, 1980).

McKinnis, R., 'An Analysis of Mark 10.32-34', *NovT* 18 (1976), pp. 81-100.

Maddox, R., *The Purpose of Luke–Acts* (FRLANT, 126; Göttingen: Vandenhoeck & Ruprecht, 1982).

Malbon, E.S., 'Galilee and Jerusalem: History and Literature in Marcan Interpretation',
    CBQ 44 (1983), pp. 243-55.
—'The Jewish Leaders in the Gospel of Mark: A Literary Study of Marcan
    Characterization', *JBL* 108 (1989), pp. 259-81.
Mann, C.S., *Mark* (AB, 27; Garden City, NY: Doubleday, 1986).
Marshall, I.H., *1 and 2 Thessalonians* (NCB; London: Marshall, Morgan & Scott,
    1983).
—*The Gospel of Luke* (NIGTC; Exeter: Paternoster Press, 1978).
—*Luke: Historian and Theologian* (Grand Rapids: Zondervan, 1978).
—'The Resurrection in the Acts of the Apostles', in W.W. Gasque and R.P. Martin
    (eds.), *Apostolic History and the Gospels* (Exeter: Paternoster Press, 1970),
    pp. 92-107.
Martin, R.A., *Syntactical Evidence of Semitic Sources in Greek Documents* (SBLSCS, 3;
    Cambridge, MA: SBL, 1974).
Marxsen, W., *Der erste Brief an die Thessalonicher* (Züricher Bibelkommentare, NT,
    11.1; Zürich: Theologischer Verlag, 1979).
Masson, C., *Les deux épîtres de Saint Paul aux Thessaloniciens* (CNT, 11a; Neuchâtel:
    Delachaux & Niestlé, 1957).
Matera, F.J., 'Responsibility for the Death of Jesus according to the Acts of the
    Apostles', *JSNT* 39 (1990), pp. 77-93.
Meeks, W.A., *The First Urban Christians: The Social World of the Apostle Paul*
    (London: Yale, 1983).
Michel, O., 'Fragen zu 1 Thessalonicher 2, 14-16: Antijüdische Polemik bei Paulus', in
    W.P. Eckert, N.P. Levinson and M. Stöhr (eds.), *Antijudaismus im Neuen
    Testament? Exegetische und systematische Beiträge* (Abhandlung zum christlich-
    jüdischen Dialog, 2; Munich: Chr. Kaiser Verlag, 1967), pp. 50-59.
Miller, R.J., 'The Rejection of the Prophets in Q', *JBL* 107 (1988), pp. 225-40.
Mohr, T.A., *Markus- und Johannespassion: Redaktions- und traditionsgeschichtliche
    Untersuchung der Markinischen und Johanneischen Passionstradition* (ATANT,
    70; Zürich: Theologischer Verlag, 1982).
Moessner, D.P., 'Jesus and the "Wilderness Generation": The Death of the Prophet
    like Moses according to Luke', in K.H. Richards (ed.), *Society of Biblical
    Literature Seminar Papers 1982* (Chico, CA: Scholars Press, 1982), pp. 319-40.
—' "The Christ Must Suffer": New Light on the Jesus–Peter, Stephen, Paul Parallels in
    Luke–Acts', *NovT* 28 (1986), pp. 220-56.
—'The "Leaven of the Pharisees" and "This Generation": Israel's Rejection of Jesus
    according to Luke', *JSNT* 34 (1988), pp. 21-46.
—*Lord of the Banquet: The Literary and Theological Significance of the Lukan Travel
    Narrative* (Minneapolis: Augsburg Fortress, 1989).
—'Luke 9.1-50: Luke's Preview of the Journey of the Prophet like Moses of
    Deuteronomy', *JBL* 102 (1983), pp. 575-605.
—'Paul in Acts: Preacher of Eschatological Repentance to Israel', *NTS* 34 (1988),
    pp. 96-104.
Morgenthaler, R., and C. Brown, 'Generation', in C. Brown (ed.), *The New
    International Dictionary of New Testament Theology* (Grand Rapids: Zondervan,
    1978), II, pp. 35-39.
Moule, C.F.D., 'The Christology of Acts', in L.E. Keck and J.L. Martyn (eds.), *Studies
    in Luke–Acts* (Nashville: Abingdon Press, 1966), pp. 159-85.

—'The Gravamen against Jesus', in E.P. Sanders (ed.), *Jesus, the Gospels and the Church: Essays in Honor of William R. Farmer* (Macon, GA: Mercer University Press, 1987), pp. 177-95.

—*An Idiom Book of New Testament Greek* (Cambridge: Cambridge University Press, 2nd edn, 1959).

Mowery, R.L., 'Pharisees and Scribes, Galilee and Jerusalem', *ZNW* 80 (1989), pp. 266-68.

Müller, K., 'Möglichkeit und Vollzug jüdischer Kapitalgerichtsbarkeit im Prozess gegen Jesus von Nazaret', in K. Kertelge (ed.), *Der Prozess gegen Jesus: Historische Rückfrage und theologische Deutung* (QD, 112; Freiburg: Herder, 1989), pp. 41-83.

Müller, U.B., *Prophetie und Predigt im Neuen Testament: Formgeschichtliche Untersuchungen zur urchristlichen Prophetie* (SNT, 10; Gütersloh: Gerd Mohn, 1975).

Munck, J., *Christ and Israel* (ET; Philadelphia: Fortress Press, 1967).

Munro, W., *Authority in Paul and Peter: The Identification of a Pastoral Stratum in the Pauline Corpus and 1 Peter* (SNTSMS, 45; Cambridge: Cambridge University Press, 1983).

Neill, S., and T. Wright, *The Interpretation of the New Testament 1861–1981* (Oxford: Oxford University Press, 2nd edn, 1988).

Neusner, J., *A History of the Mishnaic Law of Damages* (5 vols.; Leiden: Brill, 1983-85).

Neyrey, J.H., *The Passion according to Luke: A Redaction Study of Luke's Soteriology* (New York and Mahwah: Paulist Press, 1985).

Nickelsburg, G.W.E., 'The Genre and Function of the Markan Passion Narratives', *HTR* 73 (1980), pp. 153-84.

—*Resurrection, Immortality, and Eternal Life in Intertestamental Judaism* (HTS, 26; London: Oxford University Press, 1972).

Nock, A.D., *Conversion: The Old and the New in Religion from Alexander the Great to Augustine of Hippo* (Oxford: Clarendon Press, 1933).

O'Brien, P.T., *Introductory Thanksgivings in the Letters of Paul* (NovTSup, 49; Leiden: Brill, 1977).

O'Fearghail, F., 'Israel in Luke–Acts', *Proceedings of the Irish Biblical Association* 11 (1988), pp. 23-43.

—'Rejection in Nazareth: Lk 4.22', *ZNW* 75 (1984), pp. 60-72.

O'Neill, J.C., 'The Six Amen Sayings in Luke', *JTS* NS 10 (1959), pp. 1-9.

—*The Theology of Acts in its Historical Setting* (London: SPCK, 2nd edn, 1970).

O'Toole, R.B., *Acts 26: The Christological Climax of Paul's Defense (Ac 22.1–26.32)* (AnBib, 78; Rome: Biblical Institute Press, 1978).

—*The Unity of Luke's Theology* (Good News Studies, 9; Wilmington, DE: Michael Glazier, 1984).

Okeke, G.E., 'I Thessalonians 2.13-16: The Fate of the Unbelieving Jews', *NTS* 27 (1981), pp. 127-36.

Orchard, J.B., *Matthew, Luke and Mark* (Manchester: Koinonia Press, 1976).

—'Thessalonians and the Synoptic Gospels', *Bib* 19 (1938), pp. 19-42.

Overbeck, F., 'Introduction to the Acts from De Wette's Handbook', in E. Zeller, *The Contents and Origin of the Acts of the Apostles Critically Investigated* (ET; Edinburgh: Williams & Norgate, 1875), I, pp. 1-81.

Pearson, B.A., 'I Thessalonians 2.13-16: A Deutero-Pauline Interpolation', *HTR* 64 (1971), pp. 79-94.

Pesch, R., *Die Apostelgeschichte* (EKKNT, 5; 2 vols.; Zürich: Benziger Verlag; Neukirchen–Vluyn: Neukirchener Verlag, 1986).

—*Das Evangelium der Urgemeinde* (Freiburg: Herder, 1979).

—'Das Evangelium in Jerusalem', in P. Stuhlmacher (ed.), *Das Evangelium und die Evangelien* (WUNT, 2.28; Tübingen: Mohr [Paul Siebeck], 1983), pp. 113-55.

—*Das Markusevangelium* (HTKNT, 2; 2 vols.; Freiburg: Herder, 1976).

—'Die Passion des Menschensohnes: Eine Studie zu den Menschensohnworten der vormarkinischen Passionsgeschichte', in *idem*, R. Schnackenburg and O. Kaiser (eds.), *Jesus und der Menschensohn: Für Anton Vögtle* (Freiburg: Herder, 1975), pp. 166-95.

—'Der Schluss der vormarkinischen Passionsgeschichte und des Markusevangeliums: Mk 15,42–16.8', in M. Sabbe (ed.), *L'Evangile selon Marc: Tradition et rédaction* (BETL, 34; Gembloux: Duculot, 1974), pp. 365-409.

—'Die Überlieferung der Passion Jesu', in K. Kertelge (ed.), *Rückfrage nach Jesus* (QD, 63; Freiburg: Herder, 1974), pp. 148-73.

Petrie, S., ' "Q" Is Only What You Make It', *NovT* 3 (1959), pp. 28-33.

Plummer, A., *A Critical and Exegetical Commentary on the Gospel according to S. Luke* (ICC; Edinburgh: T. & T. Clark, 1896).

Pobee, J., 'The Cry of the Centurion—A Cry of Defeat', in E. Bammel (ed.), *The Trial of Jesus: Cambridge Studies in Honour of C.F.D. Moule* (SBT, 2.13; London: SCM Press, 1970), pp. 91-102.

Preuschen, E., 'Das Wort vom Verachteten Propheten', *ZNW* 17 (1916), pp. 33-48.

Radl, W., *Paulus und Jesus in lukanischen Doppelwerk: Untersuchungen zu Parallelmotiven im Lukasevangelium und in der Apostelgeschichte* (Europäische Hochschulschriften, 13.49; Frankfurt: Peter Lang, 1975).

Rau, G., 'Das Volk in der lukanischen Passionsgeschichte: Eine Konjektur zu Lk 23, 13', *ZNW* 56 (1965), pp. 41-51.

Reicke, B., 'Die Entstehungsverhältnisse der synoptischen Evangelien', *ANRW*, II.25.2, pp. 1758-91.

—'Jesus in Nazareth—Lk 4, 14-30', in H. Balz and S. Schulz (eds.), *Das Wort und die Wörter: Festschrift G. Friedrich* (Stuttgart: Kohlhammer, 1973), pp. 47-55.

—*The Roots of the Synoptic Gospels* (Philadelphia: Fortress Press, 1986).

Rese, M., 'Die Aussagen über Jesu Tod und Auferstehung in der Apostelgeschichte', *NTS* 30 (1984), pp. 335-53.

Richard, E., 'Jesus' Passion and Death in Acts', in D.D. Sylva (ed.), *Reimaging the Death of the Lukan Jesus* (BBB, 73; Frankfurt: Hain, 1990), pp. 125-52, 204-10.

Richardson, P., 'The Israel-Idea in the Passion Narratives', in E. Bammel (ed.), *The Trial of Jesus: Cambridge Studies in Honour of C.F.D. Moule* (SBT, 2.13; London: SCM Press, 1970), pp. 1-10.

Richardson, P., and P. Gooch, 'Logia of Jesus in 1 Corinthians', in D. Wenham (ed.), *The Jesus Tradition Outside the Gospels* (Gospel Perspectives, 5; Sheffield: JSOT Press, 1985), pp. 39-62.

Riesenfeld, H., 'The Text of Acts x.36', in E. Best and R.McL. Wilson (eds.), *Text and Interpretation: Studies in the New Testament Presented to Matthew Black* (Cambridge: Cambridge University Press, 1979), pp. 191-94.

Rigaux, B., *Saint Paul: Les épîtres aux Thessalonians* (EBib; Paris: Gabalda, 1956).

Robinson, J.A.T., 'The Most Primitive Christology of All?', *JTS* NS 7 (1956), pp. 177-89.

—*Redating the New Testament* (London: SCM Press, 1976).

Roloff, J., 'Anfänge der soteriologischen Deutung des Todes Jesu (Mk x.45 und Lk. xxii.27)', *NTS* 19 (1972–73), pp. 38-64.

—*Die Apostelgeschichte* (NTD, 5; Göttingen: Vandenhoeck & Ruprecht, 1970).

—*Das Kerygma und der irdische Jesus: Historische Motive in den Jesus-Erzählungen der Evangelien* (Göttingen: Vandenhoeck & Ruprecht, 1981).

Ruether, R.R., *Faith and Fratricide: The Theological Roots of Anti-Semitism* (New York: Seabury, 1974).

Ruppert, L., *Jesus als der leidende Gerechte? Der Weg Jesu im Licht eines alt- und zwischentestamentlichen Motivs* (SBS, 59; Stuttgart: Katholisches Bibelwerk, 1972).

—*Der leidende Gerechte: Eine motivgeschichtliche Untersuchung zum Alten Testament und zwischentestamentlichen Judentum* (FB, 5; Würzburg: Echter Verlag, 1972).

—*Der leidende Gerechte und seine Feinde: Eine Wortfelduntersuchung* (FB, 6; Würzburg: Echter Verlag, 1973).

Salmon, M., 'Insider or Outsider? Luke's Relationship with Judaism', in J.B. Tyson (ed.), *Luke–Acts and the Jewish People: Eight Critical Perspectives* (Minneapolis: Augsburg, 1988), pp. 76-82.

Sand, A., *Das Evangelium nach Matthäus* (RNT; Regensburg: Pustet, 1986).

Sanders, E.P., *Jesus and Judaism* (London: SCM Press, 1985).

—*The Tendencies of the Synoptic Tradition* (SNTSMS, 9; London: Cambridge University Press, 1969).

Sanders, E.P. (ed.), *Jesus, the Gospels and the Church: Essays in Honor of William R. Farmer* (Macon, GA: Mercer University Press, 1987).

Sanders, E.P., and M. Davies, *Studying the Synoptic Gospels* (London: SCM Press, 1989).

Sanders, J.T., *The Jews in Luke–Acts* (London: SCM Press, 1987).

—'The Parable of the Pounds and Lucan Anti-Semitism', *TS* 42 (1981), pp. 660-68.

—'The Prophetic Use of the Scriptures in Luke–Acts', in C.A. Evans and W.F. Stinespring (eds.), *Early Jewish and Christian Exegesis: Studies in Memory of William Hugh Brownlee* (Scholars Press Homage Series, 10; Atlanta: Scholars Press, 1987), pp. 191-98.

Sandmel, S., *Anti-Semitism in the New Testament?* (Philadelphia: Fortress Press, 1978).

Schade, H.-H., *Apokalyptische Christologie bei Paulus: Studien zum Zusammenhang von Christologie und Eschatologie in den Paulusbriefen* (GTA, 18; Göttingen: Vandenhoeck & Ruprecht, 1981).

Schenk, W., *Der Passionsbericht nach Markus: Untersuchungen zur Überlieferungs- geschichte der Passionstraditionen* (Gütersloh: Gerd Mohn, 1974).

Schenke, L., *Studien zur Passionsgeschichte des Markus: Tradition und Redaktion in Markus 14.1-42* (FB, 4; Würzburg: Echter Verlag, 1971).

Schippers, R., 'The Pre-Synoptic Tradition in I Thessalonians II 13-16', *NovT* 8 (1966), pp. 223-34.

Schmidt, D., '1 Thess. 2.13-16: Linguistic Evidence for an Interpolation', *JBL* 102 (1983), pp. 269-79.

Schmeichel, W., 'Christian Prophecy in Lucan Thought: Luke 4, 16-30 as a Point of Departure', in G. MacRae (ed.), *SBL Seminar Papers* (Missoula, MT: Scholars Press, 1976), pp. 293-306.

Schneider, G., *Die Apostelgeschichte* (HTKNT, 5; 2 vols.; Freiburg: Herder, 1980–82).

—'Das Verfahren gegen Jesus in der Sicht des dritten Evangeliums (Lk 22,54–23,25): Redaktionskritik und historische Rückfrage', in K. Kertelge (ed.), *Der Prozess gegen Jesus: Historische Rückfrage und theologische Deutung* (QD, 112; Freiburg: Herder, 1989), pp. 111-30.

—*Verleugnung, Verspottung und Verhör Jesu nach Lukas 22, 54-71* (SANT, 22; Munich: Kösel, 1969).

Schnelle, U., 'Der erste Thessalonicherbrief und die Entstehung der paulinischen Anthropologie', *NTS* 32 (1986), pp. 207-24.

Schoeps, H.J., 'Die jüdischen Prophetenmorde', in *Aus frühchristlicher Zeit* (Tübingen: Mohr [Paul Siebeck], 1950), pp. 126-43.

Schreiber, J., 'Die Bestattung Jesu: Redaktionsgeschichtliche Beobachtungen zu Mk 15.42-47 par', *ZNW* 72 (1981), pp. 141-77.

Schubert, P., 'The Final Cycle of Speeches in the Book of Acts', *JBL* 87 (1968), pp. 1-16.

Schütz, F., *Der leidende Christus: Die angefochtene Gemeinde und das Christuskerygma der lukanischen Schriften* (BWANT, 89; Stuttgart: Kohlhammer, 1969).

Schweizer, E., 'Concerning the Speeches in Acts', in L.E. Keck and J.L. Martyn (eds.), *Studies in Luke–Acts* (Nashville and New York: Abingdon Press, 1966), pp. 208-16.

—*Erniederung und Erhöhung bei Jesus und seinen Nachfolgern* (ATANT, 28; Zürich: Zwingli-Verlag, 1962).

Senior, D., *The Passion Narrative according to Matthew* (BETL, 39; Leuven: Leuven University Press, 1975).

Sherwin-White, A.N., 'The Trial of Jesus', in D.E. Nineham (ed.), *Historicity and Chronology in the New Testament* (Theological Collections, 6; London: SPCK, 1965), pp. 97-116.

Simon, M., *Verus Israel: A Study of the Relations between Christians and Jews in the Roman Empire (135–425)* (ET; Oxford: Oxford University Press, 1986).

Slingerland, D., 'The Composition of Acts: Some Redaction-Critical Observations', *JAAR* 56 (1988), pp. 99-113.

—' "The Jews" in the Pauline Portion of Acts', *JAAR* 54 (1986), pp. 305-21.

Sloyan, G.S., *Jesus on Trial: The Development of the Passion Narratives and their Historical and Ecumenical Implications* (ed. J. Reumann; Philadelphia: Fortress Press, 1973).

Soards, M.L., *The Passion according to Luke: The Special Material of Luke 22* (JSNTSup, 14; Sheffield: JSOT Press, 1987).

—'Tradition, Composition, and Theology in Jesus' Speech to the "Daughters of Jerusalem" (Luke 23, 26-32)', *Bib* 68 (1987), pp. 221-44.

Sparks, H.F.D., Review of *Synopse des quatres évangiles en français*, by P. Benoit and M.-E. Boismard, *JTS* NS 25 (1974), pp. 485-89.

—'The Semitisms of the Acts', *JTS* NS 1 (1950), pp. 16-28.

Stählin, G., *Die Apostelgeschichte* (NTD, 5; Göttingen: Vandenhoeck & Ruprecht, 13th edn, 1970).

Stanley, D.M., ' "Become Imitators of Me": The Pauline Conception of Apostolic Tradition', *Bib* 40 (1959), pp. 859-77.

—'Imitation in Paul's Letters: Its Significance for his Relationship to Jesus and to his Own Christian Foundations', in P. Richardson and J.C. Hurd (eds.), *From Jesus to*

Paul: Studies in Honour of Francis Wright Beare (Waterloo, Ontario: Wilfrid Laurier University Press, 1984).

Stanton, G.N., *Jesus of Nazareth in New Testament Preaching* (SNTSMS, 27; Cambridge: Cambridge University Press, 1974).

Stauffer, E., *New Testament Theology* (ET; London: SCM Press, 1955).

Steck, O.H., *Israel und das gewaltsame Geschick der Propheten: Untersuchungen zur Überlieferung des deuteronomistischen Geschichtsbildes im Alten Testament, Spätjudentum und Urchristentum* (WMANT, 33; Neukirchen–Vluyn: Neukirchener Verlag, 1967).

Stendahl, K., *Paul among Jews and Gentiles* (Philadelphia: Fortress Press, 1976).

Stoldt, H.-H., *History and Criticism of the Marcan Hypothesis* (ET; Macon, GA: Mercer University Press, 1980)..

Stolle, V., *Der Zeuge als Angeklagter: Untersuchungen zum Paulusbild des Lukas* (BWANT, 102 [6.2]; Stuttgart: Kohlhammer, 1973).

Stonehouse, N.B., *The Witness of Luke to Christ* (London: Tyndale Press, 1951).

Stowers, S., 'The Synagogue in the Theology of Acts', *ResQ* 17 (1974), pp. 129-43.

Strathmann, H., 'λαός', *TDNT*, IV, pp. 29-57.

Strobel, A., *Die Stunde der Wahrheit: Untersuchungen zum Strafverfahren gegen Jesus* (WUNT, 21; Tübingen: Mohr [Paul Siebeck], 1980).

Stuhlmacher, P., 'Das paulinische Evangelium', in *idem* (ed.), *Das Evangelium und die Evangelien* (WUNT, 2.28; Tübingen: Mohr [Paul Siebeck], 1983), pp. 157-82.

Talbert, C.H., 'Martyrdom in Luke–Acts and the Lucan Social Ethic', in R.J. Cassidy and P.J. Scharper (eds.), *Political Issues in Luke–Acts* (Maryknoll, NY: Orbis Books, 1983), pp. 99-110.

—'Shifting Sands: The Recent Study of the Gospel of Luke', *Int* 30 (1976), pp. 381-95.

Talbot, C.H., and E.V. McKnight, 'Can the Griesbach Hypothesis Be Falsified?', *JBL* 91 (1972), pp. 338-68.

Tannehill, R.C., *The Narrative Unity of Luke–Acts: A Literary Interpretation*. I. *The Gospel according to Luke* (Philadelphia: Fortress Press, 1986).

—'Rejection by Jews and Turning to Gentiles: The Pattern of Paul's Mission in Acts', in J.B. Tyson (ed.), *Luke–Acts and the Jewish People: Eight Critical Perspectives* (Minneapolis: Augsburg, 1988), pp. 83-101.

—Review of *Luke–Acts and the Jews: Conflict, Apology and Conciliation*, by R.L. Brawley, *Bib* 70 (1989), pp. 278-82.

Taylor, V., *The Formation of the Gospel Tradition* (London: Macmillan, 2nd edn, 1949).

—*The Gospel according to St Mark* (London: Macmillan, 1952).

—'The Origin of the Markan Passion Sayings', *NTS* 1 (1954–55), pp. 159-67.

—*The Passion Narrative of St Luke: A Critical and Historical Investigation* (SNTSMS, 19; Cambridge: Cambridge University Press, 1972).

Tiede, D.L., 'Contending with God: The Death of Jesus and the Trial of Israel in Luke–Acts', in B.A. Pearson *et al.* (eds.), *The Future of Early Christianity: Essays in Honour of Helmut Koester* (Minneapolis: Fortress Press, 1991).

—'The Exaltation of Jesus and the Restoration of Israel in Acts 1', in G.W.E. Nickelsburg with G.W. MacRae (eds.), *Christians among Jews and Gentiles: Essays in Honor of Krister Stendahl on his Sixty-Fifth Birthday* (Philadelphia: Fortress Press, 1986), pp. 278-86. Also in *HTR* 79 (1986), pp. 278-86.

—' "Fighting against God": Luke's Interpretation of Jewish Rejection of the Messiah Jesus', in C.A. Evans and D.A. Hagner (eds.), *Anti-Semitism and Early Christianity: Issues of Faith and Polemic* (Minneapolis: Fortress Press, 1993), pp. 102-12.

—' "Glory to Thy People Israel": Luke–Acts and the Jews', in J.B. Tyson (ed.), *Luke–Acts and the Jewish People: Eight Critical Perspectives* (Minneapolis: Augsburg, 1988), pp. 21-34.

—*Prophecy and History in Luke–Acts* (Philadelphia: Fortress Press, 1980).

Tilborg, S. van, *The Jewish Leaders in Matthew* (Leiden: Brill, 1972).

Townsend, J.T., 'The Gospel of John and the Jews: The Story of a Religious Divorce', in A. Davies (ed.), *Antisemitism and the Foundations of Christianity* (New York: Paulist Press, 1979), pp. 72-97.

Trocmé, E., 'The Jews as Seen by Paul and Luke', in J. Neusner and E.S. Frerichs (eds.), *'To See Ourselves as Others See Us': Christians, Jews, 'Others' in Late Antiquity* (Chico, CA: Scholars Press, 1985), pp. 146-61.

Tuckett, C.M. (ed.), *Synoptic Studies: The Ampleforth Conferences of 1982 and 1983* (JSNTSup, 7; Sheffield: JSOT Press, 1984).

Turner, M.M.B., 'Jesus and the Spirit in Lucan Perspective', *TynBul* 32 (1981), pp. 3-42.

Tyson, J.B., *The Death of Jesus in Luke–Acts* (Columbia, SC: University of South Carolina Press, 1986).

—'The Problem of Jewish Rejection in Acts', in *idem* (ed.), *Luke–Acts and the Jewish People: Eight Critical Perspectives* (Minneapolis: Augsburg, 1988), pp. 124-37.

—'Scripture, Torah and Sabbath in Luke–Acts', in E.P. Sanders (ed.), *Jesus, the Gospels and the Church: Essays in Honor of William R. Farmer* (Macon, GA: Mercer University Press, 1987), pp. 89-104.

—'Source Criticism of the Gospel of Luke', in C.H. Talbert (ed.), *Perspectives on Luke–Acts* (Edinburgh: T. & T. Clark, 1978), pp. 24-39.

Vanhoye, A., 'Les juifs selon les Actes des Apôtres et les Epîtres du Nouveau Testament', *Bib* 72 (1991), pp. 70-89.

Vawter, B., 'Are the Gospels Anti-Semitic?', *JES* 5 (1968), pp. 473-87.

Veltman, F., 'The Defense Speeches of Paul in Acts', in C.H. Talbert (ed.), *Perspectives on Luke–Acts* (Edinburgh: T. & T. Clark, 1978), pp. 243-56.

Via, E.J., 'According to Luke, Who Put Jesus to Death?', in R.J. Cassidy and P.J. Scharper (eds.), *Political Issues in Luke–Acts* (Maryknoll, NY: Orbis Books, 1983), pp. 122-45.

Walaskay, P.W., *'And So We Came to Rome': The Political Perspectives of St Luke* (SNTSMS, 49; Cambridge: Cambridge University Press, 1983).

Walker, W.O., 'The Burden of Proof in Identifying Interpolation in the Pauline Letters', *NTS* 33 (1987), pp. 610-18.

—'I Corinthians 11.2-16 and Paul's View of Women', *JBL* 94 (1975), pp. 94-110.

Walker, W.O. (ed.), *The Relationships among the Gospels: An Interdisciplinary Dialogue* (San Antonio: Trinity University Press, 1978).

—'Text Critical Evidence for Interpolations in the Letters of Paul', *CBQ* 50 (1988), pp. 622-31.

Weatherly, J.A., 'Anti-Semitism', in J.B. Green, S. McKnight and I.H. Marshall (eds.), *Dictionary of Jesus and the Gospels* (Downers Grove, IL: Inter-Varsity Press, 1992), pp. 13-17.

—'The Authenticity of 1 Thessalonians 2.13-16: Additional Evidence', *JSNT* 42 (1991), pp. 79-98.

—'The Jews in Luke–Acts', *TynBul* 40 (1989), pp. 107-17.

—Review of *Lord of the Banquet*, by D.P. Moessner, *EvQ* 63 (1991), pp. 270-73.

Weeden, T.J., Sr, 'The Cross as Power in Weakness (Mark 15.20b-41)', in W.H. Kebler (ed.), *The Passion in Mark: Studies on Mark 14–16* (Philadelphia: Fortress Press, 1976), pp. 115-34.

Weiser, A., *Die Apostelgeschichte* (ÖTKNT, 5; 2 vols.; Gütersloh: Gerd Mohn, 1981).

Wellhausen, J., *Das Evangelium Lucae* (Berlin: Georg Reimer, 1904).

Wenham, D., *The Rediscovery of Jesus' Eschatological Discourse* (Gospel Perspectives, 4; Sheffield: JSOT Press, 1984).

—'Paul and the Synoptic Apocalypse', in *idem* and R.T. France (eds.), *Studies of History and Tradition in the Four Gospels* (Gospel Perspectives, 2; Sheffield: JSOT Press, 1981), pp. 345-75.

—'Paul's Use of the Jesus Tradition: Three Samples', in *idem* (ed.), *The Jesus Tradition Outside the Gospels* (Gospel Perspectives, 5; Sheffield: JSOT Press, 1985), pp. 39-62.

Wenham, J.W., 'Synoptic Independence and the Origin of Luke's Travel Narrative', *NTS* 27 (1980–81), pp. 507-15.

West, T.G., *Plato's Apology of Socrates: An Interpretation, with a New Translation* (London: Cornell University Press, 1979).

Wickenhauser, A., *Die Apostelgeschichte* (RNT, 5; Regensburg: Pustet, 4th edn, 1961).

Wilch, J.R., 'Jewish Guilt for the Death of Jesus—Anti-Judaism in the Acts of the Apostles?', *Lutheran Theological Journal* 19 (1984), pp. 49-58.

Wilckens, U., *Die Missionsreden der Apostelgeschichte* (WMANT, 5; Neukirchen–Vluyn: Neukirchener Verlag, 3rd edn, 1973).

Wilcox, M., ' "Upon the Tree"—Deut. 21.22f.', *JBL* 96 (1977), pp. 85-99.

—*The Semitisms of Acts* (London: Oxford University Press, 1965).

—'A Foreword to the Study of the Speches in Acts', in J. Neusner (ed.), *Christianity, Judaism and Other Greco-Roman Cults: Studies for Morton Smith at Sixty* (SJLA, 12; Leiden: Brill, 1975), I, pp. 206-25.

—'Semitisms in the New Testament', *ANRW* II.25.2, pp. 978-1029.

Wilson, S.G., *The Gentiles and the Gentile Mission in Luke–Acts* (SNTSMS, 23; Cambridge: Cambridge University Press, 1974).

—'The Jews and the Death of Jesus in Acts', in P. Richardson and D. Granskou (eds.), *Anti-Judaism in Early Christianity* (Studies in Christianity and Judaism, 2; Waterloo, Ontario: Wilfrid Laurier University Press, 1986), pp. 155-64.

—*Luke and the Law* (SNTSMS, 50; Cambridge: Cambridge University Press, 1983).

Winter, P., *On the Trial of Jesus* (ed. T.A. Burkill and G. Vermes; SJ, 1; Berlin: de Gruyter, 2nd edn, 1974).

Zehnle, R.F., *Peter's Pentecost Discourse: Tradition and Lukan Reinterpretation in Peter's Speeches of Acts 2 and 3* (SBLMS, 15; Nashville and New York: Abingdon Press, 1971).

Zmijewski, J., *Die Eschatologiereden des Lukas-Evangeliums* (BBB, 40; Bonn: Peter Hanstein, 1972).

INDEXES

INDEX OF REFERENCES

OLD TESTAMENT

PSEUDEPIGRAPHA

JOSEPHUS

INDEX OF AUTHORS

JOURNAL FOR THE STUDY OF THE NEW TESTAMENT

Supplement Series